THE COMPLETE BOOK OF
Home-Made Preserves

THE
COMPLETE
BOOK OF

Home-Made Preserves

REVISED EDITION IN
ASSOCIATION WITH
THE WOMEN'S INSTITUTE

JILL NICE

HarperCollins*Publishers*

First published in 1982 by
William Collins Sons & Co. Ltd

This revised edition published in 1995 by
HarperCollins*Publishers*
Reprinted 1996

A catalogue record for this book is
available from The British Library

ISBN 0 00 4127706

Illustrations by Vana Haggerty

Printed and bound in Great Britain by the Bath Press, Bath

for Ben and Lotte

and with thanks to my mother 'Min' without whose help and stalwart support this book could never have been written.

Jill Nice lives by the sea in Dorset with her family and four cats. Brought up on the East Coast in an environment of country-loving good cooks, she was encouraged to experiment with the abundance of fruit, vegetables, herbs and flowers that grew in the family garden. This developed into a lasting passion which has found its natural outlet in devising original and elegant uses for nature's bounty.

Jill turned her love of cooking into a business selling preserves and farmhouse bakes. Combining her love of natural produce and beautician training, she also branched out with a partner into natural cosmetics and simple herbal remedies.

She believes passionately that making your own good things and putting today's harvest by for tomorrow, are fundamental human instincts which can make a creative and rewarding hobby of a healthy and economic necessity. To that end she has travelled extensively in search of new ideas to write about and to use in her talks and demonstrations, and has become an acknowledged authority in her field. She continues to cook, write and paint for pleasure and profit and has recently started Sugar 'n Spice, a club for cooks who share her passion for preserving.

Jill Nice has written two other books: *Looking Good Naturally* and *Herbal Remedies and Home Comforts,* and broadcasts frequently on radio and television.

Contents

Introduction

Preserving is a most ancient and skilful form of good husbandry; born of necessity it continues to thrive with anachronistic persistence and the reason for this success can be attributed to many things.

In the battle for survival the desire to put food by when it was available in quantity was a driving force and, in earlier days, the methods of doing so – drying and cold storage – must have been somewhat primitive but the impulse continues and still exists today to urge us into the same thrifty habits aided and abetted by deep freeze and refrigerator.

Experimenting has played its part to improve upon necessity. With the discovery of salt, sugar, wine, vinegar, oils and spices, food could be kept longer and made more palatable but these 'preservatives' were expensive and were used predominantly in the great houses and courts where many startling and exaggerated recipes were evolved. In the country houses and farms, however, the precious ingredients were used with care to give simple recipes of long lasting and undoubted value. As people of all nations travelled more widely, as new countries were discovered and trade routes established, exciting fruit and vegetables were also discovered and ideas and opinions exchanged to encourage the growth of these food plants, until eventually in the latter half of the twentieth century with the escalation of air freight and practical commercial storage we can all enjoy a wider variety and greater availability of much produce hitherto denied us.

Today, with the great interest in cookery and helped by the many excellent words written on the subject, we are encouraged to take our choice. Not only do we have the traditional preserves from the British Isles – strawberry jam, apple cheese, herb jellies, lemon curd, chunky marmalades and so on – but exciting chutneys invented by travellers from India, syrupy conserves from the Middle East, delicious preserved fruits from France – plums in brandy and peaches in wine, pretty pickles packed into patterns from Italy, quince paste from Spain, rich tomato purée from the Mediterranean, preserved red peppers from Hungary, practical and tasty recipes from the USA. The choice is boundless.

For you, the cook who treats preserving as a creative hobby – as colourful as painting, pottery or photography – there is a never ending supply of materials to experiment with: lavender from the garden to make softly scented sugar, herbs to flavour vinegar and oil both therapeutic and flavoursome, crystallized primroses and violets to decorate those special cakes, oddly shaped exotic fruit to make strange and elegant surprises, end of season vegetables for gaudy mustard pickles and piccalilli, sloe and blackberry cordial with fruit garnered from the hedgerows.

Once bitten by the bug your enthusiasm will know no bounds except those imposed by economy but here there is another advantage; this hobby can be pursued within the limits of your purse strings – for example, rhubarb and carrot marmalade tastes as superb as a rich Seville marmalade yet costs very little. In fact, if you grow your own produce it is merely a matter of pennies and this is the great joy of home preserving. You can, even within a limited income, treat your family to homemade goodies which far surpass the commercial product in flavour and cost. You can indulge your taste for making things whether simple or flamboyant – in quantity or one delicious pot at a time – have great fun doing it and then sit back smirking with satisfaction whilst everybody polishes off the end result and tells you how clever you are!

So pick up your pots and pans, raid the garden, market or greengrocers, turn the pages and get busy – if you are anything like me you will get hot and bothered, become incredibly imaginative, discover fabulous ideas, improvise like mad, swear when things go wrong and generally have a lovely, rewarding time.

Safety in the Kitchen

Boiling jam, syrup or chutney can cause some of the worst scalds and burns imaginable, so never, ever leave your children alone in the kitchen when you are preserving, or better still, do not let them in at all when they are small.

Try to use preserving pans with two-hand grips, not long handles. In this way you avoid catching the handle as you move around and it also gives you a firm two handed grip on the pan. A side-to-side handle across the pan can also be dangerous if it catches on its hooks and tips the contents on your floor, front or feet. Unless handles are absolutely insulated, wear kitchen gloves for holding them.

Always use the back rings of the cooker and keep the pan away from the front where it can tip over and where you have to lean across it. Long-handled, wooden spoons are invaluable, for wood does not conduct heat and the long handle will guard you against popping bubbles of erupting jam, etc. Wear an oven glove to protect your hand and do not wear flowing sleeves which will catch on, or trail in, the pan. A plastic measuring jug and funnel make filling jars much easier and if you stand the jars on a thick cloth or wooden board, this will prevent them from slipping or cracking. Wipe up any liquid or pieces of skin etc., which may have dropped on the floor and try to think of wearing flat-soled shoes.

Jars and Containers

Clean, dry, sterile jars and bottles are suitable for all preserves, pickles, chutneys and sauces. Domestic jars, i.e., second-hand jam jars, are accustomed to some heat, but you must make sure that you warm the jar first. Do this by standing the clean jar upside down in a cool oven and then bring gently up to 130°C/250°F (gas mark 1). If you put a cold glass jar straight into a hot oven or boiling water, it will crack. The same applies to transferring hot jars or jars full of hot preserve on to a cold surface, so lay a wooden board or thick cloth where you intend to place the jars.

Decorative glass jars are a different thing and should be carefully tested for their strength before using.

A word about jar sizes. Most British jam jars on the market are known as 1lb (450g); when you come to fill them however, you will find that they take approximately 12oz (350g). It is difficult to give a definite idea of how many jars will be needed since much depends on the type of fruit or vegetable used and the cooking time. Apple jam will fill more jars than a highly reducible fruit such as strawberries, and the same applies to jams containing commercial pectin. Chutneys and pickles vary considerably depending on the amount of liquid used and the thickness required. It is always wiser to use very small jars or pots for more unusual preserves such as herb jellies which may not be eaten very quickly and which may deteriorate once opened. Therefore you may take it that an ordinary jam jar referred to is the conventional 12oz-size (350g), a medium jar is 6oz (175g) and a small jar is approximately 2-3oz (50-75g). Large jars, generally speaking, hold 2lb (900g).

Jars can be sealed with wax discs and paper. Twist-top lids can be used to seal any preserve which does not contain vinegar – vinegar corrodes metal and not only makes a nasty mess, but renders the contents unobtainable. However, many jar and bottle caps are now plastic-lined. Twist-tops and plastic tops are available from W.I. offices. Strictly speaking, corks should not be used in herb vinegars as they tend to draw out flavour. Bottle corks can be obtained from some ironmongers and chain or department stores. Make sure that they are clean and dry before using. When potting with Kilner or preserving jars, always use new bands and the lids and screw or clip seals provided with the jars.

An old-fashioned and very competent way of sealing preserves is to pour a thin layer of melted paraffin wax over the contents, but this has its disadvantages: the preserve must be really thick and well set and it is also a rather fiddly business.

Some of the recipes for pickles refer to the use of earthenware jars. Although earthenware jars are the traditional containers for pickled fruits and fruits in alcohol, certain facts must be established. First, do make sure that the container is fully glazed and non-porous, otherwise your lovely juice will disappear. Secondly, if it is glazed, it must not be a lead glaze. Lead reacts against vinegar, alcohol and certain fruit with a high acid content to become potentially dangerous. Those attractive old-fashioned earthenware containers picked up on second-hand stalls and in markets may be lead glazed, for on the continent and in Britain this was predominantly used in the past. Scandinavian countries favoured a borax or salt glaze and this is the one used most frequently nowadays. A rough guide is the appearance: borax and salt glazes are usually a greyish stone speckled colour. Hopefully, those fashionably produced jars with pickles emblazoned across them have been made for just that purpose and, one would assume, are safe, but if you are not sure, do not use them.

Clean and polish your containers after you have filled them, label them clearly with the contents and date and store them in a cool, dry place. Now you can sit back quite smugly and enjoy the sight of rows of glowing, glistening and glorious preserves which are the fruits of your imagination and hard work.

Preserving Pans

You can have a nerve-racking time trying to detect what has gone wrong with the preserve you have just made which either looks incredibly murky, has stubbornly refused to set, or has acquired a distinctly unpleasant taste. The answer may lie in the pan you used to cook it in and a few pointers will save you time and trouble.

Preserving pans should be large enough to take all the ingredients with plenty of room for the contents to rise up, without boiling over, preferably heavy based and/or copper clad to ensure a good overall distribution of heat and to prevent burning. The wider the pan, the more quickly the liquid evaporates – hence a rapid set.

Do not leave preserves, chutneys, pickles, etc., to stand overnight in the pan, always transfer to a large china bowl. Keep your pans bright, clean, free of burnt offerings and clear of odours. Keep them out of cupboards where they can become musty.

Copper pans, although beautiful to look at, are not the very best to use for preserving. Red fruit will lose its colour when cooked in copper, although green fruit will remain bright and clear – a good example of this is gooseberries. Blackcurrants will lose much of their high vitamin C content, as do many fruit, and may obstinately refuse to set. Never cook pickles or chutneys in a copper pan as the vinegar reacts dangerously against it. Those dear old recipes which suggested that gherkins thrown into a copper pan full of boiling vinegar obtain a bright green colour were positively lethal. Fruit or vegetables containing a high oxalic acid content, such as rhubarb, spinach, sorrel, should not be cooked in copper either.

Brass pans have the same disadvantages as copper, added to which brass leaves an unpleasant aftertaste in some cases.

Aluminium pans Again, do not use aluminium to cook rhubarb, spinach, sorrel, blackcurrants and other high vitamin C fruit, nor for making pickles, chutneys, etc., containing vinegar. It is now thought that prolonged cooking in an aluminium pan may constitute a health hazard.

Enamel pans are satisfactory in all preserve making, but they must be free from scratches or chips and I also find that the contents tend to burn more easily.

13

Iron pans should never be used.

Cast iron pans with a good enamel finish and flame-proof casseroles may be suitable but are never very large.

Stainless steel pans with copper-clad bottoms are the most satisfactory all round, but unfortunately I can never find one big enough.

Utensils

The correct utensils make life easier for the cook, they also prevent mistakes and accidents. This is a quick check list of both essentials and non-essentials. Try to have them ready before you start, otherwise you may find that the jam has burnt while you search for the wooden spoon.

Good large scales or weighing machine.

Measuring jug with dry and liquid measures and preferably made of heatproof glass or rigid polythene. Also to be used for filling the jars. If you use stainless steel or enamel, you will find that the handle may get very hot.

A selection of china, heatproof glass or rigid polythene basins or bowls, including several large ones. Do not leave juice to drip into, or fruit and vegetables to stand overnight in, metal basins.

Sharp vegetable knife and a chopping knife.

Potato peeler and corer.

A couple of large flat china dishes.

A jelly bag or large squares of clean muslin and a spare piece to cut up for spice bags.

Wooden spoons: one long-handled for stirring volcanic mixtures; one wide and deep for scooping; one flat and short for sieving; one ordinary one for general bashing about.

Perforated or slotted spoon ideally wooden. If you use metal, make sure you do not leave it to stand in the pan as it will leave an aftertaste.

Large nylon sieve. Do not use metal if you can help it, for it may react against some vegetables and fruit to leave a taste of 'bad pennies'.

A potato masher, preferably wooden, for pulping.

14

A mallet or blunt instrument for cracking kernels etc.

Pestle and mortar or equivalent, for pounding and grinding. If you decide to use the end of a rolling pin in a basin, take care not to use too much force – I have knocked the bottom out of more basins than I care to count.

Jam thermometer, very handy, as it cuts out guesswork.

Jam funnel and a narrow sauce funnel. Neither of these are essential, but an absolute godsend. Rigid polythene is best.

Liquidizer, again very handy, but most liquidized pulps have to be sieved as well, so it only cuts out the hard labour.

Measuring spoon.

Wooden board, clean cloths and oven glove.

Sterilizing Sauces

This process is used for the final stages of all the sauce and purée recipes. It is an invaluable process to learn and is not nearly as terrifying as it sounds.

The jars to use are the four piece preserving jars with rubber bands, glass lid, screw or clip top. Before you start cooking your fruit take your clean dry jars and pop them into a cool oven, bring the heat up to 130°C/250°F, gas mark ½. Put the tops of the jars to boil for 10 minutes, bringing the heat up from cold. Just before they are done drop the rubber bands in as well. Pour the boiling pulp into the jars. Put on the rubber bands and the tops. Fasten the tops of the jars with screw bands or clips. When using screw bands give a bare half turn back again to allow for the expansion of the jars. Put a wire rack or false bottom in a preserving pan, sterilizer or zinc pail. Stand the jars in the receptacle making sure that they do not touch and fill the container with very hot water. Bring to the boil and boil for 5-8 minutes. Remove the jars and place on a wooden board or a cloth. Tighten the screw tops immediately. Test after 24 hours by removing the clip or screw band – you should be able to lift the containers by the glass tops. If the jar does not fall off then the seal is complete. If it does fall off then you will either have to scrape the contents from the floor or eat it within the next few days.

Mould and Allied Problems

Apart from the problems such as the incorrect use of sugar, fermenting caused by over-ripe or bruised fruit, poor colour due to the wrong pan being used, the most common problem of storing jam is that of a mould forming on top.

The most likely cause is an oversight during the potting process. Jars must be scrupulously dried, clean (and by clean I mean sterile, but please do not wash out with disinfectant) and, unless stated otherwise, hot. The jar should be filled carefully to ensure that no air bubbles are trapped and the preserve should reach almost to the top. Jam and jellies shrink on cooling and, not only does this look a bit off, it also means that the chances of a mould forming are greater.

Another cause I have found is sealing the jar when the preserve is warm. Do one of two things as the recipe states: either seal it as soon as you have potted, providing the jam etc., is boiling, or if you have waited for it to cool (as in the case of whole fruit preserves) to give a better dispersal of fruit, then allow it to become quite cold before sealing. The jar should be sealed with a wax disc, a cellophane dustcover secured with a rubber band, or with a twist top (no wax disc) or a plastic top (no wax disc). Cellophane lids should be checked from time to time during keeping to make sure that they have not perished. Store all preserves in cool, dry cupboards, away from bright lights, damp, steam and well off concrete floors.

Oil

Oil is not used extensively in preserving, being restricted mainly to an air-tight, flavourless suspension for fruit or vegetables as indicated in Basil Preserved in Oil (p.77) and also as a seal for some preserves and pastes. The most acceptable oils for most people are those which are nearly flavourless, such as sunflower and nut oil – corn oil is a fair substitute but rather heavy and safflower oil is superb but expensive. One oil which is used a lot in the Mediterranean, and which has many proprietary names, is rape seed oil. Fine olive oil is lovely and very fruity, therefore only of use if either you like the taste or if it does not mask other subtle flavours. Walnut and hazelnut oils are too exclusive and expensive to reach the general public and there are several other oils such as sesame and mustard seed oil which are more widely used in Asia, although there is a spectacular Italian fruit pickle called Mostarda di Frutta, which lists mustard seed oil amongst its ingredients.

There are plenty of delightful herb oils in this book – thyme, rosemary, marjoram, etc., which have many uses from basting meats and fish to making subtle and delicate salad dressings, but two of the finest mixed herb oils are those which I have come across in France. In these particular recipes the very pure grape seed oil is used, but sunflower or nut will substitute quite well.

MIXED HERB OIL METHOD 1

Take a selection of fresh dry herbs on small branches, balancing a mixture suitable for a definite purpose, for example, thyme, rosemary, basil, fennel and bay, make a pleasant oil for meat. Add a sliver of garlic, several green or black peppercorns and a little sea salt. For a hotter mixture a few tiny red chilli peppers can be added. Arrange these ingredients in an attractive bottle and fill up with a fine oil. Seal tightly and leave for one month on a sunny windowsill before using.

MIXED HERB OIL METHOD 2

6 tablespoons mixed fresh herbs of
   your choice
6 black or green peppercorns

$\frac{1}{4}$ teaspoon sea salt
sliver garlic (optional)
600ml/1 pint oil

attractive bottles – Spanish green glass are particularly nice

Put all the ingredients, except the oil, into a pestle and mortar and pound them well. Turn them into a dry sterile jar and add the oil. Seal tightly and leave on a warm windowsill to macerate for 1 month. Every time you go by, give the jar a good shake. Strain through a fine muslin and pour into the bottles, add an attractive little bouquet of the fresh herbs in sprigs, a few extra peppercorns, a tiny piece of garlic and, for a particularly bright appearance, several tiny red chilli peppers. The effect should be clear, glowing and quite exciting. Seal tightly. Stronger than Method 1, for a hotter effect several red chillies can be pounded with the other ingredients to start with.

A bottle each of herb oil and herb vinegar make very good looking and acceptable presents, particularly if the recipient is a gourmet. Label clearly to avoid confusion.

Pectin

Soluble gum like carbohydrate, it is the setting agent in jams and jellies and is formed in fruit from pectose during ripening or in fruit and fruit juice by heating. Without pectin, your jam is a sweet stew – your jelly a syrup. The more pectin there is in fruit the more sugar and sometimes water you can use, hence more jam. Therefore, it follows that fruits like apples are frequently used with fruit that have a low pectin content in order to give a mild tasting bulk that also has good setting properties. For example, Apple and Blackberry, Apple and Marrow, Apple and Strawberry.

Some fruit, although looking juicy and ripe and coming into the category of high pectin fruit, will curiously refuse to set. This can be caused by weather conditions – if the fruit has not had much sun it will not be as high in pectin as expected. The same problems may occur if the fruit is too ripe. These things rarely happen, but if you should be in doubt there is a pectin test you can resort to before you add the sugar. Take 1 teaspoon of the cooked fruit juice from the pan, cool it in a heatproof glass and add 3 teaspoons of methylated spirits, shake the two together. If the result is a nice, jelly-like clot that means that there is plenty of pectin present. Small, broken clots show a medium pectin content and if no clots form, then there is a very poor pectin content and you will have to resort to more devious methods. Do keep the methylated spirits away for utensils, ingredients and naked flames. Another way of losing the valuable setting properties when making jelly is to leave the draining fruit juice too long before using it. The result will be syrupy. Pectin Extract can be obtained for a rainy day in several ways and it is extremely useful to have by you.

PECTIN SYRUP OR EXTRACT FROM APPLES

To prepare the extract: take the fruit, wash and cut up, taking care to discard damaged parts. Place in a preserving pan and just cover with water. Stew gently for about 1 hour until the fruit is well pulped and mushy. Turn the pulp into a jelly bag and leave to drain into a deep bowl overnight. The next day, cover the juice and leave in a cool place. Take the pulp and replace it in a preserving pan, add enough water to make a mash and simmer again for about 1 hour. Once again, turn into a jelly bag and leave overnight. The next day, mix the two extracts, return to the pan and bring to the boil, boil for 5 minutes. If the syrup is very watery, boil hard to reduce it to a good thick consistency. Pot and seal immediately in hot, dry, sterile bottles or jars. Sterilize for 5 minutes.

PECTIN EXTRACT

An economical idea is to keep all the peelings and cores from the cooking of apples instead of throwing them away. Put these in a pan, just cover with water and stew. Alternatively, put them into an earthenware crock or casserole, just cover with water and put them into the oven when it is being used for other cooking. When they have been simmered for about 2 hours, strain off the liquid and pot or bottle in hot, dry, sterile containers.

EASY PECTIN EXTRACTION FROM APPLES, REDCURRANTS OR GOOSEBERRIES

Take fruit and water in the proportions of 1 kilogram to 1 litre/2lb 4oz to 1¾ pints. Wash but do not peel or core the fruit and put it into a pan with the water, boil together for 25-30 minutes, pulping and mashing well as you go. Turn into a clean jelly bag and leave to drain right through without prodding. Either use the resulting extract immediately or return it to the clean pan and bring just to the boil. Remove from heat and pot in small, hot, dry, sterile preserving jars. Sterilize for 1-5 minutes. (see Spiced Apple Ketchup, p.50). In any of these cases, the syrup should be kept in a fridge.

COMMERCIAL PECTIN

Commercial pectin can be used to improve on or gain a set when using medium or low pectin fruit. It can also be used to make a more economical jam from all fruit and for making freezer jams. There are specific recipes for these within this book.

Handy check for a set: drop a little boiling jam on to a very cold plate, after a few seconds you should be able to tilt the plate without the jam or jelly running.

Each of the fruit mentioned in this book, under separate headings, generally has some indication of the type of pectin content to be expected, so I have not given a separate list.

Salt

There are several varieties of salt on the market.

Table salt contains magnesium carbonate to give it free running properties, but I feel this makes it unsuitable for clear pickles and bottling.

Block salt, hard to come by now, was once so frequently used that it was known as common or kitchen salt. This is very pure and is excellent for preserving, particularly when salting vegetables, e.g., beans. It has to be scraped from the block and finely broken up.

Rock salt, in either crystal or block form is very good but not as pure as block salt.

Bay salt, sea salt or *gros sel*, crystals of sea water caused by evaporation under natural or artificial heat, is the salt that I find most satisfactory for nearly all preserving.

Maldon salt, flat flakes of salt from natural processes, is the very best, but also the most expensive.

Never neglect the addition of salt in your recipes, unless of course you are on a salt-free diet, for salt brings out the flavour in food which might otherwise be dull and lifeless. This strange property is why fortunes have been made and the prosperity of nations founded upon salt – you do not realise how vital it is until you are deprived of it and then a terrible craving sets in. Apart from which, it was at one time the only method of preserving foodstuffs.

Salt is particularly important in the making of chutneys and pickles for many reasons. Strong brine acts as a preservative and prevents the process of discolouration if used with care. Salt sprinkled on such vegetables as cucumber rids them of excess moisture, and softens hard skins and removes bitter juices from vegetables or fruit such as aubergines. Salt gives a unique pungency to lemons and limes which is totally unlike their natural flavour and it combines with herbs and spices to give magical effects from the most basic ingredients.

Some recipes require a lot of salt and some very little and I would stick to the quantities given. Remember, when reducing pulp, purée and paste, that the salt becomes stronger and more concentrated as well.

Celery salt, garlic salt, onion salt are all well known kitchen standbys, but how about making your own herb salts? Take a bunch of fresh mixed herbs, choosing a selection that is suitable for a specific purpose. For instance, use the more delicate herbs in creamy sauces, pungent herbs which will go well with meat and fish, the aromatic herbs for pizzas and cheese dishes. Make sure that the herbs are dry and clean, and chop them finely. Either put them into a liquidizer or mix very thoroughly by hand in a bowl or pestle and mortar with ¾ cupful salt to each cup of chopped herbs. The salt should be either sea salt or block salt with no additives. Spread the mixture out thinly on a baking tray and pop in a cool oven to dry – as the temperature must be very low, leave the door ajar. Store in wooden boxes and label clearly.

Salt should be kept in non-porous stoneware jars or wooden boxes and a few grains of rice added to it will keep it dry, especially if you keep it near the cooker as you are bound to. Damp salt becomes concentrated and can cause mayhem for the careful cook.

Spices, Seasoning and Flavourings

This may sound a very jumbled heading, but one subject relates to another. All too frequently dishes and, in this case, preserves, etc., are ruined because of a basic misunderstanding of the terms.

Starting with flavouring – a good, simple example of this is onion (flavoured) vinegar where the onion is the principal and the vinegar the vehicle. Garlic and tomato chutney is another more complex example – garlic will be the predominant flavour and the tomato the substance for carrying that flavour, but in either case one will not exist without the other. Without spices or seasoning, however, the recipe will be at best very ordinary, at worst unpalatable. The skilful blending of spices and/or herbs in varying proportions will relate to the other ingredients and enhance them. Strange combinations can have amazing and agreeable results, for example: lemon, garlic and horseradish; orange and coriander; prunes and cloves; gooseberry and elderflower; ginger and cardomum. The real truth of a seasoning is that its presence should not be noticeable as a single unit, but only as a contribution to the whole, however slyly it may change the main ingredients.

Important rules apply to spices in preserve making. Where it is possible, freshly grind your own spices as you need them, e.g., peppercorns, allspice, nutmeg. When you have to use commercially ground spices, make sure that they are really fresh, otherwise you will gain nothing from them. So buy in small quantities and keep in dark, airtight jars.

Generally speaking, it is preferable to use whole spices tied together in a muslin bag for all preserves – jams, chutneys, pickles, relishes, etc., unless the recipe states otherwise. Ground spices are acceptable in jams and chutneys, but should never be used in clear preserves, bottling, clear pickles, vinegars or oils, nor added to jellies after they have been drained through a muslin. The reason for this is quite simple – the taste will not be impaired but the result will be as murky as a fish pond and, in some cases, a thick sediment will form at the bottom of the jar or bottle which will look very nasty indeed – you may know that the product is good but others will view it with grave suspicion.

All the herbs, both leaf and seed, that you are likely to come across in preserving have been dealt with under separate headings, as have ginger, mustard and salt. The following spices are those that you will require at some time in jam, chutney, or pickle making, therefore I have not gone into the lengthy details of their other culinary virtues.

Allspice the dried brown berry of *Pimenta dioica* which grows in tropical America and the West Indies. Similar in appearance to a peppercorn and tasting of cloves, nutmeg and cinammon, it is also known as Jamaica pepper. Particularly useful for all preserves, pickles, chutneys, etc., also used in marinades, cakes and a thousand other forms of cooking.

Cardomum so many different seeds are sold under this name – grains of paradise, Guinea grains, Malagueta pepper, false cardomum, etc., but the true cardomum is from either the *eletharia cardomum* or *amomum cardomum* which are both plants of the ginger family. The tiny black brown seeds are contained within a creamy green pod and the flavour is distinctly that of eucalyptus, pleasantly aromatic if you like it, but distasteful if you do not. Used mainly in curry powders, it combines well with ginger, coffee and many spices. It is also a popular spice in the Near and Far East, Germany and the Scandinavian countries. Although not frequently made the most of, cardomum is a very useful spice in pickling where the taste has been likened to that of a cross between juniper and coriander.

Cinnamon a very valuable spice in preserving jams, chutneys and pickles. Use either the stick, which is in reality the outer bark of a tree *Cinnamomun zeylanicum* and which curls into those little scrolls naturally as it dries, or use as a ground spice and try to buy a good brand which has not been adulterated with inferior substitutes. Imported from Ceylon.

Cloves the dried flower buds of *Caryophyllus aromatica*, dried and imported from Zanzibar, the name derives from the French *clou* or nail. Cloves are tremendously important in preserving, for they are compatible with a vast array of fruit, vegetables, herbs and spices. Prunes, plums, walnuts, apples, oranges, pears and onions can all be pierced with a clove before pickling, spicing or crystallizing. Nearly all spice mixtures contain cloves, either ground or whole.

Mace the delicate golden filigree blades of mace are the dried aril or net surrounding the nutmeg, which in turn, is the stone of the peach like fruit of *Myristica Fragrans*. Mace is expensive both in the blade or ground and anything cheap is, in all probability, not much good. A distinctive taste which is necessary to many pickles. Impossible to home grind.

Nutmeg the stone of the *Myristica Fragrans* fruit which comes from the Dutch East Indies. The nut is very hard and can be grated easily to a fine powder, using a nutmeg grater or equivalent. Small graters were once made for this specific purpose, so great was the vogue enjoyed by the nutmeg. It is an essential spice in many sweet pickles, where although it does not predominate, would certainly be missed if left out. More useful than, and can be substituted for, mace. Ground nutmeg can be used but it goes stale very quickly and lacks much of the true flavour.

Peppercorns black, white, pink and green are all the same berry of *Piper nigrum*, the pepper vine from the Malayan and South Indian forests, Burma and Assam, which produces long spikes of small berries which turn from green to red on ripening. The black peppercorn is the berry picked just as it is beginning to ripen. It is then dried slowly, becoming wrinkled and dark. The outer skin is the aromatic part of the corn. The white peppercorn is the berry when it is allowed to ripen completely and then dried out. An inferior version is the inside of the black peppercorn after the outer skin has been soaked off, leaving the small smooth white centre. Both white and black peppercorns are best when freshly ground in a peppermill. The black is hot, spicy and aromatic, the white has more of a 'peppery' quality. Green peppers are the fresh green berries picked before they are ripe, they are then packed in jars, tins or frozen. Deliciously hot and juicy, green and pink peppercorns are used most frequently in pâtés and sausages and are really superb in some pickles. No kitchen should be without black or white pepper – freshly ground – it is the premier spice and should be used with flair and imagination in both sweet and savoury dishes. One friend of mine adds several black peppercorns to bottled pears, they discolour a little but add something special. Whole black and white peppercorns are in all mixed pickling spices.

Saffron the dried pistils of *Crocus sativus* or Autumn Crocus. A medieval spice from Asia Minor and astronomically expensive. An integral part of paella, risotto and bouillabaisse. It is very rarely used in preserves.

Turmeric a bright yellow spice mildly pungent, warm and aromatic. An important ingredient in all curry powders and also the most important addition to mustard pickles and piccalillies, it gives no heat but an agreeable spiciness and, of course, the hectic colour. Always buy good quality turmeric and use it quickly. Like ginger, turmeric is the dried root of a plant – in this case *Curcuma longa*. It is always ground to a fine powder when you buy it.

Vanilla the dried seed pod of a Mexican orchid, *Vanilla planifolia*, now grown commercially. Slim, black and sticky looking pencil, covered with a rime of frost which is characteristic of the best vanilla pods, vanilla has a million sweet and delicious uses from flavouring, milk, ice cream, chocolate and sugar. A vanilla pod can be used time and again if it is carefully dried and put away in an airtight jar or a jar of sugar, so although it is not cheap it is an investment. Vanilla's principal uses in preserving are in the syrups for bottled fruits, whole fruit preserves and in jam, although in the latter, a vanilla extract or essence can be used, but do make sure that it is a good one. Vanilla extract is either a synthetic reproduction or the result of broken pods being soaked in alcohol.

Sugar

White sugar is produced from either the sugar cane which has been established in its use for some two thousand years and which grows in the tropical regions of the world, or from sugar beet which grows in more temperate climates and has a less romantic or barbaric history, depending on your point of view. There is no difference in the sugar from either cane or beet, but I prefer cane sugar for preserving.

For the purpose of this book, it is enough to say that sugar, like honey, wine and spices, was used in early kitchens as a means to disguise or improve upon mediocre and stale food and was considered a costly and exotic spice. It took hundreds of years for it to become the everyday commodity that it is now. Sugar is a preservative, but only when it is used in conjunction with a pectin and/or acid.

Jams and jellies with inadequate sugar will invariably give poor results. You may have to overboil the jam to compensate for the lack of sugar and this will give a bad colour and taste. The preserve will probably not keep and it will either become winey, sour or grow an unappetizing mould. Jams and jellies with too much sugar will be oversweet and lacking in flavour. They will also crystallize during cooking or whilst the preserve is being stored.

The proportions of sugar to fruit are important and the recipes should be followed in this respect, but here are a few rough guide lines:

The ratio of sugar to HIGH PECTIN FRUIT can be as high as $1\frac{1}{4}$kg/$2\frac{1}{2}$lb sugar to 1kg/2lb 4oz fruit

The ratio of sugar to LOW PECTIN FRUIT is approximately 800g/1lb 12oz sugar to 1kg/2lb 4oz fruit

The ratio of sugar to MEDIUM PECTIN FRUIT is 1kg/2lb 4oz sugar to 1kg/2lb 4oz fruit

Certain important steps to be taken with sugar will ensure a clear, bright jam or jelly with a good set and no problems afterwards. Always warm the sugar before adding it to the pan of hot fruit or juice which will not only keep the colour good, but also help the sugar to dissolve more rapidly. The sugar must be thoroughly stirred in and dissolved off the source of heat before the preserve is brought to the boil – if you do not do this, you will find that you have crystals forming in the jam or, worse still, it will catch on the bottom of the pan and burn and there is no salvaging that little error. This applies to chutneys, pickles and sauces as well as to sweet preserves.

Do not boil for longer than you have to once the sugar has been added. Unless stated otherwise, the boiling should be as rapid as possible to prevent the fruit skins hardening in reaction to the sugar and to keep a good, bright colour and fresh flavour.

Do not stir too much or leave the spoon in the pan once the sugar has been added and brought to the boil, it may make it more difficult to achieve a set. Take care not to boil past the point of setting – a thing worth remembering is to remove the pan from the heat as you test for a set, otherwise you may well bubble past the setting point.

There are many sugars on the market and I will run through the advantages or otherwise, of each.

Preserving sugar: the best to use in jams and jellies as it dissolves quickly and does not form a scum. It also keeps the preserve a good clear colour, but is more costly than granulated sugar. *Preserving sugar containing PECTIN* is easily available; although more costly, it does ensure a set without excessive boiling.

Loaf or *broken lump sugar*: almost as good as preserving sugar for the same reasons, but not often seen in shops nowadays.

White granulated sugar: cheaper than preserving sugar, but does not dissolve so easily and often forms a scum which will impair the appearance, although not the taste. In this case, skim before potting.

White caster sugar: expensive to use in everyday preserving, but necessary in some more exotic recipes and to crystallize flower blossoms, etc. If you do not have caster sugar to hand in an emergency, then whirl some granulated sugar around in a blender for a second or two.

Icing sugar: do not use in preserving, as it has additives to give the hardening property.

Light brown sugar, *soft brown sugar* and *demerara*: sugar from the cane, but less refined than white. All of these sugars can be used in preserves, but as they do not form a set when used alone (there are exceptions), they should be used in conjunction with white sugar. When converting a recipe stating white sugar, use $\frac{1}{4}$-$\frac{1}{2}$ of brown sugar instead of white, depending on whether the fruit is high pectin or if you prefer a soft or firm set. Brown sugars, however, do cloud and colour jams and jellies and also change the flavour, so it is best to use them with dark strong fruit, for example: damsons and plums. They can be used very satisfactorily in conjunction with brown malt vinegar when making chutneys. Once again, as in all preserves, do make sure the sugar is dissolved before bringing to the boil.

Soft, dark brown sugar, Moscovado, Mollasses, Barbados: very dark, rich sugars which will flavour and colour quite strongly – better used in chutneys, etc. They will not form a set if used alone in jams and jellies, so substitute $\frac{1}{4}$-$\frac{1}{2}$ of the white sugar for the brown, depending on the fruit and whether you like a firm or soft set.

Sugar substitutes in this group do not include dietary sweeteners, which come under a separate heading. All of the following can be substituted for sugar, in part:

Golden syrup: a very refined by-product of white sugar which gives a lovely taste to preserves and a golden colour to pickles. It also fractionally changes the consistency. Syrup will not give a good set by itself, so substitute $\frac{1}{4}$-$\frac{1}{2}$ of the white sugar for syrup, again depending on the fruit and the firmness of set required. Always warm the tin before measuring and pouring – it will make life so much easier.

Treacle: thick, brown, gooey stuff. Use only sparingly to give a dark colour and strong flavour. Very few jams use treacle in the ingredients, but it is occasionally useful in chutneys, etc.

Corn and *Maple syrup*: more familiar to American and Canadian readers. Substitute only $\frac{1}{4}$-$\frac{1}{2}$ of the white sugar for syrup and remember that both dark corn syrup and maple syrup colour quite distinctively and maple syrup has a strong taste – it is also extremely costly.

Honey: absolutely delicious in preserves. It is much sweeter than sugar and has a unique 'wild' quality that it imparts to any preserve in which it is used. If you are lucky, you may be able to buy those lovely blossom honeys – for example, clover, eucalyptus, sage, rosemary, thyme, lime, heather and orange, but use them carefully to blend with the fruit, for their taste comes through quite distinctly. Mixed blossom honeys are the most economical, although maybe not quite so exciting to experiment with. Honey added to jam makes it a subtly different preserve, but it will not set if used alone, therefore substitute $\frac{1}{4}$-$\frac{1}{2}$ of the sugar for honey, depending on the fruit (or flowers) used and the consistency of the set preferred.

Molasses, etc: very thick and black and of no value in fruit and vegetable preserving.

Glucose: can be used with sugar in the crystallizing process for fruit in the proportions of ¼ of the sugar being substituted by glucose throughout each stage of the recipe. This gives a glossier appearance, but I do not think it makes that much difference.

Dietary Jams

Most dietary jams are made for people on a sugar-free diet, and the quantities given below are only intended as a rough guide to the sweetener:fruit ratio needed. Any recipe should be made with a strict regard for personal medical advice.

No matter how high the pectin or acid content in the fruit, sugar substitute does not have the reaction needed to give a good set. Having said that, varying degrees of success can be achieved and occasionally a preserve may be made with no sweetener at all. Gelatine is also a totally innocuous setting agent which may be used in jellies to give a light spreadable set, but take care not to overdo it as you do not want fruit jelly in pudding form!

Do not make any of these preserves in large quantities for they do not keep well. The most satisfactory way of ensuring that they will keep is to sterilize them – see Sterilizing Sauces, p.15. It is really very simple, suitable, economical and well worth the tiny extra effort.

USING SUGAR SUBSTITUTE ONLY

FOR FRUIT HIGH IN PECTIN

450g/1lb fruit   10 saccharine tablets or 500g/1lb 2oz
200ml/7fl. oz water   powdered sugar substitute

FOR FRUIT LOW IN PECTIN

450g/1lb fruit   8 saccharine tablets or 400g/15oz
1 tablespoon lemon juice   powdered sugar substitute

FOR CITRUS FRUIT

450g/1lb fruit

1.15 litres/2 pints water

2 tablespoons lemon juice

22 saccharine tablets or 900g/2lb powdered sugar substitute

Make as for any jam or marmalade recipe adding the crushed saccharine or powder at the moment when the sugar would normally be added. Make sure that it has dissolved properly before continuing as for given recipe. Pot and seal. Sterilize for 5 minutes. See Sterilizing Sauces, p.15.

USING SUGAR SUBSTITUTE AND GELATINE

FOR FRUIT HIGH IN PECTIN

450g/1lb fruit

200ml/7fl. oz water

10 saccharine tablets or 500g/1lb 2oz powdered sugar substitute

15g/½oz powdered gelatine

FOR FRUIT LOW IN PECTIN

450g/1lb fruit

4 tablespoons water

8 saccharine tablets or 400g/15oz powdered sugar substitute

15g/½oz powdered gelatine

FOR CITRUS FRUIT

450g/1lb fruit

600ml/1 pint water

juice of 2 lemons

8 saccharine tablets or 400g/15oz powdered sugar substitute

15g/½oz powdered gelatine to each 600ml/1 pint pulp

Make as for any jam or marmalade recipe, adding the crushed saccharine or powder at the moment when the sugar would normally be added. Make sure that it has dissolved before continuing as for the given recipe. Dissolve the gelatine in a little warm water or preferably syrup from the cooking fruit, add it to the pan after the cooking time is reached. Stir well and remove from heat. Pot and seal. If you have made any quantity sterilize it for 5 minutes to ensure it will keep. See Sterilizing Sauces, p.15.

Vinegar

Malt vinegar, either brown or white, is achieved from a fermentation of malt, the white being distilled, the brown coloured with caramel. This vinegar is the one which most home preservers favour, for it is economical and can be purchased in large quantities from 1-5 litres and is easily available. Although malt vinegar is harsh and uncompromising, it is quite suitable for the more robust pickles, chutneys and sauces where refined flavours would be lost. White vinegar is mainly used in conjunction with white sugar where a light, clear or decorative appearance is necessary, for example, green tomatoes, red chillies, pieces of lemon and so on, will show to better advantage if white vinegar is used.

Wine vinegar, the true and historic vinegar, is made from red or white wine. Centuries ago in Orleans, the great casks of stored wine suffered from the inclusion of air, becoming soured over a period of time, thus causing great disaster and financial loss. Eventually the value of this unpalatable wine was discovered and vinegar of Orleans is still made from casks of wine carefully controlled and scientifically worked out, whilst other companies produce a less expensive wine vinegar by more modern methods. Wine vinegar is better than malt vinegar in delicate pickles (if there is such a thing), but do not be misled into thinking that because it is more expensive and of better flavour, it must necessarily be better for all pickles as this is not so. Wine vinegar has a different effect on some combinations of fruit, vegetables, spices, etc., and may give a sour note. One of the very best uses it can be put to in preserving is in herb vinegars.

Cider vinegar is produced from cider in much the same way, but not, I believe, by such complex methods as wine vinegar. It varies enormously in quality and price and the flavour can be pleasant and mellow. It is much more useful in nearly all preserves than wine vinegar and is, if you can afford it, a better substitute for malt vinegar, particularly if you prefer natural foods. If you run out of cider vinegar in an emergency, half white vinegar and half dry cider will give you a reasonable facsimile and this is a mixture which I frequently use in preserves that are well cooked. Cider vinegar is excellent for making herb, fruit and flower vinegars, although it does have a clear golden colour which might be a disadvantage.

Spiced vinegars. Many recipes call for this and it is very handy to have a large container of a ready-made spiced vinegar put to one side – it saves a lot of hassle later on. Most of them are made from malt vinegar, although occasionally a recipe may specify a spiced wine or cider vinegar and the method is simple. A quantity of mixed pickling spices are boiled together with a quantity of vinegar in a stainless steel pan. The pan is removed from the heat, covered and left to get cold. It can then either be strained before using or the whole spices added to the pickle, but not to a chutney. If it is to be kept, it should be poured into a suitable container and sealed with a non-metal lid. The spices added to the vinegar will make it much stronger than if you strain it. There is a remarkable selection of vinegars both mild and fiery throughout this book to be found under pickled cabbage, beetroot, onion, etc.

Flavoured vinegars. There are many recipes for malt vinegars flavoured with garlic, onion, shallot and horseradish. White malt vinegar flavoured with cucumber, wine vinegars with tiny red chillies or green peppercorns added to the bottle and, of course, the vinegars left over from such goodies as pickled artichokes or onions. All these are of inestimable value in the kitchen. A few drops added to salad dressings, marinades, stuffing, dips, chutneys and pickles all give your own special unique touch and, of course, are very economical and will give a fillip to the most everyday food. For example, children will love fish fingers even more with onion vinegar.

Herb vinegars are most usually made with white vinegar, red or white wine vinegar or cider vinegar, and there are many recipes in this book for achieving these delightful and subtle concoctions. Use attractive bottles for a never ending supply of unusual and inexpensive presents which will give great pleasure to you and the recipient. The most exciting thing about making herb vinegars is the experimenting. Do not just take the recipes that I have given – try mixing and blending your own favourites – how about a few cloves or blade of mace in a tarragon vinegar (makes a smashing dressing for chicken salad)? Several coriander seeds with lemon thyme are spicy and different. The therapeutic effects of wandering about the garden selecting your herbs and then going through the leisurely business of preparing the vinegar and waiting for it to mature are very good for exhausted mothers and career women alike.

Flower vinegars. If making herb vinegars is soothing, imagine the delightful pleasure in making fragrant vinegars, perfumed and colourful with names from an Elizabethan garden – gilly flowers, clove carnation, rose, lavender, marigold. White vinegars are used to make these ancient lovelies as the liquid becomes transformed by the colour of the petals. One word of warning – do not use flowers with a bulb or corm base, unless you are absolutely sure that they are not harmful. And always check any flower that you use to make sure that it is not one of the nasties.

Fruit vinegars more old-fashioned brews concocted by those housewifely ladies of another era. Again, use white vinegar, cider vinegar or red or white wine vinegar and, usually, soft fruit. The results can be put not only to culinary use, but to medicinal as well. With hot water and honey added if necessary, children will find them a soothing and novel antidote for minor snuffles and sore throats. Inevitably, the originality is half the cure.

The following recipes will give you some idea of the fun you can have experimenting with herbs and spices in vinegar. Use only small quantities to start with and try several herbs together to suit yourself. You may like to leave the whole leaf of the herbs intact or a fresh sprig may be added to each jar for extra flavour and for the very attractive effect. Generally speaking half the weight of dried herbs to fresh are sufficient, if you do have to use them, but then the vinegar should be strained through fine muslin before bottling. Herb vinegars make the most charming and unusual presents and when made at home are very reasonable in cost.

FOUR HERBS VINEGAR

borage	chives
mint	white vinegar
basil	

large, dry, sterile heat-resistant jar with non-metal lid

Pick the herbs before they flower and early in the morning. Make sure that they are clean and dry. Bruise them well and pack them into the jar. Bring the vinegar to the boil and pour it over the herbs whilst it is still hot but not boiling. Seal and leave to infuse for 14 days, shaking every day. Strain, bottle and seal with corks.

A very aromatic vinegar.

SPICED HERB VINEGAR

1 tablespoon fresh basil leaves	1 litre/1¾ pints cider or red wine
1 tablespoon fresh rosemary leaves	vinegar
1 tablespoon fresh mint leaves	1 teaspoon dill seed
1 tablespoon fresh tarragon leaves	¼ teaspoon whole cloves
2 tablespoons fresh marjoram leaves	½ teaspoon black peppercorns
4 bay leaves	¼ teaspoon whole allspice

large, dry, sterile heat-resistant jar with non-metal lid

Boil the vinegar and allow it to cool just a little. It should be warm but not boiling when it is used. Blend all the herbs and spices together with a pestle and mortar, crushing the whole spices well. Put into the jar and cover with the vinegar. Seal and leave to infuse on a sunny windowsill for 1 month, shaking or stirring once a day. Strain through a fine muslin. Bottle and cork tightly.

If you have to use dried herbs, 15g/½oz dried herbs equals approximately 2 tablespoons of fresh.

MIXED HERB VINEGAR

1 litre/1¾ pints vinegar
1 celeriac root
1 shallot
50g/2oz fresh mixed herbs of your
   own choice

25g/1oz fresh tarragon
1 tablespoon fresh chives
1 teaspoon black peppercorns
1 teaspoon celery seed

large dry sterile jar with non-metal lid

Boil the cider vinegar and leave to cool. Scrub and dice the celeriac. Peel and slice the shallot. Wash and chop the herbs. Put all the ingredients into the jar and leave for 1 month in a cool place, shaking each day. Strain, bottle and seal with a cork.

HERBS AND WINE VINEGAR

600ml/1 pint cider vinegar
600ml/1 pint dry red wine
3 cloves garlic
branch of tarragon

small branch of thyme
small branch of oregano
1 teaspoon black peppercorns

large dry, sterile, jar with non-metal lid

Bring the cider vinegar to the boil and leave to get cold. Peel and cut the garlic and bruise it well with the herbs and peppercorns. Put all of these into a jar with both the wine and the cold vinegar, seal tightly and leave on a warm windowsill to infuse for 1 month, stirring once a day. Strain through a muslin, bottle and seal with corks.

Dried herbs may be used instead of fresh and basil can be substituted for the oregano.

CHILLI VINEGAR

1 litre/1¾ pints vinegar   6 whole cloves
25g/1oz cayenne pepper

hot, dry sterile jar with non-metal lid

Boil the vinegar and add the cayenne and cloves. Pour into the jar, seal and leave for 1 month. Strain through a filter. Bottle and cork.

TREACLE VINEGAR

Mix 6 tablespoons of best treacle with 3 tablespoons of boiled white wine vinegar. Bottle and cork.
  Dilute with cold water as a remedy for sickness!

LEMON VINEGAR

1 litre/1¾ pints white vinegar   4 bay leaves
2 lemons

dry, sterile, wide-necked bottle or jar with non-metal lid

Pour the vinegar into a stainless steel pan. Wash the lemons and pare the rind from them with a potato peeler. Add the peel to the pan with the bay leaves and boil for 5 minutes. Cover and leave to get cold. Bottle, including the peel and bay. Leave to macerate for 4 weeks. The vinegar can then either be strained and bottled or used as it is, depending on the strength you require.
  The bay leaves are optional but give a very unique flavour.

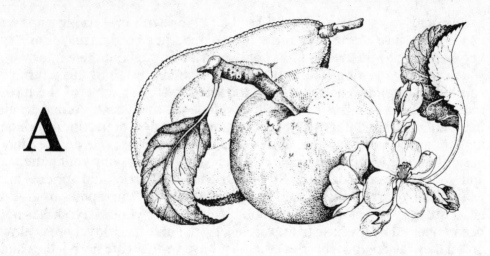

A

Apple

Apples are the most ancient, widespread, carefully cultivated fruit within the temperate regions of the world. I am speaking not just of the delightful heavy pink and white blossomed trees spreading across the garden and orchard, nor of the patio pots of miniature trees, the lazy meadows of dark cider apples, the scarlet and pink crab apples standing above country hedgerows, but of the vast holdings of apple trees marching side by side as industry to supply the western world with its most popular fruit.

The names of the old-fashioned apples ring with their rustic beginnings – Devonshire Quarrenden, Cornish Gilliflower, Rosemary Russet, Tom Putt and many others – but out of the three thousand named varieties there are relatively few that are familiar to us. The golden green Bramleys and Nonsuch which cook to a fluffy whiteness, Russels, Pippins, Pearmains and Reinettes – autumn and winter apples good for storing, with russety dry skins that whisper as you rub them, smooth, crisp apples with shiny scarlet skins and earthy names like James Grieve, George Cave and Ellinsons Orange, crisp, green imported apples such as Newton Wonder and Sturmer Pippin, and others – Worcester Lord Lambourne, Egremont and Laxton – the names trip off the tongue to remind us of another age of quiet country orchards and dedicated men forever searching for the perfect apple.

As far as the housewife is and always was concerned, the apple trees are her greatest allies, providing fruit which is available longer throughout the seasons than any other, which can be stored, dried and bottled, whose windfalls and unripe fruit can be put to as much use as a perfect eater. A fruit that can be baked, boiled, steamed, sieved and stood on its head, dressed up and dressed down, baked in cakes or cooked with meat, fish, cheese and so on and so forth. To the person with preserving on their mind, apples are all the virtues rolled into one; they bottle, freeze and dry very well to give an everlasting supply of fruit throughout the winter with which to make golden flans, soft steamed puddings, charlotte, crumble and betty – not as you may think a comedy act, but some of the most traditional and comforting British puddings at their best. Added to all these culinary advantages, apples contain a great deal of pectin. Although a plain apple jam may seem a trifle anaemic, it can provide an excellent basic for other less co-operative or luxury fruit, thus saving your patience and your purse considerably. Strawberries, blackberries and apricots are examples of some fruits which combine admirably with apples to give a good quantity of smooth, spreadable, well set jam whose flavour has not been impaired by the base fruit. Apple jelly not only has a lovely rosy glow but makes (as do gooseberries) the best base for delicate herb jellies and as a suspension for such things as white peaches and wild strawberries.

Apples like tomatoes are glut fruit. Under-ripe, windblown or as they come they seem to arrive from every source at the same time, cookers and eaters alike and hopefully the price drops in the shops at the same time. Super for you, take full advantage of it and get busy! Apples make mouthwatering chutneys, for there is no fruit or vegetable that they will not work with, crisp and colourful pickles, delicious thick fruity sauces and ketchups, butters, cheeses and marmalades to eat with crisp bread, cold meats and any way your imagination stretches. For so little expenditure you can transform a simple salad or a quick snack into a feast of new flavours and exciting discovery. It is also worth remembering that if you own a deep freeze now is the time to freeze some apples to use at a later date, perhaps when you have more or when other ingredients are more easily available. Good apples without bruises, mould or insects present will also store very well in barrels or on shelves. What more can I say of such perfect fruit?

PLAIN APPLE JAM

1kg/2lb 4oz cooking apples   1kg/2lb 4oz white sugar
2 lemons

6 hot, dry, sterile jam jars

The basic proportions for apple jam are 1kg/2lb 4oz fruit to 1kg/2lb 4oz white sugar. No water is needed unless specifically stated.

Wash, peel, core and dice the apples, discarding any damaged or wormy pieces. Keep the peelings and cores. Pare the rind from the lemons with a potato peeler and keep that. Put the fruit in a shallow bowl and sprinkle with the sugar and lemon juice. Cover with a clean cloth and leave to stand overnight. Tie the cores, peelings and lemon rind, pulp and pips into a muslin bag and put in the fridge. The next day put the contents of the bowl and the muslin bag into a preserving pan and cook slowly, stirring well until the fruit is soft. Bring to the boil and boil until a set is obtained, taking great care not to burn. Pot and seal immediately.

A rather anaemic jam, but good for pies and tarts. This is the most basic of jam recipes and will therefore lend itself to some enterprising additions. A variety of spiced apple jams, for example, Apple and Cloves, Apple and Cinnamon, are made very simply by adding a quantity of whole spice or spices to the stewing fruit. Experiment with a mixture of spices or something different, lemon and orange zest, coriander, mace, cardomum, ginger, but remember always to tie them into the bag of peels or pips. Apple and Ginger Jam is made very simply by adding a good piece of root ginger to the bag of peelings and stirring 25-50g (1-2oz) of chopped preserved ginger into the cooked jam. Whenever chopped fruit, nuts or peel is added to the jam at the end of cooking, leave to cool before potting, stirring well to disperse the additions and seal when quite cold. Preserved angelica, finely chopped good quality candied peel or pineapple are all very pleasant sweeteners to apple jam and make marvellous fillings for flaky pastry, sprinkled with chopped nuts and rolled up before cooking. Absolutely delicious, served hot with thick cream. 25-100g/1-4oz of chopped nuts, hazel, brazil, walnut, almond or pistachio added to basic apple jam make mouthwatering fillings for simple and economic flans and turnovers and are equally good with cold meats such as pork, or spread in cheese sandwiches. Use your own flair and imagination to raise this humble glut fruit into the cordon bleu class at no great extra cost.

APPLE AND DAMSON JAM

1kg/2lb 4oz cooking apples	450ml/¾ pint water
1kg/2lb 4oz damsons	1.5kg/3lb 6oz white sugar
9 hot, dry sterile jam jars	

Wash, peel, core and chop the apples. Wash the damsons. Put the fruit in a preserving pan with the water, bring to the boil, reduce heat and simmer gently. As the fruit cooks the damson stones should rise to the surface: remove all of these. A few of the kernels from the damson stones may be added to give a nice nutty flavour to the jam. Boil the stones first for a minute or two. Place them between two pieces of cloth and crack them with a hammer or rolling pin. The few kernel which you may obtain are then put in the pan with the softened fruit. Stir in the warmed sugar over a gentle heat until it is dissolved. Bring to the boil and boil rapidly until a set is obtained. Pot and seal.

This jam sets very well and has a lovely sharp flavour.

APPLE AND FIG JAM

1kg/2lb 4oz cooking apples
500g/1lb 2oz tin of figs

550g/1lb 4oz white sugar
1 lemon

6 hot, dry sterile jam jars

Wash, peel, core and chop the apples. Keep the peel and cores and tie them in a muslin bag. Drain the figs and chop them, reserving the liquid. Place figs and apples in a preserving pan with the muslin bag. Measure the syrup from the figs and make up to 300ml/½ pint with water if necessary. Add the liquid to the fruit and simmer gently until the apples are soft. Add the warmed sugar and the juice from the lemon. Stir over a low heat until the sugar has dissolved, bring to the boil and boil rapidly until a set is obtained. Remove the muslin bag giving it a good squeeze. Pot and seal.

A nice, fresh-looking jam with a slightly Oriental flavour.

APPLE AND PINEAPPLE JAM
USING FRESH PINEAPPLE

1kg/2lb 4oz cooking apples
900g/2lb fresh pineapple (weighed
   after peeling)

150ml/¼ pint water
1350g/3lb white sugar
1 lemon

9 hot, dry, sterile jam jars

Wash, peel, core and dice the apples. Dice the peeled pineapple. Place with the water in a preserving pan and simmer until soft. Stir in the warmed sugar and the juice from the lemon. Heat gently, stirring continuously until the sugar has dissolved. When the sugar has dissolved bring to the boil and boil rapidly until a set is obtained. Pot and seal immediately.

APPLE, PEAR AND QUINCE JAM

1kg/2lb 4oz cooking apples	4 lemons
1kg/2lb 4oz cooking pears	1.15 litres/2 pints water
900g/2lb quince or 1kg/2lb 4oz if using	3kg/6lb 12oz white sugar
Japonica quince	

18 hot, dry, sterile jam jars

Wash, peel, core and chop the fruit, keeping it in separate piles and keeping the peel and cores. Pare the rind from the lemons and put it with the peel and cores into a muslin bag. Place the quince, pears and muslin bag in a large preserving pan with the water. Simmer until nearly soft. Add the apples and continue to cook until all the fruit is soft. Remove the muslin bag giving it a good squeeze. Add the warmed sugar and the juice from the lemons. Heat gently, stirring well until all the sugar is dissolved. Bring to the boil and boil hard until a set is obtained. Pot and seal straight away.

Quince adds a subtle and distinctive taste and has been a much neglected fruit in cooking. Any recipe using apples or pears will benefit from the addition of quince. Reduce all the quantities of the above recipe proportionately for manageable results, unless of course you are going into business.

BASIC APPLE JELLY

1kg/2lb 4oz cooking apples	white sugar
1.15 litres/2 pints water	

The quantities of sugar are basically 450g/1lb sugar to 600ml/1 pint of apple juice obtained. Preserving sugar is without doubt the best sugar to use for jelly and indeed for jam, but as jellies are transparent the colour is clearer and there is less scum after cooking. These are good basic weights and measurements to use should you wish to make your own experiments and the following is the basic method. Wash the fruit and chop it up. Simmer with the water until very soft. Place in a thick muslin bag or jelly bag. I find that two or three layers of scrupulously clean muslin tied corner to corner, laid over a colander and placed high over a deep bowl is an adequate substitute for a professional jelly bag. The muslin must always have been boiled and be immaculately clean. Leave the pulp to stand in the bag overnight. Do not, a cardinal rule this, do not be tempted to prod, poke or squeeze during this phase. If you do, your jelly will be cloudy but if your economical soul is despairing at the waste read on. The next day measure the juice and take 450g/1lb warmed sugar for every 600ml/1 pint of liquid. Heat the liquid gently and stir in the sugar, keep stirring until all the sugar has dissolved. Boil rapidly until a set is obtained. Skim, pot and seal.

If you add herbs or ginger etc., the jelly should be allowed to cool first so that these do not sink to the bottom of the jelly. When you do this ensure that the jelly is quite cold before sealing (unless otherwise stated) as condensation causes mould. In apple jellies, as in other jellies using high pectin fruit, the boiling of the pulp may be done twice and the two liquids mixed. Follow the recipe as above to the point where the first liquid has been taken. Cover the juice then stand in a cool place. Put the remaining pulp in the preserving pan with half the original amount of water, i.e., 600ml/1 pint water to 1kg/2lb 4oz fruit. Boil again. Leave to strain overnight and the next day mix with the first liquid. Measure all the juice and take 450g/1lb warmed sugar to each 600ml/1 pint juice. Continue recipe as above. Cheese may be made from the fruit pulp if you do not go through the double boiling process.

For some variations and experiments, there are some delightful herb and spice jellies to be made by the simple addition of a few little extras.

To make herb jellies, apart from those more complicated recipes given within this book, take a bunch of fresh bright herbs picked before the sun is at its height. Divide the bunch in half and wash and dry well. The first half of the bunch goes into the gently stewing fruit. The second half is chopped and added to the jelly just before potting but remember to allow the jelly to cool a little, stirring well to disperse the leaves before pouring it into the jars. The jelly must be cold before sealing. With some herbs an attractive spray can be popped into the jar of half set jelly instead of chopping it up – this looks particularly good with rosemary, thyme, hyssop, sage etc., and, again, the jelly must be cold before sealing.

Spiced jellies are so easy. Take the whole spice of your choice, root ginger, coriander seeds, whole cloves, cinnamon stick or a mixture of several, and put them into the pan of stewing fruit where they will impart their delicious perfume.

Delicacies such as chopped preserved angelica or ginger can be added to the cooked jelly just before removing from the heat but remember to cool and stir before potting and seal when cold. Several drops of flavouring, for example oil of peppermint, can be added to the jelly before potting to give a fresh and unusual preserve but remember to use caution and a light hand. Now you have the basic methods they can be adapted to include gooseberries, blackcurrants, greengages, even oranges, lemons, grapefruit and grapes.

40

APPLE CASSIS JELLY

1kg/2lb 4oz cooking apples   1 litre/1¾ pints water
350g/12oz blackcurrants   white sugar

8 small, hot, dry, sterile jars

Wash and chop the apples. (The more unripe the apples the better the jelly. Windfalls are suitable if not too damaged.) Wash and pick over the blackcurrants and string them – a fork placed at the top of the cluster and pulled through quickly usually does this with the minimum of trouble and damage. Simmer apples and currants together with the water in a covered pan until they are soft and mushy. Place in a jelly bag and leave to drip overnight. The next day measure the juice and for every 600ml/1 pint juice take 450g/1lb sugar. Return the juice to a preserving pan and heat gently. Add the warmed sugar and stir continuously until the sugar has dissolved. Bring to the boil and boil rapidly until the setting point is reached. Skim. Allow to cool a little. Pot. Seal when cold.

APPLE AND MINT SAUCE JELLY

1kg/2lb 4oz cooking apples   white malt vinegar
water   white sugar
large handful of fresh garden mint

6 small, hot, dry, sterile jars

Wash and chop the apples roughly. Put them in a saucepan and barely cover with water. Simmer until very soft. When cooked, turn into a jelly bag and leave to drip overnight. The next day wash the mint and place in a blender with the vinegar (150ml/¼ pint to every 600ml/1 pint of apple juice gained). Or chop the mint and make up into a sauce with the vinegar. Add the mint sauce to the apple juice and for every 600ml/1 pint liquid weigh 450g/1lb of sugar. Heat the liquid gently in a large saucepan, add the warmed sugar and stir until it is dissolved. Bring to the boil and boil rapidly until a set is obtained. This will take longer than usual because of the addition of the vinegar. Allow to cool before potting. Seal when cold.

This is a lovely jelly with lamb and has the added advantage over mint sauce that it does keep very well and is highly preferable to the bright green, commercial variety.

APPLE, PARSLEY AND OREGANO JELLY

1kg/2lb 4oz cooking apples
25g/1oz fresh parsley
15g/½oz fresh oregano
600ml/1 pint water – scant measure

450ml/¾ pint wine vinegar
450ml/¾ pint tarragon vinegar
white sugar
extra fresh parsley and oregano

9 small, hot, dry, sterile jars with non-metal lids

Wash and chop the apples. Wash and shake dry the parsley and oregano and chop roughly. Put the apples, herbs and water into a stainless steel pan and simmer gently until the apples are quite soft. Add the two vinegars and boil for 10 minutes. Turn the whole lot into a clean jelly bag and leave to drain overnight into a china bowl. The next day measure the juice and for each 600ml/1 pint take 450g/1lb warmed sugar. Return the juice to the pan and heat gently, add the sugar stirring well until it has dissolved. Bring to the boil and boil hard until a set is obtained. Remove the pan from the heat and skim. Wash, dry and finely chop the remaining herbs and add them to the jelly. Leave to cool a little and stir well before potting.

Soft-set, very herby jelly that improves on keeping. Eat with cold white meats, especially good in chicken sandwiches.

APPLE PRESERVE

1kg/2lb 4oz apples
1 lemon

800g/1lb 12oz white sugar
450ml/¾ pint water

6 hot, dry, sterile jam jars

Wash, peel, core and cube the apples (either good, hard cooking apples, presentable windfalls or unripe eaters). Put them to stand in a bowl of water with a dash of the lemon juice. Put the sugar and the water into a preserving pan and heat gently until boiling, stirring well. Remove from the heat and stir in the rest of the juice from the lemon. Drain the apple cubes and pat dry (empty the whole lot into a colander, then onto a clean dry cloth and cover with another cloth, and pat). Return the syrup to the heat and immediately drop the apple cubes into it. Bring to the boil and boil for about 40 minutes. When the syrup is thick and the apple cubes are transparent the preserve is ready. Remove from heat. Allow to cool before potting so that the fruit is evenly distributed. Seal when cold.

Do not worry if the syrup does not set as firmly as in jam – it's not meant to.

APPLE AND BLACKBERRY PRESERVE

1kg/2lb 4oz cooking apples   white sugar
800g/1lb 12oz blackberries   lemons
water

8 hot, dry, sterile jam jars.

Wash and chop the apples. Wash and pick over blackberries taking care to discard any mouldy ones. Put all the fruit in a preserving pan with a tablespoon or two of water to prevent burning. Cook very gently, giving an occasional stir. When tender pass through a hair sieve and weigh the purée. For every 450g/1lb pulp take 350g/12oz sugar and the juice of 1 lemon. Return all the ingredients to the clean pan and heat gently, stirring constantly until the sugar has dissolved. Simmer for about half an hour or until the preserve has thickened to set. Pot. Seal when quite cold.
 For people who don't like pips this is a winner.

APPLE AND SAGE PRESERVE

1kg/2lb 4oz cooking apples   1 teaspoon freshly ground pepper
1 small onion   2 teaspoons dried sage
4 tablespoons water   1 small teaspoon Worcester sauce
100g/4oz caster sugar   1 dessertspoon vinegar
1 teaspoon salt   25g/1oz butter

3 medium size preserving jars

Wash the apples and chop them roughly. Peel and slice the onion. Put the apples and onion in a saucepan, add the water, cover and simmer gently until it is very soft. Stir in the remaining ingredients and continue to cook until well mixed. Pass through a sieve and return to the heat. Bring to the boil and pour into the prepared jars. Continue as for Sterilizing Sauces, p.15.

APPLE CHUTNEY USING A PRESSURE COOKER

1kg/2lb 4oz cooking apples
350g/12oz onions
50g/2oz preserved ginger
150ml/¼ pint malt vinegar

1 teaspoon salt
¼ teaspoon cayenne
500g/1lb 2oz brown sugar

5 hot, dry, sterile jars with non-metal lids

Peel, core and cut up the apples. Peel the onions and slice finely. Chop the preserved ginger. Remove the trivet from the cooker and place all the ingredients, except the sugar, in it. Stir well, cover and bring to H/15lb pressure in the usual way. Cook for 10 minutes and allow the pressure to reduce at room temperature. Remove cover. Add the sugar and stir gently over a low heat until the sugar is dissolved. Bring to the boil and boil steadily until the chutney is the consistency of thick jam. Pot and seal immediately.

APPLE AND APRICOT CHUTNEY

100g/4oz dried apricots
1kg/2lb 4oz apples
225g/8oz onions
225g/8oz sultanas

1 dessertspoon salt
pinch cayenne
300ml/½ pint malt vinegar
225g/8oz soft brown sugar

5 hot, dry, sterile jars with non-metal lids

Wash the apricots well. Leave to soak overnight in a large bowl, well covered with water. The next day wash, peel, core and chop the apples, peel and chop the onions, wash and chop the sultanas. Drain and chop the apricots. Put all the ingredients into a heavy pan and heat gently, stirring well until the sugar has dissolved. Bring to the boil, turn down the heat and simmer gently until the chutney is very thick. Pot and seal.

Leave for at least 2 months before eating. Pleasant, mild and colourful.

FRENCH APPLE CHUTNEY

1kg/2lb 4oz unripe or sour apples   50g/2oz onions
100g/4oz demerara sugar   1 large clove garlic
600ml/1 pint malt vinegar   6 dried chillies
15g/½oz mustard seed   50g/2oz ground ginger
50g/2oz raisins   15g/½oz salt

3 hot, dry, sterile, jars with non-metal lids

Wash, peel, core and chop the apples. Put them in a stainless steel pan with the sugar and vinegar all but 1 tablespoon. Simmer until the apples are soft. Wash the mustard seed with a little of the vinegar and dry in a cool oven. Stone and chop the raisins. Peel and mince the onions, garlic and chillies. Pound the mustard seed with the ginger and salt in a mortar. Add all the ingredients to the apples and mix well together. Bring to the boil and simmer until very thick. Pot and seal.

My sister, living in the Calvados area of Normandy, makes this chutney from the small apples usually reserved for cider making. These give a very unique flavour. Try under-ripe windfalls for a very good interpretation of this chutney and leave for at least 3 months before eating. I kept one jar for over a year and it was delicious.

APPLE AND MINT CHUTNEY

1kg/2lb 4oz apples   600ml/1 pint malt vinegar
450g/1lb onions   1 teaspoon mustard powder
225g/8oz tomatoes   1 teaspoon cayenne pepper
100g/4oz stoned raisins   225g/8oz soft brown sugar
large bunch fresh mint   2 teaspoons salt

4 hot, dry, sterile jars with non-metal lids

Wash, peel, core and chop the apples. Peel and chop the onions. Peel the tomatoes (drop them in boiling water and then rinse in cold), and chop them. Wash and chop the raisins and mint. Put all these in a stainless steel pan with half the vinegar. Cook slowly until soft. Meanwhile mix the mustard and cayenne to a paste with a little of the vinegar and add this to the pan. When all the ingredients are soft stir in the sugar, salt and remaining vinegar and heat gently, stirring well until the sugar has dissolved. Bring to the boil and boil rapidly until the chutney is nice and thick. Allow to cool slightly before potting. Seal when cold.

This chutney is mild and pleasantly aromatic.

APPLE AND WALNUT CHUTNEY

1kg/2lb 4oz apples
50g/2oz walnuts
1 large orange
1 small lemon

450g/1lb soft brown sugar
2 whole cloves
450ml/¾ pint malt vinegar

4 hot, dry, sterile jars with non-metal lids

Wash, peel, core and chop the apples. Chop the walnuts. Grate the rinds from the orange and lemon. Squeeze the juice from them and put this with the rind and all the other ingredients into a stainless steel pan. Bring gently to the boil, stirring well until the chutney is nice and thick and the nuts are soft. Allow to cool a little before potting. Seal when cold.

Instead of walnuts try chopped Brazil nuts which give a totally different flavour. They are extremely exotic and make this chutney something to be reserved for Boxing Day and eaten with turkey.

CHARITABLE CHUTNEY

500g/1lb 2oz prunes
1kg/2lb 4oz green apples
500g/1lb cooking pears
500g/1lb 2oz green tomatoes
500g/1lb 2oz raisins
225g/8oz preserved ginger

450g/1lb onions
2 cloves garlic
1 tablespoon sea salt
½ teaspoon cayenne pepper
1100g/2lb 8oz soft brown sugar
300ml/½ pint brown malt vinegar

10 hot, dry, sterile jars with non-metal lids

Put the prunes in a bowl with a good quantity of water and leave to soften for 4 hours. Drain, remove stones and mince. Peel, core and mince the apples and pears. Mince the tomatoes, raisins and ginger. Peel and mince the onions and garlic. Put all the ingredients except the sugar and vinegar into a large stainless steel pan and bring gently to the boil stirring all the while. Cover and cook without burning for approximately 1½ hours or until soft. Dissolve the sugar in the vinegar and add it to the fruity mixture. Bring to the boil stirring constantly and boil gently and uncovered until thick and smooth. Pot and seal.

A very fruity, mild chutney which matures well.

APPLE AND RASPBERRY CURD

1kg/2lb 4oz cooking apples
2 lemons
water
350g/12oz raspberries

2 large fresh eggs
150g/5oz unsalted butter
400g/14oz caster sugar

8 medium size, hot, dry, sterile jars

Wash, peel, core and slice the apples. Place in a pan with just enough water to cover with the juice and grated rind of the lemons. Simmer until very soft. Wash the raspberries and place in a pan without water. Heat very gently until the juices begin to flow and the fruit is mushy. Pass through a fine sieve. When the apples are cooked pass them through a fine sieve. Combine the two fruits in a large basin. Beat the eggs well and add to the fruit. Melt the butter without letting it become oily and add this to the other ingredients. Add the sugar. Place the basin in a large saucepan containing hot water. Heat gently, beating the mixture well until it thickens enough to coat the spoon. Do not allow to boil otherwise you will ruin the curd. Pot and seal immediately.

Other soft fruit, for example, loganberries, mulberries and blackberries can be used instead of raspberries.

SPECIAL HOT RELISH

1kg/2lb 4oz apples
1 litre/1¾ pints vinegar
75g/3oz sea salt
½ large head garlic
175g/6oz seedless raisins

175g/6oz fresh chilli peppers
75g/3oz mustard seed
1 large piece root ginger
350g/12oz soft brown sugar
600ml/1 pint water

5 hot, dry, sterile jars with non-metal lids

Peel, core and chop the apples and put into a stainless steel pan with half the vinegar. Cook until soft. Drain well but do not throw the vinegary juice away. Turn the apples into a large bowl and sprinkle with the salt. Peel and grate the ginger, peel and finely chop the garlic, chop the raisins and chillies. Crush the mustard seed. Add all these ingredients to the bowl of apple. Put the sugar and water into a pan and boil together to make a thin syrup and add this while still boiling to the bowl, stir in the vinegary juice and remaining vinegar. Mix well. Pot and seal.

Keep at least 2 months before using. Very, very hot and an excellent accompaniment to grills, barbecues, etc., especially if there is plenty of cooling liquid to hand!

PEPPERED APPLE RINGS

1kg/2lb 4oz crisp eating apples
1 lemon
4 medium size green peppers

900ml/1½ pints cider vinegar
50g/2oz brown sugar
1 tablespoon juniper berries

3 hot, dry, sterile jars with wide necks and non-metal lids

Wash, peel, core and slice the apples (Newton Wonders for choice) into rings. Drop into a bowl of cold water to which you have added a few drops of the lemon juice to prevent discolouring. Wash, seed and cut the peppers into rings. Put the vinegar, sugar and juniper berries into a stainless steel saucepan and bring gently to the boil, stirring well until the sugar has dissolved. Boil hard. Drain and pat the apple rings dry and pack into the jars in alternate layers with the peppers. This makes a rather nice jazzy effect. Pour the boiling syrup over the contents of the jars to cover completely. Seal straight away.

Leave for at least 2 months before broaching. A crispy, sophisticated relish with a unique flavour from the juniper berries.

SPICED PICKLE

1kg/2lb 4oz cooking apples
500g/1lb 2oz pickling cucumbers
500g/1lb 2oz melon rinds
100g/4oz allspice berries

50g/2oz whole cloves
long stick cinnamon
1.75 litres/3 pints malt vinegar
1kg/2lb 4oz Demerara sugar

8 hot, dry, sterile jars with non-metal lids

Wash and cut the apples and cucumbers into cubes but do not peel. Cut the melon rind (see Melon for preparing melon rind) into pieces and put into a stainless steel pan with very little water. Cook for 15 minutes. Add the apple and cucumber, cook for a further 10 minutes and turn into a colander; leave to drain well. Bruise the spices and tie into a muslin bag and place this in a stainless steel pan with the vinegar and sugar. Boil together for 10 minutes. Add the fruit and vegetables and bring to the boil, simmer for 5 more minutes and then remove with a perforated spoon, drain well and pack into the jars. Reboil the vinegar for 10 minutes until syrupy, discard the muslin bag and pour the vinegar into the jars to cover completely. Seal.

A crunchy pickle which is best made in smaller quantities than those given and eaten fairly quickly.

SWEET SPICED APPLE PIECES

1kg/2lb 4oz apples
600ml/1 pint water
150ml/¼ pint ginger wine
1kg/2lb 4oz white sugar
5mm/¼ inch stick cinnamon

1 piece mace
1 piece root ginger
6 whole cloves
1 lemon

5 hot, dry, sterile jars with non-metal lids

Wash and core the apples (hard crisp Newton Wonders are worth trying). Cut into neat pieces, quarters or eighths depending on the size of the apples. Place in a bowl of water with a dash of lemon juice. Take a large stainless steel pan and in it heat the water, ginger wine, sugar, cinnamon, mace, well bruised ginger and cloves. Stir well until the sugar has dissolved. Bring to the boil and boil rapidly for 10 minutes. Strain the liquid into a large, clean pan. Pare the rind from the lemon with a potato peeler. Drain and dry the apple pieces. Bring the syrup to the boil and add the apple and lemon rind, reduce the heat and simmer gently until the fruit is soft taking care not to break, because the pieces will become a purée. Put a few fresh pieces of the various spices into the jars and, using a perforated spoon, carefully pack the jars with the apples. Keep warm. Bring the syrup to the boil again and boil hard until it is thickens to about the consistency of thin honey. Pour the boiling syrup over the fruit making sure that it is well covered. Seal. If you prefer, you can cut the fruit into rings instead of pieces. Keep for at least 3 months before eating.

SPICED APPLE KETCHUP

1kg/2lb 4oz apples	1 teaspoon salt
1 large onion	½ teaspoon curry powder
1 clove garlic	¼ teaspoon cayenne powder
200ml/7fl. oz brown vinegar	½ teaspoon turmeric
1 teaspoon pickling spice	100g/4oz brown sugar

6 clean, heatproof bottles with corks or screw lids

Before you start the recipe, clean the bottles with a bottle brush, sterilize by placing them on a wire rack in a deep container, completely fill and cover the bottles with cold water and bring to the boil. When ready for the contents take them out, empty them and place them on a wooden board or thick cloth.

Wash and chop the apples. Peel and chop the onion and garlic. Add these to all the other ingredients except the sugar and cook in a stainless steel saucepan until it is a thick pulp. Pass through a nylon sieve, return the purée to the pan and add the sugar. Heat gently, stirring well until the sugar has dissolved. Bring to the boil and boil until it is very thick. Pour into the prepared bottles with the aid of a funnel. Do this while the ketchup is still boiling hot and the bottles are straight from the sterilizer. Fill to 2cm/¾ inch from the top. Wrap twists of newspaper around the bottles to support them and replace them in the sterilizer, making sure that the water level comes to just above the level of the ketchup in the bottle. Lightly cork, or if using screw tops place a disc of waxed paper on top of each bottle. Bring to the boil again and boil for 10 minutes. Prepare melted candle or paraffin wax. Remove bottles from the sterilizer, placing on wooden board and thick cloth. Push corks down hard or replace wax discs with fresh ones. Brush round the top of bottle and cork with melted wax to make an airtight seal and cover with foil. If using screw caps, make sure that they are clean, pour a teaspoon of wax over the disc of paper and then screw down tight with lid or cap.

This looks like a lot of bother, but it keeps for ages and is a great improvement on commercial brands. Actually it is much easier than it sounds.

CONSERVE OF FLOWERS

1kg/2lb 4oz cooking apples   600ml/1 pint water
100g/4oz sweet scented flower petals   white sugar

10 small, hot, dry, sterile jars

I have included this recipe under apples because the base is predominantly apple and it would be a great pity to miss this delightful conserve by being frightened off by the title.

Wash and cut the fruit into small pieces, put in a preserving pan with the water and simmer gently. Wash the flower petals well, taking care to remove the odd greenfly. Add the petals and continue to cook until the fruit is mushy. Turn into a jelly bag and leave to drain overnight into a deep bowl. The next day measure the juice and for each 600ml/1 pint liquid take 450g/1lb sugar. Bring the juice gently to the heat and add the warmed sugar, stirring continuously until it is dissolved. Bring to the boil and boil rapidly until a set is obtained. Pot and seal immediately.

Half the pleasure in making this recipe is the delight of picking bunches of the sweetest scented garden flowers that you can find – roses, violets, carnations and so on, depending which are in season. I have only made this recipe up with small quantities, as from an aesthetic point of view 100g/4oz of petals is quite a lot of flowers. Do make sure that you don't include any poisonous varieties!

Crab Apple

The best and most tasty herb jellies are made with crab apples, those delightful little wild or ornamental apples, to be found in hedgerow and garden. The trees vary in size and in the spring have beautiful heavy blossom, but the great joy is the colours of the fruit in the autumn. These range from the pale pink and green of the wild fruit to the pink, yellow, orange and deep flame of the ornamental variety. Some of these are quite edible, although they are usually hard and sharp, but they do make absolutely lovely jellies, even varying in the colour of the end product. They lend their sharp, almost perfumed taste, to the herb jellies and make a delicious savoury.

Angelica, apple mint, spearmint, costmary and borage are all excellent herbs to use with crab apples. You can of course experiment with other herbs using any of the formulas given below, using your own discretion for whether or not you use vinegar or lemon, and so on. Mint, sage and stronger flavoured herbs are better used with the ordinary cooking apples, but either variety makes up an end result which must have the advantage over any commercial product. Always make the jelly in small jars as once it is opened it will not keep for ever and it is not wolfed quite as quickly as bread-spreading jellies. Four small pots of herb jellies in a presentation box makes a smashing present.

Crab apples are very hard and they require a lot of cooking, more water and much hefty mashing with a wooden spoon or spud basher. Always chop them up very small or do the initial cooking in a pressure cooker, although this can mean you won't get so much juice.

All the following recipes can be made with ordinary cooking apples, the sharper and more unripe the better.

HEDGEROW HARVEST JAM

450g/1lb crab apples
450g/1lb blackberries
450g/1lb elderberries
225g/8oz sloes

225g/8oz haws
100g/4oz hazelnuts (optional)
1.5litres/2¾ pints water
1.75kg/4lb white sugar

8 hot, dry, sterile jam jars

Wash the fruit. Peel, chop and core the crab apples. Hull and pick over the blackberries. Remove the elderberries from the stalks – use the prongs of a fork for this. Prick the sloes several times with a needle and remove tops and tails from the haws. Chop the nuts. Put the prepared fruit and nuts into a pan with the water and cook until soft. While cooking watch for the sloe stones and remove them as you go. Add the sugar, stirring well until it has dissolved. Bring to the boil and boil hard until a set is obtained. Pot and seal.

A lovely jam to prepare and to make, tasting of those wood-smoke autumn flavours. A slight word of warning – use only good dry fruit and try to ensure that you have enough crab apples to give a firm set for blackberries and elderberries are notoriously low in pectin. Sloes give a very special taste to the jam and haws will help with the set. I could have included rosehips but as many of you will know, rosehip seeds have irritating little hairs on them and are better left to use in syrup or jelly. However, if you do use them you must carefully remove every last seed and piece of pith contained in the fleshy case and rinse very well. Cherry plum, bullace, wild cherry may all be added in the same way as sloes.

CRAB APPLE AND ROSEMARY JELLY

1kg/2lb 4oz crab apples
water
large handful of fresh rosemary sprigs

white wine vinegar
white sugar

small, hot, dry, sterile jars

Wash and chop the apples up small. Place in a preserving pan and cover with water. Cook until mushy and soft, adding more water if necessary. When soft, turn into a jelly bag and leave to drip overnight. The next day wash the rosemary, keeping back a few sprigs. Heat the liquid gently in a covered pan, add the rosemary and simmer gently for five minutes. Remove from heat, cover and leave to stand. When the house is filled with the pungent, aromatic smell of the rosemary you should have a good infusion. More prosaically, allow about 20 minutes. Strain, measure the liquid and for every 600ml/1 pint taken, measure 150ml/$\frac{1}{4}$ pint vinegar. Mix the liquids together, measure, and for every 600ml/1 pint then obtained take 450g/1lb sugar. Reheat the liquid gently and add the warmed sugar, stirring well until it has dissolved. Bring to the boil and boil rapidly until a set is obtained. This takes a little longer than usual because of the addition of the vinegar. Skim. Wash and dry the remaining rosemary. When the jelly has cooled a little, half-fill the pots, cool a little more and place a sprig of rosemary upright in the jar. The jelly should be set enough to support it. Fill to the top with jelly. Seal when cold.

This to my mind is the nicest of the herb jellies and is superb with lamb. If you like the smell of rosemary, then making this jelly will be a perfect pleasure.

APPLE PARADISE JELLY

1kg/2lb 4oz crab apples
450g/1lb cranberries
450g/1lb quinces

water
white sugar

small, hot, dry, sterile jars

Wash and chop the fruit. Put in a saucepan and just cover with water. Put on the lid, bring to the boil and then reduce heat. Simmer gently until the fruit is very soft. If you need to add water add just enough to ensure that you have lots of juice for a nice jelly. You will probably have to get to work with the old elbow grease and a wooden 'masher' as both crab apples and quinces are both notorious in the length of time they take to cook. Alternatively you could use a pressure cooker but you do not get quite so much delicious juice for your jelly. When fruit is very soft turn it into a jelly bag and allow to drip overnight. The next day measure the juice and for every 600ml/1 pint gained take 450g/1lb warmed sugar. Return juice and sugar to the pan, heat gently, stirring well until the sugar has dissolved. Bring to the boil and boil rapidly until a set is obtained. Pot and seal straight away.

If you use a pressure cooker for cooking the fruit proceed as follows. Wash and chop the crab apples and quinces. Wash the cranberries. Remove the trivet from the pressure cooker, put all the fruit in with 750ml/1¼ pints of water, cover with lid and cook for 8 minutes at M/10lb pressure in usual way. Allow to reduce at room temperature. Continue making the jelly as described above.

This jelly has a tart and unique flavour. It can be used as a savoury jelly but if you make it with ordinary cooking apples it becomes a sweeter bread and butter jelly.

SPICED CRAB APPLE PRESERVE

1kg/2lb 4oz crab apples
1 lemon
1 piece root ginger
small stick cinnamon
3 whole cloves

1 teaspoon whole allspice
1 teaspoon mustard seed
600ml/1 pint white vinegar
675g/1lb 8oz white sugar

4 hot, dry, sterile jars with wide necks and non-metal lids

Wash the crab apples and remove the stalks. Pare the rind from the lemon and tie this with the spices into a muslin bag. Wrap this in a cloth and bash it hard with a rolling pin. Put the vinegar and sugar into a preserving pan and heat gently until the sugar has dissolved, stirring well all the time. Add the muslin bag to the syrup. Bring to the boil and add the crab apples. Reduce the heat and simmer gently until the fruit is cooked (test for this by piercing a large one with a thin knitting needle, if it passes through without difficulty then they are ready). Remove with a perforated spoon and pack into the jars. Keep warm. Bring the syrup to the boil and boil hard until it is nice and thick. Pour over the fruit immediately, making sure that the apples are completely covered. Seal straight away.

SPICY APPLE BUTTER

1kg/2lb 4oz cooking or crab apples
450ml/¾ pint water
450ml/¾ pint cider
½ teaspoon ground cloves

½ teaspoon ground cinnamon
½ teaspoon ground nutmeg
soft brown sugar

small hot dry, sterile pots or moulds

Wash and chop the apples roughly. Simmer in the water and cider until very soft. Pass through a fine sieve. Measure the pulp and to each 600ml/1 pint of purée take 350g/12oz sugar. Return the fruit to the pan and heat gently until the purée is well thickened. Stir in the sugar and spices and simmer, stirring constantly until the mixture has become almost dry and no excess moisture remains. Pot and seal immediately.

If you substitute white sugar for brown when using crab apples you will obtain a much sharper butter which is also superb. Alternatively substitute 1½ teaspoons of ground ginger for the other spices for a good Apple Ginger Butter.

APPLE AND ROSEHIP CHEESE

1kg/2lb 4oz cooking or crab apples
300ml/½ pint pure fresh orange juice
150ml/¼ pint water

50g/2oz ripe rosehips
900g/2lb soft brown sugar

small, hot, dry, sterile moulds

Wash and chop the apples and put them into a preserving pan with the orange juice and water. Wash and slice the rosehips, tie them into a treble thickness muslin bag and add this to the pan. Cover and simmer until very soft. Remove the muslin bag. Pass the contents of the pan through a fine sieve and measure the resulting purée. For each 600ml/1 pint take 450g/1lb warmed sugar. Return the purée to the pan and heat gently, add the sugar stirring well until it has dissolved. Continue to cook at a gentle bubble stage, stirring frequently until the cheese is thick and almost moisture free. Pot and seal.

Marvellous on toasted brown bread, wholemeal scones or thin brown bread and butter.

Apricot

Apricots are a highly desirable fruit for preserving as they give beautiful, rich, amber goodies, reminiscent of warmth and sunshine, of hot foreign places and enclosed English gardens.

Make your fresh apricots into luxury preserves. Remember, too, that when you are travelling home from the continent by car, a tray of apricots bought at the roadside can be a year-long investment in summer sunshine. Fresh apricots start coming into the shops in January and continue a fair part of the year, arriving from South Africa, Mediterranean countries and the Middle East. They vary enormously in quality and price. Always use the best apricots, ripe, pinky-gold, firm and undamaged. To spend effort and money on mediocre fruit is an awful waste of time.

Dried apricots can be used with excellent results for jams and chutneys. Again, they vary in quality, the large, fat, expensively packed variety usually coming from California and the loose packs of smaller apricots coming from all over the place. If you are lucky you should be able to buy 3kg/7lb wholesale bags at a much cheaper price – ask your nearest Health Food stockist if he can help. They are an invaluable standby.

Preserves made with apricots are rich and sweet, blending well with citrus fruits, other dried fruits or nuts and making delicious chutneys. Their glowing colour makes them attractive to look at as presents when brandied or crystallized. The only problem with the luscious apricot is that it is very low in pectin, and is therefore quite often used with other high pectin fruits such as apples. Unless you use a commercial pectin the jam made with apricots is very runny, but I prefer this as it spreads better and goes further. The basic idea with fresh apricots is to use as little water as possible: about 6 tablespoons to the juice of two lemons for a weight of 1kg/2lb 4oz unprepared fruit, and 1kg/2lb 4oz white sugar. Make sure to add the pips of the lemons in a muslin bag.

With dried apricots, remember that they swell to at least twice their original volume and weight. It is essential to leave them to soak overnight in a large bowl with a good quantity of water. Use the juice and pips of 3 lemons to about 1.75 litres/3 pints of water for 450g/1lb dried fruit. The amount of sugar varies but it is usually 1350g/3lb to 450g/1lb dried apricots. They are usually cooked in the water they were soaked in, but do throw away the unmentionable bits at the bottom.

You should find the following exotic recipes enough to keep you experimenting everlastingly.

BASIC APRICOT JAM USING FRESH FRUIT

1kg/2lb 4oz fresh, ripe apricots

2 lemons

6 tablespoons water

1kg/2lb 4oz white sugar

6 hot, clean, sterile jam jars

Wash the apricots. Cut them in half and remove the stones, cracking at least half of them. To do this drop them in boiling water for a few minutes, wrap them in a cloth and bash them with a rolling pin. Blanche the kernels, skin them and split them – a tedious process but worth it in the end. Squeeze the lemons, reserve the juice and put the pips in a muslin bag. Put apricots, water, lemon juice and muslin bag into a preserving pan. Bring gently to the boil, reduce the heat and simmer slowly and carefully until the fruit is soft. It may be be necessary to add a dash more water, so watch it like a hawk. When the fruit is mushy and thickened remove the muslin bag, and add the kernels and the warmed sugar. Stir gently over a low heat until the sugar has dissolved and then bring to the boil and continue boiling rapidly until a set is obtained. Skim. Pot and seal.

The kernels are a necessary refinement adding the strange, nutty flavour so revered by connoisseurs.

DRIED APRICOT JAM USING A PRESSURE COOKER

450g/1lb dried apricots

1 lemon

1350g/3lb white sugar

100g/4oz blanched, split almonds

7 hot, dry, sterile jam jars

Wash and soak the apricots overnight in a deep bowl and well covered with water. The next day drain the fruit and reserve the water, throwing away the gritty bits at the bottom. Take the trivet from the cooker, put in the fruit and 600ml/1 pint of the reserved water. Cover and pressure cook for 10 minutes at M/10lb pressure. Allow the pressure to reduce at room temperature. Squeeze the juice from the lemon, add this with the sugar to the fruit. Heat gently, stirring well until the sugar is dissolved. Bring to the boil, add the almonds and boil hard until a set is obtained. Pot and seal immediately.

APRICOT AND ORANGE JAM

450g/1lb dried apricots
4 large oranges
1 lemon

1.75 litres/3 pints water
white sugar
25g/1oz blanched almonds

7 hot, dry, sterile jam jars

Using a potato peeler, pare the rind from the oranges and lemon ensuring that it is very thin and that no pith is taken. Drop the pared fruit into a bowl of boiling water and leave for 1 minute.

Remove and take the pith cleanly from the oranges and lemon. Tie the pips in a muslin bag. Put the rind and flesh through a coarse mincer. Place in a bowl and cover with 900ml/1½ pints cold water. Leave both bowls to stand overnight.

The next day put the contents of the bowls into a preserving pan and simmer for 30 minutes. When the fruit is tender, remove the muslin bag and weigh the pulp and take an equal quantity of warmed sugar. Return fruit and sugar to the preserving pan and heat gently, stirring well until the sugar has dissolved. Bring to the boil and boil rapidly until a set is obtained. Remove from the heat and stir in the chopped almonds. Allow to cool a little before potting. Seal when cold.

APRICOT AND PINEAPPLE JAM

450g/1lb dried apricots
1 lemon
600ml/1 pint water

425g/15oz tin of pineapple pieces
1600g/3½lb white sugar

8 hot, dry, sterile jam jars

Wash and chop up the apricots. Squeeze the juice from the lemon and tie the pips in a muslin bag. Put the apricots, lemon juice, muslin bag and water into a deep bowl and allow to stand overnight. The next day drain the apricots, reserving the liquid except for the bits of nasty. Drain the pineapple and add the syrup to the liquid from the apricots. Place this with the apricots and the muslin bag in a preserving pan and simmer gently until the fruit is soft. Remove the muslin bag and add the pineapple pieces. Heat gently until the pineapple is transparent. Add the warmed sugar and stir gently over a low heat until it has dissolved. Bring to the boil and boil rapidly until a set is obtained. Pot and seal.

APRICOT BUTTER AND BUTTERS IN GENERAL

Fruit butters are very similar to fruit cheeses but do not have so much sugar added. If you have a great glut of fruit then they are certainly worth making. The pure fruit butters are soft, creamy and superb with ice cream and cold puddings. Children and the elderly particularly love them for they have no difficult skin or pips to cope with. They are also very nutritious. The spicy butters are gorgeous spread in sandwiches with cold meat or eaten on toast and on crusty wholemeal bread. Most fruit make good butters. Apricots, both dried and fresh, cherries, peaches, green-gages, strawberries, raspberries and green grapes all produce a well flavoured butter following the recipe and method for spiced apricot butter but omitting the spices.

Plain apple or apple and plum can take more sugar (350g/12oz instead of 225g/8oz). Cherries should be left with the sugar and lemon juice, to stand overnight before cooking and the chopped kernels added to the butter to give a lovely almondy taste. Try experimenting with new fruits and flavours of your own to achieve some splendid results.

APRICOT BUTTER WITH SPICES

1kg/2lb 4oz fresh, ripe apricots
6 tablespoons water
caster sugar
2 lemons

ground cinnamon
ground cloves
ground allspice

small pâté dishes, moulds or pots

Wash, halve and stone the fruit. Put into a pan with the water and simmer very slowly until soft. Pass through a coarse sieve or a liquidizer. Measure the purée and for every 600ml/1 pint take 225g/8oz of warmed sugar, and 1 teaspoon of each of the spices. Grate the rind from the lemons and put this with the juice, the purée, sugar and spices back into the pan. Cook slowly stirring frequently until nearly dry and very thick. Pot and seal immediately.

APRICOT CURD

450g/1lb fresh apricots
water
2 lemons

4 large fresh eggs
100g/4oz unsalted butter
450g/1lb caster sugar

10 small, hot, dry, sterile jars

Wash the fruit and put in a small saucepan with very little water and cook until soft, adding a little more water if necessary. Take out the stones and pass the pulp through a fine sieve. Put the purée in a double saucepan, add the juice and grated rind from the lemons, the butter and sugar. Heat gently until the sugar has dissolved, add the beaten eggs and stir the mixture until it thickens. Pot and seal.

A most delicate and lovely curd may be made by substituting fresh peaches for the apricots.

RICH APRICOT MARMALADE

150g/5-6oz dried apricots
5 large sweet oranges
1 large grapefruit
1 large lemon

800g/1lb 12oz white sugar
800g/1lb 12oz brown sugar
1.15 litre/2 pints water

9 hot, dry, sterile jam jars

Wash apricots and chop them well. Wash oranges, grapefruit and lemon, cut them up and put the pips in a muslin bag. Put the rest of the citrus fruit through a coarse mincer. Place minced fruit, apricots and muslin bag in a deep bowl. Cover with the water and leave overnight. The next day transfer the contents of the bowl to a preserving pan and cook gently for about 2 hours. Test to see if the peel is soft. Remove the muslin bag and add the warmed sugar. Stir well on a low heat until the sugar has dissolved then bring to the boil and boil rapidly until a set is obtained. Allow to cool a little before potting. Seal when cold.

A very tangy, rich marmalade.

APRICOT CONSERVE

1kg/2lb 4oz fresh, ripe apricots   1kg/2lb 4oz white sugar
2 lemons

6 hot, dry, sterile jam jars

Wash and halve or quarter the apricots depending on size, and discard the stones. Place in a pan with the juice from lemons and sugar. Heat gently, stirring very carefully until the sugar has dissolved. Bring to the boil and boil rapidly until a set is obtained. Take great care not to burn. Allow to cool a little before potting. Seal when cold.

APRICOT CONSERVE WITH RUM

450g/1lb dried apricots   1350g/3lb white sugar
water   rum
1 lemon   50g/2oz blanched almonds

8 hot, dry, sterile jam jars

Wash the apricots well, chop them up and put them in a large bowl just covered with water. Leave to stand overnight. The next day put the apricots and the liquid that they have been soaked in, except for the gritty bits, into a preserving pan. Cook gently until the fruit is soft. Add the juice from the lemon and the warmed sugar, stir over a low heat until the sugar has dissolved. Bring to the boil and boil rapidly until a setting point is reached. Take off the heat and stir in a generous noggin of rum. Bring to the boil again for one minute. Remove from the heat and stir in the split almonds. Skim. Allow to cool before potting. Seal when cold.

MARDI'S APRICOT CONSERVE

450g/1lb dried apricots   50g/2oz seedless raisins
2 large sweet oranges   1500g/3lb 6oz white sugar
2 lemons   50g/2oz chopped nuts
1.75 litres/3 pints water

10 hot, dry, sterile jam jars

Wash the apricots well. Chop or mince the oranges, keep the pips and tie them with the pips from the lemons into a muslin bag. Squeeze the lemon juice and reserve it. Put the apricots, oranges and muslin bag in a deep bowl, cover with the water and allow to stand overnight. The next day turn the contents of the bowl into a preserving pan, add the raisins (large, fat, loose ones) and simmer until all the fruit is soft. Remove the muslin bag and add the warmed sugar and lemon juice. Stir gently over a low heat until the sugar has dissolved. Bring to the boil and boil rapidly until a set is obtained. Allow to cool a little and then add the chopped nuts, stir well. Pot. Seal when cold.

A very pleasant and unusual preserve. I am not sure whether 'Mardi' is connected with the *Mardi Gras* or if she was a long forgotten and exotic lady of my forbears' aquaintance.

ALCOHOLIC APRICOTS

450g/1lb dried apricots
175g/6oz soft, light brown sugar

1 lemon
300ml/½ pint cheap brandy

2 large, hot, dry, sterile preserving jars

Wash the apricots well (buy only the large good quality ones). Put them in a pan and just cover with water. Simmer very gently for about 5 minutes. Remove from the heat and allow them to cool in their juice until they are just tepid. Drain the apricots and reserve the liquid. Pack them loosely into the jars allowing room for them to expand in the delicious syrup. Keep warm. Pare the rind from half of the lemon with a potato peeler and cut it into strips. Put this into the pan with 150ml/¼ pint of the reserved liquid and the sugar. Heat gently, stirring well until the sugar has dissolved. Bring to the boil and boil hard for 5 minutes. Pour over the fruit making sure that it is equally distributed. Fill each pot up to the top with the brandy ensuring that all the fruit is well covered. Seal. Keep the jars in a dark place and give them a little shake every now and again.

The alcohol seeps into the fruit, plumps it up and is absolutely delicious. You can also use alcohol like sherry and vermouth for a unique flavour. Other dried fruit such as peaches, prunes or even raisins are delicious preserved in this fashion. Eat either in an open flan or as they are, warmed in their own syrup, with cream.

PICKLED APRICOTS

1kg/2lb 4oz large ripe apricots	3cm/1 inch piece cinnamon stick
1 level tablespoon whole allspice	1 level tablespoon grated nutmeg
1 level tablespoon whole cloves	350ml/12fl. oz wine vinegar
blade mace	500g/1lb 2oz white sugar

4 hot, dry, sterile jars with wide necks and non-metal lids

Drop the apricots into boiling water for one minute, take them out, plunge them into cold water, then drain and peel them. Tie the spices into a muslin bag. Put the fruit, nutmeg, spice bag, vinegar and sugar into a large stainless steel pan and heat gently, stirring carefully for 5 minutes. The apricots should look transparent. Remove with a perforated spoon and pack carefully into jars. Keep warm. Reboil the syrup until it is very thick. Remove the muslin bag giving it a good squeeze. Pour the syrup over the fruit making sure that it is well covered and that there are no air bubbles. Seal immediately.

Cider vinegar can be used to give a spicier result. Small golden peaches can be picked in the same way. Excellent with smoked meats, salt beef, etc.

COUNTRYMAN'S APRICOT CHUTNEY

Dried apricots lend themselves particularly well to chutney, blending with the other fruits to make the most delicious and extravagant concoctions. If you can buy the 3kg/7lb bags of dried apricots through your local health food store or grocer then you are onto a winner. They are a marvellous investment, much more economical than the larger more expensive variety, and extremely adequate for chutney.

450g/1lb dried apricots	small piece green root ginger
1 large onion	50g/2oz raisins
3 cloves garlic	600ml/1 pint white vinegar
1 teaspoon coriander seed	350g/12oz demerara sugar
1 teaspoon salt	

3 hot, dry, sterile jars with non-metal lids

Leave the apricots to soak overnight in a deep bowl and well covered with water. Drain them the next day. Peel and chop the onions and garlic. Wash the raisins. Grate the root ginger and use 1 teaspoon. Grind the coriander in a mortar. Put all the ingredients into a large, stainless steel pan. Heat gently, giving an occasional stir to prevent the sugar sticking. Continue to simmer gently until the whole mixture is well cooked and as thick as jam. Try to keep the apricots whole. Pot and seal immediately.

Leave for at least 2 months. A very good aromatic chutney and simply super with cold ham or tongue.

CURRIED APRICOT CHUTNEY

450g/1lb dried apricots
1 onion
2 tablespoons water
675g/1lb 8oz brown sugar
1 level teaspoon curry powder

1 level teaspoon cinnamon
1 level teaspoon ground allspice
pinch cayenne pepper
600ml/1 pint wine vinegar

4 hot, dry, sterile jars with non-metal lids

Wash and chop the apricots. Leave to stand overnight in a deep bowl well covered with water. The next day peel and chop the onions and stew them gently in the water with 1 tablespoon of the sugar until they are tender. Strain the apricots and put them with all the ingredients including the onion mixture, into a stainless steel pan. Heat gently, stirring well until the sugar has dissolved. Bring to the boil and then simmer gently until the chutney is thick (about 2 hours). Stir occasionally to prevent burning. Pot and seal immediately.

CRYSTALLIZED APRICOTS

The following recipe is a fairly simple method of crystallizing and is useful for those of us who do not have the time for the more professional method which, although foolproof, can take days and days to achieve by which time you have lost interest or half the fruit has been thieved.

1kg/2lb 4oz large, ripe, fresh apricots   water
1kg/2lb 4oz white sugar

hot, dry, sterile jars with wide necks (lids are not necessary)

Wipe the apricots with a damp cloth and pierce with a silver needle. Put the sugar with 300ml/½ pint water into a large pan and heat gently stirring well until the sugar has dissolved. Boil until it becomes a thick syrup but do not burn otherwise you will have caramel. Put the apricots into the syrup and boil for 10 minutes. Remove from the heat and pour out into a heatproof basin. Submerge, cover and leave for 24 hours. Put the syrup and apricots back into the saucepan. Boil for 1 minute and then take out the fruit using a perforated spoon and pack it carefully into the jars. Continue to boil the syrup hard until it is the consistency of thick honey. Pour it over the fruit in the jars dividing it equally. Cover and leave the fruit for 24 hours. Drain the syrup from the jars. Reboil the syrup again and pour over the fruit. Cover and leave. Repeat this process until there is no syrup left leaving 24 hours between each boiling. The sugar must have completely impregnated the fruit. Place the apricots on a sponge rack and leave to dry in a warm place at a constant temperature of 100°C/200°F or gas mark $\frac{1}{4}$. The top of an airing cupboard with the door ajar is an ideal place providing you do not forget and lay the clean laundry on top. Finish off with the following process for crystallizing or glacéing.

Skewer each apricot and dip it quickly into boiling water. Drain off excess moisture and then roll in fine caster sugar. Shake off excess and store between layers of waxed paper in a large, roomy box.

HOW TO GLACÉ

Place 900g/2lb of white sugar in a pan with 300ml/$\frac{1}{2}$ pint water. Heat gently, stirring well, until the sugar has dissolved. Bring to the boil, turn down to barely simmer and cover the pan tightly. Have ready a pan of boiling water, spear the fruit and dunk it into the continuously boiling water for 20 minutes. Drain. Pour some of the syrup into a wide cup and keep the rest tightly covered and simmering in the saucepan. Dip the fruit, one at a time, into the syrup and leave to drain on a wire sponge rack. Finish all the fruit in this way. As soon as the syrup becomes cloudy or bitty replace it with the fresh hot syrup. Dry the fruit on the sponge rack at a temperature of 100°C/200°F or gas mark $\frac{1}{4}$. Keep the damp down during glacéing and try to work on a dry day as humidity seems to affect the process. Store in an airy box between layers of waxed paper.

I hope that the end product of these endeavours will be as tantalizingly delicious as the fantastic crystallized fruits of Provence. Other fruit which come in those lovely boxes and on which you might well try this method of crystallizing are small golden peaches, small ripe dessert pears and purple figs which are only just ripe, otherwise they might well split.

TO DRY APRICOTS

Not only apricots but peaches, plums and greengages dry well by the following method. It would of course be marvellous if they could be dried out in the sun in the traditional fashion but this is just not possible in our unreliable climate.

1kg/2lb 4oz whole, ripe, unblemished apricots

Wipe the fruit with a damp cloth. Halve and stone the apricots and peaches, cutting if possible with a silver knife which helps prevent the fruit discolouring. Plums and greengages can be left whole. Place the fruit flat side up on a sponge rack covered with a layer of muslin. Put into a very cool oven, leaving the door ajar. The top of a warm, spacious airing cupboard would do equally well but the door must be left ajar. Should the fruit show signs of cracking the temperature must be reduced even further. Keep the fruit in this state for at least 2 hours a day for six days. If you have a solid fuel range then you can leave them in every night with the door ajar for 6 nights. I am sure that you know what dried apricots look like – they should be soft and springy and have no surplus moisture when squeezed. The same applies to plums and greengages but they do take longer to dry than apricots and peaches so please be patient. Leave in a cool dark place for a couple of days before storing them.

Artichoke

There are three different types of artichokes which may be grown satisfactorily in the British Isles.

The Globe artichoke (*Cynara scolymus*), is the blue-green thistly plant which can be grown, well mulched and manured, with considerable success in most gardens. The flower buds are the edible delicacy so beloved by gourmets. The roots, which are woody and gnarled are not edible, having a very strong purgative effect; unfortunately wood lice are absolutely crazy about them so you must be sure to guard against these invaders.

The Jerusalem artichoke (*Helianthus tuberosus*), is also a very decorative garden plant but difficult to get rid of once firmly established. Its English name is probably a corruption of the Italian name *girasole articiocco* – sunflower artichoke. The roots are the edible part of the plant, very nobbly, difficult to peel and with a unique, rather smokey, nutty taste.

The Chinese artichoke (*Stachys sieboldi*), is unfortunately rarely grown in Britain. It only does well in the southern counties, as frost does not agree with its temperament. The tubers are small, slim and golden orange with a glorious nutty flavour, rather delicate and dry – similar to salsify. Both salsify and Chinese artichokes are much neglected in Britain but seeds or plants can be bought from any good nurserymen.

PICKLED JERUSALEM ARTICHOKES

1kg/2lb 4oz Jerusalem artichokes	2 lemons
water	4 bay leaves
sea salt	1.15 litres/2 pints white vinegar

3 hot, dry, sterile jars with non-metal lids

Wash the artichokes and scrub well with a small brush. Peel them (this is a nobbly, nasty, difficult business but they must not have any skin left on them). Cut the large ones in half and drop them into boiling water to which you have added 50g/2oz of salt. Cover and cook until just tender; do not overcook because they are liable to disintegrate. While they are cooking take the peel from the lemon in thin strips with a potato peeler, taking no pith with it. Put this with the bay leaves and vinegar into a stainless steel pan and boil for 15 minutes. Allow the vinegar to cool, drain off and keep the peel and bay leaves. When the artichokes are cooked drain them well and pack them carefully into the jars, dispersing the peel and bay leaves decoratively amongst them. Pour the cold vinegar over the contents of the jars, completely covering. Seal.

Keep for at least 4 weeks before using. I think this pickle goes superbly well with smoked fish. The lemon gives a strange pungency to the delicate nutty flavour of the artichoke and it also has the added advantage of looking attractive and unusual. Don't throw the vinegar away – not only is it excellent as a dressing for smoked fish, but it can also be used for making clear pickles, adding its own distinctive flavour.

PLAIN WHOLE ARTICHOKE PICKLE

1kg/2lb 4oz Jerusalem artichokes	600ml/1 pint malt vinegar
lemon juice	25g/1oz brown sugar
4 chilli peppers or 1 sweet red pepper	25g/1oz whole black peppers

3 hot, dry, sterile jam jars with non-metal lids

Wash and clean the artichokes, peel and quarter or slice, drop into a bowl of cold water to which a dash of lemon juice has been added (to prevent discolouration). Wash the chilli peppers. (If you prefer a milder pickle, use one sweet red pepper, washed, deseeded and cut into rings.) Put the other ingredients into a stainless steel pan and bring to the boil and boil for 5 minutes. In the meantime, drain and pat dry the artichokes and peppers or chillis and pack the jars with them. Cover with the hot vinegar and seal immediately.

Another lovely pickle and extremely decorative to give as presents.

STORING JERUSALEM ARTICHOKES

If you have to lift the artichokes before you are ready to use them, they may be stored in sand. Brush dirt and soil from the artichokes and three-quarter-fill a heavy box, tub or container with free running, clean, dry sand – not sand from the beach. Put a good layer of sand on the bottom of the box and then a layer of artichokes and so on, finishing with sand. Store in a dry place and help yourself when you need them.

Asparagus

Only if you grow your own asparagus is it really worth preserving in any form, for it is a luxury and very expensive at any time. However it is a plant that is worth growing, for once established (from seed it takes three years), it gives no trouble and progresses rapidly. Always choose sticks of asparagus that are full grown, fat and straight.

PICKLED ASPARAGUS

450g/1lb asparagus spears
300ml/½ pint dry white wine
300ml/½ pint white wine vinegar

½ teaspoon grated nutmeg
3 blades mace
¼ teaspoon white pepper, freshly ground

2 tall, dry, clean sterile jars with non-metal lids

Wash the asparagus carefully in cold water and cut off the thick base ends, leaving the green, delicate part. Cut them no longer than 13cm/5 inches (do not throw the end bits away – use them for flavouring soups, stews etc.); leave in a bowl of slightly salted water for 2 hours. In the meantime, pour the wine, vinegar and spices into a stainless steel saucepan and boil hard for about 10 minutes. Leave to get cold. Drain the asparagus. Now, bearing in mind that the spears must not be damaged, put it into a large preserving pan that gives plenty of room, just cover with water, bring to the boil and remove from the heat immediately. Have ready some dry, clean cloths. Remove the asparagus carefully and lay it on the cloths to drain. When they are cold pack the spears carefully into the jars making sure that the heads are all facing the same way, up or down. Pour the cold, prepared vinegar over them, making sure that they are well covered and there are no air bubbles. Cover and seal immediately.

Do not keep this pickle too long – a couple of weeks is enough. It is a real delicacy, made with gentle and subtle flavourings and, although expensive, is superb with delicately flavoured cold meats or fish, e.g., Parma ham, smoked salmon etc.

Aubergine

A native of South America, the aubergine made its journey to Europe with the conquistadores via Spain, thence to Italy and the Mediterranean basin and on into Asia, but despite its romantic background it can be grown quite well in Britain. Different varieties of aubergine are suitable for different purposes although the taste is always the same. Long thin aubergines, round, fat, white, striped and purple, freeze very well and makes excellent meaty chutneys. My own preference is for immersing them in oily aromatic juices or pickling them. I find that it is not possible to bottle them as they do not seem to take kindly to being drowned in mere mundane water. With typical British madness we often call it the egg plant, presumably because one variety of aubergine is white and egg-shaped.

AUBERGINE AND CAPSICUM CHUTNEY

1kg/2lb 4oz plump aubergines
1kg/2lb 4oz red peppers (capsicum)
50g/2oz sea salt
1 large tablespoon turmeric
1 large tablespoon good curry powder
900ml/1½ pints malt vinegar
1 rounded teaspoon ground ginger

1 rounded teaspoon ground cinnamon
4 bay leaves
1 tablespoon olive oil
225g/8oz shallots
2 large cloves garlic
100g/4oz soft brown sugar
salt and cayenne to taste

4 hot, dry, sterile jars with non-metal lids

Wash and cut the aubergines into small chunks. Wash and chop the peppers, discarding seeds and pith. Put the salt and turmeric into a large bowl and add the aubergines and peppers, giving them a good stir to make sure that all the vegetables are well covered with seasoning. Dissolve the curry powder in a bowl with a little of the vinegar, add the ginger, cinnamon and bay leaves. Cover and leave to stand for 15 minutes. Wash, peel and slice the shallots and garlic. Heat the olive oil in a large, heavy frying pan. Add the aubergines, peppers, shallots and garlic and cook for 10 minutes, giving it an occasional stir. Add the sugar, stir well and add the curry mixture. Blend well together and simmer gently for a further 10 minutes, taking care not to burn. As the mixture is not very moist you should watch it carefully. Add the rest of the vinegar, stir well and simmer gently until thick. Test for seasoning and add more salt and cayenne to taste. Pot and seal.

Store for at least 2 months before using. A good, chunky chutney, very much like a piccalilli but more fiery and more real taste coming through. Excellent with cold meat.

AUBERGINE AND PEPPER RELISH

1kg/2lb 4oz fleshy aubergines
900g/2lb red peppers
900g/2lb cooking apples
900g/2lb onions
4 red chillies
3cm/1 inch piece of root ginger

2 tablespoons coriander seeds
1.15 litre/2 pints brown malt vinegar
2 teaspoons sea salt
350g/12oz sultanas
675g/1lb 8oz soft brown sugar

9 hot, dry, sterile jars with non-metal lids

Wash the aubergines and chop into small pieces. Wash the peppers, discard the seeds and pithy parts, chop finely. Wash, peel, core and chop the apples into small dice. Wash, peel and shred the onions. Wash and chop the chillies (keep your fingers away from your eyes and mouth – the oil from chillies is very burning). Bruise the ginger and slightly crush the coriander seeds; tie chillies, ginger and coriander into a muslin bag. Place peppers, apples and onions in a large stainless steel pan with the muslin bag and half the vinegar. Bring to the boil, cover and simmer until the onions are tender. Add the aubergines, salt, washed sultanas, sugar and the remainder of the vinegar. Bring to the boil again and simmer until well thickened, giving an occasional stir to prevent sticking. Remove the muslin bag and pour into jars. Seal.

Avocado

The Avocado pear has grown enormously in popularity and availability since the last war. Originating from Central and South America it is a pear-shaped vegetable (not a fruit) of the Persea family with a tough, leathery green skin and soft, pale green flesh which is usually eaten as a savoury. It is considered a useful vegetable because of the very high protein and fat content which with the high percentage of vitamins A and B, makes it an invaluable dietary addition. Avocado should only be eaten when very soft and as they do not travel very well are rather expensive. However they are now being produced in quantity closer to our own shores, in Israel and Mediterranean areas, so this problem is being largely overcome.

Avocado do not cook well, so generally speaking they should only be heated through. For this reason the chutney recipe that I have given below specifies unripe fruit which will not become harsh and unpleasant when cooked. Nevertheless, take the precaution of testing and tasting throughout the process and if you have to use ripe fruit, add it at the very end and just heat through once.

Grow your own Avocado trees from the stones – they usually prosper very well. I plant them, fat end down, into a pot of good soil with the tips poking out, and keep them well watered.

AVOCADO CHUTNEY

1kg/2lb 4oz unripe, very green and
   hard avocados
3 limes
2 small oranges
1 clove garlic
1 shallot
1 sweet red pepper
300g/11oz soft light brown sugar

100g/4oz seedless raisins
450ml/¾ pint cider vinegar
long stick cinnamon
1 teaspoon curry powder
1 teaspoon ground ginger
1 teaspoon dried mustard powder
1 teaspoon ground black pepper

4 hot, dry, sterile jars with non-metal lids

Wash and dry the limes and oranges and slice very thinly. Peel the garlic and shallot, seed the pepper and put these through a mincer. Put all the ingredients except the avocados into a stainless steel pan and simmer for 1 hour. Skin the avocados, remove the stone and cut the flesh into small cubes. Add the flesh to the pan and cook for about 20 minutes, although it may take a little longer so keep on tasting and testing to ensure that you do not overcook. When it is thick and soft remove the cinnamon. Pot and seal.

    Store for at least 2 months before using. Keep in a cool place and serve with fish and cold meats.

B

Banana

The everyday banana found in all British food shops from the corner grocer to the hypermarket is only one humble member of a family boasting hundreds of varieties. Still relatively cheap to buy, it is very high in starch and carbohydrate, easy to eat, a meal in itself and an invaluable, highly nutritive food source.

Bananas come to us throughout the year from the Canaries, Israel, South America and the West Indies. I prefer not to use bananas for preserving as I find them too bland and sweet for my taste. However, children love them in jam and the good but rather soft chutney makes a fine accompaniment to curry. Another banana-type fruit is the plantain, which is larger with coarser flesh and excellent for making fritters, etc. Weights for bananas can be rather misleading. All these recipes are given for unpeeled fruit but you can reckon that one unpeeled, medium size banana weighs approximately 100g/4oz and peeled, 75g/3oz. You should get about nine unpeeled bananas to 1kg/2lb 4oz.

BANANA JAM

1kg/2lb 4oz bananas
1 lemon

600ml/1 pint apple juice
225g/8oz white sugar

5 small, hot, dry, sterile jars

Peel and slice the bananas. Squeeze the juice from the lemon and put this with the apple juice and sugar into a preserving pan. Heat gently, stirring well until the sugar has dissolved. Add the bananas and bring to the boil, stirring well. Simmer gently until nice and thick. Pot and seal.

This jam sets very well owing to the use of the high pectin apple juice, which you can of course make yourself from all those leftover apple peels and cores (see Pectin Syrup or Extract p.19).

BANANA PRESERVE WITH RUM

1kg/2lb 4oz bananas
1 lemon
1 tablespoon rum

350g/12 oz white sugar
175g/6oz Barbados sugar
1 teaspoon ground cinnamon

small, hot, dry, sterile jam jar

Peel bananas and slice them into a bowl. Grate the rind and squeeze the juice from the lemon. Mix these in a bowl with the rum and sprinkle over the bananas, turning them very gently as you do so. Mix the sugars together. Take a fresh bowl and put the sugar and bananas in layers into this. Cover and leave for 24 hours. The next day turn the whole lot into a preserving pan with the cinnamon. Heat gently, stirring well, until the sugar is completely dissolved. Bring to the boil and boil for 5 minutes, stirring continuously. The preserve will be thick, rich and brown. Remove from heat and leave for 10 minutes before potting. Seal.

A very good addition to an ice cream sundae with lots of nuts.

PICKLED BANANAS

1kg/2lb 4oz bananas
250g/9oz demerara sugar
2 blades mace

3cm/1 inch stick cinnamon
6 cloves
300ml/½ pint malt vinegar

3 hot, dry, sterile jars with non-metal lids

Tie the spices in a muslin bag and put these with the vinegar into a preserving pan. Heat gently until just warm. Add the sugar stirring well until it is dissolved. Bring to the boil and boil for 15 minutes. Peel and slice the bananas into 5mm/¼ inch strips crossways. Add them to the syrup and cook gently until tender. Pack into jars with a perforated spoon, strain the syrup and pour over the fruit making sure that it is well covered and that there are no air bubbles. Seal.

Very good with cold rice salads.

BANANA AND DATE CHUTNEY

350g/12oz cooking apples
675g/1lb 8oz onions
600ml/1 pint malt vinegar
1 rounded teaspoon ground allspice,
  turmeric, ginger and coriander

1 level teaspoon cayenne
1kg/2lb 4oz bananas
350g/12oz cooking dates
75g/3oz crystallized ginger
3 teaspoons salt

4 hot, dry, sterile jars with non-metal lids

Peel, core and chop the apples. Peel and chop the onions. Put apples and onions with a third of the vinegar into a stainless steel preserving pan. Cook gently until soft. Make a paste in a small china bowl with the spices and 1 tablespoon of the vinegar, cover and leave to stand. Peel and chop the bananas. Chop the dates and the crystallized ginger. Add these to the preserving pan with the spicy paste. Stir well and continue to cook very gently until the chutney is thick and pulpy. Stir in the salt, sugar and remaining vinegar. Simmer gently until very thick. If the chutney shows signs of sticking or burning, add more warm vinegar. Like most chutneys, it needs careful watching. When it is well cooked, bring to the boil just once. Stir well. Pot and seal.

A very tasty chutney, slightly curried and hot. A good accompaniment to cold lamb or chicken.

Barberry

Barberry bushes, like many other indigenous shrubs, are on the decline in Britain. In East Anglia, where I once lived, they grow quite frequently in the long shady lanes leading to the marshland. The barberry is of the *Berberis* family, grows to about 2½ metres/8 feet in height, and is very prickly with serrated oval leaves and long clusters of very scarlet, slightly translucent oval berries. Bearing in mind how many of these very scarlet berries are highly poisonous be sure of your facts beforehand. The local people believed them to be deadly because of their appearance. In fact they make a very pleasant, slightly tart jelly or jam, not unlike that of the rowan, and, because the berries are high in pectin and acid make a good jelly. Pick the fruit in the autumn when it is very ripe.

BARBERRY JELLY

1kg/2lb 4oz barberries
300ml/½ pint water

white sugar
lemons

3 hot, dry, sterile jam jars

Wash the berries and run the clusters through the prongs of a fork to remove the main stalk. Put the fruit into an earthenware dish in a warm oven until the juices run. Warm the water and when the fruit is very soft remove it from the oven, add the water and cook for a further 15 minutes. Leave to strain in a muslin bag overnight. The next day measure the liquid gained and for each 600ml/1 pint take 450g/1lb sugar and the juice of 1 lemon. Put the barberry juice, and sugar into a pan, heat gently stirring well until the sugar has dissolved. Add the lemon juice, bring to the boil and boil hard until a set is obtained. Pot and seal.

An orangey-red jelly, very good with cold game, particularly venison.

Basil

The basil (*Ocimum basilicum*) used for culinary purposes is the soft leaf basil and is, without doubt, one of the most delicious and useful herbs. It is an absolutely necessary ingredient for all those marvellous Mediterranean dishes, particularly in pesto sauce, certain soups and all, but *all*, tomato dishes. Rather than dry it, which I think is a shame, keep a pot going all the winter until the next one comes along or preserve in oil which retains that wonderful flavour better than anything. It also freezes remarkably well. Apple and Basil Jelly is another successful way of having your herbs and eating them. Bush basil (*Ocimum minimum*) is used only as a border bush in the garden and not as a herb.

BASIL JELLY

See Tarragon Jelly, p.352, but use white vinegar.

BASIL PRESERVED IN OIL

a large quantity of very fresh basil
best quality olive oil

a good preserving jar

Pick the leaves from the stalks. Wash and drain them without bruising, dry in a clean cloth. Pack into a jar and completely cover with olive oil. Seal jar securely. Basil, fresh, frozen or dried keeps its flavour very well but in oil it is particularly successful, though unfortunately it tends to be a little bit slippery. The oil can be used afterwards, its slight flavour making it good for salad dressing.

FREEZING BASIL

Pick fresh basil before the midday sun takes its toll. Strip leaves from stalks and pop into small polythene packets, sealed very tightly to prevent the smell spreading. Label, freeze and store. A handy tip: if you are using crushed leaves in a recipe, crush the frozen herb in the packet and add it straight away to the dish. Freezer-life is about six months.

DRYING BASIL

Again, pick fresh basil before the sun is high. Remove the best leaves and tops. Tie them loosely into a muslin bag and dip them in boiling water for half a minute. Remove, pat dry without damaging leaves and spread them on trays. It is best, if possible, to dry this herb fairly quickly in an airy, light and warm room, failing that a warm oven 100°C/200°F or gas mark $\frac{1}{4}$ will have to do. Turn the leaves from time to time to make sure that they are evenly dried. Do not leave in direct sunlight otherwise you will lose the volatile oils. Pack in airtight jars. Seal well.

Sweet Bay or Laurus

The bay tree that grows in my coastal garden is a giant, and a pretty useful one too according to folk legend – the bay is associated with honour, fame and victory, and is a protector and a healer. Take heart, however, for even a small bush must bring you all these qualities and grown in a tub, indoors or out, they are very cooperative. Either grow your bush from a cutting, pruning strategically at the right time, or buy a sturdy standard or half standard from a nursery.

DRYING BAY LEAVES

Hang a simple bunch in a dry place close at hand. Either use them as you go along or store them in an airtight jar. Essential and imaginative in making white sauces, milk puddings, in a bouquet garni, in stews, in poaching and sousing fish and as decoration on pâté and terrine. Be discreet when using it and remember that a fresh leaf is twice as powerful as a dried one.

Bean

What a beautifully evocative word 'bean' is, summing up the best in British vegetables. Everybody, no matter how small their garden space, should be able to grow at least one variety and reap a modest crop, for beans are accomodating, good-natured and productive. The three main British varieties of bean are:

Broad bean: white, scented flowers with long, large, soft, green pods, velvet-coated inside providing soft hollows for the large, flat green or white bean. When young the bean may be cooked whole in the pod but when they are mature the bean alone is eaten. They bottle, pickle and freeze very well and older beans may be dried with great success.

78

French beans, dwarf or *stringless beans*: these are smooth, roundish and easy to prepare requiring only topping and tailing – the nearest bean we have to a Haricot vert.

Runner or *scarlet beans*: the variety most commonly grown in Britain. They have to be strung and sliced before cooking and make excellent pickles and chutney. This is a bean which can produce a tremendous crop in a good summer.

New and exciting varieties of bean now to be found in a good seedsman's range are Haricot beans, Dutch Brown bean, Tic bean, Green Soya bean, Navy bean and Lima bean. It seems that the possibilities are endless. Hot house beans come into the shops in March – August and one variety or another from home and abroad continues throughout the year. There are an enormous amount of named varieties of each type of bean to choose from. Some have purple pods, others beautifully scented flowers; some are giants others dwarfs. Pick the variety which will suit your circumstances and conditions best.

CUMBERLAND BEAN PICKLE

1kg/2lb 4oz runner beans
2 medium size English onions
450ml/¾ pint white vinegar
50g/2oz plain flour

1 level tablespoon mustard powder
½ teaspoon ground black pepper
½ teaspoon powdered turmeric
150g/5oz white sugar

6 hot, dry, sterile jam jars with non-metal lids

Wash, string and slice the beans into thin strips crosswise. Wash, peel and slice the onions very finely. Cook together with a pinch of salt and just enough water to cover until tender. Take a good tablespoon of the vinegar, put it in a large stainless steel saucepan with the flour, mustard, pepper and turmeric, mix to a smooth paste, start to heat gently and add the remainder of the vinegar very carefully bit by bit, rather as you would a roux sauce, ensuring that there are no lumps. Simmer until the flour is cooked but do not boil. It should be of a thick, shiny, sauce-like consistency. Drain the beans and onions and add to the sauce, stir well and continue stirring until the mixture thickens again. Pot and seal immediately.

Store for at least 2 months before using. A very crisp, piccalilli-like pickle. Pleasant, hot and not too strong. Keeps well.

PICKLED BROAD BEANS

1kg/2lb 4oz broad beans
2 teaspoons salt
600ml/1 pint white vinegar
1 orange

4 cloves
2 blades mace
3 pieces root ginger
10 black peppercorns

5 dry, sterile jam jars with non-metal lids

Shell the beans (you could use up old large ones left in the garden). The recipes make allowances for shelled weight so do not be alarmed at the meagre remains of your original kilogram. Put them into a saucepan of boiling water to which you have added the salt. Boil gently until they are just soft but if they break up they will ruin the pickle. The skin should be firm but the inside soft, so bite one and see. Strain the beans and allow to cool. Pare the rind from the orange with a potato peeler, you need only a few strips; boil this with the vinegar and spices in a stainless steel pan. Boil for about 8 minutes and then strain the spices off, retrieving a few pieces of the peel. Allow the vinegar to get quite cold. Pack the beans into the jars taking great care they do not break or mash. Place a few pieces of the orange peel amongst them. Pour the cold vinegar over to cover completely making sure that there are no air bubbles. Seal. Keep at least 2 weeks before using. Do not throw away the vinegar – it may be used in making clear pickles at a later date.

This pickle makes a splendid pair with pickled Jerusalem artichokes if you are giving presents. Kidney beans may be pickled in the same way.

SALTING BEANS

Salting beans is a curiously satisfying process, presumably because it is one of the most ancient of the preserving arts. Salt only French or runner beans picked when they are fresh and young. You will need a large earthenware crock and 350g/12oz coarse salt to every 1kg/2lb 4oz beans. Do not use refined, free-running or table salt, the additives in it spoil the process. Wash and dry the beans, string them if necessary. Leave French beans whole but runner beans should be sliced. Put a layer of salt in the crock and then a layer of beans and so on and so forth until you get to the top, press down hard and finish with a good layer of salt. You can, if you wish, make one layer of salt at the bottom and one layer of salt at the top, mixing the rest with the beans before putting them in the jar. Cover and leave for a few days. The beans will shrink and you can then add in some more, pressing down well and finishing with a layer of salt. The salt takes a tremendous amount of moisture from the atmosphere and will turn damp and brine-like. This is all right, so do not throw it away.

Make sure that you have pushed the beans and salt well down leaving no air pockets. Seal firmly with a cork or a parchment disc tied down tightly (whatever you use it must be moisture proof). Stand the crock well off stone, brick or concrete floors as these draw moisture up. If your beans have turned slimy you either did not use enough salt or they needed to be pressed down harder. To cook the beans, remove some from jar, replace lid. Wash thoroughly and soak in warm water for just 2 hours. Cook in the usual way, without salt, until tender.

DRYING BROAD BEANS

Use the young, early beans for eating fresh and allow some of the later beans to mature on the plant until they are quite ripe and fully mature. Pull the whole plant up and take it in to a dry, airy place and hang it upside down with room for the air to circulate around it. When the pods are quite dry and ready they will split open naturally and the beans fall from them. Store the dried beans in airtight containers, even paper bags properly sealed will do, but do not store them in the shed because everything from wood lice to the odd mouse will chew its way through paper. I can remember very well the bitter, earthy, green smell of broad beans drying in my mother's old shed.

Beetroot

The very first, original, beetroot was grown on sandy dunes in the Mediterranean basin. The Romans discovered it and developed it into roughly its present form. It is extremely easy to grow in gardens and you can ensure, by careful planting, that you have your own beetroots in various sizes throughout the summer. It is best to lift beetroots (or beets, as our American friends confusingly call them) when they are very small; it is possible then to eat them uncooked.

Beetroots may be steamed, boiled or baked in the oven in a tightly-lidded dish with the minimum of water. Do not cook hard or too long – about two hours is long enough for a medium-sized beet. Try not to cut the green or root off too close to the beetroot or to damage or score the skin prior to cooking for if this happens the beet will bleed and lose its colour. After cooking, and while the beetroot is still hot rub your finger and thumb over the skin which will come away in your hand, taking the 'tops and tails' with it. Apart from the ruby red beetroot familiar to us all,

81

there is now a golden beetroot and a white one, both of which have deliciously edible leaves as well. As well as being used in salads, beetroot can also be eaten as a hot vegetable but in Britain we neglect this aspect. Polish, Russian and Jewish cooks are not so remiss.

BEETROOT PICKLE

1kg/2lb 4oz raw beetroot
1.15 litres/2 pints malt vinegar
3cm/1 inch piece of cinnamon stick
6 cloves

2 blades mace
7 whole allspice
4 peppercorns

3 hot, dry, sterile jam jars with non-metal lids

Wash and cook the beetroot in boiling, salted water. Allow to get cold then peel and slice or dice. Place the vinegar in a stainless steel saucepan with the spices and boil hard for one minute. Cover and leave to stand until cold. Pack the jars with the beetroot and cover with the strained vinegar. Seal tightly.

Variations on the basic theme:

A HOTTER SPICED VINEGAR

1.15 litre/2 pints malt vinegar
15g/½oz black peppercorns
15g/½oz whole allspice
15g/½oz green ginger

15g/½oz raw fresh horseradish
15g/½oz sea salt
1 teaspoon cayenne pepper or 2 dried
   chilli peppers

A SWEET BEETROOT PICKLE

For 600ml/1 pint malt vinegar, add 225g/8oz soft brown or white sugar. Mix well with the boiling spiced vinegar, stirring well to ensure that it has dissolved. Allow to cool before using.

Pickled beetroot will keep for up to six months before becoming soft. If the beetroots are very small it is possible to pickle them whole – it is then preferable to bake rather than to boil them, adding a sprinkling of sea salt to the beets before packing in the jars. The flavour is excellent.

KÜMMEL'S BEETROOT PICKLE (CARAWAY)

1kg/2lb 4oz raw beetroot
1½ teaspoons sea salt
1½ teaspoons soft brown sugar

1½ teaspoons caraway seeds
ground black pepper
900ml/1½ pints malt vinegar

a large, glass preserving jar

Wash and cook the beetroot in usual way without damaging. When cool, peel and cut into even slices. Mix together salt, sugar, caraway and black pepper to taste. Place a layer of beetroot in the bottom of the jar, sprinkle with the mixed seasoning, place another layer of beetroot on top of this, season again and continue in this fashion until seasoning and beetroot is used up. Cover completely with (cold) vinegar. Seal tightly.

I think the title is a slight British misinterpretation, as Kümmel is German for caraway.

BEETROOT CHUTNEY

1kg/2lb 4oz raw beetroot
350g/12oz onions
450ml/¾ pint white vinegar
350g/12oz cooking apples

225g/8oz sultanas
1 teaspoon pickling spice
1 small piece root ginger
350g/12oz white sugar

4 hot, dry, sterile jam jars with non-metal lids

Wash and cook beetroot without damaging. When cool, peel and dice. Peel and chop the onions, put them into a large stainless steel saucepan with a little of the vinegar, and cook until soft. Wash, peel, core and chop the apples. Wash the sultanas and tie the spices in a muslin bag and add all the ingredients to the pan with half the remaining vinegar to the onions. Cook until very soft, stirring occasionally and taking care not to burn. When ingredients are cooked, add the remainder of the vinegar and the sugar, heat gently, stirring well until the sugar has dissolved. Boil steadily until the chutney is thick. Remove spice bag. Pot and seal.

The sultanas may be omitted and the juice and rind of 1 lemon and 1 teaspoon ground ginger substituted in their place.

BEETROOT RELISH

1kg/2lb 4oz raw beetroot	800g/1lb 12oz white sugar
50g/2oz fresh ginger	100g/4oz blanched and slivered
4 lemons	almonds

5 hot, dry, sterile jars with non-metal lids

Wash and peel the uncooked beetroot and put it through a coarse mincer. Pop it into a heavy pan and barely cover with water. Simmer for about 1 hour until just tender. Chop the ginger, grate the rind and squeeze the juice from the lemons. Add these with the ginger and sugar to the beetroot. Stir well, heating gently until the sugar has dissolved. Remove from the heat. Stir in the almonds and seal.

   Keeps for 2-3 months before it discolours and the almonds go soft. A superb relish with cold turkey, pork or chicken. It has a very unusual and subtle flavour.

Blackberry

There is a great affinity between the Englishman and the blackberry, possibly because it is the most easily obtainable of the hedgerow fruit and because it can be turned to so many uses – the oldest being medicinal, curing anything from gout to whooping cough. Eventually superstition was superceded by science and as the housewife recognized the full economic potential of blackberries, thriftiness took over.

   The uses that a good cook can put blackberries to are many and varied: pies and puddings; sauces both sweet and savoury; and those pots of glorious purple red jellies and jams, dark mysterious looking chutneys, relishes, sauces and vinegars.

   Memories of purple-mouthed village children late home from school on hot autumn evenings, arms scratched and the seats out of their trousers reminds me that the hardest things to bear about blackberrying are thorns. Although you may console yourself with the thought that it really is worth the effort, bear carefully in mind that most cultivated varieties are thornless! Growing your own in the garden is no very great problem. A trellis or trellised wall set in a warm spot, a well drained soil rich in compost and kept moist are the most basic requirements. One of two particularly good varieties for garden cultivation is Himalayan Giant which has superb large, sweet fruit that are very good for dessert use or bottling and freezing. The other well tried variety is Oregon Thornless which takes a little longer to establish but again has a good crop of excellent fruit and the added advantage of a decorative ferny leaf. On the whole I prefer to keep the cultivated varieties of blackberry for bottling, freezing and eating as they are, with just a little sugar and cream. The hedgerow fruit I find better for making jams, pickles, etc., for it has a much stronger flavour and a more solid berry which is not lost in cooking.

Blackberries are very low in pectin content and it is a good idea to use home-made pectin extract, p.19, with them when making jam or jelly. How about those apple cores and peels that you should have stored in the freezer for just such a contingency? Tie those in a muslin bag and stew them with the berries. Blackberry and Apple Marmalade is a fine traditional recipe, each fruit complementing the other – the apple providing both bulk and set, the blackberry its own perfumed texture and taste. If you are prepared to make only small quantities of jelly at a time, which indeed many of you may prefer to do, make it with the natural fruit, sugar and lemon. This gives a soft preserve with the full autumnal flavour of blackberries which unfortunately will not keep long. Another lovely jelly with a delicate taste and good set is made from the unripe fruit. It is said that the young blackberry shoot picked, scrubbed and cooked may be eaten like asparagus with much the same flavour.

Lastly, a hint on how to remove those inevitable blackberry stains from your clothing. Soak in cold water and then launder, rubbing a little borax into the stain as you go. Old stains or stains on dry cleaning material may be loosened with a little neat glycerine then soak or sponge.

BLACKBERRY JAM

1kg/2lb 4oz blackberries
1kg/2lb 4oz white sugar

150ml/$\frac{1}{4}$ pint redcurrant juice or
150ml/$\frac{1}{4}$ pint apple extract

4 hot, dry, sterile jam jars

Pick over the blackberries and wash them. Put in a preserving pan with either the redcurrant or apple juice, and simmer very gently until the fruit is soft and reduced in quantity. Add the warmed sugar and heat gently, stirring well until it has dissolved. Bring to the boil and boil hard until a set is obtained. Pot and seal.

The apple or redcurrant juice gives the additional pectin necessary for a good set.

BLACKBERRY AND ELDERBERRY JAM

1kg/2lb 4oz ripe blackberries
1kg/2lb 4oz ripe elderberries

1600g/3lb 8oz white sugar

8 hot, dry, sterile jam jars

Pick over the blackberries, hull and wash them. Strip elderberries from stem, wash them and place them in a preserving pan. Give them a random mashing with a wooden spoon and then allow them to heat gently until the juices flow. Bring to the boil and simmer until soft, taking care not to burn – it may be necessary to add a tablespoon of warm water. Put them through a fine sieve. Return the blackberries and the elderberry pulp to a clean preserving pan. Cook gently for 10-15 minutes until the blackberries are soft. Add the warmed sugar and heat gently, stirring well until it has dissolved.

Glorious smoky autumnal taste to this less pippy and soft set jam.

BLACKBERRY AND ROSEHIP JAM

450g/1lb rosehips
water
1kg/2lb 4oz blackberries

white sugar
unsalted butter

4 hot, dry, sterile jam jars

Wash and cut the hips, taking care to remove all the seed. This is a terribly fiddling job so it is worth knowing that they contain, in and around them, almost invisible little hairs which must go, so persevere. Chop the hips small, put into an earthenware container, just cover with water and allow to stand for 2 days and until the flesh is tender. Wash and pick over the blackberries and put them in the container with the hips into a cool oven for a couple of hours or until the juices are flowing freely. Grease a preserving pan, place over a low heat, add the fruit and sugar and stir gently until the sugar has dissolved. Bring to the boil and boil hard until a set is obtained. Skim, pot and seal.

A superb, delicate jam which should have city-bound cooks extolling the virtues of the countryside.

BLACKBERRY JAM MADE IN THE FREEZER

1kg/2lb 4oz ripe blackberries   200ml/7fl oz commercial pectin
1.25kg/2½lb caster sugar

small, rigid polythene containers with lids

Wash and pick over the blackberries (preferably cultivated). Put them in a large glass bowl and add the sugar. Mash them well together with a wooden spoon. You could use a mixer for this process using the heavy beater on a very low speed. Leave for ½ hour giving an occasional stir. Add the pectin and stir hard for 3 minutes. Pot with 1cm/½ inch headroom. Cover and seal. Leave for not less than 5 hours at room temperature and then place in the refrigerator. The jam should have become nicely jelled after about 48 hours. Store in the freezer compartment of your refrigerator or in the freezer. Allow to thaw out at room temperature for about 1 hour before serving.

A very handy recipe to remember for all soft fruit, particularly raspberries, loganberries and mulberries, but do not try it with any other type of fruit. It does not work.

BLACKBERRY JELLY

Blackberries, to my mind, make one of the most delicious jellies. Glowing purply-red, rich with that special autumnal taste, the sight of blackberry jelly, on any winter tea table will bring a satisfied smile to the faces of those gathered around. However, it should be remembered that blackberries are high in water content, low in pectin and need very, very little water to cook in. My preferred method for cooking blackberries is to place them, with or without any other fruit which may be needed, in an earthenware casserole or dish. Add the minimum of water (1 tablespoon to 1kg/2lb 4oz blackberries). Cover and place in a warm fire oven or Aga for one day and one night, by which time the juices will have run rich and red and the fruit will be very soft. Strain off in a jelly bag overnight to obtain the ruby extract.

1kg/2lb 4oz blackberries (not   1 lemon
   over-ripe)   white sugar
150ml/¼ pint water

2 hot, dry, sterile jam jars

Wash and pick over the blackberries, put them in a preserving pan with the water and simmer until soft. An occasional mash with a wooden spoon during cooking helps break up the fruit. Turn the pulp into a jelly bag and leave to drain overnight into a clean bowl. Do not prod or squeeze or you will have a cloudy jelly. The next day measure the juice and for every 150ml/¼ pint take the juice of ½ lemon and 450g/1lb warmed sugar. Return the juice to the pan, heat gently and add the sugar and lemon juice. Stir well until dissolved. Bring to the boil and boil hard until a set is obtained (you will not get the solid, hard set; more of a soft and spreadable sort). Skim, pot and seal.

For a slightly perfumed jelly add two leaves of rose or sweet-scented geranium (absolutely complementary to the autumnal taste of blackberries), to the stewing fruit.

For a spicy blackberry jelly add 1 teaspoon of mixed spice to every 450g/1lb sugar.

Do not waste the left over pulp which can be used with great advantage for making cheeses, curds and pastes.

BLACKBERRY AND GOOSEBERRY JELLY

1kg/2lb 4oz blackberries   300ml/½ pint water
500g/1lb 2oz gooseberries   white sugar

4 hot, dry, sterile jam jars

Wash and pick over the fruit, discarding any mouldy bits and pieces. Put altogether in a pan with the water and simmer until very tender – you may need to add a little more water if the fruit dries out; mashing with a wooden spoon also helps. Turn the pulp into a jelly bag and allow to stand overnight. The next day measure the juice and for every 600ml/1 pint take 450g/1lb warmed sugar. Return juice to pan and heat gently, add sugar, stirring well until it has dissolved. Bring to the boil and boil hard until a set is obtained. Skim, pot and seal.

This is a very delicious jelly, the two flavours complementing each other well. It also sets very well, due to the high pectin content in the gooseberries. Apples may be used instead of gooseberries.

BLACKBERRY AND PEAR CONSERVE

1kg/2lb 4oz ripe blackberries
water
1kg/2lb 4oz ripe pears

2 lemons
white sugar

8 hot, dry, sterile jars

Wash and pick over the blackberries. Place three-quarters of them in a preserving pan with just enough water to cover. Allow them to simmer gently to a complete pulp. Put in a jelly bag and allow to drain overnight into a clean bowl. The next day wash, peel and core the pears, cut into small pieces and place them in the preserving pan with the remainder of the blackberries, the juice from the lemon and the lemon pips tied in a muslin bag. Measure the blackberry juice and for every 600ml/1 pint gained allow 350g/12oz warmed sugar. Add the blackberry juice to the pan of fruit and bring to the boil. Simmer for 30 minutes until soft, remove the muslin bag and add the sugar, stirring well over a low heat until it has dissolved. Bring to the boil and then boil hard until a set is obtained. Pot and seal.

A particularly delicate conserve, both blackberry and pear have such gentle flavours.

SPICED BLACKBERRIES

1cm/½ inch piece cinnamon
1 piece root ginger
1 dozen allspice berries
4 cloves

300ml/½ pint malt vinegar
1kg/2lb 4oz blackberries
450g/1lb white sugar
2 leaves rose scented geranium

4 hot, dry, sterile jars with non-metal lids

Make up a spiced vinegar by bruising the spices and tying them into a muslin bag. Put this with the vinegar into a stainless steel pan and boil hard for 5 minutes. Cover and leave to stand until cold, remove muslin bag. Wash and pick over the blackberries. Pop the vinegar and sugar into a large stainless steel pan and heat gently, stirring well until the sugar has dissolved. Add the blackberries and simmer until just tender. Remove with a perforated spoon and pack into the jars – keep warm. Boil the syrup hard until nice and thick, add a geranium leaf to each jar and pour the hot syrup over the fruit making sure it is well covered. Seal immediately.

Do not throw away any of the vinegars made in these pickles – they can be used again in many savoury recipes.

PICKLED BLACKBERRIES

1kg/2lb 4oz cultivated blackberries
300ml/½ pint white wine vinegar

450g/1lb white sugar
2 leaves rose-scented geranium

3 hot, dry, sterile jars with non-metal lids

Wash and pick over the blackberries. Put the vinegar into a stainless steel pan with the sugar and heat gently, stirring well until it has dissolved. Add the blackberries and simmer gently for 5 minutes. Do not allow the fruit to become too soft or to break up. Remove blackberries with a perforated spoon and pack into hot jars. Keep warm. Boil the vinegar until it is syrupy. Pop a geranium leaf well down in each jar and pour the hot syrup over the fruit to cover completely. Seal.

Keep at least a week before eating. One of the best recipes for pickled blackberries as it is quite a light syrup and the geranium leaves give a delicate scent.

BLACKBERRY RELISH

1kg/2lb 4oz blackberries
½ teaspoon sea salt
15g/½oz soft brown sugar
½ teaspoon mustard powder

½ teaspoon ground cloves
½ teaspoon ground nutmeg
½ teaspoon ground cinnamon
300ml/½ pint malt vinegar

dry, hot, sterile, heatproof bottles with screw lids or corks

Wash and pick over the blackberries. Put in a pan with just enough water to cover and simmer until soft. Pass through a fine sieve leaving only the pips behind. You should have a good combination of juice and purée making a thick liquid. Return it to a stainless steel pan, add the rest of the ingredients and simmer for about 15 minutes. Pour into prepared bottles to within 2cm/¾ inch of the top and then continue sterilization process (p.15).

I find that a slug of this relish in both savoury and sweet dishes gives quite a fillip.

BLACKBERRY CORDIAL

1 litre/2 pints home-made blackberry
  juice
450g/1lb white sugar or 225g/8oz mild
  flavoured honey

1 teaspoon ground cloves
1 teaspoon ground cinnamon
1 teaspoon ground nutmeg
150ml/¼ pint brandy

sterilized, heat-resistant bottles with screw caps (see Spiced Apple Ketchup, p.50)

Boil together the blackberry juice and the sugar stirring well until it has dissolved. Continue to boil away until a syrup has formed. Remove from the heat, skim and add the spices. Stir well and bring to the boil again, continue to simmer for about 20 minutes. Remove from the heat, allow to settle, strain through a muslin cloth into a hot metal container, (if it has become very cool, reheat until it is just at boiling point before pouring into the jug). Stir in the brandy and bottle to 2cm/¾ inch from the top. Sterilize as for Sterlizing Sauces, p.15.

Apart from being a very pleasant cordial this is an excellent old-fashioned remedy for tummy troubles – 1 tablespoon for children, 1 wine glass for adults. Diluted in hot water it is a good bedtime drink for fractious children of all ages, to say nothing of fractious adults! You may forego the sterilization process if you intend to use within a few days.

Blueberry

Also known as bilberry, blaeberry, hurtlebury, whortleberry, wineberry, depending on which region you live in. The wild blueberry, *Vaccinium myrtillus*, still remains relatively undiscovered to the average British housewife. This may be because it is the very devil to pick, being a low and secretive plant situated in dense, shrubby heath or moor where lying on your stomach is liable to bring you eye to eye confrontations with certain reptilian and other nasties. Commercially blueberries have not been exploited because of their rather meagre yield. However, some good nurserymen now stock bushes for the garden and I think that they are worth buying for they are compact and grow well in semi-shade, but needing an acid soil. The fruit is juicy, though a little sharp, and makes excellent eating, savoury or sweet, raw or cooked. Bottled, they make unusual puddings and pies especially when added to apples. They freeze well and make very fine jams and jellies, needing little extra water for good results. Apart from home grown blueberries, which ripen from June to July, it is also possible to buy imported Polish fruit in the shops from June to August.

WHOLE BLUEBERRY JAM

1kg/2lb 4oz blueberries
1kg/2lb 4oz white sugar

4 hot, dry, sterile jam jars

Wash the fruit and place in a heavy pan. Heat slowly – try not to break the berries but ensure that they are soft – for about 5 minutes. Add the warmed sugar, heat gently, stirring with care until it has dissolved. Boil steadily until a set is obtained (this will not take too long). Pot and seal.
   A delicious, sharp jam with a good, soft set and colour.

BLUEBERRY JAM WITH RHUBARB

1kg/2lb 4oz blueberries   1kg/2lb 4oz white sugar
225g/8oz rhubarb

5 hot, dry, sterile jam jars

Wash the fruit. String and cut the rhubarb very fine and put it in a preserving pan with the sugar. Heat very gently, stirring well until the sugar has dissolved. Bring to the boil and boil hard for 10 minutes stirring frequently. Add the blueberries, stir well and bring to the boil again. Now simmer gently until a set is obtained. Pot and seal.

BLUEBERRY SAUCE

1kg/2lb 4oz blueberries   pinch cinnamon
1 wine glass red wine   500g/1lb 2oz white sugar
5 cloves

small, hot, dry, sterile jars

Wash and stalk the berries, drain and put into a stainless steel pan with the wine, spices and sugar. Bring gently to the boil, making sure that the sugar is dissolved. Skim and simmer gently for 30 minutes. Strain the juice and return it to the pan (reserve the berries) and boil until it becomes a thick syrup. Pop the blueberries back into the syrup, stir well and bring quickly to the boil. Remove from heat. Allow to cool a little before potting. Seal.

Superb with cold meats and game, particularly good with cold spiced beef.

Borage

Borago officinalis

An easily nurtured annual growing to about 60cm/2 feet, with hairy, misty green leaves and lovely bright blue star-like flowers. It is a plant that grows well in any soil and once established will continue to seed itself for many years. When the leaves are bruised or broken they exude a very strong cucumber smell and may be chopped and sprinkled on salad or cooked with peas, beans and cauliflower. For health purposes they may be steeped in hot water and drunk as a cure for hangovers, or mixed with bran, barley and water and used to cleanse the skin. Alternatively, the whole sprig with flowers is frequently used as a decoration in fruit punches and cold drinks. The flowers alone, brewed like tea, may be taken to purify the system and also make the most exquisite candied decorations. This herb does not dry or freeze at all well and only the young tender leaves which still retain their strong fragrance should be used for the above purposes.

CANDIED BORAGE FLOWERS

borage flowers   caster sugar
egg

Pick the flowers when they are fully open but before the sun gets too hot. Use them immediately, making sure that there are no insects inside. Separate the egg yolk from the white and whisk the white until it is stiff

93

but not dry. Take a small paint brush and 'paint' each flower with the egg white. Place the sugar in a shallow dish and as each flower is painted, swish it well in the sugar to cover and give a frosted appearance. Place on waxed paper to dry and when they are well set store in an airtight tin with wax paper between the layers.

Burnet

Sanguisorba minor

Burnet is an attractive feathery herb, not very large, which is only grown and used infrequently. I find that it thrives best in pots, indoors throughout the year, although it will grow and replant from year to year in a sunny garden. The cucumber-scented leaves add fresh delight to jaded salads and summer drinks. It is a tender plant and does not dry well but it makes an excellent vinegar (see Tarragon Vinegar, p.353) and freezes well (see Freezing Basil, p.77). Be warned that for whatever purposes you may use it you should make sure that you take only the young tender inner leaves.

C

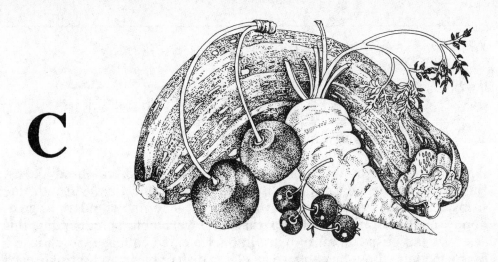

Cabbage

There are so many different types of cabbage for so many different uses, all requiring varying conditions and areas for their successful production, that I would need to devote a couple of pages to that alone. Also consider how much room you need in a garden to grow cabbages to supply winter needs and how reasonably priced and obtainable they are, bearing all that in mind I will look at cabbage with only an eye to preserving. Cabbages can be fairly easily divided into three categories:

Green Cabbage, wrinkled leaves, in many shades of green, which is used purely as a cooked vegetable with differing degrees of imagination and success.
White Cabbage, as well as being cooked, is delicious in salads and is preserved in sauerkraut. Good for freezing.
Red Cabbage, is marvellous cooked in spicy and festive ways and, traditionally, pickles. Always remember to remove the white ribs and stalks before using.

There are some very exciting cabbages grown purely for decorative purposes. Would you believe that to drink cabbage water is good for catarrh, colds and bronchitis?

PICKLED RED CABBAGE

1kg/2lb 4oz firm, red cabbage heads	cayenne pepper
sea salt	1.15 litre/2 pints malt vinegar

dry, sterile jars with non-metal lids

Wash the outside of the cabbage, throw away any discoloured leaves. Halve and quarter and remove the white stalks and ribs. Cut into fine strips across the cabbage – this way you get nice fine shreds, not great floppy hunks. Some people do this on a vegetable shredder but this destroys the crispy texture of traditional pickled cabbage, so choose a happy medium. Lay the cabbage in a large dish or basin and sprinkle each layer with salt. Cover and leave for 24 hours. The next day tip into a colander to drain off any surplus salt, rinse if necessary, and drain again. Pack the cabbage loosely into the jars and pour the vinegar over to cover, leave a short while to penetrate and press down to see if it requires topping up with more vinegar. Sprinkle $\frac{1}{4}$ teaspoon cayenne on each jar if liked. Seal.

All pickled cabbage may be eaten after two weeks but not kept longer than three months when it will start to go soft.

For variations on a basic theme prepare the cabbage as above, omit cayenne and plain vinegar, and substitute one of the following spice vinegars.

A MILD SPICED VINEGAR

1 litre/1¾ pints malt vinegar	4 blades mace
5cm/2 inches stick cinnamon	15 whole allspice
12 cloves	8 black peppercorns

A MELLOW SPICED VINEGAR

1 litre/1¾ pints malt vinegar	4 dried, crushed chillies (optional)
30g/1oz black peppercorns	1 tablespoon whole cloves
8 blades mace	1 tablespoon mustard seed
6 bay leaves	1 tablespoon whole allspice
2 pieces bruised root ginger	1 teaspoon sea salt
5cm/2 inches stick cinnamon	1 clove crushed garlic (optional)

RED CABBAGE RELISH ·

1kg/2lb 4oz firm, red cabbage heads
sea salt
1 piece bruised root ginger
1 teaspoon caraway seed

4 blades mace
1 teaspoon whole allspice
1.15 litre/2 pints white vinegar

8 dry, sterile jars with non-metal lids

Wash the outer cabbage leaves, removing any blemished pieces. Halve and quarter, cutting out the white stalk and ribs. Grate on a coarse grater and place in a deep bowl, sprinkling each layer with salt as you go. Cover and leave for 24 hours. The next day drain in a colander and hold briefly under cold running water. Shake well to remove excess moisture and leave to drain. In the meantime, tie the spices into a muslin bag and put this with the vinegar into a stainless steel pan, boil for 3 minutes, reduce to barely simmering, cover and leave for 10 minutes. Return the drained cabbage to the bowl, remove the bag from the vinegar and pour the hot spicy concoction over the cabbage, cover and leave for 24 hours giving an occasional stir. Pack into the jars making sure that the cabbage is well covered with vinegar. If it isn't, make up a little more and use this to top up. Seal.

A soft pickle which keeps well.

SALTED CABBAGE OR SAUERKRAUT

1kg/2lb 4oz hard, white cabbage
25g/1oz sea salt

caraway seeds

1 large wooden or earthenware container ·

Wash the cabbage, remove outer and blemished leaves, keep some of these and put half of them into the container, lining the bottom. Shred the firm, white head finely and place in a large basin, mix well with the salt and caraway seeds to taste. Turn the mixture into the container and cover with a few more leaves. Now place a plate or saucer on the top of the cabbage so that it fits tightly, excluding all air, weight it heavily and leave for 2-3 weeks in a warm place at a temperature of 23°C/75°F, to ferment. After a few days a salt rime and scum will rise to the surface, probably covering the plate, remove this as it occurs. If it does not occur or if the brine level drops below that of covering the plate, add one more tablespoon of salt dissolved in 600ml/1 pint water. Repeat this process if necessary. After 3 weeks the fermentation should stop and the sauerkraut is now ready for use.

Any sauerkraut that is not immediately needed should be bottled and sterilized. To do this, drain off the brine into a large stainless steel pan, bring to the boil and add the cabbage, stir well and lower the heat to simmer. When it is hot right through, pack into dry, clean jars and seal with sterile ring tops, clips or screw bands (if using bands make a half turn back after tightening to allow for expansion). Put the jars into a large saucepan with a rack in the bottom to prevent the jars coming into contact with the direct heat. Make sure that the jars do not touch. Cover with boiling water and boil gently for 25 minutes. Remove the jars from the saucepan and place on a wooden board or cloth, and tighten the screwband. Next day test for a good seal by removing band or clip and holding jar by its lid, if it holds you have a good seal. Replace the bands or clips and store. Do not keep if the seal is faulty.

All cabbage when allowed to mature becomes particularly odoriferous. Fermenting sauerkraut is no exception but it is very good with hot boiled German sausage.

Cape Gooseberry, Golden Berry, Chinese Lantern

Those pretty little lanterns of scarlet and gold usually seen in cottage gardens and dried flower arrangements contain a small golden berry which makes a delicate conserve in the tradition of the French Mirabelle. The correct seed to plant in your garden is that of *Physalis peruvianus edulis* and the fruit is ready to be picked when the husk is golden and the berry is quite yellow.

Cape gooseberries may be crystallized and glacéed – follow the method given for Crystallized Apricots, page 64. They also make delicious sweets if boiled very briefly in thick syrup and wrapped in home-made marzipan.

CAPE GOOSEBERRY CONSERVE

1kg/2lb 4oz cape gooseberries   300ml/½ pint water
1kg/2lb 4oz white sugar   2 lemons

Make sure that all the papery-thin husk is removed and pierce the small fruit with a silver needle. Put the sugar, water and the juice from the lemons into a preserving pan. Stir well over a low heat until the sugar has dissolved. Boil well until a syrup is formed, add the cape gooseberries and boil steadily withot breaking the skins but ensuring that the fruit is just tender and the syrup thick. Allow to cool a little before potting. Seal.

Caraway

Carum carvi

This is an umbelliferous garden grown plant with creamy flowers, not unlike Queen Anne's Lace, and soft ferny green leaves. As it grows to a height of 60cm/3 feet in two years it is best to keep it to the back of the garden, preferably in full sun.

Although the seeds are usually the only part of the herb harvested, the young leaves may be chopped and scattered on soups and salads. The seeds themselves have a much more interesting reputation. Tasting mildly like aniseed they should be gathered before they ripen and dry too much as they are at their best when clear and green and retaining much of their pungent aroma. An oil was at one time made from caraway to aid digestive and tummy troubles, and it was probably with this in mind that seedcake made with caraway was a staple part of nursery tea.

Caraway is used a great deal in Middle European cooking, in savoury dishes such as sauerkraut, roast meat, dumplings, goulash, bread, and in France, in cream dishes and specialist cheeses. In England, of course it is used in biscuits, cakes and pickles whilst a sprig of caraway lends excitement to a dish of baked fruit. The roots of caraway, scrubbed, boiled and glazed are delicious. A few seeds tucked in your husband's pocket will stop him from straying and the same applies to your pigeons! It would seem worth growing a pot on your windowsill as a double insurance, being one of those seeds that does grow happily indoors.

After you have gathered the seeds, dry them by laying them on a tray in a dry airy room or preferably lay them out in the sun each day for five days. Pot them in a dark jar, or, if in a clear jar, keep them in a dark place. Leave some seeds on the plant to replant the following year, if they do manage to seed themselves successfully in the autumn you should have plants big enough to provide good seed heads next summer.

CARAWAY VINEGAR

a good tablespoonful of fresh caraway
  seeds

600ml/1 pint white or white wine
  vinegar

a dry, sterile, attractive, glass jar with non-metal lid

Grind the seeds to release the aromatic oils, using a pestle and mortar, the end of a rolling pin or crushing between sheets of greaseproof paper – all work well. Tip them into the jar and add the vinegar. Seal and leave to stand on a warm windowsill for 2 weeks. Shake each day. Using a funnel and filter paper, or two layers of muslin over a nylon sieve, strain the vinegar until it is clear. Pop it back into the clean, dry bottle and seal.

Coriander, dill and fennel are other examples of seeding herbs which may be used in the same way to make these very pleasant vinegars. A dash of herb vinegar added to salads makes for great variety.

Carnation

The very lovely, highly scented, spicy gilly flower of medieval days, whose petals were used in a variety of ways from the medicinal to the culinary. You can still chop them and use them in salads or thin biscuits, or try adding a few to brandied fruits.

One of the finest ways to use the clove-scented carnation petals is in a soft and delicate vinegar. Follow the method as for Tarragon Vinegar, p.353, using the proportions of two cups of flower petals to 600ml/1 pint white wine vinegar. These gentle herb and flower vinegars are delightful with cold foods and salads of a less rumbustious nature.

Carrot

A hardy biennial vegetable coming to the western world firstly as a weed, then as animal fodder and finally through the invention of the French as the carrot in an infinite variety of shapes and sizes that we find so invaluable, not only as a bulk providing filler but also giving us a high percentage of vitamin A or carotene in our diet, the natural and healthy way. There are many varieties of carrot that you may grow and many are the uses to which they may be put – large coarse carrots being excellent and economical for stews, soups, hashes, with eggs and cream, baked and roast, in cakes and pudding, preserves (the Arabians particularly treasure carrot jam), wines and even sweetmeats.

I prefer to buy the larger carrots which are cheap and obtainable throughout the year. The really covetable carrots you should try to grow are the baby carrots which do not produce so much in terms of weight but more than make up for this in flavour and quality. They need little cooking and just dressed in a delicate glaze or fine sauce are good enough to eat without an accompaniment, but you may prefer to eat them raw in a salad. These small carrots freeze and bottle well and require very little preparation. Cut off the tops and place them in a saucer of water and the lovely fern-like fronds will decorate your windowsill for ages.

Because most people have small gardens or are even reduced to a window box or sill, I will give you only a few of those small, tender varieties that are practical and productive to grow in restricted circumstances. A small round variety called Konfrix will grow in almost any soil conditions, even window boxes, whilst Little Gnome positively thrives in pots and boxes on the windowsill. Two varieties hitherto only available in France where they were tried and tested are Muscatelle which is a deliciously sweet, small carrots that children like and a round little carrot known as Rubin, both of these varieties do particularly well in the south of England. Another small carrot which is very sweet is Sucram and a carrot that is the gourmet's delight is a variety known as Little Finger.

Carrot seed is very fine and light and if watered too heavily may be washed away, for this reason many people prefer to buy pelleted seed although there is not much choice in this area. Sage bushes grown in proximity to carrots keep carrot fly at bay and carrots grow particularly well where last year's Brassica crops were cultivated.

CARROT PRESERVE

1kg/2lb 4oz large carrots
3 lemons
600ml/1 pint water

1kg/2lb 4oz white sugar
blanched almonds
6 tablespoons brandy

4 hot, dry, sterile jam jars

Wash and peel the carrots, slice or chop them. Grate the rind and squeeze the juice from the lemons. Reserve the pips and tie them in a muslin bag and put these with the carrots in a preserving pan. Just cover with water. Stew gently until soft. Remove the muslin bag, drain the carrots and put them through a sieve or electric blender, return the pulp to a clean pan with the warmed sugar, lemon rind and juice, heat gently stirring well until the sugar has dissolved. Blanch and split the almonds and stir them, with the brandy, into the slightly cooled jam. Pot and seal.

Angelica or preserved ginger may be substituted for the almonds. Although it is not imperative to add the brandy it does improve both the keeping quality and the flavour of the jam, creating a more luxurious preserve.

CARROT AND RHUBARB CONSERVE

1kg/2lb 4oz young carrots
1kg/2lb 4oz young rhubarb
2 lemons
225g/8oz candied citron peel

water
2kg/4lb 8oz white sugar
50g/2oz preserved or crystallized
   ginger

10 hot, dry, sterile jam jars

Wash the carrots and cut into small pieces. Wash the rhubarb and cut into chunks without stringing. Grate the rind from the lemons removing the pith as this makes the conserve bitter. Cut up the pulp and tie the pips into a muslin bag. Place rhubarb and carrots in a preserving pan with the lemon juice pulp and pips, just cover with water and stew gently until tender. If necessary, shred or chop the candied peel and ginger and add these with the grated rind and warmed sugar to the pan, stir well over a low heat until the sugar has dissolved and then bring to the boil and boil hard until a set is obtained, stir frequently to ensure that it does not burn. Pot and seal.

Two sweet oranges and candied orange peel may be substituted for the lemons and citron peel. This gives a sweeter conserve.

SUNSET MARMALADE

1kg/2lb 4oz carrots	4 limes or lemons
1kg/2lb 4oz cooking apples	1kg/2lb 4oz white sugar
500g/1lb 2oz peaches	675g/1lb 8oz clear honey

8 hot, dry, sterile jam jars

Wash, scrape and dice the carrots. Peel, core and dice the apples. Peel, stone and dice the peaches. Grate the rind and extract the juice from the lemons. Put all the ingredients into a large preserving pan and stir well, heat very gently, continue to stir until the sugar has melted. Bring to the boil and simmer, stirring frequently to prevent burning. When the mixture is thick and transclucent it is ready for potting. Seal.

Extra sugar may be substituted for the honey – 1750g/3lb 12oz altogether – this may turn out to be an economic necessity! A very fine preserve from America.

SPICED CARROTS

1kg/2lb 4oz young carrots	1 tablespoon whole cloves
600ml/1 pint white vinegar	2 teaspoons ground cinnamon
600ml/1 pint water	2 teaspoons sea salt

3 hot, dry, sterile jars with non-metal lids

Put the vinegar, water, spices and salt into a stainless steel pan. Boil for 5 minutes, cover and leave to cool. Wash, peel and cut the carrots into halves or quarters lengthwise, cook in just enough water to cover until tender. Drain and leave to cool then pack into jars, strain the vinegar and pour it over the carrots to cover completely. Seal.

Leave at least 2 weeks before using, very good in *hors d'ouevres*.

MILD CARROT CHUTNEY

1kg/2lb 4oz carrots
bay leaf
1.15 litre/2 pints malt vinegar
100g/4oz sultanas

small pieces of green ginger or 2
   teaspoons ground ginger
2 teaspoons mixed spice
1 tablespoon black peppercorns
225g/8oz white sugar

2 hot, dry, sterile jars with non-metal lids

Wash, peel and grate or mince the carrots, put in a stainless steel pan with the bay leaf and half the vinegar. Stew gently until the carrots are becoming mushy, add the remainder of the vinegar and the rest of the ingredients. Stir well until the sugar has melted, bring to the boil and then simmer until thick. Stir occasionally, remove bay leaf, pot and seal.

   Very mild, sweet chutney.

STORING CARROTS

Store as for Jerusalem Artichokes, p.68, but lift before October and make sure that there are no worm or fly in them.

Cauliflower

Cauliflowers are a familiar sight throughout the year in greengrocer's shops in every part of Britain. There is the true cauliflower which has a large white, tight head of unopened flowers surrounded by leaves and a slightly coarser, duller relative which is a form of broccoli. There are many varieties of both vegetable which are both treated in the same culinary fashion. Cauliflowers are so easily obtainable that unless you have a large garden or allotment it is better to buy a good quantity from a market or shop when they are at their cheapest. Dressed in a variety of ways they still make an economical meal and also freeze very well which makes them worth stocking up. Do not waste the stalks – use them for making soup, or as with cabbage stalks, dressed in a creamy sauce, well seasoned with nutmeg and garnished with fried breadcrumbs.

CAULIFLOWER PICKLE

1kg/2lb 4oz firm, white cauliflower
100g/4oz sea salt
1.15 litre/2 pints water
1 teaspoon mixed black and white
   peppercorns
½ teaspoon mustard seed

¼ teaspoon ground nutmeg
6 cloves
1 piece of ginger
blade mace
a few red chillies
1.15 litres/2 pints white vinegar

3 dry, sterile jars with non-metal lids

Wash the cauliflower, break into neat florets, discard the leaves and any discoloured pieces. Do not throw away the stalks (see above). Put the florets in a basin, dissolve the salt in the water and cover the cauliflower with this brine. Cover the whole lot with a cloth and leave for 24 hours. In the meantime, crush or bruise the spices and put them with the vinegar into a stainless steel pan, bring to the boil and boil for 3 minutes, remove from the heat, cover and allow to cool.

The next day turn the cauliflower into a colander, rinse briefly under cold, running water and drain thoroughly. Pack into jars, strain the vinegar, keeping back a few chillies which should be popped, for effect, into the pickle. Cover the cauliflower completely with vinegar, making sure that there are no air bubbles. Seal.

A pleasantly mild, crispy pickle. For various other spiced vinegars suitable for pickling cauliflower see Pickled Red Cabbage, page 96, but for aesthetic reasons it is advisable to substitute the malt vinegar for white. For a further variation on a theme add 4 teaspoons of sugar to 1.15 litres/2 pints of the vinegar in the previous recipe. Do this while the spicy vinegar is still boiling and make sure that it is well dissolved. This will give you Sweet Pickled Cauliflower.

PICKLED CAULIFLOWER AND ONION

1kg/2lb 4oz cauliflower
100g/4oz sea salt
500g/1lb 2oz silverskin or small white
   onions

25g/1oz mixed pickling spice
a few red chillies
150g/5oz white sugar
1.15 litres/2 pints white vinegar

3 hot, dry, sterile jars with non-metal lids

Wash the cauliflower, remove stalks and leaves and break into nice neat florets. Put in a large basin and sprinkle with 50g/2oz of the salt, cover and allow to stand overnight. In the meantime, put the onions in another bowl and pour boiling water over them, making sure that they are well covered. Leave to stand for a few minutes, drain and cover with cold water. Peel (doing it like this makes the job easier and stops streaming eyes). Put the onions into a large pan and dissolve the remaining salt in 600ml/1 pint cold water, cover the onions with this brine (you may need to make up more brine in the given proportions). Cover and leave overnight. The next day turn both vegetables into a colander and rinse under cold running water. Leave to drain. Tie spices in a muslin bag and put them with the sugar and vinegar into a large stainless steel pan. Heat gently, stirring well until the sugar has dissolved, bring to the boil, remove the spice bag and add the vegetables. Bring to the boil again, stir well and immediately pour into the jars making sure that the vegetables are pressed down and well covered with the vinegar. Seal.

A crispy, light pickle very good with Caerphilly or Wensleydale cheeses.

Celeriac

Apium rapaceum

Root celery is not unlike a white swede to look at. This extremely pleasant and agreeable vegetable may be eaten raw or cooked. Grated raw and bathed in a smooth cream and lemon dressing it is available in every charcuterie in France and is absolutely delicious, having a smooth subtle flavour. Cooked, it is used in soups and stews as any other root vegetable and I find that because it has a mild taste children like it and eat it without protest. It may also be diced, lightly boiled and served hot with butter and black pepper or allowed to cool and served with a vinaigrette dressing. Although not terribly common in the shops they do appear from September to March either home grown or imported from France.

PICKLED CELERIAC

1 large head of good, firm celeriac
1 large onion
15g/½oz sea salt

1 teaspoon ground ginger
150ml/¼ pint white vinegar
600ml/1 pint water

2 dry, sterile jars with non-metal lids

Boil the vinegar, salt, ginger and water together in a stainless steel pan, leave to cool. Wash, scrub and trim the celeriac, cut into thick slices. Peel and slice the onions. Fill the jars with layers of celeriac and onion and cover with the vinegar water solution, making sure that there are no air bubbles. Seal.

This is a pickle which does not keep long. I prefer another variation on this recipe which is made by using the same ingredients and method but substituting a flavoured vinegar like onion vinegar, for both vinegar and water (make sure you use a white vinegar). This is a strong type of pickle which goes well with cold roast beef.

STORING CELERIAC

Lift in October and store as for Jerusalem Artichokes, p.68.

Celery

As I have consigned more than one crop of celery to the devil I do not consider that any advice I have to offer on the subject of growing it to be helpful. You need a large garden and a sense of purpose. I prefer to wait for the dirty, sooty, home-grown garden stuff to come into our local greengrocers round about November; I then enjoy the fruits of other people's labours! I do not consider the pale and anaemic polythene wrapped variety to be worth buying. The dirty celery when well washed, proves itself to have good, firm, white sticks tinged with green, to be crisp and well textured with a strong flavour. There is absolutely no part of celery which cannot be used in a variety of ways in sauces, soups, stews, salads, as a herb or pickled, frozen and bottled. When you consider the exotic price of tinned celery hearts you will see my point. The garden celery, even bought at shop prices is well worth bottling or freezing as a luxury vegetable and of course if your garden is large enough and your husband is good at digging it is worth trying to grown your own. Wild celery is a slightly different vegetable and although it used to grow profusely in East Anglia I have not seen it freely in the south of England. It is very similar to some of the nasty damp dwellers like hemlock so I advise you to look long and carefully at a reliable handbook on the subject. The smell and flavour of wild celery is extremely strong and pungent but the leaves when dried make fine flavouring for stews.

There is a variety of celery called Cut Celery which is not a true celery, forming no bulb but many leaves which can be used as greens or flavouring.

GARDEN PICKLED CELERY

2 heads garden celery
1 green or red pepper
4 pieces root ginger

4 blades mace
1.15 litre/2 pints white vinegar
4 teaspoons sea salt

4 fairly tall, dry, sterile jars

Wash the celery well, removing soot, insects and any bruised or damaged pieces. Cut off the green tops (these may be dried and used instead of celery seed). Divide the pieces and cut them into neat sticks to fit the jar with 3cm/1 inch headroom. Wipe dry. Wash the pepper, removing seed and pith and cutting the flesh into long strips. Tie the spices into a muslin bag and place in a stainless steel pan with the vinegar and salt. Bring to the boil and boil for 10 minutes. Add the celery and pepper, reboiling for another 3 minutes. Remove the vegetables with a perforated spoon and pack carefully into the jars, keeping the celery upright and the pepper prettily popped in. Allow the vinegar to cool. If you want a milder vinegar remove the spice bag now, otherwise leave it where it is until the vinegar is used. When the vinegar is quite cold pour it over the celery to completely cover. Seal.

Keep for 2 weeks before using but it does not last for a long time. Do not throw the vinegar away after you have eaten the celery, it is very tasty.

CELERY AND TOMATO RELISH

2 heads garden celery
250g/9oz tomatoes
1 red pepper
200ml/7fl. oz white vinegar
140g/5oz white sugar

2 teaspoons sea salt
$\frac{1}{2}$ teaspoon mustard powder
$\frac{1}{2}$ teaspoon ground allspice
$\frac{1}{2}$ teaspoon ground cinnamon
$\frac{1}{2}$ teaspoon celery seed

6 hot, dry, sterile jars with non-metal lids

Wash the celery thoroughly. Remove the leaves and chop the stalks. Drop the tomatoes into boiling water, then into cold. Skin and chop them. Wash and chop pepper removing seed and pith. Put the vinegar into a stainless steel pan with sugar and spices, bring gently to the boil, stirring well until all is dissolved and boil together for 5 minutes. Add the vegetables, bring to the boil again and then simmer gently for about 40 minutes giving an occasional stir. Pot and seal.

A softer, sweet relish that goes particularly well with mild cheeses.

CELERY VINEGAR

1 head of garden celery
1.15 litre/2 pints white vinegar

1 tablespoon white sugar
1 tablespoon sea salt

large, hot, dry, sterile jar with non-metal lid

Wash and scrub the celery, taking great care to remove soot and other unmentionables, cut into small pieces. Put the vinegar, sugar and salt into a stainless steel pan, bring to the boil. Remove from heat. Pack the celery into jars and cover completely with the vinegar. Seal tightly and leave for 2 weeks to macerate. Strain through a fine sieve. Bottle and seal.

Chamomile

Anthemis nobilis

A sweet scented decorative plant with white or yellow daisy head, yellow eye and bright green feathery leaves. Pick the flower heads when they are just beginning to turn down, dry them and use for making soothing tea to calm ruffled nerves, raving insomnia and toothache. Makes lovely pot pourris, old-fashioned cosmetics and has been a standby for years as a hair lightener.

DRYING CHAMOMILE FLOWERS

Laying the heads on a greaseproof-covered tray, well spread out in a single layer, leave in a warm airy room until very dry. Gather them up and store in a dark container or place.

Cherry

How I envy anyone who has been lucky enough to inherit a mature, healthy, cherry tree in their garden for although it is perfectly possible to buy a small established tree from a nursery they take quite a time to reach any size and the crop which they may produce can be totally ravaged by birds in one day, whereas with a large tree there is at least a one for you, one for me ratio. On the other hand, of course, it is possible to cover a small tree with a bird net.

To own a cherry tree is to have glorious pink and white floral display in the garden in the early summer. However, the more beautiful the display the less productive the variety and it is usually the ornamental trees which have the heaviest blooms. The sparser, more gentle blossoms are those which yield the fruit from which the finest and most mouth watering of preserves are made. The White Heart or Biggareau varieties of cherry are those which go from white, through yellow and scarlet to black and include the White Hearts and Napoleons but these are, in my opinion and with the exception of one or two recipes, totally wasted as a preserve fruit. They become pale, insipid and flaccid, lack any setting qualities at all and are generally a waste of time. They may be used with other fruit in Summer Pudding or compôte and are bottled or frozen with this in mind but their great beauty is that they are delicious raw. The May Duke variety is another group of cherries which are primarily a dessert fruit although they do freeze, bottle and stew with good results and can be adapted to some preserves as they keep their flavour better. These cherries are a very bright red.

The Morello cherry is the fruit that has the unique distinction of turning any humble jam into food for the Gods. It looks delectably ripe, juicy and transparent either glowing red or nearly black but take a bite and it is fiendishly tart and acid. Although it lacks good setting properties it retains both shape and flavour when cooked and produces glorious ruby red and purple preserves particularly to be found on the continent. Morello cherries are also known as sour cherries. One Morello tree in the garden is enough, for, unlike the sweet cherry, they are self-fertile and they are much more amenable to less perfect soil conditions than other cherries. When picking Morellos take care to cut the stalk from the branch not to pull or tear, consequently each cherry should have its own little piece of stalk attached and if the fruit is really ripe it should be possible, by gentle easing, to bring the stone from the cherry on the end of the stalk.

It is more likely however that whatever the variety it will be shown in your greengrocers to be either a dessert or cooking cherry, with no complications. Apart from home produce from the British Isles cherries appear in the shops from the continent, Canada and the USA which spreads the season from April to August.

Stones may be removed from the cherry either with a little patented gadget not unlike an apple-corer; by cutting the fruit in half; by slitting the cherry to encourage the stone to drop out during cooking, or by easing gently on the stalk and hoping to pull both out together. Always keep a container under the fruit during any of these processes in order to catch the juices which must be added to the preserve. The almondy kernels, when added to the fruit impart a strange flavouring which is entirely complimentary to the cherry and is the sign of a particularly good preserve. Cherries go well with all food from the savoury, in *hors d'oeuvres*, to sweet simple fruit salads or rich creamy *torten*.

When making preserves with cherries it is as well to remember that the fruit have so little pectin or acid in them that they should be cooked in the minimum of water. A very careful watch has to be kept on fruit that is cooked on the open heat, to prevent it burning and much better results can be obtained by keeping the fruit whole, putting it in an earthenware casserole with very little water and leaving in a low oven (a fire oven is of course more economical) until the fruit is tender but still retaining its shape. This can also be achieved by putting the cherries in a heatproof bowl with very little water and standing in a pan of boiling water over a low heat.

Although it may be more sensible, particularly if you have children, to remove the stones from the cherries when making jams it is aesthetically more correct to leave them in as they contribute to a better flavour, set and appearance.

CHERRY JAM

1kg/2lb 4oz Morello or May Duke cherries

2 lemons
800g/1lb 12oz white sugar

4 hot, dry, sterile jam jars

Wash the cherries and remove the stones, crack a few of these (it is best to wrap them in a cloth) and remove the kernels. Tie the remaining stones in a muslin bag with the rind and pips from the lemon. Put muslin bag, cherries and juice from the lemons into a preserving pan and heat gently. When the juices begin to flow, simmer until tender; if the fruit is very firm, add 3 or 4 tablespoons of water to prevent burning. Remove the muslin bag giving it a good squeeze and add the kernels and the warmed sugar stirring well until it has dissolved. Bring to the boil and boil until a set is obtained. Skim. Pot and seal.

If you do not want the fiddle of removing the stones then cook the cherries whole skimming the stones from the pan as the fruit cooks and they rise to the top. Crack a few and add the kernels to the jam before adding the sugar.

CHERRY AND APPLE JAM

1kg/2lb 4oz dessert cherries   150ml/¼ pint water
675g/1lb 8oz cooking apples   1350g/3lb white sugar

7 hot, dry, sterile jam jars

Wash the cherries. Wash, peel, core and chop the apples and tie the peels and cores into a muslin bag. Put apples, bag and water into a large preserving pan and cook until the fruit is soft, add the cherries and continue to cook gently until they are tender but unbroken. Remove with a perforated spoon any stones which rise to the top, retrieve the muslin bag and add the warmed sugar, stir well until it has dissolved. Bring to the boil and boil hard until a set is obtained.

The apples give bulk and set to a good spreadable, economical jam.

CHERRY AND GOOSEBERRY JAM

1kg/2lb 4oz Kentish Red or Morello   2kg/4lb 2oz white sugar
  cherries   2 lemons
1kg/2lb 4oz ripe red gooseberries

9 hot, dry, sterile jam jars

Wash the fruit, top and tail the gooseberries and stalk and stone the cherries. Put both fruits into a preserving pan with the juice from the lemons, bring very gently to the boil and then simmer for about 25 minutes. Add the warmed sugar and stir well until it has dissolved. Bring to the boil and boil steadily until a set is obtained, try not to boil too furiously otherwise you will harden the gooseberry skins. Skim, pot and seal.

A very bright and colourful jam with a good set.

CHERRY JELLY

1kg/2lb 4oz very ripe cherries
water

apple juice
white sugar

8 medium size, hot, dry, sterile jars

Wash the cherries and put them in a dish or pan with a little water, either cook very gently on the top of the cooker or put into a low oven to become soft and juicy – you may have to mash them a bit to break them up. When the cherries are very tender turn them into a jelly bag and leave to drain overnight into a clean bowl. The next day measure the juice and for every 600ml/1 pint cherry juice take 300ml/½ pint apple juice and 450g/1lb warmed sugar. Return both juices to the pan, heat gently and add the sugar, stir well until it has dissolved. Boil hard until a set is obtained. Skim. Pot. Seal when cold.

CHERRY AND ORANGE CONSERVE

1kg/2lb 4oz black cherries
2 large, sweet, thin-skinned oranges
2 lemons
1 stick cinnamon

1 teaspoon whole cloves
900g/2lb white sugar or 450g/1lb white sugar and 450g/1lb soft brown sugar

4 hot, dry sterile jam jars

Wash and stone the cherries, crack a few stones and reserve the kernels. Cut the orange into very thin slices and remove the pips. Cut the lemons, squeeze out the juice, reserve it and remove the pips. Tie cherry stones, lemon and orange pips and the spices into a muslin bag. Lay the orange slices in a large preserving pan and just cover with water, add the muslin bag and simmer until the oranges are soft. Remove the muslin bag and add the cherries, kernels, lemon juice and the warmed sugar. Heat gently, stirring well until the sugar has dissolved. Bring to the boil and boil hard until a set is obtained. Pot and seal.

The spices may be omitted for an equally unusual and tasty conserve.

CHERRY CHUTNEY

1kg/2lb 4oz Morello cherries (or an equally sour cherry)
900ml/1½ pints malt vinegar
175g/6oz cooking apples
350g/12oz onions
fair size piece of root ginger
1 tablespoon pickling spice
2 teaspoons sea salt
350g/12oz white sugar
225g/8oz walnuts or almonds

4 hot, dry, sterile jars with non-metal lids

Wash the cherries, remove the stalks and put in a stainless steel pan with 400ml/14fl. oz of the vinegar. Simmer until the fruit is tender and the stones rise to the top, seek out any that still remain. Wash, peel, core and chop the apples. Peel and chop the onions; bruise the spices and tie them in a muslin bag. Add apples, onions, spices and salt to the cherries in the pan. Cook until very soft. Remove spice bag. Dissolve the sugar in the remaining vinegar and add it to the chutney, stir well and boil steadily until nice and thick. Chop the nuts and stir them in. Pot and seal. Keep for at least 2 months before using. A sharp chutney that goes very well with cold game.

CHERRY CHUTNEY USING TINNED FRUIT

2 × 500g/1lb 2oz tins of cherries
900ml/1½ pints red or white wine vinegar
1 cinnamon stick
10 cloves
piece root ginger
500g/1lb 2oz brown sugar
250g/9oz seedless raisins

3 hot, dry, sterile jars with non-metal lids

Drain the cherries (the juice can be used to make a jelly). Put the vinegar into a stainless steel pan with the spices and boil together for 20 minutes. Allow to cool and strain before using. Put cherries, sugar, raisins and cold vinegar back into the pan, heat gently stirring well until the sugar has dissolved and then boil for 30 minutes. Cool. Pot. Seal when cold.

Keep at least 2 weeks before using. Excellent with cold meats, chicken or game.

CONFITURE OF CHERRIES WITH BRANDY

1kg/2lb 4oz Morello or May Duke   7 tablespoons redcurrant juice
   cherries   2 tablespoons brandy
800g/1lb 12oz white sugar

4 hot, dry, sterile jam jars

Wash and stalk the cherries. Put a little of the sugar to cover the bottom of a preserving pan, place a layer of cherries on this, then a layer of sugar and so on until all the sugar and fruit is used up. Sprinkle with the fruit juice (apple juice will do at a pinch) and place over a low heat. Bring gently to the boil, shaking the pan constantly but never stirring the contents with a spoon. Boil rapidly, still giving the pan a shake. Skim. When the syrup has reached setting point and the cherries look clear and cooked take a narrow wooden spoon and very carefully stir in the brandy. Remove from the heat and allow to cool a little before potting. Seal.

    This is a confiture in the true tradition of continental preserves without being too sweet. The whole fruit suspended in the jelly gives it a good potential as a sophisticated sauce for home-made ice cream, custards, soufflés or crêpes.

SOUR PICKLED CHERRIES

1kg/2lb 4oz Morello cherries   2 blades mace
600ml/1 pint white wine vinegar   1 teaspoon black peppercorns
2 teaspoons coriander seed

3 dry, sterile, jars with non-metal lids

Wash the cherries and pack them into a large, sterile jar. Cover them with the vinegar, place a clean saucer on the top and leave for a week. Bruise the spices and tie them in a muslin bag. Strain the vinegar from the fruit and put it in a stainless steel pan with the spice bag, bring to the boil and boil hard for 10 minutes. While you are waiting for the vinegar to boil, pack the cherries into the jars. Allow the vinegar to cool, retrieve the spice bag and pour the vinegar over the cherries to cover.

    Keep for at least one month before using.

CHERRY STALK TEA

Do not throw away those cherry stalks – pop them into a polythene box and keep them in the refrigerator. When you are feeling a trifle jaundiced first thing in the morning, pour a cupful of boiling water on to a dozen of them. The resulting brew is very cleansing and therapeutic.

Chestnut

Every town and country child must have had a memory or two of either searching the peaty ground for those spiky green clusters with their glimpses of glossy brown or the bright charcoal burners on the city streets releasing the tempting smell of roasting chestnuts. Ineradicably one of the great memories of childhood, but as we grow older the more sophisticated delights of chestnut stuffing, marron glâcé and rich and creamy puddings take over. Do not confuse the Spanish chestnut with the horse chestnut, which when pickled in vinegar and stood for days in a cool oven provides small boys with championship conkers. The Spanish chestnut should more rightly be called the Italian chestnut for the Romans, who ground the nut to a flour or *pollenta*, carried it with their expeditionary legions throughout Europe and to this day chestnut flour is still frequently used in cake making.

Wild chestnuts may be fun to gather but they do not give a worthwhile harvest for the cook, so better to leave them for the squirrels. The large, sweet chestnuts which are in our shops during November-December, come from France and Italy and these are the ones to use for preserving, abundant, cheap and fully ripe.

CHESTNUT PRESERVE

1kg/2lb 4oz sweet chestnuts   6 tablespoons orange flower water
1kg/2lb 4oz white sugar   vanilla essence

5 medium size, hot, dry, sterile jars

Prepare the chestnuts by wiping them and making a small horizontal slit on the curve. Boil them in a little water until tender, peel whilst hot, carefully removing both skins. Drain them and return to the pan with the sugar, orange flower water and a few drops of vanilla essence. Heat gently, stirring well until the sugar has dissolved, bring to the boil and then simmer until the chestnuts have disintegrated and the mixture is quite thick. Pot and seal.

CONSERVED CHESTNUTS WITH JELLY

1kg/2lb 4oz sweet chestnuts   crab apple jelly
white sugar

Wipe the chestnuts and make a small horizontal slit on the curve, put them in a pan with just enough water to cover. Boil until tender and peel while still hot, removing both outer and inner skin. Put the chestnuts through a fine sieve or liquidizer, weigh the resulting purée and for every 450g/1lb take 450g/1lb sugar and 225g/8oz crab apple jelly. Put the sugar into a preserving pan with a few drops of water and allow to melt gently stirring well all the time and taking great care not to burn, when it is a syrup remove from the heat and stir in the jelly until melting, add the chestnut purée. Spread this paste on to a flat baking tray, making a layer of about 5mm/$\frac{1}{4}$ inch thick. Place the tray in a very cool oven, keep the door ajar and leave overnight. The next day cut into squares and remove from the tin, turning them on to a sieve or colander, jostle them about occasionally to allow a good movement of air and leave until completely dry. Store in a dry tin.
   Absolutely delicious, as you can imagine.

CANDIED CHESTNUTS
OR MARRON GLÂCÉ

1kg/2lb 4oz sweet chestnuts   600ml/1 pint water
1kg/2lb 4oz white sugar   vanilla pod or a few drops of essence

Prepare the chestnuts by making a horizontal slit on the skin, put in a pan with a little salted water, cover and cook until just tender. Drain and remove outer and inner skin whilst still hot, taking great care not to break the chestnut. Place the sugar, water and vanilla in a preserving pan and boil to a very thick syrup, transfer the chestnuts into the syrup and boil very carefully for 10 minutes. Pour nuts and syrup into a deep bowl, cover with a clean cloth and leave for 24 hours. The next day return the chestnuts and syrup to the pan and boil for 5 minutes, once again transfer nuts and syrup to the bowl, cover and leave for 24 hours. Repeat this operation three times more making five times in all or until the syrup is used up. Cover a wire rack with greaseproof paper and place the chestnuts on this, pop them into a cool oven, leaving the door ajar and allow them to dry completely. Store between sheets of greaseproof paper in an airtight tin. Keep cool and dry.

Should such a thing be even remotely possible, do not keep long. During the process of making *marron glâcé* some of the chestnuts may, inevitably, fall apart. Collect the pieces with a perforated spoon and mould them into small balls which will make equally acceptable sweets.

STORING CHESTNUTS

Remove thick outer husks if they still have them, wipe the nut clean and dry and store in any mouse-proof container in a cool, dry place.

Chilli

The chilli pepper referred to is the small pointed, scarlet and green, pungently hot variety of capsicum, which as children we called the Devil's dancing cap. Every country that I have ever been to has had some other ramification of the name and this lack of ethnic knowledge has led to some very nasty assaults on my taste buds, nevertheless I still consider it indispensible to the spice cupboard, but only in careful quantities.

It is perfectly possible to grow chilli peppers in this country but in a greenhouse or conservatory and one or two seedsmen do stock chilli seeds. Look for the names of Cayenne Chilli, Hot Peppers or Mexican Chilli. These chillies grown from seeds may be dried and ground to provide chilli powder, or used fresh in chutneys and hot spicy dishes. They may also be pickled whole and used in *hors d'oeuvres* to shock the unwary. When cutting chillies take care not to touch the lips, eyes or other sensitive areas with your fingers as the residual oils cause a painful burning sensation – douse any affected area with lots of cold water. I do not think that there is any particularly lasting damage involved but it is, like onion oil, very uncomfortable.

Chillies come into our shops from Africa, the Canaries and France during February to July.

CHILLI SAUCE

10 whole dried chillies or 6 whole
   fresh chillies
450g/1lb onions
450g/1lb ripe tomatoes
450g/1lb cooking apples
225g/8oz sultanas
2 fat cloves garlic

1 dessertspoon sea salt
1 dessertspoon whole mustard seed
1 dessertspoon whole allspice
1 dessertspoon whole cloves
225g/8oz soft brown sugar
600ml/1 pint cider or wine vinegar

8 small, hot, dry, sterile jars with non-metal lids

Wash and shred the chillies and tie them in a muslin bag. Peel and chop the onions; wash and chop the tomatoes; wash, peel, core and chop the apples. Chop the sultanas, peel and crush the garlic. Bruise the spices and tie them in another muslin bag. Put all the ingredients into a large stainless steel pan and heat gently, stirring well until it comes to the boil. Reduce the heat and simmer gently until the mixture is very thick, taking care to prevent burning or sticking. When it has cooked enough remove the muslin bags and put the pulp through a food mill or mincer (although the mincer is very messy it gives a chunkier sauce which I prefer). Return to pan and reheat to boiling, giving an occasional stir. Pot and seal.

    A hot sauce, wonderful for barbecues and it can be made hotter or milder by the amount of chillies used.

PIRI PIRI SAUCE

a handful of fresh hot chillies
1 lemon

bay leaf
300ml/$\frac{1}{2}$ pint olive oil

a small stone jar with tight lid

Slit the top from each chilli. Finely pare a shred of peel from the lemon. Put all the ingredients into the jar and leave to stand in a very gentle heat (a tepid oven) until the mixture has infused. Seal and keep at least 24 hours before using. It will obviously be better the longer you keep it.

    Use for basting grilled meat and fish.

CHILLI VINEGAR

1.15 litre/2 pints white vinegar
1 teaspoon whole cloves

100g/4oz fresh red or green chillies or
50g/2oz dried red chillies

hot, dry, sterile jar with a wide neck and non-metal lid

Simmer the vinegar and cloves in a stainless steel pan for 2 minutes. Remove from heat, cover and allow to stand whilst preparing the chillies. Wash the chillies and slice in half lengthwise. Strain the vinegar and return to the pan, bring to the boil add the chillies. Bring quickly to the boil and pour into the jar. Seal and leave in a dark place. The vinegar made with dried chillies takes 2 weeks to mature, with fresh red chillies it takes 5-6 weeks to mature and with the green chillies about 8 weeks to mature. When it has obtained a pungency to curl your hair, strain the vinegar through muslin and bottle it in sterile bottles with corks. Seal tightly.

A very good vinegar for making dressings to go with particularly bland food. Cold fish will benefit from a mere spot and it may be added to a quantity of vinegar when making pickles. The thing to beware of with chilli vinegar is that you do not immediately notice how hot it is as the heat of chillies is more of a sensation than a taste.

SALTED CHILLIES

a quantity of fresh unmarked chillies
sea salt

a large earthenware crock

Wash and dry the chillies well. Starting off with a layer of salt and then a layer of chillies, fill the jar up completely, finishing with salt. Seal with a cork or parchment tied down firmly. Stand the crock in a dry place well above stone, brick or concrete surfaces which will draw up the moisture.

To use the chillies, remove from the jar and shake off excess salt.

DRIED CHILLIES

Make sure that your chillies have matured to a dark red pod. Pick them with a piece of stalk attached and thread a string through this, knotting after each stalk. Hang them in a hot sunny place, either the garden where the sun is at its hottest or in the greenhouse in which you grew them. A hot dry area with plenty of glass like a bay window might do at a pinch. When dry the pods will be shrunken, dark and bend without snapping. They may be kept on the string and used as you need them but if your kitchen is damp or steamy, store in an airtight jar.

Clementine

A small, sweet, juicy, orange-type fruit, thin skinned and pithless, segmented like satsumas and tangerines but with rather more pips. They are reasonably priced and worth making into a preserve although it is more like a sweet orange jam than a marmalade. Clementines are available in the shops from December to February and arrive from Cyprus, Spain and Morocco.

CLEMENTINE MARMALADE

1kg/2lb 4oz clementines
2 large lemons

1.15 litre/2 pints water
1550g/3lb 8oz white sugar

5 hot, dry, sterile jam jars

Wash and cut the clementines very finely – or mince them. Keep the pips. Remove the juice from the lemons and reserve it. Retrieve the pips and tie them in a muslin bag with the clementine pips. Place the fruit, bag and water in a deep bowl, cover and leave to stand overnight. The next day turn the contents of the bowl into a preserving pan and simmer gently with a lid on for about 1½ hours or less if the fruit was minced. When the peel is soft remove the muslin bag and add the lemon juice and warmed sugar. Heat gently stirring well until it has dissolved. Bring to the boil and boil hard until a set is obtained, do not put the lid on once the sugar has been added. Pot and seal.

A very good breakfast preserve that children will love.

Coconut

The coconut which we buy from our greengrocers round about the festive season is the mere nut from an enormous husk-covered phenomenon which is grown in the tropics where it has an important economic value, providing fibre, food, drink and oil for those countries. We only receive the fully mature fruit in Britain but the young, green coconut is considered a great delicacy. Although British housewives use desiccated coconut fairly frequently in sweet and cake making, it is rarely used in the making of preserves and the fresh coconut is generally purchased with a view to keeping the bird population happy. However, both desiccated and fresh coconut make an excellent preserve which, although it does not keep long, is marvellous on biscuits and cakes and much more effective and delicate than the usual heavy jam and coconut covering on commercial products. Thin, home-made, almond biscuits sandwiched together with coconut preserve and lightly topped with lemon icing are delicious. Use either creamed coconut or the milk from well soaked desiccated coconut in curries, not the fresh milk which does not have the same effect. Save that for delicious drinks from the innocent to the evil.

COCONUT JAM

1 fresh coconut	vanilla pod or a few drops of vanilla
white sugar	essence
water	a pinch of cinnamon – optional

6 small, hot, dry, sterile jars

Make holes in the two little eyes at the top of the coconut, drain off the milk and break the shell in half (do not throw the empty shells away, fill them with fat and bird seed and hang them in the garden for the birds), remove the flesh, grate it, weigh it and take an equal amount of sugar. Place the sugar in a preserving pan with a minute drop of water, stir gently over a very low heat until the sugar has melted, bring to the boil and add the vanilla, cinnamon (if used) and coconut. Simmer for about 1½ hours, stirring frequently. Remove the vanilla pod. Pot and seal.

Keep the milk for making drinks or puddings or freeze it for use at a later date.

COCONUT PRESERVE
USING DESICCATED NUT

450g/1lb desiccated coconut
300ml/½ pint water
1 tablespoon rose water

450g/1lb white sugar
1 tablespoon lemon juice
50g/2oz blanched almonds

6 medium size, hot, dry, sterile jars

Put the coconut into a large bowl, mix the rose water with half of the water and fold it well into the coconut with a fork. Do not stir but lift lightly until all the coconut is moist, add a little more of the water, cover and leave to stand overnight by which time the coconut will be soft. Put the sugar into a preserving pan and add the juice from the lemon and the rest of the water. Melt gently over a low heat and then boil to a syrup, add the coconut and stir well, bring very carefully to the boil again, as soon as it boils remove from the heat. Chop the almonds and stir them into the preserve. Allow to cool a little. Pot and seal.

Both these preserves should retain the pure white colour therefore it is essential that they do not overcook or burn. Orange water may be added instead of rose water. Do not keep long.

Coriander

Coriandrum sativum

One of the most ancient of herbs discovered by the Chinese thousands of years ago and used by them as a vegetable – the roots may be cooked and eaten like carrots – and as a flavouring, for the round seed heads, once dried make a very important contribution to the spice range. The leaves also give a good but different taste. The best way to preserve them is by freezing (see Freezing Basil, page 77.) Coriander is one of the herbs often referred to as an Oriental Spice and as nothing else is quite like it, it is worth growing in the garden. The plant is a hardy annual reaching a height of about 45cm/18 inches with pale, frondy leaves, small pink flowers and a rather foetid smell. It requires a light fertile soil and plenty of sunshine to thrive in. The seeds should be picked and treated in the same way as caraway but do make sure that they are well and truly dried and brown before using them otherwise they can be rather nasty. Store in dark jars or a dark place and use for seasoning in curries and chutneys, cream cheeses, milk puddings, meat dishes, salads, biscuits, bread and homemade marmalade, where it is especially good.

CORIANDER CORDIAL

15g/½oz dried coriander seed
rounded teaspoon caraway seed
1cm/½ inch cinnamon stick

600ml/1 pint water
225g/8oz white sugar
600ml/1 pint brandy

dry, sterile, glass bottle with stopper

Crush the spices a little and put them in the bottle with the brandy. Seal and leave to steep on a nice warm windowsill for 3 weeks. Make a syrup by boiling the water and sugar together until it is well dissolved and thick. Take 600ml/1 pint of this and strain the brandy into it. Mix well and return to bottle. Seal.

Caraway Cordial, similar to kümmel but not quite, can be made by the same method omitting the spices and using only 25g/1oz caraway seed.

Sweetcorn or Indian Corn

Although most gardens are not large enough to accommodate any quantity of sweetcorn it can be grown with surprisingly good results when planted carefully. Rich clumps of soil raised up and mounded around each plant and kept well watered will yield strong healthy plants with good ears of maize. Underneath and between the plants you can grow cucumbers, squashes of all sorts and dwarf beans; they make very good bedfellows both enjoying the same conditions and each offering the other protection against the elements. Grow on in peat pots and plant out in May.

Maize or sweetcorn is one of the most ancient cultivated crops and can take many shapes and forms from the tiny multi-coloured decorative cobs

– which incidentally are nearest to the true first maize known to fourth-century Indians – to the large, hard variety grown in endless miles for maize crops and animal food. In between somewhere comes the variety which we buy fresh from the greengrocer or tinned and frozen from the supermarket. Either frozen or tinned corn may be used in the recipes given here but make sure that the corn is well thawed or drained first (never throw away the liquid from a tin of sweetcorn, it makes the basis of an excellent bisque). Fresh corn should have the husk and silk removed before blanching the cob in boiling water for 10 minutes, dipping quickly into freezing water to cool and removing the kernels with a sharp knife.

You may expect to see fresh corn from Britain, the continent and USA in the shops from July-October.

CORN PICKLE

1kg/2lb 4oz corn kernels
1 cucumber
3 onions
4 firm tomatoes
1 pepper, green or red
300ml/½ pint cider vinegar

150ml/¼ pint water
2 level tablespoons sea salt
½ teaspoon ground black pepper
½ teaspoon turmeric powder
1½ teaspoons mustard powder
225g/8oz white sugar

4 hot, dry, sterile jars with non-metal lids

Wash the kernels under cold running water. Peel the cucumber and onions and cut into small dice. Skin the tomatoes (drop them into boiling water and then into cold, this makes it much easier), deseed and dice the pepper. Put all the ingredients except the sugar and tomatoes into a stainless steel pan, heat gently and then add the sugar, stirring well until it has dissolved. Bring to the boil, still stirring, and boil for 5 minutes. Reduce the heat, cover and simmer for 1 hour – take care not to burn. Add the tomatoes, stir well and cook for another 5 minutes. Pot and seal.

Keep for at least 2 months before using. A very nice soft pickle which children will like.

CORN AND PEPPER RELISH

1kg/2lb 4oz corn kernels
900g/2lb green peppers (about 6)
900g/2lb red peppers
1kg/2lb 4oz spanish onions
2 level tablespoon whole mustard seed

1 level tablespoon whole cloves
600ml/1 pint cider vinegar
1 level tablespoon sea salt
675g/1lb 8oz white sugar

9 hot, dry, sterile jars with non-metal lids

Rinse the corn kernels under a cold tap. Wash and chop the peppers removing seed and pith. Drop corn and peppers into a pan of boiling water for 3 minutes (blanching). Drain. Peel and chop the onions, bruise the spices, tie them into a muslin bag and put this with the vinegar, salt and sugar into a large stainless steel pan. Bring to the boil, stirring well until the sugar has dissolved and then boil to a thin syrup, which will take about 5 minutes. Add the vegetables, stir well and bring to the boil. Remove the muslin bag. Pot, making sure that the vegetables are pressed well down and covered with syrup. Seal.

This relish can be eaten immediately; if kept too long it will soften and become dark. The vegetables should be crisp giving a relish that has a good bite. Goes very well spread on home-made hamburgers.

Courgette

Known confusingly as courgette in France, Zucchini or Zucchini Squash in America and originally, baby marrow in Great Britain, the courgette has now taken on a new lease of life as a gourmet vegetable. It has proved itself so adaptable and easy to grow that it is fast becoming an established favourite and every garden should boast a few plants.

Courgette have a mellow, buttery flavour and retain both firmness and delicacy of flesh throughout cooking. I find them an excellent vegetable to use in clear mixed pickles as they have more bite and flavour than the popular marrow for which I often substitute them. They also look attractive, having a range of colour from white through green and striped to yellow. Never peel them, half their beauty is in their soft edible skin. Courgettes may be cooked in a variety of ways, from being gently sautéed in butter or made into glorious multicoloured ratatouille, used raw or cooked in salad. Even the flowers have a unique use of their own – like marrow flowers. Take the male or barren flower either leaving it as it is or stuffing it with a fine mixture of mince and rice and dip it into a light batter, and deep fry. A truly delicious recipe from Italy. If you have a good crop of courgettes the possibilities to experiment with may be endless.

Apart from the true French courgette there are these other specialist varieties to choose from.

Black Beauty a black variety with pure white flesh.
Golden Courgette a glorious yellow vegetable which when very young, may be eaten raw.
White Courgette a pure white courgette.

Pick any of these small enough and they may be cooked whole. Allow them to become large and you have a better than average marrow. Courgettes are available in the shops more or less throughout the year and come from the continent or Africa. I also feel that if you are lucky enough to take your car to Europe it is one of those vegetables well worth buying in quantity on your way home for they do make the most superb pickles and freeze very well in made up dishes, yet they never seem to yield crops in the glut proportions which makes pickling an economic proposition.

PICKLED COURGETTE

1kg/2lb 4oz courgettes	25g/1oz mixed pickling spice
100g/4oz sea salt	dill seeds or head
1.15 litre/2 pints water	1.15 litre/2 pints white wine vinegar

3 dry, sterile jars with non-metal lids

Wash the courgettes and slice into 3cm/1 inch pieces. Pop them into a deep bowl and make up a cold brine with the salt and water, but do make sure that the salt has dissolved. Cover the courgettes with brine, lay a clean cloth over the top and leave for 24 hours. In the meantime, tie the spices into a muslin bag and put them in a stainless steel saucepan with the vinegar. Bring to the boil and boil for 5 minutes. Cover and leave to get cold. The next day, drain the courgettes and pack them into the jars, sprinkling the dill seeds or placing the heads amongst them, remove the spice bag from the vinegar which may then be poured over the courgette to cover. Make sure that there are no air bubbles. Seal.

A very pleasant crunchy pickle which goes well with cold lamb.

Cowslip

I deplore the devastation wreaked upon our scant wild flower population by the wholesale gathering of flower heads for the making of wine etc. However, certain plants and many areas are now heavily protected by government legislation so the recipes I have given, using wild flowers, are given for their unique and antique interest only and with the plea that even if they grow in profusion and are not protected, pick only a very, very few to experiment with and pick only here and there over a large area to prevent decimation on one site.

COWSLIP SYRUP

175g/6oz cowslip heads   450g/1lb white sugar
600ml/1 pint water

small, hot, dry, sterile stoppered bottles

Make sure that you only use fresh flower heads and, that they are free from insects. Put them in a heatproof bowl and pour the boiling water over them. Cover with a lid and leave to stand for 24 hours. The next day strain the cowslip infusion into a saucepan, heat gently and add the warmed sugar, stir well until it has dissolved. Boil gently until it is a syrup. Bottle and seal.

COWSLIP VINEGAR

1 cup of cowslip heads
250ml/8fl. oz white wine vinegar

small, dry, sterile bottles with non-metal lids

Follow the method given for Tarragon Vinegar, p.353.

CANDIED COWSLIPS

275g/10oz fresh cowslip heads   water
225g/8oz white sugar

Make sure that you collect your flowerheads on a dry day and before the sun is high. Put the sugar into a heavy, wide-based pan, heat gently to warm and add a little hot water at a time until the sugar is just moist and able to melt without browning and no more. Boil gently until the syrup has begun to candy. Remove it from the heat, shake in a few flowers at a time until they are all covered, dry and frosted (stir with a great deal of care). Shake off surplus sugar. Put in jars and seal tightly.

Primroses may be candied in the same way.

Cranberry
Vaccinium oxycoccus

I was first introduced to cranberries by a Polish friend who was a chef and I thought then that it seemed extraordinary to me that Europe, which gave birth to the cranberry, no longer gives it more than a passing glance at Christmas. Admittedly, the small, sharp berry grown in the wilds of northern Europe does not evoke such enthusiasm as the fat pink variety imported from North America where it enjoys privileged tradition alongside the huckleberry and blueberry. The recipes that I have given are either fairly ancient British recipes or traditional Baltic or North American ones and I give them in the hope that we may see more imports, not in the silly little plastic boxes but in some quantity, for, although the cranberry is tart and nasty to eat raw, and low in pectin, it does make the most delicious pies and pastries and excellent sharp preserves which have a completely unique flavour. The most traditional use, of course, is in sauce or jelly to eat with turkey at Thanksgiving and we have the American settlers to thank for its survival at all. Some hypermarkets stock large plastic bags of frozen cranberries and these should be gently defrosted, keeping the juice to add to the liquid, and used as the fresh fruit. Fresh cranberries come into our shops from September to December.

A relative of the cranberry is the very tiny Mountain Cranberry (*Vaccinium villis idaea*) which enjoys the same habitats and shares the same appearance and flavour as the more sophisticated variety. If you come across enough to wish to cook them, treat as for cranberry.

CRANBERRY AND APPLE JELLY WITH THYME

1kg/2lb 4oz cranberries
1kg/2lb 4oz cooking or crab apples
1 large bunch of fresh thyme

2 lemons
water
white sugar

10 small, hot, dry, sterile jars

Wash the cranberries, wash and slice the apples, take two-thirds of the thyme and wash and rub this to release the oils. Squeeze the juice from the lemons and reserve, put the pips into a preserving pan with both fruits, the thyme and just enough water to cover. Simmer gently until all the fruit is very soft (a bit of mashing may be necessary here). Turn into a jelly bag and leave to drain overnight into a clean bowl. The next day measure the juices and for every 600ml/1 pint take 450g/1lb warmed sugar and 2 tablespoons of the lemon juice and heat gently, stirring well until it has dissolved. Bring to the boil and boil hard until a set is obtained. Wash and dry the remaining thyme and either chop it or select some small sprigs. Skim the jelly. If you are using chopped thyme this is the moment to stir it in, leave for 5 minutes before potting. However, for a very decorative effect small sprigs of thyme may be suspended in the cooling jelly by allowing the jelly to become slightly cool before half-filling the jars, popping in a neat piece of thyme and allowing to cool a little more before filling up each jar. Make sure that you only seal it when the jelly is cold.

Dried thyme (75g/3oz) may be used if fresh is not available. This recipe may also be used to give a good Cranberry and Apple Jelly by omitting the thyme completely or you may substitute other precious herbs of your choice.

CRANBERRY CONSERVE

1kg/2lb 4oz cranberries
2 large sweet oranges
600ml/1 pint water
100g/4oz large seedless raisins

100g/4oz shelled walnuts
500g/1lb 2oz soft brown sugar
200g/7oz white sugar

5 hot, dry, sterile jam jars

Wash and stem cranberries, wash and finely slice the oranges, removing pips and put both fruit into a preserving pan with the water. Simmer gently until tender. Wash and chop the raisins, chop the walnuts and add these with the warmed sugar to the conserve, heat gently, stirring well until the sugar has dissolved. Bring to the boil and boil hard until a soft set is obtained. Pot and seal.

A very pleasant mixture of tastes. This conserve would make a very good present with a pot of Mardi's Conserve (see p.61).

CRANBERRY CHUTNEY

1kg/2lb 4oz cranberries
900g/2lb cooking apples
375g/13oz large raisins
15g/½oz mixed pickling spice

2 teaspoons sea salt
2 teaspoons mixed spice
600ml/1 pint vinegar
500g/1lb 2oz white sugar

5 hot, dry, sterile, jars with non-metal lids

Wash the cranberries, wash, peel, core and chop the apples and wash and chop the raisins – alternatively all three may be coarsely minced. Tie the pickling spice into a muslin bag. Put cranberries, apples, raisins, spices, salt and spice bag into a stainless steel pan with half the vinegar. Boil gently until all the fruit is soft, dissolve the sugar in the remainder of the vinegar and add to the fruit. Stir well and boil gently until thick, remove muslin bag. Pot and seal. Store for at least 2 months.

CRANBERRY CHEESE

1kg/2lb 4oz cranberries
600ml/1 pint water

600g/1lb 6oz white sugar

small, hot, dry, sterile moulds

Wash the cranberries and put them in a preserving pan with the water. Simmer until they pop and are soft. Pass through a fine sieve, return to the pan and heat gently, add the warmed sugar and continue to cook gently, stirring well until the paste is very thick and leaving the sides of the pan. Pot and seal.

Rather a tart cheese; cut it into slices to eat with cold game. Not a cheese to be eaten with puddings as a sweet.

A very good cheese may be made by adding 100g/4oz large raisins and 100g/4oz chopped walnuts with the sugar. This cheese is then turned out of its mould, which should be larger than usual, decorated with glazed orange slices and served with rich game or liver pâté.

Cress or Land Cress

The garden variety of cress which we buy in the shops as mustard and cress is also known as peppergrass. The tiny, dark seeds may be made into a very refreshing, slightly hot vinegar.

CRESS VINEGAR

15g/½oz cress seeds
1 litre/1¾ pints white or white wine vinegar

large, hot, dry, sterile jar with non-metal lid

Put the vinegar into a stainless steel pan, bring it to the boil and allow it to cool. Dry the seeds in a warm oven and then pound them in a mortar or the equivalent until they are a fine powder. Turn them into the jar, add the vinegar, seal and leave in a cool dark place, giving a stir or a shake every day for 10 days. Strain the vinegar through a muslin cloth into sterile bottles with corks. Seal tightly.

Cucumber

This enormously popular salad vegetable is world wide and its history and origin become a little confused in the mists of time. However, it would appear from recipes that over the centuries the northern countries have perfected the ridge and pickling cucumbers and in the hotter and more temperate countries the dark, smooth-skinned variety has been favoured. While this vegetable is very good in salads it does not lend itself to the delicious range of pickles, some of them very ancient, that the ridge and pickling cucumbers do. Many of these recipes are basically a simple extension of preserving a glut vegetable and the cucumbers are steeped in brine or vinegar, with additions, to keep them for as long as possible. Cucumbers are usually left for a short period of time in some kind of salt preparation and it is as well to remember that a dry brine gives a crisper end result than a wet brine. I find it a good idea to pot the pickles using whole cucumbers in coloured or opaque jars to prevent colour loss. They look particularly good in light green glass if you are thinking in terms of present giving.

Some of the slightly more unusual varieties of cucumber worth mentioning are:

Zeppelin A greenhouse cucumber that improves with the length of time that it stays on the vine, gradually turning to a beautiful deep gold. This is useful when you need to extend the picking time.

Burpless Another greenhouse cucumber which grows to a good size, has a smooth, dark green appearance and whose name speaks for itself.

Both of these cucumbers are best eaten raw in salads but they, and other greenhouse varieties may be preserved in a few of the recipes given below.

Pablo *Perfection Ridge* *King of the Ridge* *Long Green*	All these are ridge or garden cucumbers which are distinguishable from the greenhouse variety by their appearance which is shorter and thicker with a light green, warty looking skin. They also retain their shape and flavour well and keep for a longer time. Ridge cucumbers may also be eaten raw and are useful in most of the preserves.
Rhineland Pickling *Venlo Pickler*	Small pickling cucumbers grown specifically for that purpose, similar in appearance to the ridge cucumber and adapting well in conditions in either garden or greenhouse. Usually a prolific cropper it is frequently known as the Gherkin. Of all the cucumbers I find this little fellow the easiest and most worthwhile to grow in the garden.

Cucumbers are not the greatest of preservers but they do frequently appear in glut proportions so it is as well to have some ideas beyond the salad bowl. Do not try to freeze or bottle them, it will not be the greatest success mainly because they have a high water content. All the recipes for ridge cucumbers are also suitable for gherkins and I will give a little more information on that under Gherkin.

It is not very often that one comes across ridge or pickling cucumbers in the greengrocer's shop. It is far more likely to be the greenhouse variety that faithfully reappears throughout the year from Great Britain, the Canaries and Holland. They may sometimes be expensive but they are rarely unobtainable, which is, I think, a good argument for concentrating your energies on growing the ridge and pickling kind. An incidental piece of information which may come in handy – 1 large, fat, long cucumber of the greenhouse variety can easily weigh 675g/1lb 8oz

---

CUCUMBER CONSERVE

1kg/2lb 4oz large cucumbers   50g/2oz root ginger
1kg/2lb 4oz white sugar

6 small, hot, dry, sterile jars

Peel the cucumbers and slice thinly. Lay in a deep dish and cover with the sugar. Cover the bowl with a clean cloth and leave for 24 hours. The next day strain off the sugary juices and pour them into a preserving pan. Bruise the ginger and tie it in a muslin bag. Bring the syrup gently to the boil and continue to simmer briskly for 45 minutes. Add the cucumber and boil gently without stirring for a further 10 minutes. Remove from heat, cover and leave overnight. The next day bring to the boil again and boil gently for 15 minutes. Remove muslin bag. Pot and seal.

Try to keep the slices of cucumber reasonably whole. This is a very proper and inoffensive preserve, very cool to look at and with no very strong taste beyond the ginger. If kept too long it will discolour.

SWEET GOLDEN PICKLE

1kg/2lb 4oz ridge cucumbers (King of the Ridge, Fablo)   75g/3oz soft, light brown sugar
350g/12oz onions   1 tablespoon mustard seed
3 red or green peppers   1 teaspoon celery seed
25g/1oz sea salt   ½ teaspoon turmeric
600ml/1 pint white or white wine vinegar   small blade of mace

4 hot, dry, sterile jars with non-metal lids

Wash, peel and dice the cucumbers. Peel and finely chop the onions, wash and dice the peppers removing seed and pith. Put all the vegetables into a bowl and sprinkle with the salt. Cover and leave for 2 hours. Turn into a colander and rinse under cold running water, drain well. Place the sugar, vinegar and spices in a large stainless steel pan, bring gently to the boil stirring until the sugar has dissolved then boil for a further 2 minutes. Add the drained vegetables and bring to the boil mixing well. The vegetables should be tender and retain their shape and colour without becoming mushy. Pot and seal.

A very pleasant aromatic pickle which children like and one which goes particularly well with mild cheeses.

PICKLED CUCUMBER

1kg/2lb 4oz cucumbers
25g/1oz sea salt

50g/2oz mixed pickling spice
1.15 litre/2 pints white vinegar

2 large, dry, sterile jars with non-metal lids

Wash the cucumbers; if they are very small leave whole, otherwise cut into manageable pieces. Put in a bowl sprinkling with the salt as you go. Cover and leave overnight. In the meantime bruise the spices and tie them into a muslin bag, put this in a stainless steel pan with the vinegar and boil together for 5 minutes. Remove from the heat. Cover and allow to cool. The next day turn the cucumbers into a colander and rinse briefly under cold running water. Drain well and pack into jars. Remove spice bag from the vinegar, which should then be poured over the cucumber to cover. Make sure that there are no air bubbles. Seal.

For Sweet Pickled Cucumbers, add 4 teaspoons of white sugar to the vinegar after you have removed it from the heat, making sure it is well dissolved. For a hotter pickle, use the seasoning and add a few dried chillies to the jars.

Gherkins may be pickled the same way.

DILL PICKLES WITH FENNEL

1kg/2lb 4oz small, young, tender
  cucumbers, ridge or pickling
50g/2oz sea salt
1.15 litre/2 pints water
4 teaspoons sea salt
1.15 litre/2 pints white vinegar

a good quantity of fresh fennel stalk
  and seeds
coriander seeds
1 tablespoon black peppercorns
1 tablespoon dill seeds

4 dry, sterile jars with non-metal lids

Wipe the cucumbers and cut them into thick chunks. Make a cold brine with the salt and water, making sure that the salt is dissolved. Place the cucumbers in a deep bowl and cover with the brine, leave for 2 hours. Meanwhile, boil the vinegar and salt together in a stainless steel pan and leave to cool. Wash the fennel and chop into manageable pieces. When the cucumbers are ready, drain and rinse them and pack into jars well interspersed with the fennel, spices and dill seed. When the jar is nearly full, cover the contents with the cold vinegar solution. Seal.

Keep for one month before using. A very good recipe to use for gherkins.

HOT CUCUMBER PICKLES

1kg/2lb 4oz large cucumbers
50g/2oz sea salt
1.15 litre/2 pints water
1 tablespoon sea salt
1.15 litre/2 pints white wine vinegar
4 whole cloves
1 tablespoons black peppercorns
large piece root ginger

piece fresh horseradish
225g/8oz shallots
1 clove garlic
a few sprigs fresh tarragon or 1
   tablespoon dried tarragon
2 bay leaves
dried chilli peppers to taste

6 hot, dry, sterile jars with non-metal lids

Wash and peel the cucumbers, cut in half lengthwise and then into 3cm/1 inch chunks. Make a brine by boiling the 50g/2oz salt and water together in a large pan, add the cucumber to this and boil for 1 minute. Turn into a colander and drain, put into an earthenware crock, sprinkle with 1 tablespoon of salt and cover with the vinegar. Place a clean cheesecloth over the top and leave for 3 days, then drain off the vinegar and pour it into a stainless steel pan, add the cloves, peppercorn and bruised ginger. Boil hard for 1 minute allow to cool. Wash and slice the horseradish, peel and finely slice the shallots and garlic, tear the bay leaf into pieces and bruise the chillies. Turn out the cucumbers and pack them in alternate layers with the shallots, horseradish and garlic, into the jars. Intersperse well with the tarragon and bay, put a few chillies down the side of the jars. Cover with the cold vinegar – do not strain. Seal.

A good crisp pickle and very, very hot. If you like a softer pickle, add the cucumber to the boiling vinegar for 1 minute before packing into jars. A good pickle with oily smoked fish.

136

CUCUMBER AND TOMATO PICKLE

1kg/2lb 4oz cucumbers
2 teaspoons sea salt
450g/1lb onions
900g/2lb ripe tomatoes
1 green pepper
1 red pepper
325g/11½oz sultanas
bunch of fresh mint

900ml/1½ pints cider vinegar
1 teaspoon curry powder
1 teaspoon mustard powder
½ teaspoon cayenne powder
½ teaspoon paprika
½ teaspoon ground black pepper
½ teaspoon ground ginger
450g/1lb white or soft brown sugar

7 hot, dry, sterile jars with non-metal lids

Wash and peel the cucumbers, place in a bowl and sprinkle with the salt. Peel and chop the onions very fine. Plunge the tomatoes into boiling water, then into cold and the skins should come off as by magic, chop the pulp. Wash the peppers and dice, removing pith and seeds. Wash and chop the sultanas, and wash and finely chop the mint (or put it into a liquidizer with a little of the vinegar) Put the vinegar and spices into a large stainless steel pan and bring to the boil. Drain and remove excess salt from the cucumbers and add these to the pan with the other vegetables, sultanas, mint and sugar. Heat gently, stirring well until the sugar has dissolved. Bring to the boil. Pot and seal.

   Keep for at least 1 week before using. This is a really delicious sweet and crunchy pickle.

RUSSIAN CUCUMBERS IN SALT

1kg/2lb 4oz small cucumbers
sea salt
black peppercorns
cloves

juniper berries
fresh tarragon sprigs
fresh fennel or dill

hot, dry, sterile heatproof crock or jar

Wash and dry the cucumbers (do not use any larger than 12cm/5 inches) and put into the jar, sprinkling each layer with a liberal poultice of the herbs and spices to taste and leaving 3cm/1 inch headroom. Boil the water and pour over the top of this mixture to cover, place a heavy non-metal weight on top of a plate to ensure that the cucumbers are totally submerged beneath it and leave to macerate for 8 days.

   A mild and aromatic pickle, fresh and savoury and unlike the usual pickled cucumbers. Gherkins also submit to this treatment very well.

Currant

The currants referred to on the next few pages are the members of the *Ribes* family which are edible, that is the blackcurrant, redcurrant and whitecurrant not to be confused with the black and shrivelled little object which is the dried corinth grape. The jams, preserves, pickles and beverages which may be made from these three currants are among the very best to be offered in the culinary world; some are strong and rich, full of sharp flavour, others delicate and subtle. Not only do they taste good but they have the most glorious appearance, are full of vitamins, give a good yield per kilogram and always set remarkably well. What more could one ask of any fruit?

Blackcurrant

Blackcurrants are one of the most worthwhile fruits to grow in your own garden, since the increase in commercial uses for blackcurrants means that very few reach the open market. This is a great pity as not only is the blackcurrant a very high source of natural vitamin C it is also an asset in the kitchen, making superb summer pudding, compôte, ice cream and glorious jams and jellies. It freezes and bottles with excellent results and you can make your own syrups and juices to keep you free from colds throughout the winter. The blackcurrant has an extraordinarily high pectin content which, as you know, gives advantages in making preserves but again one disadvantage is the hard skin on the fruit. This can be alleviated by long and gentle stewing and by making sure that the fruit is well cooked before adding the sugar, thus preventing the currants from becoming hard and gritty.

Blackcurrant bushes give a fairly high yield for their size, making them an investment in even a pocket handkerchief garden. They are unobtrusive and decorative, and they don't mind a certain amount of shade so may be grown beneath trees and shrubs without adverse results, but the soil must be rich, well weeded and moist. Two varieties which I have found to be successful are Baldwin, which has a nice compact bush and bears good-sized fruit particularly high in vitamin C, and Wellington XXX which bears its large, sweet, well flavoured fruit earlier than Baldwin. This bush has a more vigorous, spreading habit which makes the fruit easier to reach but takes up more room. Pruning is essential and may be done when the fruit is being picked. Cut the fruiting branch to just below the lowest bunch of currants then carry the branches off to the sunniest part of the garden, put your feet up and remove the fruit in your own good time. Not such a back-breaking task!

The bush and leaves of all the *Ribes* family, including the Flowering Currant have that rather curious 'catty' smell and if the leaves are dried in much the same way as you would dry large leaf herbs, and one or two dropped into a brewing pot of Indian tea, you will have an interesting and stimulating potion.

BASIC BLACKCURRANT JAM

1kg/2lb 4oz blackcurrants
900ml/1½ pints water

1500g/3lb 6oz white sugar

7 hot, dry sterile jam jars

Remove the currants from the stems – the easiest way to do this is to pull the stem through the prongs of a fork, wash them and place in a stainless steel pan. (You should not use copper as it reacts against the high acid content in blackcurrants.) Add the water and bring to the boil, reduce the heat and simmer gently, stirring occasionally until the skins are very soft, test and taste to make sure. When the fruit is cooked and the contents of the pan reduced by half add the warmed sugar, heat gently, stirring well until it has dissolved. Bring to the boil and boil hard until a set is obtained. Skim. Pot and seal.

Using less water (but not less than 600ml/1 pint) gives a thicker, stronger flavoured jam. 2 tablespoons of rum added to the jam just before it is removed from the heat makes a very mellow preserve.

BLACKCURRANT JAM USING A PRESSURE COOKER

1kg/2lb 4oz blackcurrants
300ml/½ pint water

1kg/2lb 4oz white sugar

4 hot, dry, sterile jam jars

Remove the currants from their stalks and wash them. Remove the trivet and place the currants and water in the cooker, cover and bring to M/10lb pressure. Cook for 3 minutes, then allow pressure to reduce at room temperature. Remove lid and stir in the warmed sugar. Return to the heat, stirring well to make sure that the sugar has dissolved. Bring to the boil (do not cover) and boil hard until a set is obtained. Pot and seal.

A pressure cooker is an ideal way to cook blackcurrants as the skins are very hard and require long cooking to ensure that they are not tough. This process in a pressure cooker takes only 3 minutes compared with at least 30 minutes by conventional methods.

BLACKCURRANT AND APPLE JAM

1kg/2lb 4oz blackcurrants
450g/1lb cooking apples

water
1600g/3lb 8oz white sugar

7 hot, dry, sterile jam jars

Remove currants from the stems, wash and put them in a stainless steel pan with just enough water to prevent them sticking, heat gently and simmer until the fruit is soft. Peel, core and slice the apples and cook in another pan with just enough water to prevent burning. The blackcurrants will take longer to cook and both fruits must be watched to ensure that they do not burn. When the fruits are cooked, mix the pulps together (if you prefer your blackcurrants pipless put them through a fine sieve before adding to the apples). Return to a clean pan and add the warmed sugar, heat gently, stirring well until it has dissolved. Bring to the boil and boil hard until a set is obtained. Skim. Pot and seal.

A superb, economical jam with good set and colour.

SUMMER JAM WITH BRANDY

450g/1lb blackcurrants
450g/1lb redcurrants
450g/1lb cherries
450g/1lb gooseberries

1.15 litre/2 pints water
2700g/6lb white sugar
6 tablespoons brandy

10 hot, dry, sterile jam jars

Stalk the currants. Stone the cherries, take the stones, crush them and tie securely in a muslin bag. Top and tail the gooseberries. Put all the fruit into a preserving pan with the water, bring to the boil and simmer until the fruit is tender and the skins are soft. Remove the muslin bag and add the sugar, stirring well until it has dissolved. Bring to the boil and boil hard until a set is obtained. Stir in the brandy, bring briefly to the boil and remove from the heat immediately. Pot and seal.

Very fruity jam with an excellent set and an all-time favourite. Use small quantities of fruit as it appears in the shops just to say that you have tried it.

BLACKCURRANT JELLY

Blackcurrants make superb jelly, mainly because of the high pectin content but also because of the sharp, strong flavour and good colour. It is not necessary to leave the blackcurrant pulp in the bag for longer than 1 hour or so when draining. Unlike other fruit the blackcurrants have a tendency to set in the bag and although this does not affect the jelly it does mean that no more juice will come through from that particular boiling. If you are not making a cheese with the pulp just boil it up again with half the original quantity of water and gain more juice. One advantage blackcurrant jelly has over the jam is its lack of pips which makes it particularly good for children. There is no need to stalk the currants.

1kg/2lb 4oz blackcurrants (not
  over-ripe)

900ml/1½ pints water
white sugar

6 medium size, hot, dry, sterile jars

Wash the currants and place them in a stainless steel pan with 600ml/1 pint of the water. Bring to the boil and then continue to simmer for 1 hour. Use a wooden spoon to give them a good mashing during cooking. When they are very soft and pulpy turn them into a jelly bag and leave to drain into a clean bowl for 1 hour. Reserve the juice and return the pulp to the pan with the remaining 300ml/½ pint water. Simmer for 30 minutes and then turn the pulp back into the jelly bag and leave to drain for a further hour. Mix the two juices together, measure them and for every 600ml/1 pint take 450g/1lb warmed sugar. Return to the pan, heat gently and add the sugar, stirring well until it has dissolved. Bring to the boil and boil hard until a set is obtained. Skim. Pot and seal.

A scented geranium leaf added to each pot gives a very good touch.

TWO LIVELY LITTLE RECIPES USING BLACKCURRANT JELLY

150g/5oz home-made blackcurrant
   jelly
200ml/7fl.oz home-made chilli sauce

4 tablespoons home-made horseradish
   sauce

Mix all together and eat with lamb or tongue.

Currant jelly, stirred with a fork, sprinkled with grated orange and decorated with fresh mint to be eaten with lamb.

SPICED BLACKCURRANT JELLY

1kg/2lb 4oz blackcurrants
900ml/1½ pints water
200ml/7fl.oz cider vinegar

5cm/2 inch cinammon stick
12 cloves
white sugar

8 small, hot, dry, sterile jars

Wash the currants and put them in a stainless steel pan with the water and bruised spices, bring to the boil and then simmer for 1 hour. Turn into a large fine-mesh sieve and press juice gently through with a wooden spoon but do not use enough force to push the fruit through. Mix the juice with the vinegar, measure it and for every 600ml/1 pint gained take 450g/1lb warmed sugar. Return juice to the clean pan, heat gently and add the sugar, stirring well until it has dissolved. Bring to the boil and boil hard until a set is obtained. Skim. Pot and seal.

BLACKCURRANT VINEGAR

1kg/2lb 4oz blackcurrants   white sugar
1.15 litre/2 pints white vinegar

hot, dry, sterile bottles with sterile corks

Wash fruit and put it in a large earthenware crock. Add the vinegar, cover and leave to stand for 5 days, stirring occasionally. Strain the fruit through a single layer of muslin or a fine-mesh sieve. Measure the juice gained and for every 600ml/1 pint take between 225g/8oz and 450g/1lb depending on how sweet your tooth is. Put sugar and juice into a stainless steel pan, heat gently, stirring well until the sugar has dissolved then boil for 10 minutes. Bottle, leaving 2cm/$\frac{3}{4}$ inch headroom, seal.

Blackcurrant vinegar may be mixed with sugar and hot water and taken as an antidote for tickly throats. It is also a very unusual dressing for winter salads, e.g., grated red cabbage and walnuts. Both Raspberry and Blueberry Vinegar can be made in the same way. Delicious and unusual.

DRYING BLACKCURRANTS

1kg/2lb 4oz fat, ripe, fresh blackcurrants

Pick over currants, wash them and put them in a large sieve. Dip them for 30 seconds into rapidly boiling water (to soften the skins). Plunge them into cold water. Place between sheets of kitchen towels and pat dry. Place on shallow trays and lay them out in the sun to dry, or place them in a cool oven at 49°C/120°F. After one hour increase to 54°C/130°F and after one hour again, increase the temperature to 60°C/140°F or gas mark $\frac{1}{4}$. Keep at that temperature until the currants are hard and rattle on the trays.

Although I have told you how to dry currants it really is rather a pity to preserve them in this way as they are very hard and never really regain their texture or shape even with long soaking. However, having said that, there is an ethnic delight based in North America called *pemmican*, a substantial preserved food compounded of dried meat, fat, currants etc., which explorers use on long treks and expeditions. It is also the most reliable method of drying many useful small fruit, e.g., blueberry, elderberry which make excellent flavouring, something akin to juniper.

Red and White Currants

The last time that I saw either red or white currants in any quantity at all was in a market place in north west France many years ago which would seem to indicate that commercially these currants are no longer a viable proposition. However a few bushes planted in your own garden will provide you with many delightful and delicious surprises as these little fruit are an essential ingredient for a good summer pudding, compôte or simple stewed fruit. Being very high in acid and pectin they make superb delicate preserves leaving nothing to artifice. Being a bit pippy however they are used more frequently in jellies than in jams. The delicate conserve in which wild strawberries are suspended in white currant jelly is a masterpiece both visually and gastronomically. The scarcity of these fruits will lead you, as it has done generations of housewives before you, to use them with great care and imagination. Redcurrant extract (see below) is used frequently as a natural setting agent in preserves made of fruit with a low setting content, i.e., cherries, raspberries etc. It also forms a basis for some of the most delightful herb jellies where its clear rosy colour and light sharp taste can only add enchantment to your most precious herbs. I do not find that red or white currants bottle well; they shrink and become anaemic and unhappy looking, which is a great waste of this valuable and versatile fruit. The lesson to be learnt is never ever cook red or white currants too long for not only do you eradicate much of the fine and subtle flavour but colour and shape also. Redcurrant preserves or those containing red currants will set almost as soon as the sugar has become absorbed. Another small culinary point which is worth knowing is that the green or unripe currants from both the red and white bushes may be picked and cooked with surprisingly good results, requiring far less sugar than the ripe fruit – try a few pieces of sweet cicely instead of sugar. So do not despair if your currant branches are threatening to break under the weight of unripe fruit, all is not lost.

REDCURRANT EXTRACT

Make a redcurrant extract by washing the fruit and placing it in a preserving pan with 600ml/1 pint water to every kilogram of fruit. Simmer gently, giving an occasional mash with a wooden spoon if need be, until the fruit is very soft and allow to drain overnight into a clean china bowl until every drop of juice is extracted. Return to the clean pan and bring to the boil. Pot immediately in hot, dry, sterile jars. Seal tightly and keep in a cool place. Pectin Extract may be sterilized as for Spiced Apple Ketchup, p.50, just to be on the safe side.

NORMANDY REDCURRANT JELLY

1kg/2lb 4oz ripe redcurrants　　　　caster sugar
water

6 medium size, hot, dry, sterile jars

Wash the fruit and put them in a preserving pan, do not worry about the stalks. Add a few tablespoons of water to prevent sticking and heat very gently until the juices begin to flow, taking great care not to burn. In the meantime, put the caster sugar into a liquidizer and powder it; failing that crush it down in a bowl. Add the sugar to the pan, bring gently to the boil, stirring well and boil hard for 8 minutes removing the scum as it rises. Gently press the jam into a fine nylon sieve but do not rub hard. Pour the jelly into the jars. Seal and keep in a cool place.

This really is a delightful soft jelly which comes from northern France. Try mixing soft creamy cheese with redcurrant jelly and a little sugar which is absolutely delicious.

REDCURRANT AND MARJORAM JELLY

1kg/2lb 4oz redcurrants
300ml/½ pint water
150ml/¼ pint cider or wine vinegar
white sugar

50g/2oz fresh marjoram or 25g/1oz dried marjoram
a few sprigs of fresh, or 15g/½oz dried marjoram

8 small, hot, dry, sterile jars with non-metal lids

Wash the fruit. Wash and chop the 50g/2oz fresh marjoram, if used. Put the currants, water, vinegar and fresh or dried marjoram into a stainless steel pan and boil gently until the fruit is very soft. Turn into a jelly bag and allow to drain into a clean bowl overnight. The next day measure the juice and for every 600ml/1 pint take 450g/1lb warmed sugar. Return the

145

juice to the clean pan, heat gently and add the sugar, stirring well until it has dissolved. Bring to the boil and boil hard until a set is obtained. You may now do one of two things. Either half-fill the jars with the jelly, keeping some back to top up and when it is nearly cool pop in a washed, dried, neat sprig of marjoram and fill up with some of the remaining jelly – this will give the effect of the herb being suspended in the jar. Or you may stir the 15g/½oz of chopped, dried marjoram into the hot jelly, leaving it to cool for 5 minutes before potting. Seal when cold.

This recipe may be made with 450ml/¾ pint water, omitting the vinegar completely. An excellent jelly with cold pork or veal.

REDCURRANT AND CHERRY CONSERVE

1kg/2lb 4oz redcurrants   1500g/3lb 6oz white sugar
1kg/2lb 4oz ripe cherries   300ml/½ pint water

8 hot, dry, sterile jam jars

Wash the redcurrants and place in a preserving pan, heat gently until the juices begin to flow and the fruit is soft. Mash well and turn into a muslin bag, leave overnight to drain into a clean bowl and resist the temptation to prod or press. The next day stone the cherries, put the sugar and water into a preserving pan and boil carefully until a syrup is formed, add the cherries and continue to boil carefully until very thick. Add the juice from the redcurrants and boil again until a set is obtained. Pot and seal.

A lovely preserve, too good to eat on bread and butter, better perhaps in a soft Genoese sponge or just with fresh cream when you feel like spoiling yourself. The same recipe can be made with blackcurrants and black cherries for a dark, rich preserve.

REDCURRANT MARMALADE

1kg/2lb 4oz redcurrants   225g/8oz large seedless raisins
2 large, thin-skinned sweet oranges   1kg/2lb 4oz white sugar

5 hot, dry, sterile jam jars

Wash the currants, wash and thinly slice the oranges, wash and chop the raisins, then put all the fruit into a preserving pan. Warm through, and when it is beginning to simmer add the warmed sugar and bring gently to the boil, stirring well until the sugar has dissolved. Boil for 20 minutes when a set should be obtained. Pot and seal.

An incredibly delicious mixture of flavours.

SPICED RED AND WHITE CURRANTS

1kg/2lb 4oz red and white currants
725g/1lb 10oz sugar
200ml/7fl. oz white vinegar

1 teaspoon ground cinnamon
1 rounded teaspoon ground cloves

6 medium size, hot, dry, sterile jars with non-metal lids

Wash and string the fruit. Put sugar, vinegar and spices into a stainless steel pan and boil gently for 5 minutes to make a thick syrup. Allow to cool. Add the fruit and bring to the boil, boil together for 20 minutes trying not to break the fruit. Pot and seal.

You may use either redcurrants by themselves, blackcurrants or a mixture of red, white and black for this preserve. A delicious and useful recipe for using odds and ends of currants left on bushes or after jam making.

PICKLED REDCURRANTS

1kg/2lb 4oz redcurrants
225g/8oz white sugar
600ml/1 pint white wine or white wine
    vinegar

50g/2oz sea salt
2 fresh bay leaves

6 medium size, hot, dry, sterile jars with non-metal lids

Put aside at least six neat bunches of redcurrants (110g/4oz), making sure that they are washed and dried. Wash the remaining fruit. Place the sugar, vinegar, wine, salt and bay leaves in a stainless steel pan, heat gently and boil to a syrup, add the bulk of the fruit and boil until it is soft, mushy and richly red. Skim and allow to cool. Strain through a nylon sieve pressing the fruit down well in order to get the maximum of juice without the pulp – this is easier said than done for the cool jelly will be trying to set, but persevere. Return the syrup to the pan, bring to the boil again, skim. The syrup should now be clear and bright; if not, continue to boil and skim until it is. Pop a good bunch of the prepared currants into each jar and pour the hot syrup over them to cover completely. Allow to cool a little so that the fruit will not rise to the top. Seal.

The fruit will be whole, crisp and juicy, set in a soft jelly of delicate flavour. A really remarkable preserve that looks too good to eat.

WHITE CURRANT JELLY WITH WILD OR ALPINE STRAWBERRIES

1kg/2lb 4oz white currants   sugar
water   225g/8oz wild or Alpine strawberries

4 medium-size hot, dry, sterile jars

Wash and remove the stalks from the currants. Put into a preserving pan with half a glass of water. Bring gently to the boil and simmer carefully until the skins are broken and the fruit is soft. Put through a fine sieve without pressure. Measure the juice and for every 600ml/1 pint take 550g/1lb 4oz warmed sugar. Return the juice to the pan, heat gently and add the sugar, stirring well until it has dissolved. Bring to the boil and boil until a set is obtained. Remove from heat and add the washed and dried strawberries. Stir well and leave to cool a little. Pot. Seal when cold.

The delicate and exquisite flavour of wild strawberries is enhanced by the subtlety of the white currant jelly. Red currants may be substituted for white currants.

D

Damson

The plum from Damascus, but now seen as a heavy mature tree carrying masses of white blossom and a good crop of small dark purple fruit with a golden-green flesh. It is possible and worthwhile to buy a ready established young tree of two or three years. Ask your nurseryman for his advice and bear in mind that this dense tree can be grown with good effect as a hedge. The joys to be had from owning and preserving one of these lovely old trees are manifold. Damsons fruit best when grown in proximity with other varieties of plum unless you have one of the self-pollinating varieties. The fruit is quite sour when eaten raw and is best when preserved or bottled. In fact the sharp rich jams, jellies and cheeses that are made with the damson are some of the great classical country recipes of Britain and, of course, being very high in pectin content, the damson is the housewife's friend. Damson mixed with apple, perhaps bottled together and transformed into a sweet suet crust pudding, is a delight on a cold winter's night. Like so many traditional British fruit the damson is nutritious, tasty, economical and fast disappearing – how long ago is it since you saw fresh damsons for sale in your greengrocers? When they do appear in the shops it is usually from August-October as they are one of the latest fruiting plums.

A good hint for removing stones from hard plums, damsons, sloe, bullace etc., is to stir in a knob of unsalted butter after the set has been obtained, and they should then slide merrily to the surface.

149

BASIC DAMSON JAM

1kg/2lb 4oz damsons   1kg 350g/3lb sugar
450ml/¾ pint water

5 hot, dry, sterile, jam jars

Wash the damsons and, if you wish, you can slit the skins to facilitate the removal of stones. Place them in a preserving pan with the water and simmer until the fruit is very soft. Using a perforated spoon try to remove as many stones as is possible. Add the warmed sugar and heat gently, stirring well, until it has dissolved. Bring to the boil and boil until a set is obtained – you will find that the jam thickens quite quickly and in order to avoid burning has to be watched and stirred frequently. At this stage, any remaining stones quickly rise to the surface. Pot and seal.

If you can manage to crack a few of the stones, add the kernels to the jam before potting. They give an indefinable special something to the preserve.

DAMSON JAM USING A PRESSURE COOKER

1kg/2lb 4oz damsons   1kg 350g/3lb white sugar
300ml/½ pint water

5 hot, dry, sterile, jam jars

Wash the damsons and prick them with a fork. Remove the trivet from the cooker and put in the fruit and water. Cover and bring to M/10lb pressure for 5 minutes. Allow pressure to reduce at room temperature. Mash the fruit to ensure it is very soft and remove as many stones as possible. Add the warmed sugar and heat gently stirring well until it has dissolved, bring to the boil and boil rapidly until a set is obtained. Do not replace the lid on the cooker once the sugar has been added. Pot and seal.

DAMSON JELLY

1kg/2lb 4oz damsons   white sugar
600ml/1 pint water

6 medium size, hot, dry, sterile jars

Wash the damsons and simmer them with the water in a preserving pan.
When the fruit is very soft, turn it into a clean jelly bag or two or three
layers of very clean muslin spread over a colander and leave to drain into
a clean bowl overnight. The next day measure the juice and for every
600ml/1 pint gained take 450g/1lb warmed sugar. Return the juice to the
pan, heat gently and add the sugar, stir well without boiling until it has
dissolved. Bring to the boil and boil hard until a set is obtained. Pot and
seal.

 Damson Jelly may also be made in the same proportions and in the same
way as for Blackcurrant Jelly, p.141. This is particularly good when using
less ripe fruit and gives a higher yield.

PRESERVED DAMSONS

1kg/2lb 4oz fat, ripe damsons 1kg/2lb 4oz white sugar
water

4 hot, dry, sterile, jam jars

Wash the damsons. Place them in a preserving pan with just enough water
to cover. Heat very gently and simmer for 10 minutes, then remove them
from the pan with a perforated spoon, drain and lay them on a shallow
dish, then sprinkle with half the sugar. Leave to stand in a cool place
overnight. Immediately after you have done this, add the remaining sugar
to the damson juice, heat gently stirring well until it has dissolved and then
boil for 10 minutes. Skim, cover and allow to stand overnight. The next
day turn the damsons with all their attendant stickiness into the juice, heat
gently and simmer for 30 minutes. Remove the damsons with a perforated
spoon, pack into the jars and bring the syrup to the boil again. Boil hard
until it reaches a setting point. Pour over the damsons to cover. Seal.

 A whole fruit preserve suitable to flans and syrups.

FRUIT CHEESES AND DAMSON CHEESE
IN PARTICULAR

Damsons make the best cheeses ever and, although they are not so fleshy as some fruit and have tough skins and large stones, the pulp is rich and well flavoured with fine setting properties. Other fruit which make glorious full flavoured cheeses with a sharpness and bite and can be made by the same method (although not requiring long oven cooking unless the skins are hard and requiring no water for soft fruit, are as follows: blackcurrant, sloe, plum, quince, apple and plum, apple and mulberry, rhubarb and blackcurrant, apple and blackcurrant. Medlars and goose-berry both make unique and very sophisticated cheeses by the same method but need less sugar – 350g/12oz instead of 450g/1lb. Loganberry, raspberry and mulberry cheeses, extravagant and gorgeously creamy, need no water in the cooking although a little lemon juice may come in handy. Apples and black grapes make totally different cheeses both in flavour and cost but again lemon juice must be added for flavour or set, 1 lemon to each 450g/1lb pulp. Apple cheese is also improved by the addition of a little ground spice, so try ginger, cinnamon or cloves.

The best cheeses have a slightly crusty appearance and often improve with keeping. They should be potted into moulds and turned out before eating.

DAMSON CHEESE

1kg/2lb 4oz damsons   white sugar
water

small, hot, dry, sterile moulds

Wash the damsons and put them into an earthenware dish with about 1 tablespoon of water, just enough to prevent hardening. Cover and place in a slow oven overnight. The next day, when the juices have run and the fruit is soft, pass through a fine sieve, crack some of the stones, chop the kernels and add them to the purée which should now be weighed, and for every 450g/1lb gained take 450g/1lb warmed sugar. Return both to a clean pan and heat gently, stirring well until the sugar has dissolved. Bring to the boil and boil until the cheese is very thick and leaves the side of the pan, with no surplus moisture. Pot and seal.

Leave for quite a while before using. This cheese is a little sharp with a pleasant almondy taste more for the cold buffet table than the nursery. It also keeps very well despite a rather crusty appearance. It is perfectly possible to use the pulp left over from damson jelly instead of fresh fruit.

PICKLED DAMSONS

1kg/2lb 4oz damsons
500g/1lb 2oz soft brown sugar
long stick cinnamon

1 tablespoon whole cloves
50g/2oz root ginger
1 litre/1¾ pints malt vinegar

4 hot, dry, sterile, jars with non-metal lids

Wash the damsons, discarding any blemished fruit, lay them in a non-porous earthenware dish and sprinkle with sugar as you go. Crumble or bruise the spices and infiltrate these among the fruit. Just cover with vinegar, put into a low oven, and leave to cook very gently until the fruit is soft but not broken and the juices are running freely. Remove the dish from the oven and leave to cool. When very cold strain the damsons and return them to the dish, boil the juice in a stainless steel pan and pour it over the fruit. Cover and leave for 24 hours. Repeat this process 10 times and then leave for one week. The damsons will end up wrinkled and dark and the syrup will be very thick. Pack the fruit into the jars and boil up the syrup once again. Pour over the fruit. Seal.

    An extremely exotic looking pickle with a really fine sharp flavour. Marvellous with game. Also to be recommended when made with blue or purple cooking plums.

DAMSON AND DRIED FRUIT CHUTNEY

1kg/2lb 4oz damsons
1 onion
1 clove garlic (optional)
150g/5oz seedless raisins
75g/3oz dates
25g/1oz preserved ginger

350g/12oz soft brown sugar
600ml/1 pint malt vinegar
1 teaspoon sea salt
¼ teaspoon ground allspice
¼ teaspoon ground ginger

3 hot, dry, sterile jars with non-metal lids

Wash the damsons, slitting the skins; peel and chop the onions and garlic, chop the raisins and dates. Put all the ingredients into a large stainless steel pan and simmer for about 2 hours on a low heat. Remove the stones with a perforated spoon as they rise. When the chutney is very thick remove from heat and allow to cool a little before potting. Seal when cold.

    Store for at least 2 months before using. This is a sharp, rich chutney with a good colour.

Date

I have recently noticed the advent of fresh dates into the occasional delicatessen or greengrocer's shop and not only fresh but also the whole sticky fruit is now being sold in bulk, not in highly expensive boxes – these I believe are imported from Israel. Both the fresh dates and the boxes and blocks come from North Africa. The date itself is as old as history and the unique shape of the date palm is probably the first tree shape any of us draw. The soft, sticky fruit comes from inside a green or red outer skin and is dried and either elegantly boxed or compressed into a slab for our consumption. Many of you may also have seen date palms and fruit in such holiday islands as Majorca. Dates are very sweet and nutritious and make really excellent preserves, chutneys etc., for not only do they give a good, thick, rich texture, but the amount of sugar necessary is often much reduced. Dried dates also contribute much to superb puddings especially when mixed with apples and as the block variety are relatively cheap they are also economical. The large, sticky, single dates are a highlight on the Christmas table when wrapped or stuffed with a mixture of home-made marzipan and chopped nuts. Fresh dates preserved in syrup are a Middle Eastern delicacy now becoming possible in northern Europe thanks to more imaginative importers and a greater demand.

DATE JAM

1kg/2lb 4oz cheap block dates	2 lemons
1 litre/1¾ pints water	½ teaspoon ground cinnamon
500g/1lb 2oz white sugar or	½ teaspoon grated nutmeg
100g/4oz soft brown sugar and	50g/2oz unsalted butter
400g/14oz white sugar	

4 hot, dry, sterile jars

Chop the dates (if they are in a block they should have no stones to remove). Put them into a preserving pan with the water, mash well with a wooden spoon to get a good mix. Bring slowly to the boil and simmer for 10 minutes. Grate the rind and extract the juice from the lemons, add these to the pan with the warmed sugar, spices and butter. Heat gently beating well until the sugar and butter are dissolved, simmer, stirring continuously until the mixture is thick and smooth. Pot and seal.

Not only is this a very good nursery jam especially on brown toast, but it is excellent in gooey biscuits and pastries and children love it. The spices may be omitted.

HOT DATE CHUTNEY

1kg/2lb 4oz cheap block dates
250g/9oz sultanas
2 dried red chillies
500g/1lb 2oz onions
4 cloves garlic

1 teaspoon sea salt
1 teaspoon ground ginger
1 teaspoon ground black pepper
750ml/1¼ pints malt vinegar

4 hot, dry, sterile jars with non-metal lids

Put the dates, sultanas, chillies and peeled onions and garlic through a fine mincer. Place them in a stainless steel pan with the seasonings and vinegar and, stirring well, bring to the boil. Simmer gently, giving an occasional stir, for about 1½ hours. Pot and seal.

Store for at least 2 months before using. A rich, very hot chutney that will guarantee a good head of steam! Do not think you have forgotten the sugar as the dates provide the sweetness and it is therefore economical.

DATE AND APRICOT CHUTNEY

500g/1lb 2oz dried apricots
1kg/2lb 4oz block dates
250g/9oz preserved ginger
4 cloves garlic

500g/1lb 2oz fat, seedless raisins
500g/1lb 2oz white sugar
50g/2oz sea salt
1.15 litres/2 pints white vinegar

6 hot, dry, sterile jars with non-metal lids

Put the apricots into a large deep bowl, cover well with water and leave to soak for 24 hours. The next day chop the dates and ginger, peel and grind the garlic to a pulp, wash the raisins and drain the apricots. Put all of these into a stainless steel pan with the sugar and salt, just cover with the vinegar (use more than 2 pints if necessary) and cook until soft and thick, about 2 hours. Pot and seal.

Store for at least 2 months before using. A much milder, chunkier chutney which goes very well with curry or cold chicken, tongue or spiced beef.

DATE AND ORANGE CHUTNEY

1kg/2lb 4oz block dates
625g/1lb 6oz onions
625g/1lb 6oz thin-skinned oranges
350g/12oz sultanas
1kg/2lb 4oz brown sugar

350g/12oz thick, dark treacle
75g/3oz sea salt
½ teaspoon cayenne
2.25 litres/4 pints malt vinegar

8 hot, dry, sterile jars with non-metal lids

Mince the dates, peel and mince the onions, wash and cut the oranges and put through the mincer after removing the pips (if the oranges have a lot of pith you will have to peel them first and then remove the pith, putting fruit and peel through the mincer afterwards). Wash the sultanas. Put the sugar, treacle, seasoning and vinegar into a stainless steel pan and heat gently, stirring well until sugar has dissolved, bring to the boil and add the fruit and onions. Bring to the boil again and then simmer until thick and smooth. Pot and seal.

Although this is a mild and pleasant chutney, for a really unusual and sophisticated chutney substitute the oranges for lemons. Store for at least 2 months before using. A much milder, chunkier chutney which goes very well with curry or cold chicken, tongue or spiced beef.

E

Elderberry

Sambucus nigra

The elderberry is a most prolific and abundant tree which grows in the British Isles. Steeped in folklore, it has been the friend and enemy of countrymen from time immemorial. The weird, damp, acrid smell of the tree and leaves and its skeletal appearance in winter suggest its sombre connections with witchcraft. But in the spring it is a mass of frothy, white, sweet-scented blossoms which, more than any other flower has lent itself to magic cures and, more prosaically, some very modern ones too.

Elderflowers, used in preserves, give an extraordinary muscat flavour to even the most mundane fruit, raising it straight away to the luxury class. They make really beautiful wine, refreshing drinks, soothing tisanes and may also be fried in batter! Pick the flowers while they are fresh and open on a hot day before the sun is at its fullest. Never wash them for it destroys their fragrance and try to ensure that the bitter stalk is not immersed for long in the preparation.

Elderberries, small and reddish-black, are in umbrella-like clusters which when ripe turn upside down. The crop is often so heavy that the whole bough bends with the weight. The taste of raw elderberries is sharp yet sickly but they make up very well with other hedgerow fruit to give good preserves and interesting spicy ketchups and sauces. Make sure that you pick the fruit on a dry day when the berries are bursting with juice and have not begun to deteriorate in any way. Weigh the fruit off the stems unless otherwise stated. The best way to remove the stalks without damaging the berries too much is to pull them through the prongs of a fork.

ELDERBERRY FOUR FRUIT JELLY

1kg/2lb 4oz elderberries
350g/12oz apples
350g/12oz damsons
350g/12oz blackberries
1 teaspoon whole cloves
1 teaspoon whole allspice

piece of root ginger
piece of cinnamon stick
750ml/1¼ pints water
white sugar or half white sugar and
   half soft brown

12 medium size, hot, dry, sterile jars

Wash all the fruit removing hulls, stems and other unwanted pieces. Chop the apples. Bruise the spices and put them with the fruit and water into a preserving pan. Cook gently, giving the occasional judicious mashing, until the fruit is very soft and pulpy. Turn into a jelly bag and leave to drain overnight into a clean bowl. The next day measure the juice and for every 600ml/1 pint gained take 450g/1lb warmed sugar. Return the juice to the pan and heat gently, add the sugar stirring well until it has dissolved. Bring to the boil and boil hard until a set is obtained. Pot and seal.

    The elderberries give plenty of juice and the damsons and apples give a good set, making a very pleasant and tasty autumn preserve.

ELDERBERRY AND THYME JELLY

1kg/2lb 4oz elderberries
bunch of fresh thyme

2 small lemons
white sugar

6 small, hot, dry, sterile jars

Wash the fruit removing stalks, wash the thyme and put both the elderberries and two-thirds of the herb into a preserving pan, add the pulp (not the pith), rind, juice and pips of the lemons, mash well and simmer until soft. Turn into a jelly bag and leave overnight. The next day measure the juice and for every 600ml/1 pint take 350g/12oz warmed sugar, return the juice to the pan and heat gently, add the sugar stirring well until it has dissolved. Bring to the boil and boil hard until a set is obtained. Remove from the heat. Chop the remaining thyme and stir into the jelly. Allow to cool before potting. Seal when cold.

    This recipe may also be made using apple and elderberry. Delicious with liver and added to dark savoury sauces.

SPICED ELDERBERRY AND APPLE JELLY

1kg/2lb 4oz elderberries
800g/1lb 12oz cooking or crab apples
400ml/14fl. oz water

1 orange
½ cinnamon stick
white sugar

6 medium size, hot, dry, sterile jars

Wash the elderberries removing the stalks. Wash and chop the apples and place both in a preserving pan with the water, cover the pan and simmer until very soft. Turn into a jelly bag and leave to drain overnight. The next day pare the rind from the orange and tie this with the cinnamon stick into a muslin bag. Measure the juice and for every 600ml/1 pint take 450g/1lb warmed sugar. Return the juice and muslin bag to the pan, heat gently and add the sugar stirring well until it has dissolved. Bring to the boil and boil rapidly until a set is obtained. Remove the muslin bag, squeezing it well. Pot and seal.

A soft, tasty jelly which is one of the best elderberry recipes. Blackberry and apple also make up very well with orange and cinnamon as added flavouring.

ELDERBERRY AND CRAB APPLE CHUTNEY

1kg/2lb 4oz elderberries
1kg/2lb 4oz crab apples
350g/12oz sultanas
350g/12oz onions
750ml/1¼ pints vinegar
1½ teaspoons ginger

1½ teaspoons ground cinnamon
1½ teaspoons ground allspice
1½ teaspoons cayenne pepper
25g/1oz sea salt
350g/12oz white or soft brown sugar

7 hot, dry, sterile jars with non-metal lids

Wash the elderberries and remove the stalks if necessary. Wash, peel, core and chop the apples and wash the sultanas. Peel and finely chop the onion and cook it in a stainless steel pan with the remainder of the ingredients except the sugar. Add half the vinegar, stir well and cook gently until the chutney is thick and smooth. Stir occasionally to prevent burning. Dissolve the sugar in the remainder of the vinegar and add it to the chutney. Stir well and bring to the boil, continue to simmer until the chutney is thick, smooth and free from excess moisture. Pot and seal.

A good recipe for slightly under-ripe berries. Plain cooking apples can be substituted for crab apples but try to ensure that they are firm and sharp. Store for at least 2 months before using.

FORTIFIED ELDERBERRY SYRUP

1kg/2lb 4oz elderberries
200ml/7fl. oz water
1 small egg

white sugar
brandy

1 large, hot, dry, sterilized bottle

Wash the elderberries and remove stalks if necessary, put them in an earthenware casserole with the water, cover and leave in a warm oven until the fruit is very soft and the juices just beginning to run. Turn into a jelly bag and leave to drain overnight into a clean bowl. The next day measure the juice and for every 600ml/1 pint take 450g/1lb warmed sugar. Return the juice to the pan but before you heat it separate the white of the egg and beat it to a light froth (not a meringue). Add this to the juice and bring to the boil, which has the effect of clarifying the juice to a pristine liquid. Remove the scum. Add the sugar to the juice and bring gently to the boil, stirring well and skimming frequently. Simmer for about 5 minutes. Bottle, leaving a good 3cm/1 inch headroom. Tip 1 teaspoon of brandy into the bottle. Seal.

Dilute before using. A marvellous country cold cure as good for the soul as for the sinuses.

PONTACKS SAUCE

1kg/2lb 4oz ripe elderberries
1 litre/1¾ pints red wine vinegar or red wine (claret)
2 tablespoons black peppercorns
225g/8oz shallots

2 teaspoons sea salt
2 blades mace
1 teaspoon whole cloves
2 large pieces of root ginger

hot, dry, sterile bottles with corks

Wash the berries removing the stalks if necessary and put them into an earthenware casserole with the peppercorns. Boil up the vinegar or wine and pour it over the fruit, cover with a lid and put into a warm oven overnight. The next day peel and mince the shallots and put them with the remaining spices into a stainless steel pan. Add the strained juice from the elderberries and bring to the boil. Boil gently for about 10 minutes. Remove from the heat, cover and allow to cool. Strain carefully, return the sauce to a clean pan and return to the boil just once more. Bottle and seal.

A very good elderberry sauce which is excellent with fish and offal or try a dash in a casseroled liver and bacon. It is said to keep for seven years. Substitute malt vinegar for the wine vinegar or red wine if economy imposes.

ELDERBERRY VINEGAR

1kg/2lb 4oz elderberries   1kg/2lb 4oz white sugar
1.5 litres/2¾ pints white vinegar

hot, dry, sterile bottles with corks

Wash and strip the berries from the stalks if necessary, pack them into sterile jars and cover with vinegar. Seal with a non-metal lid and leave in a nice warm place for up to a week, shaking occasionally. Strain the vinegar from the fruit and put it into a stainless steel pan. Heat gently, add the sugar and stir well until it has dissolved. Bring to the boil and boil for about 10 minutes. Bottle and seal.
    Very good in hot water with added honey and a *soupçon* of something special to alleviate a cold.

ELDERFLOWER TEA

elderflowers   100g/4oz opaque container or box,
50g/2oz good quality mild-flavoured   with a tight lid
  tea

Pick the flowers when they are in full bloom on a hot dry day. Shake them and blow on them to remove any creatures and strip the flowers from the stalks with finger and thumb or through the prongs of a fork. Put the tea into the container and fill it up with the dry, clean flowers. Every day, twice a day, turn the flowers and tea out onto clean paper, stir and return to the container. When the flowers are dried out completely you may either add the mixture to a larger quantity of tea as it will be very concentrated or add a touch to your normal brew as required.
    Many other flowers and leaves may be used in this manner to make aromatic tea, for example – peppermint, verbena, rose geranium, orange blossom.

F

Fig

You could, on reading the delights in store for you on the following pages, rush out and buy a fig tree, for they grow well in warm areas of the British Isles, positively flourishing under glass or against a sunny wall. However, I will dampen your spirits and say that they will not provide the abundance of ripe, purple fruit that they do in their native country. Anyone who has sampled the delights of the sweet odoriferous flesh of the fresh ripe fig picked from a Mediterranean hillside will consider that it is a philistine thing to preserve them in any way at all. However, there will undoubtedly be quite a harvest of green or unripe fruit for you to experiment with and these make delicious and unusual jams, jellies and even chutney.

Dried figs in blocks are the most economical jam and chutney makers, while the whole dried fruit may be treated with more reverence. Tinned green or golden figs also make a worthwhile and elegant preserve. Fresh and tinned figs go wonderfully well with a little preserved ginger and syrup. The fresh fig was known in mythical times as the food of the Gods and it is truly the most ambrosial of fruit, its cultivation ancient and widespread. The varieties obtainable in Britain are Brown Turkey which grows best against a wall, having brown-purple fruit, and White Marseilles, a bush variety which has greenish white fruit. Have a go at growing your own fig tree in a large pot or tub – you will be surprised at the results achieved. However, consult a good nurseryman before making your choice. Figs, fresh and dried, come to us from Guernsey, France, Greece and Turkey.

FRESH FIG JAM

1kg/2lb 4oz under-ripe fresh figs 250ml/8fl. oz water
3 lemons   800g/1lb 12oz white sugar

4 hot, dry, sterile jam jars

Wash the figs. Remove the stalks and slice the fruit in half. Cut the lemons and take the grated rind, pulp and pips from one and a half of them and tie into a muslin bag. Take the juice from all 3 lemons and put it into a preserving pan with the figs, water and muslin bag. Bring to the boil and then simmer until the fig skins are soft. Remove the muslin bag giving it a good squeeze and add the warmed sugar, heat gently, stirring well until it has dissolved. Bring to the boil and boil hard until a set is obtained, about 15 minutes. Pot and seal.
 Very handy for unripe British fruit.

FIG AND APPLE JAM WITH DRIED FIGS

1kg/2lb 4oz dried block figs 1 litre/1¾ pints apple juice
600ml/1 pint water   900g/2lb white sugar
3 lemons

5 hot, dry, sterile jam jars

Wash the figs, chop them up and put into a preserving pan with the water. Squeeze the juice from the lemons and add to the fruit. Cook until very soft. Warm the apple juice and add this with the warmed sugar to the revolting-looking mixture in the pan. Heat gently stirring well until the sugar has dissolved. Bring to the boil and boil hard until a set is obtained. Pot and seal.
 Surprisingly delicious and awfully good for you.

FRESH FIG CONSERVE WITH SHERRY

1kg/2lb 4oz fresh figs
1 lemon
200ml/7fl. oz pure orange juice

1kg/2lb 4oz white sugar
3 tablespoons sweet sherry

5 hot, dry, sterile jam jars

Wash the figs, cut out the stalks and chop roughly. (If you wish to keep the figs whole, drop them into boiling water for one minute and do not chop.) Squeeze the juice from the lemon and put this with the figs and orange juice into a preserving pan. Bring to the boil and then simmer gently until the figs are tender (about 15 minutes). Add the warmed sugar, heat gently stirring well until it has dissolved. Bring to the boil and boil hard until a set is obtained, stir in the sherry, bring to the boil once more. Pot and seal.

This conserve may be made with whole dried figs but leave them to soak overnight before starting.

FRESH FIG PRESERVE

1kg/2lb 4oz fresh ripe figs
2 lemons

1kg/2lb 4oz white sugar

5 hot, dry sterile jam jars

Wash the figs and cut the stalks off. Squeeze the juice from the lemons and put this with the figs and sugar into a preserving pan. Heat very gently, carefully stirring or shaking the pan until the sugar has dissolved and a syrup is formed. Boil until a set is obtained taking care not to burn. Pot and seal.

One of the very nicest preserves. Fresh, delicate and with a good taste of the fresh fig.

SWEET PICKLED FIGS

1kg/2lb 4oz fresh ripe figs
600ml/1 pint apple vinegar

900g/2lb white sugar
1 tablespoon whole cloves

5 hot, dry, sterile jars with non-metal lids

Wash the figs, leave a little piece of stalk on the end and peel if the skins are blemished. Put the vinegar, sugar and cloves into a stainless steel pan and heat gently, stirring well, until the sugar has dissolved. Bring to the boil, when it is thick and syrupy add the figs. Boil gently for 3 minutes. Remove with a perforated spoon and pack into the jars. Reboil the syrup and pour over the fruit to cover. Seal.

If you can manage to buy figs that are slightly blemished at a reduced price this recipe is particularly useful. A pleasant and unusual accompaniment to ham and continental sausages.

DRIED FIG PICKLE

1kg/2lb 4oz whole dried figs
1kg/2lb 4oz demerara sugar
600ml/1 pint vinegar

1 tablespoon ground cinnamon
1 tablespoon ground mace
1 tablespoon ground allspice

4 hot, dry, sterile jars with non-metal lids

Wash the figs and put them in a large deep bowl, cover well with water and leave overnight. The next day drain and rinse the figs and pat dry. Put sugar and vinegar into a stainless steel pan, heat gently, stirring well, until they make a thin syrup. Bring to the boil and add the spices, stir well and boil for 1 minute. Add the figs and simmer gently for about 1 hour or until the fruit is soft without breaking, and the syrup is thick. Pot and seal.

Particularly good with rich, spiced meats and strong cheese.

G

Garlic

Allium sativumis

Garlic is one of the most universally loved, hated, abused, overworked
or neglected seasonings in creation. Some cooks consider a mere dash of
garlic salt to be more than adequate to a dish whereas to others a whole
bulb will cause them no grief. I feel that a fresh clove rubbed around a
salad bowl, a mere sliver added to the lamb, is usually enough to add a
gourmet touch. However, there are many delicious recipes like aïoli of
which it is the life and, when sizzled lightly in olive oil, garlic achieves
a magic quality. Never attempt to freeze garlic or to freeze dishes heavily
seasoned with garlic as it becomes overwhelmingly strong and somewhat
rancid. The very best garlic to buy is that which has been grown in the
Mediterranean and tied out in the sun to dry to a bleached whiteness.

Garlic is an absolute essential to the home preserver to be used in both
fruit and vegetable chutneys and pickles where its underlying pungency
brings out the best in other ingredients. Apart from which it is said to be
good for the digestion, reduces the cholesterol level and keeps colds at
bay to say nothing of vampires and evil spirits. It is also considered to be
an aphrodisiac whilst paradoxically guaranteeing to keep all non-garlic
eaters at a distance!

Ransoms (*Allium ursinum*) and Hedge Garlic (*Alliaria petiolata*) are
both wild plants which smell very strongly of garlic. Use the leaves as
seasoning for sauce and salads etc., where it gives a mild and delicate
reminder of the real thing.

PIQUANT GARLIC KETCHUP

25g/1oz garlic cloves
25g/1oz anchovies
8 dried red chillies
4 teaspoons ground cloves

4 teaspoons ground allspice
1 lemon
1 litre/1¾ pints malt vinegar
300ml/½ pint soy sauce

dry, sterile bottles with corks

Put the peeled garlic and all the dry ingredients together with the anchovies into a pestle and mortar or equivalent and pound to a paste. Grate the rind from the lemon and squeeze out the juice. Add both of these to the bowl and mix further. Turn into a stainless steel pan, add the vinegar and soy sauce, bring to the boil stirring well and simmer for 30 minutes. Allow to get cold and pass through a fine sieve. Bottle and seal tightly.

Piquant is hardly the adjective to describe this sauce!

GARLIC VINEGAR

1 large bulb of garlic – between 10 to
   15 cloves
1.15 litre/2 pints vinegar

1 teaspoon black peppercorns
1 teaspoon whole cloves

large, dark, hot, dry, sterile bottle and cork

Peel and mash the garlic either in a pestle and mortar, garlic press or on a plate with the flat of a knife. Bring the vinegar (cider, malt or white wine etc., depending on your preference) and spices to the boil in a stainless steel pan and pour it into the bottle, add the crushed garlic. Seal and shake the bottle well. Leave in a cool, dark place for 1 week for a mild vinegar or 2 weeks for a pungent brew. Strain through a filter paper or muslin. Bottle and seal.

The spices may be omitted but the result is not so mellow.

SALTED GARLIC

a quantity of large garlic cloves
sea salt

earthenware jar with air-tight lid

Make sure that the garlic is completely unmarked, peel and thinly slice
the cloves. Pack them into a jar, sprinkling a layer of salt between each
layer of garlic. Seal and keep in a cool dark place. I have known the pot
to be buried in the garden for storing.

Leave for 3 months before using when they should have become
transparent. Shake off the salt and fry lightly in olive oil.

DRYING GARLIC

Using the little topknots left by the withered leaves, tie the bulbs together
in a long string and hang them in a hot, dry place, preferably in full sunlight
to bleach and dry.

Geranium

The pungent, breath-catching scent of geranium leaves is unmistakable
and through the centuries the lemon, rose and peppermint-scented
varieties have been used to perfume everything from soap to cream
cheese. It is one of those things that you either love or loathe. If you love
the scent, dry the leaves to make a pot pourri or use them fresh to flavour
those tiny heart-shaped cream cheeses which can be eaten with fine sugar
and fresh strawberries. You could also preserve them throughout the year
in gentle and fragrant jellies, see under Apples, Blackberries etc.

ROSE GERANIUM AND BAY LEAF JELLY

1 handful rose geranium leaves
1 bay leaf
1 small lemon

600ml/1 pint apple juice made from
    cooking or crab apples
2 tablespoons white wine vinegar
350g/12oz white sugar

4 medium size, hot, dry, sterile jars

Make sure that the geranium and bay leaves are clean. Pare the rind from half the lemon with a potato peeler and chop it very finely. Put all the ingredients except the sugar into a stainless steel pan and bring gently to the boil, simmer for 10 minutes and add the warmed sugar, stirring well until it has dissolved. Bring to the boil and boil hard until a set is obtained. Pour straight through a nylon sieve. Pot and seal.

    A clean dry geranium leaf or a tiny twist of lemon peel can be added to the half set jelly for decorative purposes. It also adds to the distinctive and delicious flavour of this unusual preserve. The vinegar can be omitted for a delicately perfumed tea-time jelly.

Gherkin

The gherkin is a small variety of pickling cucumber. Although the immature fruit of the ridge cucumber are frequently used in pickles with good results, the gherkin variety is the most suitable. For prolific, quick maturing and reasonably trouble-free plants try Dobie's Prolific and Venlo Pickler. The recipes for gherkins are under Cucumbers with the exception of the one below which makes a very good, simple pickle.

GHERKINS AU NATUREL

1kg/2lb 4oz firm, fresh, green gherkins
1.15 litre/2 pints white wine vinegar

4 dry, sterile jars with non-metal lids

Bring the vinegar to the boil in a stainless steel pan and then leave to get cold. Fill a large preserving pan with water and bring to the boil, reduce the heat to keep the water hot but not boiling or even simmering. Brush the gherkins and remove the flower ends and stalks. Plunge them into the hot water and stir briskly for 15 minutes, watching the water very carefully. If you let it boil you will have a disaster in the form of boiled cucumbers. Remove the gherkins with a perforated spoon, drain and pack into the jars. Leave to cool. Cover with the cold vinegar and seal.

Very good pickle that is ready in 2-3 days.

Ginger
Zingiber officinale

An important and endlessly useful spice, ginger is completely universal, being used in everything from flavouring cakes to spicing fish. It came originally from South China and both of the recipes given below are oriental methods of preserving fresh ginger. The fresh root or green ginger when grated or pounded has a much better flavour than dried root and powdered ginger and is obtainable from good greengrocers or oriental food stores. However, it does not keep well. The powdered ginger is usually from Jamaica and the humble ground ginger is from West Africa.

Ginger is used an enormous amount in making preserves and it should be remembered that you will only get the best out of your spices if they are really fresh.

PRESERVING GINGER IN SYRUP

450g/1lb fresh, young ginger roots   100ml/3fl. oz water
250g/9oz white sugar   white sugar

2 dry, sterile decorative jars with lids

Take the ginger roots and plunge them into a pan of boiling water, keep at simmering point until tender. Drain and allow to cool a little before peeling and cutting into manageable pieces. Place in a china bowl and cover with cold water, leave to stand for 5 days changing the water twice a day (these changes of water are necessary to reduce the heat of the

170

ginger). Drain well. Make a thick syrup by boiling the 250g/9oz sugar with the water, leave to get cold. Replace the ginger in the bowl and immerse in the cold syrup, cover with a plate and leave for a further 5 days. Drain the syrup, measure it and for every 600ml/1 pint take a further 50g/2oz sugar – return to the pan and boil to a thick syrup. Allow to cool. Pack the ginger into the jars and cover with the cold syrup. Seal.

PICKLED GINGER

450g/1lb fresh ginger roots   600ml/1 pint white vinegar
25g/1oz sea salt   100g/4oz white sugar

2 hot, dry, sterile jars with non-metal lids

Wash and scrub the ginger, peeling away any discoloured patches. Put the roots in a china bowl, mix in the salt, cover and leave for 3 days. Drain and shake well, pack into jars. Put the sugar and vinegar into a stainless steel pan and bring to the boil, boil hard until syrupy and pour over the ginger to cover completely making sure that there are no air bubbles. Seal.

Keep for at least 6 weeks before using, but the longer you keep it the better.

STORING GREEN GINGER

Green ginger is expensive and once the tin or jar has been opened, it does not keep at all. Put it into a clean dry jar and cover with dry sherry. Seal tightly and keep in the refrigerator. The sherry left in the jar afterwards is not bad either!

Gooseberry

In my formative years I discovered that nothing much grew under the gooseberry bush except compost and thorns. I also learnt that some gooseberries can be eaten raw whilst others will take the roof off your mouth unless cooked. The best varieties to grow are those which crop heavily early in the year and may be picked off while still unripe and used for bottling and jam making, leaving a substantial quantity on the bush to swell and ripen for dessert fruit. This short list will give you some idea of a few of the many varieties and their special points.

Keepsake   a hard green berry. Good for preserving and dessert. Matures early.
Lancashire Lad   a very dark red berry. Excellent in whole fruit preserves and bottling. Matures mid-season.
Careless   a pale green berry. Suitable for all jams, chutneys, bottling and freezing. Matures mid-season.
Leveller   a large smooth golden green berry. Has a justifiable reputation as a dessert fruit. Matures mid – to late season.

The gooseberry is a hardy, deciduous shrub of the *Ribes* family, and well worth the effort in any garden for in a good year the rewards can reach glut proportions. They are also one of the great preserving fruit with plenty of pectin giving good economical jams with few problems. The sharp flavour makes for piquant chutneys and they bottle and freeze superbly giving a never ending standby for puddings and pies in the cold winter months. Gooseberry fool made with the addition of a few elderflowers will make an ordinary pudding into something quite different. Large, firm, frozen gooseberries scalded and sliced into a winter salad make a change and gooseberry sauce with mackerel cuts the richness of that oily fish. Make Gooseberry Pectin Extract as for Apple Pectin Extract, p.19.

BASIC GOOSEBERRY JAM

1kg/2lb 4oz ripe gooseberries   1350g/3lb white sugar
450ml/¾ pint water

6 hot, dry, sterile jam jars

Wash and top and tail the gooseberries with a pair of scissors. Put them in a pan with the water, bring to the boil and reduce to simmer. Cook until the fruit is soft, breaking down with a wooden spoon if need be. It will take about 45 minutes for the gooseberries to cook. Add the warmed sugar and stir well until it has dissolved. Bring to the boil and boil hard until a set is obtained. Pot and seal.

Red gooseberries turn a much darker shade of red if cooked longer. This is a traditional sharp jam, for a Spicy Gooseberry Jam add ½ teaspoon ground nutmeg and ½ teaspoon of ground cinnamon with the sugar.

NORMANDY GOOSEBERRY JAM

1kg/2lb 4oz ripe red or yellow
  gooseberries
unsalted butter

1kg/2lb 4oz white sugar
2 tablespoons water

4 hot, dry, sterile jam jars

Wash and top and tail the gooseberries. Grease the preserving pan lightly with the butter and put in the sugar and water. Heat very gently until the sugar has dissolved and then allow it to become a syrup, increasing the heat until it begins to bubble. Add the fruit and cook for 10 minutes. Turn the contents of the pan into a deep china bowl, cover and leave to stand overnight. The next day return the fruit and syrup to the pan and bring to the boil. Boil hard until a set is obtained. Pot and seal.

    This is an excellent method for softening the skins of the gooseberries.

GOOSEBERRY AND ELDERFLOWER JAM

1kg/2lb 4oz gooseberries
6 heads of elderflowers

450ml/$\frac{3}{4}$ pint water
1350g/3lb white sugar

6 hot, dry, sterile jam jars

Wash and top and tail the gooseberries. Make sure the elderflowers are fully open and dry, hold them upside down and shake them well to remove any nasties. Place the gooseberries in a preserving pan with the water and bring to the boil, then simmer until soft (to retain a good green colour do not overcook). Add the warmed sugar, stirring well until it has dissolved. Bring to the boil and boil to obtain a set but whilst all this boiling is going on, whirl the flower heads around in the jam. Do not worry if a few drop off in the process, they look very pretty and will not hurt. Pot and seal.

    A remarkable jam, light, sharp and lovely, pervaded with the sunny flavour of muscatel. I prefer to add the elderflowers in this way as it gives more than a hint of perfume, but the jam may pop up and scald your fingers particularly if you are not wearing a kitchen glove. So it is perfectly all right to tie the heads – no stalks – in a muslin bag and put them in with the fruit at the beginning, but remember to remove it.

GOOSEBERRY AND RASPBERRY JAM

1kg/2lb 4oz red gooseberries
175g/6oz slightly under-ripe
  raspberries

675g/1lb 8oz white sugar

4 hot, dry, sterile jam jars

Wash the gooseberries and carefully pick over the raspberries. Put both fruit into a preserving pan with just enough water to prevent sticking, heat gently, stirring well until there is enough juice to boil. Bring to the boil and continue for 10 minutes, still stirring, until the fruit is soft. Pass the whole lot through a fine sieve and return to the pan. Bring to the boil again and boil steadily for a further 40 minutes. Remove the pan from the heat and stir in the warmed sugar, continue to heat gently stirring well until it has dissolved. Bring to the boil and boil hard until a set is obtained. Pot and seal. On occasion, instead of using 175g/6oz of raspberries, I have added 300ml/½ pint of raspberry juice to the gooseberry purée just before reheating. Tinned juice is permissible but cut the sugar down to about 625g/1lb 6oz.

A soft, pipless jelly jam. Make Gooseberry and Loganberry Jam in the same way as the above method but substituting loganberries or loganberry juice for the raspberries or raspberry juice.

GOOSEBERRY AND ORANGE JELLY

Gooseberries, as has been said, are another of those very high pectin fruit which frequently arrive in glut proportions. Like apples, they make a very good basic jelly to experiment with although they have a more definite taste of their own. Nevertheless, it is a good sharp flavour and is not so strong that it will obliterate other more delicate additions, particularly herbs. Depending on the fruit you use these jellies may be rosy red or a fresh clear green and make an excellent accompaniment to savoury dishes. I have given some examples of the more complicated recipes for you to follow but try out your own ideas especially those using fresh garden herbs. The creative pleasure that it will give will be very worthwhile.

1kg/2lb 4oz gooseberries
2 large, thin-skinned sweet oranges

300ml/½ pint water
white sugar

6 medium size, hot, dry, sterile jars

Wash the gooseberries. Wash the oranges and extract the juice, put to one side. Chop the skin and pulp and put this with the water and gooseberries into a preserving pan. Simmer until the fruit is very soft. Turn into a jelly bag and leave to drain overnight. The next day add the juice from the oranges to the gooseberry juice and measure the result. For every 600ml/1 pint take 450g/1lb warmed sugar. Return juices to the pan and heat gently, add the sugar stirring well until it has dissolved. Bring to the boil and boil hard until a set is obtained. Pot and seal.

A fine fresh jelly very suitable for children.

GREEN GOOSEBERRY JELLY

1kg/2lb 4oz ripe green or yellow
  gooseberries

300ml/½ pint water
white sugar

6 medium size, hot, dry, sterile jars

Wash the fruit and put them into a preserving pan with the water, simmer until soft and pulpy. Turn into a clean jelly bag and leave to drain into a bowl overnight. The next day transfer the juice to the pan and boil for 5 minutes, then measure it. For every 600ml/1 pint gained take 400g/14oz warmed sugar. Return the juice to the pan with the sugar, heat gently stirring well until it has dissolved and bring to the boil. Boil hard until a set is obtained. Skim. Pot and seal.

Remember that green and yellow gooseberries are a variety on their own, not just under-ripe fruit.

GOOSEBERRY AND FENNEL JELLY

1kg/2lb 4oz green gooseberries
a handful of fresh fennel stalks
300ml/½ pint water

white sugar
several heads of fennel seeds

9 small hot, dry, sterile jars

Wash the gooseberries and put them into a preserving pan with the water. Wash and chop the fennel stalks and add these to the pan, cover and simmer gently giving an occasional mashing until the fruit is very soft. Turn into a jelly bag and leave to drain overnight into a bowl. The next day measure the juice and for every 600ml/1 pint take 450g/1lb warmed sugar. Return the juice to the pan and heat gently, add the sugar stirring well until it has dissolved. Bring to the boil and boil hard until a set is obtained. Meanwhile clean and dry the seed heads well. When the jelly is ready skim and remove it from the heat. Allow to cool a little and half-fill the jars. Place a fennel head in each one and fill up with the jelly. Seal when cold.

A particularly good savoury jelly that goes well with cold fish, especially mackerel.

GOOSEBERRY AND MINT JELLY

1kg/2lb 4oz green gooseberries
a large handful of fresh mint
300ml/½ pint water

white sugar
white wine vinegar

9 small, hot, dry, sterile jars

Wash the fruit and three-quarters of the mint, put both into a preserving pan with the water. Cover and simmer until soft, giving an occasional mashing. Turn into a jelly bag and leave to drain overnight. The next day measure the juice and for every 600ml/1 pint take 400g/14oz warmed sugar and 1 tablespoon wine vinegar. Return juice and vinegar to the pan and heat gently, add the sugar stirring well until it has dissolved. Bring to the boil and boil hard until a set is obtained. Wash, dry and chop the mint, stir it into the jelly and allow to cool before potting. Seal when cold.

GOOSEBERRY AND STRAWBERRY CONSERVE

1kg/2lb 4oz gooseberries
1kg/2lb 4oz strawberries

1 lemon
2kg/4lb 8oz white sugar

8 hot, dry, sterile jam jars

Wash, top and tail the gooseberries, pick over and hull the strawberries and squeeze the juice from the lemon. Put all of these with the sugar into a deep bowl and mix gently together. Cover and leave to stand overnight. The next day, turn the contents of the bowl into a preserving pan and heat gently stirring continuously until the sugar has dissolved. Bring to the boil and boil until a set is obtained. Pot and seal. These recipes using added quantities of high pectin fruit are probably the most economical types to use with strawberries.

GOOSEBERRY BUTTER

1kg/2lb 4oz green gooseberries
100ml/3fl. oz water
4 fresh eggs

225g/8oz unsalted butter
350g/12oz caster sugar
½ teaspoon ground ginger

small, clean, dry, sterile pots

Wash the gooseberries and put them into a preserving pan with the water, simmer until soft, then pass through a fine sieve. Beat the eggs and return all the ingredients to the pan (preferably to a double boiler). Heat gently beating with a wooden spoon but do not boil. When the mixture is very thick, pot and seal.

A rich soft filling excellent for cakes. Does not keep long. Many fruits may be made up like this for the same purpose.

SPICED GOOSEBERRY PICKLE

1kg/2lb 4oz gooseberries
150ml/¼ pint water
2 thin-skinned, sweet oranges
2 thick-skinned lemons
225g/8oz sultanas
large piece of root ginger

stick of cinnamon
2 blades of mace
1 tablespoon whole cloves
1350g/3lb soft brown sugar
600ml/1 pint red wine vinegar (others
   will do)

6 hot, dry, sterile, jars with non-metal lids

Wash, top and tail the gooseberries and put them in a stainless steel pan with the water. Cook until the skins are tender. Wash and thinly slice the oranges and lemons, removing pips. Wash the sultanas. Bruise the spices and tie them in a muslin bag. Put all these ingredients with the sugar and vinegar into the pan with the gooseberries. Heat gently, stirring well until the sugar has dissolved. Bring to the boil and simmer, stirring frequently until the mixture is thick. Remove the muslin bag. Pot and seal.

Store for at least 2 months before use. A delicious combination of flavours which is excellent with cold turkey, pâté, etc.

BENGAL CHUTNEY

1kg/2lb 4oz gooseberries	25g/1oz cayenne pepper
150g/5½oz seedless raisins	75g/3oz ground ginger
150g/5½oz demerara sugar	75g/3oz mustard seed
1 tablespoon sea salt	2 tablespoons golden syrup
25g/1oz onions	450ml/¾ pint malt vinegar

3 hot, dry, sterile jars with non-metal lids

Wash, top and tail the gooseberries. Put into a pan with just enough water to prevent sticking; simmer gently until the skins are just beginning to soften. Wash and chop the raisins, peel and finely chop the onions; add these with the remaining ingredients to the pan. Heat gently, stirring well until the sugar has dissolved. Simmer for about 2 hours taking care not to let it burn. The chutney should be nicely thick and smooth. Pot and seal.

This very strong chutney also works well if made with apples instead of gooseberries.

MUSCATEL SYRUP

1kg/2lb 4oz green gooseberries	750ml/1¼ pints water
1kg/2lb 4oz white sugar	3 sprays elderflower heads

hot, dry, sterilized bottles, see Spiced Apple Ketchup, p.50

Wash the gooseberries. Put the sugar and water into a preserving pan and bring slowly to boiling point, stirring well. As soon as a syrup is formed add the gooseberries and simmer until the skins are soft. Clean the elderflowers by turning them upside down and shaking. As the syrup is beginning to boil plunge the heads in, bring rapidly up to the boil and remove from the heat. Strain through thin muslin and bottle. The syrup may be sterilized (see p.15) but this not really necessary unless you wish to keep it a long time.

This syrup has the delicious fragrance of muscatel as anyone who has made elderflower wine will know. Dilute with water or soda for cooling summer drink. Do not throw the gooseberries away – sieve them to use for making a fool. Just chill and serve with fresh cream or use them in home-made ice cream.

Grape

For me to go deeply into the subject of grapes would be presumptious. Viniculture has been covered admirably and thoroughly by great men throughout history starting with Pliny, their main interest in this splendid fruit being wine – that mystical beverage which they produce. For women to tamper with the grape and actually boil it is looked upon as a sacrilege. Yet when the first Roman reduced the grape to a syrup which was used as a sugar substitute in cooking, and a flagon of this concoction fermented, it was discovered to be an interesting drink of subtle flavour and strange effect. Grape juice and syrup are still used in cooking both sweet and savoury dishes and grapes make the most delicate and delicious preserves. If you are fortunate enough to have your own vine, the best and most economical grapes to use for preserves are the thinnings from the vine – these are the unripe grapes removed in order to allow a few selected bunches to mature to perfection, You can also use the unripe fruit left at the end of the season.

The expensive imported grapes should be used in a preserve which requires the fruit to be kept whole, while grapes like Black Hamburgh are a luxury to be kept for steeping in brandy. Some varieties of green grapes turn to a glowing red when cooked, and it is important to remember that grapes require an additional setting agent, e.g., lemons. Vine leaves, like blackcurrant and oak leaves, are frequently used as firming agents – that is to say, they keep the fruit or vegetable crisp and firm – in making pickles.

Grapes come to us throughout the year from the continent, Australia, South America, Israel, USA and North and South Africa. The small, sweet, seedless, white grapes, which are the finest buy and are often sold loose, come from Cyprus. The dried grapes from Australia, California, Greece and Turkey are sold as currants, sultanas and raisins.

Oregon grape

Mahonia aquifolium

This delightful shrub, although more frequently seen in gardens, grows freely in the wild. Originally imported from North America, the Oregon grape has attractive, glossy, dark green, spiked leaves that change to red and purple in the winter and mimosa-like puffs of yellow, sweet-scented blossom. Blooming in the early spring, this lovely bush is an asset to any garden and it has an extra bonus in the rich, purple-black fruit born in the summer. These make unexpected and pleasant preserves.

The quantity and method given for preserving Currants (p.138) work very well with Oregon grapes but do not expect to achieve a good set.

GREEN GRAPE JAM

1kg/2lb 4oz unripe green grapes   1kg/2lb 4oz white sugar
water

6 medium size, hot, dry, sterile jars

Wash the grapes and put them into a preserving pan with just enough water to prevent burning. Simmer very carefully until the fruit is soft, adding a little warm water if necessary and mashing with a wooden spoon to break the fruit up. Remove any pips that rise to the surface although there are not very many in the unripe fruit. Add the warmed sugar and heat gently stirring well until it has dissolved. Bring to the boil and boil hard until a set is obtained. Pot and seal.

Preserves made with unripe grapes set considerably better.

GRAPE AND ORANGE JAM

1kg/2lb 4oz unripe green grapes   150ml/¼ pint water
2 thin-skinned, sweet oranges   800g/1lb 12oz white sugar

5 medium size, hot, dry, sterile jars

Wash the grapes and put them into a preserving pan, breaking them up a little to extract the juice. Grate the rind from the oranges, squeeze out the juice and put these with the grapes. Add the water and carefully bring to the boil. Reduce the heat and, stirring from time to time, simmer until the fruit is soft. Remove any pips which have risen to the top. Add the sugar, stirring well, until it has dissolved. Bring to the boil and boil hard until a set is obtained. Pot and seal.

    A refreshing and delicate jam.

GRAPE AND HERB JELLY

1kg/2lb 4oz black grapes   150ml/¼ pint water
large handful of savory, rosemary or   white sugar
    thyme   ½ bottle commercial pectin
1 tablespoon wine vinegar

8 small, hot, dry, sterile jars with non-metal lids

Wash the grapes. Wash the herbs and divide them in half. Reserve one half and put the other with the grapes, vinegar and water into a preserving pan. Mash well, cover and leave to simmer until the fruit is very soft, looks anaemic and has plenty of juice. Turn into a jelly bag and leave to drain overnight. Do not prod or squeeze. The next day, chop the remainder of the herbs. Measure the grape juice and for every 600ml/1 pint gained, take 450g/1lb warmed sugar. Return the juice to the pan, heat gently and add the sugar, stirring well until it has dissolved. Bring to the boil and remove from heat, stir in the pectin and boil hard for 1 minute. Skim and stir in the herbs. Allow to cool before potting. Seal when cold.

    The aromatic fragrance of fresh herbs simmering on the hob is the most evocative of summer scents.

GREEN GRAPE AND FRUIT CHUTNEY

1kg/2lb 4oz green grapes
900ml/1½ pints good wine vinegar
400g/14oz mixed sultanas, currant and
   seedless raisins
250g/9oz crystallized ginger
300g/11oz crystallized lime or citron

500g/1lb 2oz tin mangoes
15g/½oz dried chillies
3-6 cloves garlic
100g/4oz mustard seed
15g/½oz ground ginger
25g/1oz sea salt

5 large, hot, dry, sterile jars with non-metal lids

Wash and pip the grapes. Wash the sultanas, currants and raisins. Chop the ginger and the lime and put the chillies and peeled garlic through a mincer. Drain the tin of mangoes and, making sure that all surplus moisture is removed, cut into pieces. Pour the vinegar into a large stainless steel saucepan with the sugar, heat gently, stirring well until it has dissolved, boil for 10 minutes and then add the remainder of the fruit except the mangoes. Bring to the boil, stirring continuously, reduce the heat and simmer for a further 20-25 minutes. Pot and seal.

   Store for at least 2 months before using. An exotic and delicious chutney that is expensive but well worth making for special occasions or unusual presents.

BLACK GRAPE PRESERVE

1kg/2lb 4oz black grapes
400g/14oz white sugar

300ml/½ pint water

3 hot, dry, sterile jam jars

Wash the grapes and remove the pips. Put the sugar and water into a preserving pan and heat gently, stirring well, until the sugar has dissolved. Bring to the boil and cook until a thin syrup is formed, add the grapes and boil gently until the grapes are translucent without being soft and you have a thick clear syrup. Allow to cool before potting. Seal when cold.

   A few spoonfuls of this preserve served in elegant little dishes with fresh cream make a memorable party dessert.

VINE LEAVES PRESERVED IN OIL

large bunch of young vine leaves   50g/2oz sea salt
1.15 litre/2 pints water   best quality oil

dry, sterile, shallow, wide jar

Make sure that the leaves are clean and wipe them carefully. Bring the water to the boil in a large pan, add the salt and continue to blanch the leaves in this brine for 1 minute. Remove them carefully from the pan and drain and dry them on kitchen towels. Pack into the jars and cover with oil making sure that there is at least 2cm/¾ inch of oil above the top layer of leaves. Seal tightly.

These preserved leaves can be used in many French, Greek or Italian recipes. Fresh vine leaves are used frequently in pickling for they have the same firming and preserving properties as blackcurrant or oak leaves. Vine leaves can also be placed between greengages when bottling in syrup to improve the clear, green colour.

STORING GRAPES

Two very handy ways of storing grapes which may be familiar to continental readers. Using only very good quality grapes, hang bunches of them from S-shaped wire hooks attached to a line or thin wooden rod running across a space well away from walls etc., or cut bunches of grapes with a good stalk. Hang jars or small bottles by a wire hook from a wooden rail. Put water and a pinch of ground charcoal into each jar and stand the grapes in this, making sure that only the stalk is in the water. The grapes should hang well clear. The apparatus should be set up in a damp warm shed or cupboard (not a suitable atmosphere for storing any other kind of fruit) and should be checked at least twice a week for damaged fruit which must be cut away from the bunch. The grapes should last from autumn to spring.

Grapefruit

The doyenne of the breakfast table familiar to all of us, the grapefruit is usually relegated to a refreshing breakfast food, easy *hors d'oeuvres*, dieters' delight or a swift source of vitamin C. However, it can also be used to make a variety of tangy preserves and marmalade.

Grapefruits are available throughout the year and come to us from practically every hot region of the world. There are several varieties from the very thick-skinned to the thin-skinned and juicy, but one of the best type is frequently ignored because of its mottled and pitted appearance – this is the excellent pink-fleshed grapefruit which is full of juice and superbly sweet. For the purposes of the following recipes, 4 large grapefruit of the thin-skinned variety weigh approximately 1kg/2lb 4oz.

GRAPEFRUIT AND TANGERINE JELLY

1kg/2lb 4oz grapefruit	5 litres/9 pints water
500g/1lb 2oz tangerines	white sugar
4 lemons	

10 medium size, hot, dry, sterile jars

Wash the fruit and chop it up. Put it into a preserving pan with the water, cover and simmer for 2 hours or until the fruit and rind is very soft. Turn into a clean jelly bag and leave to drain overnight into a china bowl. Do not prod or squeeze or the jelly will be cloudy. The next day reserve the juice and keep it in a cool place, return the pulp to the pan and just cover with the minimum of water. Boil for 1 hour. Turn the pulp into a jelly bag and again leave to drain overnight. The next day mix both the juices, measure and for every 600ml/1 pint take 450g/1lb warmed sugar. Return the juice to the pan, bring to the boil and add the sugar stirring well until it has dissolved. Bring to the boil and boil hard until a set is obtained. Pot and seal.

Apart from being good on bread and butter this very refreshing jelly is unusual and imaginative in sponge sandwich.

GRAPEFRUIT JELLY MARMALADE

1kg/2lb 4oz grapefruit	5 litres/9 pints water
3 lemons	2775g/6lb 3oz white sugar
2 small oranges	

12 hot, dry, sterile jam jars

Dunk the fruit in boiling water and working on a large dish, remove the peel and pith separately. Shred the peel finely and reserve it. Chop the pith up with the rest of the fruit and put in a preserving pan with 2½ litres/4½ pints water. Bring to the boil, cover and simmer for 2½ hours until soft. Put the shredded peel in another pan with 1 litre/1¾ pints water, cover and cook for 2 hours until tender. Drain the liquid from the shreds, but do not throw them away. Put the juice with the pulp and turn into a thick muslin cloth laid over a colander. Leave to drain for 1 hour. Return the pulp to the pan with the remaining 1.15 litre/2 pints water and simmer for 30 minutes. Strain as before and mix the two juices together, return to the preserving pan and bring to the boil. Add the warmed sugar, stirring well until it has dissolved, pop in all the shreds and bring to the boil. Boil until a set is obtained. Allow to cool before potting. Seal when cold.

CANDIED GRAPEFRUIT PEEL

good-sized grapefruit with firm unblemished skins	salt white sugar
water	

Peel the grapefruit and cut the rind into 3cm/1 inch strips, cover with the cold water, add a pinch of salt and leave to soak overnight. The next day, drain the peel, put it in a pan and just cover with cold water. Bring to the boil and simmer for 5 minutes, strain and repeat this last process three more times. The final time, cook the rind until it is tender, strain and reserve the liquid. Cover the rind with cold water and leave until cool, then drain and weigh it. For every 450g/1lb take 450g/1lb sugar. Using approximately 150ml/¼ pint of the reserved liquid to each 450g/1lb of sugar, make a moderately thick clear syrup. Add the grapefruit peel and boil until the syrup is really thick and the peel transparent. Remove the peel with a perforated spoon and drain it on a sponge rack. Put into a cool oven and leave the door ajar. When it has dried out, is pliable and just sticky, roll it on granulated sugar. Lay out on sheets of waxed paper to dry off completely. Store in a sealed glass jar.

Do not throw the fruit away – use it to make jam or jelly.

Greengage

A very under-rated member of the plum family which is a superb dessert fruit. In our own rambling garden we grew two varieties: Cambridge Gage – a particularly good fruit for bottling, quite firm and green but a tree that needs to be grown in company with another plum such as Czar or Victoria to pollinate it, otherwise it will not set fruit – and Early Transparent Gage which is a fine self-pollinating variety which, unfortunately, does not stay on the tree long before splitting, it can be used in jam but does better as a dessert fruit. Oullins Golden Gage is a dessert fruit which bottles well but requires another variety of plum to cross pollinate.

Preserves and jams made with this green or golden yellow fruit have a sharp sweetness, an attractive colourful appearance and, because of the reasonably high pectin content, set well.

GREENGAGE JAM

1kg/2lb 4oz greengages   1kg/2lb 4oz white sugar
150ml/¼ pint water

5 hot, dry, sterile jam jars

Wash the fruit, cut them in half and remove the stones. Crack half of them and tie the broken shells with the remaining stones into a muslin bag. Blanch and skin the kernels and put them to one side. Place the greengages, water and muslin bag in a preserving pan and cook gently until the fruit is soft, adding more water if necessary. Add the warmed sugar, heat gently stirring well until it has dissolved. Bring to the boil and boil until a set is obtained. Remove the muslin bag, skim and stir in the kernels. Pot and seal.

Greengage jam is sharp and tasty and the addition of the kernels gives that almondy touch which makes a special preserve.

GREENGAGE AND RED PLUM JAM

1kg/2lb 4oz greengages
1kg/2lb 4oz red cooking plums

300ml/½ pint water
2kg/4lb 8oz white sugar

8 hot, dry, sterile jam jars

Wash and stone the greengages and plums (although stoning them is not absolutely necessary). Put both fruit in a preserving pan with the water and cook until very soft, if you have left the stones in, remove them as they rise. Add the warmed sugar and heat gently, stirring well, until it has dissolved. Bring to the boil and boil until a set is obtained, take care that it does not burn. Pot and seal.

GREENGAGE JELLY

1kg/2lb 4oz greengages
300ml/½ pint water

white sugar

6 medium size, hot, dry, sterile jars

Wash and halve the greengages. Put into a preserving pan with the water, cover and simmer on a low heat until soft, adding a little more water if necessary. Turn into a clean jelly bag and leave to drain overnight into a bowl. Do not prod or squeeze. The next day, measure the juice and for every 600ml/1 pint take 450g/1lb warmed sugar. Return the juice to the pan and heat gently to boiling, add the warmed sugar stirring well until it has dissolved. Bring to the boil and boil until a set is obtained. Skim. Pot and seal.

A very attractive, clear, golden-green jelly.

GREENGAGE PRESERVE

1kg/2lb 4oz greengages
1kg/2lb 4oz white sugar

vanilla essence

4 hot, dry, sterile jam jars

Wash, halve and stone the fruit. Lay in a deep bowl sprinkling each layer with the sugar. Finish with a layer of sugar, cover and leave to stand overnight. The next day turn into a preserving pan and heat and stir carefully until the sugar has all dissolved, try not to break the fruit up. Bring to the boil and boil for 15 minutes. Remove the fruit with a perforated spoon and pack into jars. Add vanilla essence to taste and re-boil the juice for 5 more minutes or until it is very thick and pour over the greengages to cover. Seal.

Greengage Preserve is excellent in open tarts made with a sweet short pastry and piped with fresh cream.

Guava

Guavas, with their superb pink flesh and delicate flavour, are one of those exotic fruit which until recently could only be bought in cans, but which are now available fresh from Israel and America. Slice guavas, sprinkle them with lemon or lime juice and eat them chilled for a refreshing and delicious dessert, and, like lychees and green figs, they have an extraordinary fragrance that lends itself very well to the more elegant and sophisticated preserves. Guavas, when used in jams and jellies, will always need the addition of high pectin fruit to help them set for they are very low in pectin, although high in vitamin C.

GUAVA AND LIME JELLY

1kg/2lb 4oz guavas   white sugar
300ml/½ pint water   2 whole limes

6 medium size, hot, dry, sterile jars

Wash and slice the guavas. Put them in a preserving pan with the water and simmer gently until they are very soft – this will take about 45 minutes. Turn into a clean jelly bag and leave to drain overnight into a bowl. The next day measure the juice and for every 600ml/1 pint take 450g/1lb warmed sugar and the juice of 1 lime or 1 teaspoon of lime juice. Return the juices to the pan and heat gently, add the sugar stirring well until it has dissolved. Bring to the boil and boil hard until a set is obtained. Skim. Pot and seal. Lemons may be substituted for limes.

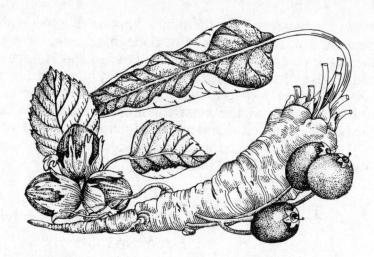

Hawthorn

Crataegus monogyna

The dense hedges and shrubs which make up best part of our countryside lanes, heavy with pink and white blossoms and pervading the air with a heady perfume, is hawthorn. The superstitious believe that the flowers brought into the house are unlucky yet in Suffolk it was traditional for a pretty servant to present the first blossoms to the mistress of the house on May Day. The dense prickly branches deter children from eating the edible leaves and berries (we used to call it the Bread and Cheese tree) although the taste is reasonably pleasant and can be made up into a palatable jelly. The blossom, however, makes up into a sweet liqueur which should be tried to be believed. Gather the flowers on a hot, dry day before noon and take them straight home and use immediately for they must not wilt or turn brown. The dark red berries are gathered when they are fully ripe but not wrinkled.

HAW AND APPLE JELLY

1kg/2lb 4oz ripe haws   white sugar
750ml/1¼ pints pure apple juice,
  preferably crab apple

8 small, hot, dry, sterile jars

Wash the haws and put them into a preserving pan with the apple juice. Simmer until soft (this could be done in a pressure cooker) and then give the berries a good mashing with a wooden spoon, turn into a muslin bag and leave to drain overnight. The next day measure the juice and for every 600ml/1 pint take 450g/1lb warmed sugar. Return the juice to the pan and heat gently and add the sugar stirring well until it has dissolved. Bring to the boil and boil hard until a set is obtained. Pot and seal.

This recipe could be made with water instead of apple juice but the result is not so soft and pleasant.

HAW SAUCE

1kg/2lb 4oz haws
600ml/1 pint white vinegar
150g/5oz white sugar

1 tablespoon sea salt
1 teaspoon white pepper, preferably ground

hot, dry, sterile bottles with non-metal lids

Wash the haws and put them in a stainless steel pan with the vinegar. Simmer until soft. Either mash well with a wooden spoon or put into a liquidizer, then pass through a sieve. Return to the pan and heat gently. Add the sugar, salt and pepper stirring well until it has dissolved. Bring to the boil and boil hard until thick – about 15 minutes. Bottle and seal.

A tasty sauce which will surprise your friends. It keeps well and is also the most economical way of using haw berries.

MAY FLOWER LIQUEUR

large bunch of fresh May flowers
50g/2oz white sugar

600ml/1 pint brandy

dry, sterile, wide-mouthed jar with tight lid

Turn the flowers upside down and shake them well to remove insects etc. Make sure that there are no stalks or pieces left on the blossom and pack loosely into the jar, sprinkling with sugar as you go. Fill the jar up with brandy, seal it and give a good shaking. Place on a sunny windowsill to be influenced by moonbeams for three weeks, giving the jar a shake every day. Store in a warm cupboard for another 3 months. Strain through a filter or muslin and bottle. Seal tightly.

Hazel Nut

The British hazel nut is really a cob or filbert (French *noix de Philbert*) so named after St Philibert whose feast day was on 22 August, the day on which the nuts are supposed to ripen. It is not a very rewarding experience to go gathering nuts from the hedgerows for not only have modern hedge cutting methods absolutely decimated the tree but the end result is very rarely worth the effort as they are frequently powdery or mouldy inside. Better to leave them to birds and squirrels. The hazel nut is steeped in tradition having the most magical properties attributed to it, but one of the best is the gently toasted nut, grated and scattered on delicious cakes and desserts and for this it is much better to rely on the imported nuts from Spain and Italy. You can also buy small trees from good nurseries. Ask for advice on planting as you need room and suitable conditions but they could make a pleasant and rewarding garden hedge.

CANDIED HAZEL NUTS

hazel nuts	water
white sugar	icing sugar

Shell the nuts, blanch and skin them. Make up a syrup in the proportions of 100g/4oz sugar to 600ml/1 pint water and simmer the nuts in this for 1 hour. Let them cool in the pan and then heat gently adding a further 50g/2oz of the sugar to the pan. Bring to the boil for 1 hour and allow to cool. Continue to repeat this process until the syrup candies when cooled. As soon as this looks like happening remove the nuts with a perforated spoon, put them on a tray. Dust well with the icing sugar and leave them in the sun or a cool oven with the door ajar, to dry. When they are dry, pack and store in greaseproof paper.

Use the candied syrup to pour over ice cream.

TO STORE HAZEL NUTS

As for Chestnuts, p.118.

Horseradish

Once you have established a horseradish plant in a quiet, undisturbed corner of the garden where it will not interfere with other plants and where its tall, bright green foliage can be best appreciated, it will thrive for ever. And wherever it is planted, potatoes will do well there, too. It is the long, white, tap root which the plant is grown for and as you will not wish to dig up the complete root every time you need a scraping, leave yourself plenty of room to hack a chunk out when you need it. The horseradish root is pungently hot, peppery and is one of those accompaniments to roast beef and smoked fish that you either love or loathe. The fumes from fresh, raw horseradish will make your eyes water and it is advisable when you have washed and scraped it to leave it to stand for an hour or so in a bowl of cold water. Too often horseradish is mixed with other harsh seasonings, e.g., vinegar or mustard, to make a sauce which burns the palate and deprives your taste buds of other pleasures. So it is preferable to mix it with cream and seasonings of a milder nature to reduce its fiery temperament. It may be preserved in a number of ways to be used at a later date in the making of pickles and relishes. It goes particularly well with beetroot and lemons and Apple or Gooseberry and Horseradish Sauce are marvellous with mackerel – mix the horseradish with a purée of these fruits instead of cream.

HORSERADISH SAUCE

1 large piece of horseradish
sea salt
white sugar

white malt vinegar
a few red, dried chillies (optional)

small, dry, sterile jars with non-metal lids

Wash, peel and grate the horseradish, popping it into cold salted water as you go to prevent discolouration. Drain well and pack into the jars filling two-thirds-full, add 1 teaspoon of salt, ½ teaspoon of sugar and a piece of chilli to each jar. Cover with the cold vinegar. Seal.

For a more basic recipe omit the sugar and chilli and cover the horseradish with boiling vinegar.

To use horseradish, drain off the surplus vinegar and use in the proportions of 1 tablespoon of horseradish to 150ml/$\frac{1}{4}$ pint fresh cream. Do not throw the vinegar away, it is quite pungent and can be used on rich fishy foods or fish and chips!

HORSERADISH AND GARLIC SAUCE

100g/4oz horseradish
100g/4oz garlic
100g/4oz ground mixed spice
1 small stick cinnamon
150ml/$\frac{1}{4}$ pint malt vinegar

1 teaspoon celery seed
150ml/$\frac{1}{4}$ pint soy sauce
140ml/scant $\frac{1}{4}$ pint pickled walnut
   vinegar
150ml/$\frac{1}{4}$ pint pickled onion vinegar

medium size, dry, sterile jars with non-metal lids

Scrub and clean the horseradish, peel the garlic and put both through a mincer. Put the spices, cinnamon and malt vinegar into a stainless steel pan and boil together, remove from the heat and cover, leave to get cold. Retrieve the cinnamon stick and mix all the ingredients with the vinegars. Pot and seal. Shake every day for 1 month.

Hair raising, to say the very least.

TO DRY HORSERADISH

Wash, peel and grate the root and lay it out on a flat tin making sure that it has plenty of room. Pop into cool oven 48°C/120°F, or gas mark $\frac{1}{4}$. turning it occasionally to ensure even drying. Pack into warm dry jars with tight fitting lids. Seal tightly.

TO STORE HORSERADISH

Make sure the roots are lifted whole and dry, brush off any surplus dirt and store as for Jerusalem Artichokes, p.68.

J

Juniper

A delightful family of coniferous trees, differing in shape, size and colour and bearing a small green berry which over a period of two years turns blue-black to give us the herb which is of such value in the kitchen. When crushed the berry releases sharply green aromatic oils which are used in a variety of ways from flavouring gin to seasoning creamy sauces. It has a unique place when cooking rich game or meat dishes, and pâté benefits enormously from its addition. The smell of juniper is similar to that of the hot sun on its foliage, a particularly evocative and optimistic fragrance. The trees are usually grown domestically for their decorative appearance although wild juniper still thrives in the further reaches of Scotland.

The following recipes are great fun but I am afraid you will not achieve the effectiveness of gin – if you do, please let me know.

LATWEGE

a quantity of juniper berries   white sugar
water

small, hot, dry sterile moulds

Wash and dry the berries and put them in stainless steel pan with just enough water to cover the bottom layer. Cook until soft but not broken and then pass through a fine sieve. Weigh the pulp and for every 50g/2oz

194

take 150g/5oz warmed sugar. Return both purée and sugar to the pan, beating well with a wooden spoon and heat gently to boiling point, boil until the mixture is thick and setting but never stop beating. Pot and seal.

This German juniper conserve is traditional with rich cold meats or wild boar and venison.

JUNIPER LIQUEUR

500g/1lb 2oz juniper berries   150ml/¼ pint water
450g/1lb white sugar   600ml/1 pint brandy

large, dry, sterile jar with tight-fitting lid

Make a thin syrup with the sugar and water. Wash and dry the berries and pack them into the jar. Pour the cold syrup over them and add the brandy. Seal the jar and give it a good shake. Leave in a warm place for 2 weeks shaking it every day, then strain the liquid through a filter or fine muslin and pour into dry, sterile bottles. Seal.

Leave for as long as possible before drinking, preferably a couple of years – an impossibility in our household.

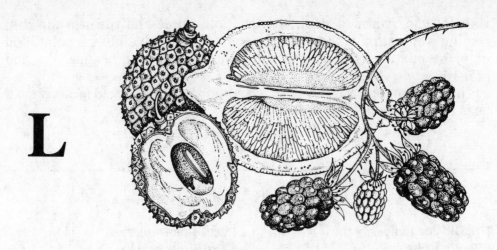

Lavender

Lavandula spica

One of the most beloved of British herbs which grows as an attractive blue green shrub in almost every part of the country. Although the leaves and flowers are most often used in pot pourris and sachets, the flowers may also be made into a soothing and aromatic herb vinegar.

LAVENDER FLOWER VINEGAR

1 litre/1¾ pints white wine vinegar
large bunches of lavender heads

dry, sterile jars with non-metal lid

Boil the vinegar and allow it to get cold. Gather the flowers before they are fully open and on a hot dry day before the sun is full. Strip the flowers from the stalks and shake to remove insects, pop them into the jar and cover with vinegar. Seal well and leave to stand on a warm windowsill for 2 weeks, stirring twice a day. Strain through muslin and taste – if you would like a stronger vinegar put some fresh lavender in the jar, making sure that it is covered with the vinegar. Leave as before. Strain again through muslin. Bottle and seal.

Rosemary or thyme flowers may be used instead.

LAVENDER SUGAR

lavender flowers
caster sugar

Use only the flower heads, bruise them well and take an equal quantity of fine sugar. Put both flowers and sugar into a glass jar, seal and leave for 1 month shaking every day. Sieve the sugar to remove flower heads before using.

Marvellous on iced biscuits, sponge cakes etc.

Lemon

It has been said that lemons, honey, garlic and olive oil will protect man from all the ills of mind, body, spirit and soul. Lemons, in the most basic way, certainly fulfill these promises for they are full of health-giving vitamin C, are pleasing to the eye and can be used in every domestic way from basting meat to whitening the skin. So varied are their uses that I would need a separate book to enumerate them. To the home preserver they are an indispensible and invaluable friend – the high pectin/acid content will ensure a set in the most lackadaisical preserve, the acidity will prevent discolouration and give sharpness and life to oversweet or sad jams and jellies. The peel is full of aromatic oils and a mere strip added to pickles gives a tangy pungency that is indefinable. The pith, however, should be treated with caution for it is very bitter and unless used with discretion can obliterate or change the character of the preserve completely. Lemon juice will alter the flavour of a delicate fruit and will improve the flavour of a dull one.

Used in their own right lemons make the most delicate, golden, herb jellies, rich lemon curds, tangy marmalades, aromatic pickles and bitter-sweet chutneys. The best lemons to buy unless specifically stated otherwise are the thin-skinned varieties for they are very juicy and there is little pith to bother about – bear in mind that the quantity of pith affects the weight of the fruit for the recipe and is uneconomical.

Lemons from Greece and Cyprus are small and round and when you buy them in British shops, fully ripe and yellow, but in their own country they are also picked when they are hard and green, hence Bitter Lemons. The juice of the large Californian lemon is higher in acid content than other varieties but generally speaking your choice should be governed by the thickness of the skin, firmness and bright golden colour for it is unlikely that you will be aware of the country of origin as they come from the continent, West Africa, Middle East, South Africa, USA and the West Indies.

A few worthwhile pieces of information to help you:

Many of the recipes require that you leave the lemon skins in salt to soften and lose their bitterness. If you have kept the slices in the refrigerator for 24 hours beforehand, or if the whole lemon has been deep frozen, then this process will not take so long. Also, the time given for macerating in the jar can be reduced for the peel will soften more rapidly. When lemons are sliced and sprinkled with salt, cover them and leave in the refrigerator.

The flavour of lemon juice kept for more than a few hours in a refrigerator will change.

Do not use commercial lemon juice with additives as a substitute for the pure juice.

6 large or 8-9 small, thin-skinned lemons should equal 1 kilogram/2lb 4oz.

There are approximately 3 tablespoons of lemon juice and 1 level teaspoon of grated rind to 1 large, thin-skinned lemon.

Zest is the finely grated lemon peel.

LEMON JAM

1kg/2lb 4oz bright, firm lemons (about   1.75 litres/3 pints water
  7 large)   1500g/3lb 6oz white sugar

8 hot, dry, sterile jars

Wash the lemons and, working on a large dish to catch the juices, cut the fruit into slices, remove the pips and tie them into a muslin bag. Put fruit, juices, bag and water into a preserving pan, cover and bring carefully to the boil, simmer until the rind is soft. Remove from the heat and add the warmed sugar, stirring well until it has dissolved. Bring to the boil and reduce the heat to keep it just boiling. (These precautions are necessary as you do not want the jam to set too quickly, nor do you want it to become too deeply coloured.) In about 10 minutes the jam will be cooked and thick. Remove the bag, squeezing well and put the pulp through a liquidizer or mincer – this is a very sticky business – return to the preserving pan. Heat gently beating well with a wooden spoon to ensure that you have a soft smooth jam. Bring to the boil stirring continuously and taking great care not to burn. Remove from heat almost immediately. Pot and seal.

A light refreshing jam with a good delicate colour.

BITTER LEMON JELLY

1kg/2lb 4oz lemons
3 Seville oranges

2.25 litres/4 pints water
white sugar

6 medium size, hot, dry, sterile jars

Wash the fruit, remove the peel with a potato peeler, chop roughly and put to one side. Working on a large dish to catch the juices, chop up the fruit, collect the pips and tie them into a muslin bag with the peel. Put the fruit, muslin bag, juices and water into a preserving pan. Simmer for 2 hours after which time retrieve the muslin bag and hang on to it, turn the contents of the pan into a jelly bag and leave to drain until all the juice is through – do not prod or poke. Measure the juice gained and for every 600ml/1 pint take 450g/1lb warmed sugar. Return juice to pan and heat to boiling point, add the sugar stirring well until it has dissolved. Pop the muslin bag into the pan and bring quickly to the boil. Boil hard for 5 minutes by which time a set should be obtained. Try not to overcook (if you sail past the setting point you will have to reboil again and this will change the colour). Remove bag. Skim. Allow to cool for 30 minutes. Pot and seal.

This tangy jelly is marvellous spread between the layers in an apple and cornflour pudding. The traditional thing to use is marmalade but as not all children, particularly small ones, like marmalade chunks, this is a happy alternative. May also be eaten as a savoury jelly with duck.

LEMON AND GINGER JELLY

1kg/2lb 4oz lemons
110g/4oz root ginger
1.75 litres/3 pints water

white sugar
100g/4oz preserved ginger

6 medium size, hot, dry, sterile jars

Wash and chop the lemons. Bruise the root ginger and tie it into a muslin bag. Place the lemons, ginger and water in a deep bowl, cover and leave to stand overnight. The next day transfer the lemons and water into a preserving pan. Bring to the boil and simmer for 2 hours. Turn into a jelly bag and leave until all the juice has drained through. Measure it, and for every 600ml/1 pint gained take 450g/1lb warmed sugar. Return its juice to the pan and heat to boiling, add the sugar, stirring well, until it has dissolved and boil until a set is obtained. Chop the preserved ginger and stir it into the jelly, bring to the boil and remove from the heat. Allow to cool. Stir well before potting. Seal when cold.

The preserved ginger may be omitted for a more economical jelly, but the taste is not as good.

BASIC LEMON CURD

Generally all curds tend to deteriorate rather quickly because of the high egg content, so it is better practice to reduce the quantities to suit your purse and your potential use of them. Keep curds in a refrigerator or in expandable (polythene) containers in the freezer for a limited time. Most curds last only two months, particularly if you add alcohol. Cooking them also has its problems for the eggs may well curdle into a scrambled sort of mess if the mixture is allowed to overheat and for this reason it is best to ensure that the bowl is only suspended over the simmering water (a very heavy-bottomed large saucepan may be used but it has its limitations). Remember also that the cooling curd will thicken even more. Always use fresh eggs as stale ones do not emulsify so readily. Caster sugar gives a smoother texture and unsalted butter makes a purer curd.

Home-made lemon curd is delightful and a totally different preserve from the citrus flavoured sweet paste of commercial products.

1kg/2lb 4oz good quality lemons	900g/2lb caster sugar
225g/8oz unsalted butter	4 large fresh eggs

4 hot, dry, sterile jars

Wash the lemons and grate the rind finely, taking care to avoid the pith. Extract the juice and sieve it through a fine mesh. Cut the butter into small pieces and put into a basin with the sugar, rind and juice. Heat the bowl over a pan of hot water, trying not to immerse the bottom of the bowl in the water and stir well with a wooden spoon until the contents are melted and blended. Beat the eggs and strain them through a sieve, add them to the mixture continually beating. Keeping the heat very low and stirring all the time cook until the mixture is thick and creamy. Watch carefully to see that it does not curdle for there is no way to put this expensive mistake right. Pot and seal, using a wax disc and cellophane cover.

Keeps for up to 2 months in a refrigerator. Although I prefer to add my eggs after the other ingredients are blended, it is satisfactory to put them all in the bowl together.

HONEYED LEMON CURD

1kg/2lb 4oz bright fresh lemons	8 fresh eggs
225g/8oz unsalted butter	4 extra egg yolks
900g/2lb clear honey (heather honey is terrific)	4 tablespoons malt whisky (optional)

6 hot, dry, sterile jars

Wipe the lemons and grate the rind finely. Extract the juice and strain through a fine sieve. Put all the ingredients, except the eggs and whisky, into a double boiler and heat gently, stirring well with a wooden spoon until they are melted. Beat the eggs and yolks together and strain into the mixture, continue to cook gently beating well until the mixture is thick and creamy. Take care not to overheat. If you have the whisky now is the time to add it, cook for a further 2 minutes. Pot and seal.

Better than anything on home-made brown bread.

LEMON SHRED MARMALADE

1kg/2lb 4oz lemons	1 large grapefruit
3.5 litres/6 pints water	white sugar

10 hot, dry, sterile jam jars

Wash and peel the lemons very finely with a potato peeler. Remove the pith. Cut the peel into hair strips and put into a small pan with 600ml/1 pint of the water, cover and simmer until soft. Chop the lemon pulp and grapefruit and put it into a preserving pan with the remaining 3 litres/5 pints water, cover and simmer for two hours or until the fruit is soft. Drain the strips and add the water to the preserving pan. Bring to the boil for about 5 minutes and turn into a clean jelly bag. Allow to drain until all the juice is through. Measure the liquid and for every 600ml/1 pint take

450g/1lb warmed sugar. Return the juice to the pan and heat to boiling, add the sugar and strips of lemon peel stirring well until the sugar has dissolved. Bring to the boil and boil hard until a set is obtained – about 15 minutes. Leave to cool a little, and stir well before potting to distribute the peel. Seal when cold.

Light, refreshing and quite elegant. Substitute 3 limes for the grapefruit for another interesting sharper jelly.

LEMON CHUTNEY AND PICKLES

Savoury preserves made with lemons occupy a very special place in my larder for they are completely unique. The strong tangy oils from the peel and the sharpness of flesh and juice give a terrific bite to the most innocuous recipe and when horseradish, ginger, vinegar or salt are blended with lemons the pungent results can be startling and only be described as green or bitter. Let me hasten to assure you that they are thoroughly edible and delicious, but perhaps appealing to more sophisticated palates.

HOT LEMON CHUTNEY

600ml/1 pint brown malt vinegar
25g/1oz mustard seed
2 tablespoons whole cloves
2 tablespoons black peppercorns
2 tablespoons whole allspice
a few dried chillies
1kg/2lb 4oz thin-skinned lemons
450g/1lb onions

100g/4oz seedless raisins
½ teaspoon powdered mustard
½ teaspoon ground ginger
1 teaspoon Tabasco sauce or chilli powder
1 teaspoon sea salt
450g/1lb Muscovado sugar

5 hot, dry, sterile jars with non-metal lids

Boil the vinegar and whole spices together in a stainless steel pan for 2 minutes. Cover and leave to get cold for at least 2 hours. Strain before using. Wash the lemons and chop them into small pieces, peel and chop the onions. Put all the ingredients except the sugar into a large stainless steel pan with half the vinegar. Cover and simmer until quite soft. Dissolve the sugar in the remaining vinegar and add to the pan. Bring to the boil stirring well and then continue to simmer, uncovered and stirring frequently until the chutney is thick and smooth. Pot. Seal when cold.

202

Very good with cold lamb, cold fish and currys. A less exciting sweeter chutney can be made with oranges. Use 750g/1lb 11oz lemons and 250g/9oz oranges, i.e, roughly 4 lemons and 3 oranges.

LEMON AND LIME PICKLE

1kg/2lb 4oz thin-skinned lemons
75g/3oz green ginger
25g/1oz green chillies

bay leaves
2 or 3 limes
2 tablespoons sea salt

large, dry, sterile jar

Wash the lemons and dry them. Working on a large dish, cut them into quarters and remove the pips. Peel the ginger and cut it into fine strips. Wash and dry the chillies and remove their seeds (unless you want a particularly demoniac result, in which case leave them in). Break the bay leaves into small pieces and extract the juice from the limes. Pack the jar with lemon quarters alternating each layer with a sprinkling of all the goodies you have just prepared, plus the juice that has run from the lemons and half the salt. Top up with the lime juice. Cover and shake well. After covering with a fine muslin, leave to macerate on a sunny windowsill for 4 days and each day pop in a little of the remaining salt. Do not be appalled by the pickle at this stage, it will taste and smell very strong and there will be a thick crust of salt on top. But do not worry, this will sort itself out, providing you refrain from stirring it. After 2 weeks the lemons will be soft and soaking in a thick juice and you can start using the pickle.

Eat as an accompaniment to curry and rice. Limes may be subjected to the same treatment but do not forget that the lime peel softens more rapidly than lemon peel.

BITTER LEMON PICKLE

1kg/2lb 4oz thin-skinned lemons
2 tablespoons sea salt
450g/1lb sultanas
25g/1oz fresh ginger
4 cloves garlic

25g/1oz fresh horseradish
300ml/½ pint cider vinegar
675g/1lb 8oz soft, light brown sugar
1 teaspoon chilli powder

4 small, hot, dry, sterile jars with non-metal lids

Wash the lemons and, working on a large dish, cut into eighths lengthwise, removing the pips as you go. Sprinkle with salt and leave in the fridge for 2 days, turning over and giving a good stir every now and again. Wash and dry the sultanas, peel the ginger if necessary, peel the garlic and wash and scrape the horseradish. Drain the lemons, reserving the liquid. Put all these ingredients through a coarse mincer and transfer them into a stainless steel pan. Add the lemon liquid, chilli powder, vinegar and sugar. Mix well and heat gently stirring all the time, when the sugar has dissolved bring to the boil and simmer until thick and soft. Pot and seal.

The finest pickle recipe I know. Electrifyingly pungent and aromatic without being harsh. Delicious with a good Cheddar and crispy bread, or with Epigrammes of Lamb.

LEMON MUSTARD PICKLE

1kg/2lb 4oz lemons	2 teaspoons ground allspice
500g/1lb 2oz onions	500g/1lb 2oz white sugar
1 tablespoon sea salt	225g/8oz seedless raisins
50g/2oz mustard seed	1.15 litre/2 pints cider vinegar

4 hot, dry, sterile jars with non-metal lids

Wash the lemons and, working on a large dish, slice the lemons finely, removing pips. Peel and slice the onions, put them with the lemons and sprinkle with the salt. Cover and leave in the fridge for 24 hours. Turn the contents of the dish into a stainless steel pan with the remainder of the ingredients. Bring gently to the boil, stirring well and simmer until soft and thick – about 1 hour. Pot. Seal when cold.

CANDIED LEMON PEEL

firm, unblemished lemons with medium-thick skins	50g/2oz white sugar for each fruit

Segment the skins into quarters and remove carefully from the fruit without taking any flesh. Pop into a large pan with just enough water to cover and simmer for 1½ hours, adding more water if necessary. Add the sugar and stir until it has dissolved. Bring to the boil, remove from the heat and leave overnight – do not cover otherwise the end result will be sticky. The next day bring to the boil again and simmer for 5 minutes, remove from heat and leave uncovered overnight. The next day bring to the boil and then simmer continuously without caramelizing until all the syrup has been absorbed. Drain the peel and lay it on a sponge rack, fill the hollows with a little of the thick syrup to give that lovely crunchy effect, cover with greaseproof paper and pop into a cool oven (48°C/120°F or gas mark ¼) with the door ajar – the airing cupboard will do if you take care not to cover your sheets with sticky syrup. Leave until dry and crystalline. Store in a wooden or cardboard box between sheets of waxy paper and do not fit an airtight lid.

Orange peel is candied in the same way. If you have fruit with a very coarse rind and a lot of pith it would be better to use the method given for Candied Grapefruit Peel, p.185.

DRIED LEMON PEEL

firm unblemished lemons

airtight jars

Wipe the lemons with a damp cloth and remove the peel with a potato peeler. Dunk it in to boiling water for 1 minute, drain well and pat dry. Lay on a drying screen and leave in a hot, dry place until the peel curls and shrivels or it can be dried in a cool oven. Although not highly recommended as a way to retain the citrus flavour, enough of its oils are kept to lightly flavour milk puddings etc.

Lime

Although limes are similar to lemons in as much as that they are small, sharp, citrus fruit, there the resemblance ends, for they are usually smaller, with much more acid and inedible when raw. However, they do make the most delicious marmalade, refreshing drinks, pungent pickles and excellent flavourings. For instance, if a recipe calls for lemon rind or peel substitute lime, but in lesser quantities, and the result is amazingly different. In any lemon pickle recipe that you may wish to adapt for limes, reduce the amount of salt used otherwise the flavour may be overwhelming. Also the rinds of limes soften more rapidly than other citrus fruits, therefore the macerating or cooking time should be reduced accordingly.

Limes come from tropical and sub-tropical climes such as South Africa and the West Indies and nowadays are widely available. There should be approximately 8-10 limes to each 1kg/2lb 4oz.

Lime flowers are the blossom from the European Lime or Linden Tree and these may be dried in the same way as chamomile flowers, p.109. Use them to make an infusion or tea which will purify the system and calm the nerves. Make Lime Blossom Tea as for Elderflower Tea, p.161.

LIME MARMALADE

1kg/2lb 4oz limes   2225g/5lb white sugar
2.75 litres/5 pints water

9 hot, dry, sterile jam jars

Wash the limes and, working on a large dish to catch the juice, either cut them up very finely or put them through a mincer. Remove the pips and tie them in a muslin bag. Put the fruit, any juices, muslin bag and water into a deep bowl, cover and leave to stand for 24 hours. The next day turn the contents of the bowl into a preserving pan, cover and simmer for 2 hours or until the peel is very tender. Remove the muslin bag and add the warmed sugar, stirring well until it has dissolved. Bring to the boil and boil hard until a set is obtained – usually about 30 minutes. Do not cover the pan once the sugar has been added. Leave to stand before potting. Stir well, pot and seal.

This recipe may be made with lemons or with an equal mixture of lemons and limes. Any of these recipes will give you a light refreshing marmalade that is a pleasant change from the conventional.

PICKLED LIMES WITH GARLIC

1kg/2lb 4oz limes   100g/4oz root ginger
2 tablespoons sea salt   25g/1oz black peppercorns
2 large cloves garlic   100g/4oz mustard seed
2 tablespoons turmeric   1.15 litre/2 pints white vinegar
8 small onions (maybe more)   12 dried red chillies
2 tablespoons whole cloves

very large, dry, sterile jar with wide neck and non-metal lid

Wipe the limes and slit them four times end to end but do not cut through. Stuff each slit with salt and a sliver of garlic. Put them in a bowl, cover and leave in a warm place for 5 days. Turn once a day, pouring their juices over them carefully to make sure that they all have a good baste. Remove the limes putting the liquid to one side, and rub separately with the turmeric. Peel and spike each onion with the cloves (there should be one onion to each lime) and pack both into the jar. Cover with the reserved juices. Bruise the spices and tie them in a muslin bag and pop it into a stainless steel pan with the vinegar. Boil for 5 minutes and pour the boiling liquid, minus bag, over the limes to cover well. Put a saucer on the top of the jar and leave to stand for 24 hours. Push the chillies down into the jar and seal.

This recipe may also be made with lemons but leave them in the bowl for 10 days instead of 5 which is the time that it will probably need for the skins to soften and the flavour to mature.

Loganberry

The loganberry is a delicious and productive cross between the raspberry and cultivated blackberry. The trailing canes grow in the same way as blackberry and for good results should be tied on to a trellis. The shape of the leaf is similar to that of the wild blackberry, whilst the cone-shaped, red fruit resembles an elongated raspberry both in appearance and flavour. If you can get hold of a plant try for a thornless variety – East Malling Thornless is a good example. Unfortunately we do not go in for loganberries as commercially as they do in America, where it was first hybridized, and where it is still called the phenomenal berry, so it may not be easy to find a supplier.

Two very good reasons for growing your own fruit are the expensive scarcity of loganberries, and the fact that the raw berry does not keep well, so should be used immediately it is picked. Over-ripe fruit does not make good preserves and the dark, purply-red fruit should be eaten in desserts where its sweet softness will be best appreciated. When using loganberries in preserves always remember to pick slightly under-ripe, dry fruit on a hot, dry day. Never use any berries touched by mould. Soak them in a bowl of cold salted water, 15g/½oz sea salt to 1.15 litre/2 pints water, to remove any pests and shake well in a colander to dry. Loganberries set fairly well but for economic necessity most recipes include those fruit which will provide bulk without eradicating the fine loganberry flavour. I have given a selection of recipes for loganberries but the quantities and methods given for most raspberry preserves will work with equally good results.

LOGANBERRY JAM

1kg/2lb 4oz slightly under-ripe   1kg/2lb 4oz white sugar
   loganberries

3 dry, hot, sterile jam jars

Soak the loganberries, shake dry and place in a preserving pan. Simmer very gently until the fruit is soft and add the warmed sugar, stirring well until it has dissolved. Bring to the boil and boil hard until a set is obtained. Throughout this process take great care not to burn. Pot and seal.
    A very simple recipe. To make an outstanding summery preserve use a mixture of cherries, redcurrants, raspberries and loganberries.

LOGANBERRY AND REDCURRANT JELLY

1kg/2lb 4oz loganberries   300ml/½ pint water
1kg/2lb 4oz redcurrants   white sugar

6 hot, dry, sterile jars

Soak and drain the loganberries, removing the stalks. Wash the redcurrants. Put both fruit into a preserving pan with the water. Bring to the boil and then simmer until soft. Turn into a jelly bag and leave to drain into a clean bowl overnight or until all the juice is through, resisting the temptation to squeeze. The next day measure the juice and for every 600ml/1 pint take 450g/1lb warmed sugar. Return the juice to the pan and boil rapidly for 1 minute, add the sugar stirring well until it has dissolved. Bring to the boil and boil hard until a set is obtained. Pot and seal.
    A gloriously glowing preserve.

Lychee

Fresh lychees originate in China but those grown for export come from South Africa. Fresh, the lychee has a hard nobbly, reddish skin and the white pulp which covers the single brown seed has a delicately perfumed taste. To ensure the very best results, choose those with brightly coloured skins free from blemishes.

The tinned lychees are the delicious small, sweet white fruit which is served as a dessert in Chinese restaurants. The fruit is also dried and the nutty, muscatel flavoured result is sold as litchie nuts.

LYCHEE JAM USING TINNED FRUIT

500g/1lb 2oz tin lychees   lemons
white sugar

3 medium size, hot, dry, sterile jars

Drain the syrup from the tin of lychees and put it in a preserving pan. Weigh the fruit and for each 450g/1lb take 225g/8oz sugar and the juice of 2 lemons. Add the sugar to the juice in the pan and heat gently stirring well until it has dissolved. Bring to the boil and continue boiling until you have a thin syrup. Mix in the fruit and the lemon juice, bring to the boil again and simmer for 10 minutes. Take care not to discolour by overboiling. Pot and seal.

Both tinned guavas and tinned mangoes may be made into preserves in the same way but an important rule applies. Do not overcook the fruit otherwise it will disintegrate.

M

Mandarin

A small, orange type fruit full of juice, thin-skinned and pithless with loose segments. The flavour of the mandarin is more distinctive than either satsuma or clementine and although it has very little pectin or acid content it is possible to make a light jammy marmalade or preserve. Originating in China or Indo-China mandarins come into our shops during October – March from Italy, North Africa and Spain.

Follow recipes given for Clementines or Tangerines, p.121 and p.355.

Mango

Mangoes are the most delicious and succulent fruit imaginable, in taste and texture not unlike a cantaloupe melon. The flesh is pinky-orange, varying in colour with the degree of ripeness, and the smooth, inedible skin is yellow-green. Juicy, sticky mangoes are usually eaten fresh but take care that the fruit you choose is plump and firm – a mango from a poor tree can be truly horrible. Mangoes have a high vitamin A and sugar content which, when raw, makes them important for their dietary contribution.

Green or unripe fruit make very good chutneys which are a traditional and important accompaniment to curries. Mango chutney should be thick, hot and sweet, the fruit soft but not disintegrating. Be careful not to overcook fresh mangoes for they can put a very nasty edge on the teeth.

Mangoes are exported from India and Kenya. Tinned mangoes can be used instead of fresh but they are softer and should not be cooked for so long. Make sure that the syrup is drained off before using and weigh the fruit after draining, and do not sprinkle tinned fruit with salt as some recipes require.

Other alternatives to use are peaches and more rarely papaya (paw-paws) – another exotic fruit. Some of the recipes require tamarind – a long pod which contains seeds covered in brown pulp. This seed and pulp is soaked and sieved to provide a paste which is used quite extensively in Indian cooking, and therefore obtainable in good Indian food shops. Barberries can be satisfactorily substituted for tamarind. The barberry has elongated bright red berries which, because of their high acidity, are seldom eaten raw. They are however, excellent in preserves and chutneys.

One mango can weigh between 150g/5oz – 675g/1lb 8oz, so for 1kg/2lb 4oz you may need only two.

FRUITY MANGO CHUTNEY

1kg/2lb 4oz mangoes
100g/4oz cooking apples
225g/8oz block dates
100g/4oz seedless raisins
100g/4oz onions
3 bay leaves
1 lemon

100g/4oz tamarind pulp
$\frac{1}{4}$ teaspoon ground nutmeg
600ml/1 pint malt vinegar
25g/1oz sea salt
2 teaspoons cayenne pepper
900g/2lb soft dark brown sugar
1 tablespoon lime juice

5 hot, dry, sterile jars with non-metal lids

Peel and quarter the mangoes. Wash, peel, core and chop the apples. Chop the dates and raisins. Peel and chop the onions and tie the bay leaves together with a long piece of cotton. Squeeze the juice from the lemon and put all the ingredients, except the sugar and lime juice, together into a large bowl, mix well and leave for 4 hours. Transfer into a preserving pan and add the sugar and lime juice. Heat gently stirring well until the sugar has dissolved, bring to the boil and simmer until thick and soft. Remove bay leaves. Pot and seal. This chutney should reach a rich mellow maturity, so keep for as long as possible before eating. If you buy fresh tamarinds, remove the fleshy seeds and stand them in a little boiling water for 30 minutes before passing through a fine sieve, discard the pips and then weigh.

211

CREOLE MANGO CHUTNEY

1kg/2lb 4oz green mangoes
3 sweet thin-skinned oranges
2 thin-skinned lemons
3 cloves garlic
200g/7oz seedless raisins
100g/4oz almonds

250g/9oz green or purple figs
250g/9oz whole dates
2 teaspoons sea salt
2 teaspoons ground black pepper
1kg/2lb 4oz soft, dark brown sugar
600ml/1 pint malt vinegar

7 hot, dry, sterile jars with non-metal lids

Peel and chop the mangoes. Wash oranges and lemons and slice finely, removing pips. Peel and chop the garlic, wash and chop raisins, blanch, skin and chop the almonds. If the figs have thick skin leave them to stand in hot water for 5 minutes and remove hard bits before chopping. Remove stones from dates and chop. Turn all the ingredients into a preserving pan and bring gently to the boil stirring well until the sugar has dissolved. Simmer for 45 minutes or until the mixture is soft and thick. Pot and seal.

A terrific combination in this thick fruity chutney. For economy's sake you may wish to use dried figs and dates. Whole dried figs should be soaked before using.

Marigold
Calendula officinalis

Pot marigold is an ancient flower used for culinary and medical purposes, apart from which the golden orange flower is the brightest and most cheerful addition to any garden or window box. Grown near roses, they keep them free from various insects although marigolds themselves are very prone to blackfly so take care to wash them well. Grow from seed and they will continue to spring up year after year, reseeding naturally. The scent and taste of marigolds is tangy and green, coming into the same category as geraniums and chrysanthemums, either loved or loathed.

Dry marigold heads as for Chamomile, p.109 and use as substitute for saffron.

Marigold Vinegar may be made in the same way as Lavender Flower Vinegar, p.196. Use only the marigold petals and watch as they gradually transform the vinegar into a glowing golden liquid.

MARIGOLD CONSERVE

100g/4oz freshly gathered marigold
  petals

400g/14oz caster sugar
1 lemon

small, dry, sterile moulds

Gather the flowers on a dry day before the sun is at its highest and use the petals immediately. After removing any unwelcome insects put the petals into a mortar or bowl and grind to a smooth pulp adding a little of the lemon juice to give it a smooth silkiness. Bit by bit add the sugar beating continually until it is all absorbed and you have a glorious golden poultice in the bowl. Pot and seal.

Marigold Conserve is guaranteed to cure melancholy. My own opinion is that much of the cure is in the gently satisfying indulgence of making flower conserves.

Sweet Marjoram

Origanum makorana

This domestic marjoram which is one of thirty different species of *origanum* will be an absolute necessity in the garden for all of those with culinary ambitions. It will modestly require little room and the seedlings, once planted into a light, warm, moist soil, will thrive with little trouble although in colder areas of Britain it is wisest to treat it as an annual and to take the precaution of growing a few plants in pots on the kitchen windowsill. The plant grows to about 60cm/2 feet in height and has grey-green leaves and small clusters of pale, purple flowers but what it lacks in appearance it makes up for in its delightful and varied uses. Fresh, the sweet, spicy leaves are strongly aromatic and give a marvellous boost to the most lifeless salad or pallid sauce. All tomato, pasta and shellfish dishes will benefit from its addition, particularly Italian dishes, and a beef joint will triumph when basted with marjoram oil. Dried, the herb can be added to an infinite variety of stuffings, breads, scones and so on *ad infinitum*. The marjoram oil or vinegar will make a mayonnaise with a difference whilst marjoram and mint tea is considered to be very therapeutic before retiring to bed.

Wild oregano or pot marjoram, *Origanum vulgara*, is very similar to the sweet or knot marjoram, but has a slightly spicier almost bitter leaf. It grows prolifically in England and may be used without fear. Oregano is Mediterranean marjoram and is used extensively in Italian cooking.

Make Lemon and Marjoram Jelly as for Lemon Jelly, p.199, adding marjoram leaves.

Make Marjoram Vinegar as for Tarragon Vinegar, p.353.

Dry and freeze marjoram leaves as for Basil, p.77.

MARJORAM OIL

6 tablespoons crushed marjoram leaves

3 tablespoons white wine vinegar

600ml/1 pint corn or sunflower oil (olive oil if not too strongly flavoured)

large glass jar with tight-fitting lid

Make sure that the leaves are fresh. Put them in a pestle and mortar and pound them well (a blunt instrument and bowl is a good substitute). Turn them into the jar and add the oil and vinegar, leaving a good space at the top to shake. Seal tightly and put on a warm windowsill to infuse gently. Shake every time you pass. Leave for 3 weeks and then strain the oil crushing the marjoram on the sieve to make sure you squeeze out the last drop of aromatic juice. If you do not feel that the oil is strong enough for your taste, repeat the process with the same oil and fresh leaves until it is satisfactory. Pour into bottles and add a fresh, clean sprig of marjoram to each bottle. Seal tightly.

Try this concoction with the leaves of basil, rosemary, thyme or mint. Fennel will give a lovely oil for making a mayonnaise to accompany fish or eggs. The method is the same. Well pounded seed herbs such as coriander also make a very flavoursome oil.

Marrow

Marrows, which are of the same family as squash, melons, cucumbers and gourds, are thought to have originated in the Americas. Although we are familiar with the long, fat, green or green and yellow vegetable which can so accomodatingly live on the compost heap, few people grow the beautiful ornamental squash such as Custard Marrow or Crookneck Squash yet they make wonderful eating, particularly stuffed and baked. Another variety trying hard to gain in popularity is the Spaghetti Marrow which, when cooked properly, has masses of curly pulp, golden buttery and sweet, which, with a good sauce, makes a meal in itself. Baby marrows are almost indistinguishable from courgettes and even marrow flowers may be stuffed and fried in batter.

Marrows are so obliging and useful that even the smallest garden should find a spot for them. I have seen them growing in baskets hanging on a wall and also in large pots, as well as the most obvious places but they will of course thrive best under prepared conditions. Select a hot, level bed and dig in plenty of compost material, grass, cuttings, etc. Mix in a fair helping of fertilizer and leave a depression where you are to plant the seeds. Cover with a layer of fine top soil and press two or three seeds into this, sideways up. Place a glass jar over the top to act as a little summer house and also to protect the tender seedling from slugs. Thin out when they are large enough and continue to protect from slugs – possibly with the help of a few saucers of beer which the slugs will imbibe with abandon and promptly drown in. Always keep the plant well watered right from the word go.

Trailing varieties of marrow are fine if you have the odd patch which needs covering but the bush variety will suit those of you who have limited space. Bring some seeds on in small pots on the windowsill during April and then by the time that you are planting your outdoor seeds in May you will have one or two established seedlings to pot out as well.

Marrow is an excellent bulk vegetable in jams, chutneys and pickles and can help to eke out precious fruits and more expensive vegetables, although it lacks setting properties.

The best marrows to use for jams and chutneys are fully matured with hard skin and golden pulp, while the smaller hard marrows are best for pickles for they will not soften so readily. Always peel and seed your marrow before weighing otherwise the results may be disastrous, and it is advisable to steam or stand the marrow overnight before adding to the pan to ensure that the cubes are not rubbery. Soggy marrow has put innumerable people off the vegetable but used in preserves it provides subtle, almost elegant, jams and creams and smooth thick chutneys which are extremely economical. Do not discard the humble marrow; while nutritionally extinct it is the preserver's good friend.

MARROW JAM

The finest marrows for preserve-making are the large, greeney-gold ones that have been left to mature fully. Use these in preference unless otherwise stated. The weights given for the marrow are taken after it has been fully prepared.

1kg/2lb 4oz prepared marrow   25g/1oz root ginger
3 lemons   1kg/2lb 4oz white sugar

5 hot, dry, sterile jam jars

Peel, seed and dice the marrow, weigh it and put it into a steamer or a colander placed over a large saucepan of water. Put on the lid and steam until just tender. Remove and place in a large bowl. Grate the rind from two of the lemons and squeeze the juice from all three. Add the juice and rind to the marrow with the bruised root ginger tied into a muslin bag. Stir in the sugar, cover and leave to stand for 24 hours in a cool place. Turn into a preserving pan and heat gently, stirring well until the sugar has dissolved completely. Bring to the boil and boil hard until the marrow is transparent and soft without breaking up. The syrup should be thick and golden. Remove muslin bag. Pot and seal.

 The marrow may be used directly without steaming first but the result is not so good as it tends to stay hard. Add the grated rind and juice of 3 sweet oranges for a super Marrow and Orange Jam. And for Marrow and Ginger Jam add 100g/4oz chopped preserved ginger.

MARROW AND PLUM JAM

1kg/2lb 4oz prepared marrow   1kg/2lb 4oz cooking plums
2kg/4lb 8oz white sugar

10 hot, dry, sterile jam jars

Peel, seed, dice and weigh the marrow and put into a deep bowl. Sprinkle with half the sugar, cover and leave overnight. The next day, turn the contents of the bowl into a preserving pan, heat gently, stirring well, until the sugar has dissolved. Simmer until tender. Wash and stone the plums and add them to the marrow with the remainder of the sugar (it may be necessary to reduce the sugar to 1675g/3lb 12oz if the plums are very ripe). Add a few plum kernels to give that lovely almondy flavour and stir well until the sugar has dissolved. Bring to the boil and boil gently until set. Pot and seal.

 A very good glut jam. The same recipe can be used for Damson and Marrow Jam.

MARROW GINGER JAM USING COMMERCIAL PECTIN

1kg/2lb 4oz prepared marrow
150ml/¼ pint water
50g/2oz root ginger
1450g/3lb 4oz white sugar

1 lemon
100g/4oz crystallized ginger
1 bottle commercial pectin

6 hot, dry, sterile jam jars

Peel, seed, dice and weigh the marrow and put it into a large preserving pan with the water. Add the bruised root ginger tied into a muslin bag; cover and simmer for 20 minutes. Chop the crystallized ginger and add it to the pan with the juice from the lemon and the warmed sugar, stirring well until the sugar has dissolved. Bring to a full boil for 2 minutes then remove the pan from the heat and discard the muslin bag. Stir in the pectin and continue to skim and stir for 1 minute, allow to cool before potting. Seal when cold.

Marrow benefits from the use of commercial pectin as it has a struggle to reach a set when cooked without other more co-operative fruit. Use this recipe as a basis for experimenting with your own added flavours.

MARROW AND BLACKBERRY CHUTNEY

1kg/2lb 4oz prepared marrow
2 teaspoons sea salt
500g/1lb 2oz blackberries
500g/1lb 2oz cooking apples
250g/9oz onions
250g/9oz sultanas

300ml/½ pint vinegar
250g/9oz sugar
1 level teaspoon ground ginger
1 level teaspoon mixed spice
1 level teaspoon mustard powder
1 level teaspoon cayenne pepper

8 hot, dry, sterile jam jars

Peel, seed, dice and weigh the marrow, put it in a colander and sprinkle with the salt, cover and leave to drain overnight. The next day rinse and shake dry. Pick over and rinse the blackberries. Peel, core and chop the apples. Peel and chop the onions. Wash the sultanas. Put the fruit and vegetables into a stainless steel pan with half the vinegar and cook until just soft, taking great care not to burn. Mix the sugar and spices with the remaining vinegar and add to the pan, stirring well until all is well mixed. Bring slowly to the boil, reduce the heat and simmer until thick and soft. Pot and seal.

TANGY MARROW CHUTNEY

1kg/2lb 4oz prepared marrow
25g/1oz sea salt
225g/8oz onions
225g/8oz apples
225g/8oz sultanas

50g/2oz candied orange peel
3 teaspoons ground ginger
½ teaspoon cayenne pepper
600ml/1 pint malt vinegar
225g/8oz white or soft brown sugar

4 hot, dry, sterile jars with non-metal lids

Peel, seed, dice and weigh the marrow, put it into a colander and sprinkle with the salt. Cover with a weighted plate and leave to drain overnight. The next day rinse and drain the marrow. Peel and chop the onions. Wash, peel, core and chop the apples and chop the sultanas and peel. Take all the ingredients except the sugar and put them in a stainless steel pan with half the vinegar and cook gently until soft. Dissolve the sugar in the remaining vinegar and add this to the pan, stirring well. Bring to the boil and simmer until thick and smooth. Pot and seal.

An excellent chutney with a very different flavour.

THREE FRUIT CHUTNEY

1kg/2lb 4oz prepared marrow
25g/1oz sea salt
1kg/2lb 4oz cooking apples
1kg/2lb 4oz cooking pears
100g/4oz onions
2 teaspoons plain flour

2 teaspoons mustard powder
2 tablespoons cayenne pepper
2 tablespoons turmeric powder
2 tablespoons ground ginger
1 litre/1¾ pints vinegar
500g/1lb 2oz sugar

7 hot, dry, sterile jars with non-metal lids

Peel, seed, dice and weigh the marrow, put it into a colander and sprinkle with the salt. Cover with a weighted plate and leave to drain overnight. The next day rinse and shake dry, place in a steamer and cook until soft. In the meantime wash, peel, core and chop the fruit. Peel and chop the onions and simmer with the fruit in a minute amount of water until quite soft. Mash the marrow and fruit well and combine all the dry ingredients except the sugar with a little of the vinegar to make a paste. Turn all of these together into a stainless steel pan, add half the vinegar and simmer until thick. Dissolve the sugar in the remaining vinegar and stir into the mixture. Simmer until the right thick smooth consistency is reached. Pot and seal.

A very fruity, rich chutney and an excellent way to use the end-of-season leftovers. It is also remarkably hot, so you might like to reduce the quantity of cayenne.

SWEET PICKLED MARROW

1kg/2lb 4oz prepared marrow
300ml/½ pint white vinegar
350g/12oz white sugar

a piece of cinnamon stick
1 teaspoon whole cloves

3 hot, dry, sterile jars with non-metal lids

Peel, seed, dice and weigh the marrow. Put the vinegar, sugar and spices into a stainless steel pan (you can tie the spices into a muslin bag and I find that in this case it is preferable, as the whole cloves tend to stain the marrow when it is in the jars, spoiling an otherwise clear golden appearance). Bring to the boil and add the marrow. Continue to simmer stirring occasionally, until the cubes are transparent without breaking up. Remove the marrow with a perforated spoon and lay on a dish to cool. Bring the syrup to the boil, again, collect any surplus syrup from the dish, add this and boil rapidly until the liquid is thick. Pack the marrow firmly into the jars, remove the muslin bag from the pan and give it a good squeeze before pouring the boiling syrup over the marrow to cover completely. Make sure that there are no air bubbles. Seal.

MILITARY PICKLE

1kg/2lb 4oz prepared marrow
1 cauliflower
450g/1lb runner beans
450g/1lb small or silverskin onions
25g/1oz sea salt
2.25 litres/4 pints malt vinegar

450g/1lb demerara sugar
12 dried red chillies
25g/1oz turmeric powder
25g/1oz ground ginger
100g/4oz plain flour

6 dry, sterile jars with non-metal lids

Make sure that the marrow is cut into small dice. Wash the cauliflower and break it into small florets. Wash, string and cut the runner beans cross-wise. Peel the onions. Lay all the vegetables on a large dish and sprinkle with the salt. Leave overnight. The next day drain the vegetables well, rinse under cold water and shake dry. Place them in a stainless steel pan with the vinegar and boil for 5 minutes. Add the sugar and chillies, stirring well until the sugar has dissolved. Bring to the boil once again. Mix the remaining ingredients to a smooth paste with a little vinegar and add it to the pan, boiling and stirring continuously. Reduce the heat to a gentle bubble and continue in this way for 30 minutes but do keep stirring to keep the mixture smooth. Leave to get quite cold. Pot and seal.

A very fiery pickle.

CANDIED MARROW

1kg/2lb 4oz prepared marrow	6 dried chilli peppers
1kg/2lb 4oz white sugar	50g/2oz caster sugar
25g/1oz root ginger	½ saltspoon cream of tartar
2 lemons	½ saltspoon bicarbonate of soda

Peel, seed, dice and weigh the marrow and place it in a bowl of cold water. Leave overnight. The next day strain the marrow and pat it dry, return it to the dry bowl and add the sugar, mixing well. Cover and leave overnight. The next day, bruise the ginger and pare the rind from the lemons. Tie these with the chillies into a muslin bag. Squeeze the juice from the lemons, put this into a preserving pan with the marrow and all its attendant stickiness. Add the muslin bag. Heat very gently stirring well until the sugar has completely dissolved and continue to simmer until the marrow is transparent and the syrup thick. Pour into a china bowl, cover and leave for 1 week. Lay a sheet of grease-proof paper over a sponge rack, remove the marrow from the syrup, drain and leave to dry on the paper. The rack should be put in a warm place – either an airing cupboard or a warm oven. When the marrow is completely dry, roll it in the caster sugar to which you have added the cream of tartar and bicarbonate of soda. Pack into a box between sheets of waxed paper.

Marvellous sticky chewy sweetmeats. ¼ teaspoon cayenne pepper may be used instead of chillies.

GINGER MARROW

1kg/2lb 4oz prepared marrow
1kg/2lb 4oz white sugar
1 lemon

large piece root ginger
50g/2oz candied peel
4 dried red chillies

4 hot, dry, sterile jars

Peel, seed and dice the marrow into 3cm/1 inch cubes. Weigh before using. Put into a bowl and mix with the sugar. Grate the rind from the lemons and extract the juice and add these to the marrow. Cover and leave for 24 hours. Bruise the ginger and cut the chillies into strips, tie into a muslin bag. Transfer the contents of the bowl into a preserving pan and add the muslin bag. Boil for 1½ hours. In the meantime, cut the candied peel into thin strips and add this to the marrow before potting. Stir well, and remove the muslin bag. Pot and seal. The marrow should retain its cube shape and be transparent and the peel should be very thin. Almost like an anglicized chow-chow.

STORING MARROWS

Cut the marrows before early frosts, leaving a good piece of stem. Keep in nets in a cool, dry place. If you cannot get hold of nets, then store small marrows on shelves but turn them over now and again and examine for mould etc.

Melon

Melons, like marrow, are the fruit of a vine. Depending on their environment they can be grown in a number of ways, but generally speaking very few can be grown out of doors in the British Isles. There is a tremendous difference in shapes and sizes, colours and taste and the best melons for dessert eating or *hors d'oeuvres* are the heavily perfumed musk and cantaloupe melons. Musk melons are frequently called netted melons because of the filigree pattern on the yellow or green rind, which in some groups has deeply marked segmentations. The flesh is green to deep salmon pink. Cantaloupe melons have thick, warty, orange rind with deeply segmented markings and deep orange flesh. Both of these varieties of melon may be grown with some success in Britain as they are reasonably hardy.

Winter melons are a larger fruit, more oval in shape and with a green to yellow rind, patterned and plain, sometimes indented. Honeydew and Spanish melons fall into this category and I find these useful for preserving as the flesh is firm, although somewhat lacking in flavour, and they are less expensive than other varieties. Ogen melons which come originally from Israel are small green and gold striped fruit with an aromatic green flesh. When other cheaper small melons are not available these make good whole pickles which are pleasantly perfumed.

Water melons are large, dark-green, smooth and shiny with glorious red flesh, crisp and refreshingly cool; they are better than a sorbet on a hot day. The preserves made from these melons are in a class of their own – crunchy, colourful and spectacular enough to make very good presents.

There are many specifically named melons all of which have a place in one or the other of these categories, – for instance Charentais melon is a cantaloupe variety, although many of the names may be unfamiliar. Melons come from South America, Cyprus, France, Holland, Israel, Spain and North and South Africa and are obtainable in one form or other throughout the year. Water melons are mostly obtainable in July and August.

A medium-size melon will weigh approximately 2kg/4lb 8oz and about a quarter of this weight is taken by rind and pips. Water melons weigh between 3-4kg/6-9lb and again a fair percentage is rind and pips. It is most important to weigh the melon after preparation to allow for this weight difference. Ninety-five per cent of a melon is water and 5 per cent sugar so whilst they are hardly fattening they do not lend much nutritional value to the diet. When preparing melons make sure that all the fibres, pips and soft flesh is removed and that the diced pieces are at least bite-sized to ensure that they do not disintegrate.

MELON CONSERVE WITH KIRSCH

1kg/2lb 4oz ripe prepared melon   150ml/¼ pint kirsch
500g/1lb 2oz white sugar

3 attractive, hot, dry, sterile jars

Peel and seed the melon removing all fibres, weigh and cut into neat cubes. Put into a bowl in layers with the sugar. Cover and leave for 24 hours. Transfer to a preserving pan with the kirsch, and taking care not to burn, bring slowly to the boil. Stir gently and frequently until the conserve is thick and golden. Pot and seal.

Very elegant and sophisticated conserve.

MELON AND PINEAPPLE PRESERVE

1kg/2lb 4oz ripe prepared melon
1kg/2lb 4oz pineapple

4 lemons
2kg/4lb 8oz white sugar

9 hot, dry, sterile jars

Peel and seed the melon removing all fibres. Weigh and cut into small neat cubes. Peel and cut the pineapple into the same size cubes; try to work on a plate to ensure that you catch some of the juice. Put both melon and pineapple into a preserving pan with the juice from the lemons and simmer very carefully taking great care not to burn. When the fruit is just tender and there is a certain amount of juice, add the warmed sugar and continue to heat gently stirring well until it has dissolved. Bring to the boil and boil gently until a set is obtained. Pot and seal.

More of a very special dessert as none of these low pectin fruit set well enough to spread.

MELON AND RASPBERRY PRESERVE

1kg/2lb 4oz slightly firm prepared
   melon
900g/2lb white sugar

1 lemon
300g/11oz raspberries

5 hot, dry, sterile jars

Peel and seed the melons removing all fibres, weigh and cut into cubes and put into a bowl, well layered with the sugar, and sprinkled with the juice from the lemon. Cover and leave for 12 hours. Pick over the raspberries, only wash if necessary and dry. Transfer the melon etc., to a preserving pan and heat very gently stirring well until all the sugar is dissolved. Bring to the boil and add the raspberries. Continue to cook gently for 30 minutes. Pot and seal.

SWEET MELON PICKLE

small slightly under-ripe melons   lemons
water   root ginger
white sugar

large sterile jar

Brush the melon and wipe with a damp cloth. Slice the melon into neat, thin triangles and remove the seeds. Boil up a large pan of water and leave the melon in this for 3 minutes. Drain well and weigh, for each 450g/1lb take 450g/1lb warmed sugar, 600ml/1 pint water, 1 lemon and 1 piece root ginger. Grate the rind from the lemon and tie the bruised ginger into a muslin bag. Turn everything into a preserving pan and bring to the boil stirring carefully until the sugar has dissolved. Simmer for 5 minutes. Remove the melon with a perforated spoon and, taking care not to break it, pack it into the jar. Bring the syrup to the boil and pour it over the fruit. Cover with a gauze cloth and leave for 3 days. Drain the syrup into the pan and bring to the boil again. Pour over the melon to cover and seal tightly.
    A very good way of bottling melon.

WATER MELON PICKLE

1 water melon   20 whole cloves
25g/1oz sea salt   4 small cinnamon sticks
2 sweet oranges   1.15 litre/2 pints cider vinegar
2 lemons   900g/2lb white sugar

6 hot, dry, sterile jars with non-metal lids

Brush the melon and wipe with a damp cloth. Cut into quarters and remove the pips, fibres and soft flesh around the seeds. Remove the soft red flesh which you can either crush and freeze or eat then and there with a little sugar. Take a very sharp knife and pare the dark green rind from the quarters leaving yourself with a neat segment of thick white rind and a thin layer of firm red flesh. Weigh the results of this endeavour and for every 1kg/2lb 4oz take the ingredients in the proportions above. Make a brine with the salt and enough water to cover the melon and leave to soak overnight in this cold solution. The next day rinse and drain the melon and shake dry. Wipe the oranges and lemons and slice them thinly, discard the pips and cut the slices into halves. Bruise the spices and tie them in a muslin bag, put this with the vinegar and sugar into a large stainless steel pan and bring gently to the boil, stirring well until the sugar has dissolved. Add the oranges and lemons and any juice you may have collected and bring to the boil again. Now add the melon, reboil briefly and remove from the heat. Using a perforated spoon, pack the fruit into the jars taking care not to include the muslin bag which should be squeezed and removed. Reboil the syrup, skim and pour over the melon to cover completely. Make sure that there are no air bubbles. Seal.

A most attractive pickle which goes well with rich meats, hot, white, bean dishes and cold buffets. Use the water melon flesh to mix with fresh blackberries and sugar for a refreshing dessert. (The same pickle can be made without the oranges and lemons but it is not so good.)

SWEET AND SOUR MELONS

1kg/2lb 4oz prepared honeydew melon   575g/1lb 4oz white sugar
300ml/½ pint cider vinegar   2 teaspoons pickling spice

3 hot, dry, sterile jars with non-metal lids

Peel and seed the melon removing the fibres. Weigh and cut into cubes. Fill a pan with water and bring to the boil, add the melon cubes and bring rapidly to the boil again. Have ready a bowl of iced water, turn the melon cubes into a colander and tip immediately into the cold water. Leave to get cold. Boil the vinegar in a stainless steel pan, drain the melon well and put it into the vinegar. Bring to the boil and boil for 2 minutes. Turn the whole lot into a china bowl and leave to cool. Cover and let stand for 48 hours. When this time has elapsed strain off the vinegar and bring it to the boil in the same pan, add the sugar and the spices tied into a muslin bag. Stir well until the sugar has dissolved and boil for 15 minutes. Skim, add the melon and boil for a further 3 minutes, remove with a perforated spoon and pack into the jars. Retrieve the spice bag and reboil the syrup once again. Skim and leave to cool. Pour over the melon to cover. Seal when cold.

Keep 2 weeks before using. A sprig of summer savory or lemon thyme popped down the side of the jar looks terrific.

SMALL GREEN MELONS IN VINEGAR

600ml/1 pint white wine vinegar
1 level tablespoon sea salt
1kg/2lb 4oz very small green melons

1 teaspoon ground white pepper
sprigs of fresh tarragon

large, dry, sterile jar with non-metal lid

Put the vinegar and salt into a stainless steel pan and boil for 5 minutes. Brush the melons and wipe with a damp cloth. Fill the jar with them sprinkling with the pepper and sprigs of tarragon as you go. When the vinegar is cold pour it over the melons to cover. Lay a gauze over the jar and leave for 48 hours. Drain the vinegar from the jar and return it to the pan, boil for 5 minutes, leave to get cold and then pour it over the melons. Seal tightly.

Leave 2 weeks before eating. Cut them by slicing from the centre outwards to make a neat slice. Very spectacular-looking pickle.

MELON CHUTNEY

1kg/2lb 4oz prepared cantaloupe
  melon
2 small oranges
1 green pepper
50g/2oz currants

675g/1lb 8oz white sugar
1 teaspoon ground allspice
$\frac{1}{4}$ teaspoon sea salt
1.75 litres/3 pints white vinegar

4 hot, dry, sterile jars with non-metal lids

Clean the melon and remove the thickest part of the outer rind and the soft flesh and pips. Take only the inner rind and about 5mm/$\frac{1}{4}$ inch of firm flesh. Weigh and cut into bite-sized pieces. Put the melon into a large preserving pan with enough water to cover, place a lid on top and simmer until just soft. In the meantime, peel, seed and chop the oranges taking care not to lose the juices. Wash, seed and dice the pepper, and wash the currants. Drain the melon and return to the pan with the rest of the ingredients, cover and simmer for 45 minutes giving an occasional stir. Uncover and bring to the boil, reduce heat and simmer, uncovered for a further 45 minutes. The chutney should be soft in a thin golden syrup. Pot and seal.

A very festive pickle-type chutney and a firm favourite with chicken terrine, bland white meats and pale honey roast ham.

STORING MELONS

As for Marrows, p.221.

DRIED MELON SEEDS

Take the melon seeds, free them from fibres, wash and dry them well and lay them on a tin baking tray. Put into a slow oven until they have turned golden brown and crisp. They burn very quickly so keep an eye on them. Delicious nibbles.

Mincemeat

Mincemeat was originally a mixture of mead, honey, available fruit, meal, spices, beef or mutton and fat all of which were cooked to a porridge-like consistency, fermented to taste and usually eaten on high days and holidays. It then gently transformed itself into rich puddings and a sweet sustaining mince of fruits, spices and meat which is still used in raised pies in regions of Britain.

The mincemeats which I have included in the following pages are those which fill mince pies made with short or puff pastry during the Christmas season. I find it more economical to make a large quantity of basic mincemeat to keep hungry children happy during the festival and a special supply of the more extravagant mincemeats to fill party pies for special occasions. There is no denying that to make mincemeat is expensive, and working on this theory I feel that as it is for a special occasion the best ingredients should be used. Whole candied peel is much better than the ready cut and the children love a few glacé cherries in mince, while candied apricots and ginger ring the changes with a festive flair. Although a luxury, muscatel raisins give a much better flavour and for economy's sake I use half of those and half of the ordinary variety. Finely chopped Brazil nuts have a more distinctive taste than almonds alone and hazelnuts give a richer result. Fresh suet is to be recommended (remove all the pieces of skin before grating, but if your butcher will not supply it console yourself with the thought that there is not all that much difference between that and the ready grated). Use plenty of juice and alcohol to keep moist but do not allow to become soggy. If mincemeat dries out after keeping resuscitate it with a little more alcohol and it is advisable to leave the made mincemeat overnight in a cool place (not cold) before adding the plonk and potting.

If you would like to ensure that your mincemeat does keep for a long time then sterilize it in this way. Use dry, sterile, preserving jars and lids, pot the mincemeat and seal it, place the jars in a roasting tin with cold water to halfway up the jars. Put into an oven and set at 130°C/250°F or gas mark 1 and leave for 1½ hours. Make sure that the seal is tight before storing in a cool dry place. To help in your calculations a 450g/1lb jar will, when full, contain approximately 400g/14oz mincemeat.

A final word about the making. A lack of mincer or grater once drove me to prepare and make my mince using only a knife, wooden spoon and rolling pin. Chopping, pounding battering and beating I macerated my mince by hand, but the mincemeat was the finest ever made.

CURRANT MINCEMEAT

450g/1lb blackcurrants

350g/12oz redcurrants

350g/12oz white currants

900g/2lb cooking apples

225g/8oz seedless raisins

150g/5oz candied peel

150g/5oz soft brown sugar

4 lemons

2 teaspoons ground mixed spice

4 hot, dry, sterile jam jars

Remove stalks and wash the currants. Wash, peel, core and chop the apples, wash and chop the raisins, chop the candied peel and extract the juice from the lemons. Put all these ingredients, with the sugar and spice, into a large stainless steel pan and heat gently stirring all the while until the sugar has dissolved, bring to the boil, reduce heat and simmer gently for 20 minutes. Pot and seal.

A refreshing, different mincemeat. Very good if you do not like the traditional mince made from all dried fruit and as it keeps a long time it can be made in the summer for use at Christmas.

FANCY LEMON MINCEMEAT

1kg/2lb 4oz lemons

1kg/2lb 4oz cooking apples

900g/2lb fat seedless raisins

450g/1lb currants

900g/2lb beef suet

225g/8oz mixed peel

4 tablespoons Seville marmalade

300ml/½ pint brandy

8 dry, sterile jam jars

228

Wash the lemons and remove the rind with a potato peeler, put it in a pan with a little water and simmer until soft. Squeeze the juice from the lemons and reserve. Wash and core the apples and bake them in the oven until they are squishy, then scoop out the pulp. Wash and dry the raisins and currants and put them through a mincer with the drained lemon rind. Shred the suet and chop the mixed peel. Put all these ingredients with the lemon juice and marmalade into a large bowl, mix well and stir in the brandy. Pot and seal.

A sharper mincemeat that makes a superb open tart.

CHRISTMAS MINCEMEAT

2 large, hard, juicy, cooking apples
1 orange
1 lemon
450g/1lb beef or vegetarian suet
100g/4oz almonds or almonds and
  brazils
225g/8oz candied peel (citron, orange
  and lemon)
450g/1lb seedless raisins (Lexia or
  muscatels)

450g/1lb yellow sultanas
450g/1lb currants
100g/4oz glacé cherries
50g/2oz glacé pineapple
50g/2oz crystallized ginger
350g/12oz soft, light brown sugar
½ teaspoon salt
½ teaspoon grated nutmeg
½ teaspoon ground mixed spice
150ml/¼ pint brandy or rum

6 dry sterile jars, wax discs, brown paper and string

Peel and core the apples. Grate the rind from the orange and lemon and squeeze out the juice. Finely shred the suet. Clean the fruit if necessary. Blanch or skin and chop the nuts and chop the peel finely. Chop the cherries, pineapple and ginger very small. Chop the raisins and put the sultanas and currants through a coarse mincer with the apples. Put all the ingredients, except the brandy or rum, into a large basin and mix well with the orange and lemon juice. Cover and leave overnight. The next day stir in the alcohol making sure that everything is very well mixed. Pot and seal with the discs which have been dipped in brandy and the brown paper tied down with string.

A superb light mincemeat which is full of pleasant surprises.

CIDER MINCEMEAT

350g/12oz hard, juicy, cooking apples
350g/12oz seedless raisins
1 lemon
150g/5½oz currants
150g/5½oz soft brown sugar
2 teaspoons ground cinnamon

1 teaspoon ground cloves
1 teaspoon ground nutmeg
75g/3oz unsalted butter
150ml/¼ pint dry cider
brandy or rum

2 hot, dry, sterile jars

Wash, peel, core and chop the apples; chop the raisins; grate the rind from the lemon and extract the juice. Put all the ingredients into a preserving pan and simmer gently giving an occasional stir for 30 minutes. Add enough alcohol to moisten without making soggy. Pot and seal.

This mincemeat does not keep for long.

Mint

Mentha

Although there are more than forty varieties of mint, we usually only come into contact with spearmint which is also known as lamb's mint or green pea mint. Yet there is also applemint, eau de cologne, pineapple, peppermint, ginger, orange, lemon, pennyroyal, wild water, corn, calamint, etc.

Many of the more delicate mints should be used in light apple-based jellies to taste them to advantage and, if touched with a tinge of artificial colour and packaged prettily, they will make the most heart-warming presents. There are very few dishes which will not benefit from the addition of a little mint and although mint with vinegar and sugar is a traditional accompaniment to roast lamb, my own preference is for a gooseberry and mint jelly. Chopped mint with honey or cream cheese makes a splendid filling for brown bread sandwiches and scented mints make refreshing drinks like Mint Julep. In parts of the Middle East mint sauce is turned into a thick syrup which with the addition of iced water becomes a sherbet. Add mint to sweet dishes as well as savoury, to jams and puddings or add mint vinegar to equal quantities of cream and good quality mayonnaise to make a superb dressing for fruit salad. Mint tea made with china tea or mint leaves, honey and lemon is a soothing and purifying concoction in a class of its own.

There is nothing so refreshing as to wander into the garden in the early morning and to crush fresh eau de cologne or spearmint beneath your nose which clears the fug away amazingly well. Mint is prolific and will grow with a certain gay abandon which takes over the garden unless severely restrained; to do this plant your mint in a large pot and bury it in the garden with the rim just above earth level, root out and replant new young shoots when the old plant grows straggly. Use only fresh young leaves for sauces etc. Domestically, mint keeps ants and moths away from the home to say nothing of fleas, and perhaps that is why cats love rolling in catmint.

A few handy hints for making mint sauces. A little hot water poured onto the chopped mint leaves will set the colour. Sugar should be dissolved with a little hot water before adding to the mint particularly if it is to be kept. Unless you intend to sterilize mint sauce for keeping do not make it up with both vinegar (or lemon) and sugar (or honey) as it will ferment if kept for any time.

A swift and easy way to make mint sauce for immediate use is to put the whole lot into a liquidizer – mint, vinegar and sugar and all – the results are then achieved in one fell swoop. Allow the fizz to settle before using.

MINT JELLIES

Although there are specific recipes given for mint jellies they usually require some special attention. The following recipe is for a basic mint jelly to be made with a variety of different fruit. Experiment also with flavoured mints, for example, apple and peppermint, gooseberry and applemint. Use any of the following fruit to make a jelly by the normal method: apple, crab apple, gooseberry, red or white currant, lemon, plum or rhubarb. Chop approximately 100g/4oz fresh mint with 1 tablespoon of white sugar and 1 tablespoon of water alternatively put them into a liquidizer. Place in a bowl, cover and leave to stand overnight (you can be doing this while the fruit is also draining). The next day measure your fruit juice and continue to make the jelly. Just before the set is reached, stir in 1 good tablespoon of the mint mixture to each 600ml/1 pint of the measured juice. Allow to cool a little before potting. Seal.

This is a particularly good way of using delicate mints which do not take to being swamped with the taste of vinegar.

MINT AND HONEY JELLY

25g/1oz mint leaves
300ml/½ pint water
450g/1lb clear honey

½ bottle commercial pectin
green colouring (optional)

4 small, hot, dry, sterile jars

Wash, dry, and chop the leaves, put them in a bowl; boil the water and pour it over the mint. Cover and leave to stand for 30 minutes. Strain the liquid and pour it into a large pan. Add the honey and heat gently stirring well, dropping in a few spots of colour if required. Bring to the boil for 1 minute and remove from the heat. Stir in the pectin, return to the heat and boil for 1 minute stirring and skimming. Pot and seal.

MINT MARMALADE

Make a basic Lemon Marmalade, p.201, adding 1 tablespoon of fresh chopped mint to each 450g/1lb marmalade. Stir in just before the set is reached.

MINT PICKLE

300ml/½ pint malt vinegar
2 teaspoons dry mustard
2 teaspoons sea salt
1 stick cinnamon
1 teaspoon black peppercorns
1 blade mace

225g/8oz soft brown sugar
225g/8oz fresh mint leaves
225g/8oz slightly under-ripe tomatoes
450g/1lb cooking apples
6 small onions
25g/1oz sultanas

3 dry, sterile jars with non-metal lids

Put the vinegar, spices and sugar into a stainless steel pan and bring to the boil, stirring well until the sugar has dissolved. Boil for 30 minutes and strain before using. In the meantime wash, dry and chop the mint, wash and cut the tomatoes into quarters; wash, peel, core and chop the apples. Peel and cut the onions into halves; chop the sultanas. Return the strained syrup to the pan and add all the ingredients except the mint. Simmer for 10 minutes and leave to get cold – it is advisable to cover the pan otherwise you may have potted wasp etc. Remove the ingredients with a perforated spoon and pack into the jars, sprinkling each layer well with chopped mint. Top up with the remaining syrup. Seal.

Leave for at least 2 months before using. A fresh and pleasant pickle which is particularly good with meat loaf and other potted meats and meat pies. White wine vinegar and white sugar may be used.

TO MAKE A MINT SAUCE FOR KEEPING

150ml/¼ pint vinegar

50g/2oz quantity of fresh young mint leaves

large, dry, sterile jar with non-metal lid

Boil the vinegar and leave it to cool. Wash, dry and chop the mint finely, pack into the jars and completely cover with the vinegar.

To re-use, remove the quantity that you require, sealing the jar tightly afterwards. Put it into a small pot, sprinkle with sugar and a tiny drop of boiling water to dissolve the sugar. Add extra vinegar if necessary.

A most unusual mint sauce can be made by using fresh, pure, lemon juice instead of vinegar and mixing with clear honey instead of sugar.

A MINT VINEGAR

100g/4oz fresh young mint leaves
1.15 litre/2 pints white wine or cider
    vinegar

225g/8oz white sugar

hot, dry, sterile bottles with corks

Wash, dry and chop the mint. Put all the ingredients into a stainless steel pan and bring to the boil for 5 minutes stirring and crushing continuously to bring out the flavour. Bottle and seal tightly.

Use in cold drinks well diluted.

TO PRESERVE MINT IN SUGAR

a large quantity of fresh mint leaves
white sugar

large, dry, stone jar with lid

Wash, dry and chop the mint. Put into the jar in layers with the sugar and fill the jar in this way finishing with a layer of sugar. Keep pressing down as you go and seal tightly. Spoon out the mint as you need it.

DRYING AND FREEZING MINT LEAVES

As for Basil, p.77.

Mulberry

The black or common mulberry is a delightful, picturesque tree, sturdy and domed with flat, broad leaves, bearing a good crop of purplish-red, raspberry-type berries which fall when they are fully ripe. This ancient tree was recorded by Roman writers in days BC, and must have arrived in Europe from Asia. In Britain it can still be found in the remnants of great parklands or in the large gardens of old family houses. If you find one, try begging a few cuttings – they may take!

The berries of the Black Mulberry make really beautiful preserves for they have a sharp flavour resembling a loganberry and give a reasonably successful set. One drawback is that the centres may be a little woody but do not let this deter you. The best way to gather the fruit without grovelling in the grass is to place a large cloth under one area of the tree at a time and shake the boughs firmly – the ripe fruit will then fall off. Remove mulberry stains from clothes in the same way as for Blackberries and take the stains off your fingers with lemon. The leaves of the White Mulberry are those used to feed silk worms.

BASIC MULBERRY JAM

1kg/2lb 4oz mulberries
1kg/2lb 4oz white sugar

4 hot, dry, sterile jam jars

Rinse the mulberries in a colander and shake them dry. Place in a deep bowl with the sugar, cover and leave overnight. The next day transfer them to a preserving pan and heat gently, stirring carefully until the sugar has completely dissolved. Bring to the boil and boil steadily until a set is obtained – about 20 minutes. Pot and seal.

Although the set is very soft I think that this is the best way to make mulberry jam. Take care not to burn and be prepared for a rather meagre yield.

SEEDLESS MULBERRY AND APPLE JAM

1kg/2lb 4oz mulberries
675g/1lb 8oz cooking apples
300ml/½ pint water
1kg/2lb 4oz white sugar

6 hot, dry, sterile jam jars

Rinse the mulberries in a colander; wash, peel, core and chop the apples and put both fruit into a preserving pan with the water, simmer until soft. Pass the fruit through a fine sieve discarding only the pips. Return the pulp to the pan and heat gently, add the warmed sugar stirring well until it has dissolved and bring to the boil, boil hard until a set is obtained. Pot and seal.

Another economical jam, try it on steamed sponge pudding with a sweet white sauce.

RED MULBERRY JELLY

1kg/2lb 4oz red but not ripe mulberries
  or a mixture of ripe and partly ripe
900ml/1½ pints water
white sugar

9 small, hot, dry, sterile jars

Rinse the mulberries in a colander and put them into a preserving pan with half the water, cover and simmer for 1 hour. Mash the fruit well and add the remaining water, simmer uncovered for a further hour. Turn into a jelly bag and leave until all the juice is drained through into a clean bowl, but do not prod or poke. Return the juice to the pan and heat gently, add the sugar, stirring well until it has dissolved. Bring to the boil and boil hard for 5 minutes. Skim. Pot and seal.

A soft-set, glowing jelly.

Mushroom

There is no pleasure quite so satisfying as a glimpse of those gleaming white caps sunk in the tussocky grass and there is no smell so autumnal as the dew-fresh earthy odour of fresh mushrooms. But never pick mushrooms, ceps or fungi without knowledgeable advice. Field mushrooms are flat with dark brown gills or slightly domed with browny pink gills while horse mushrooms are similar but much larger and smell vaguely of almonds, which may put you off. Discard any mushrooms with a greenish tinge, have white gills or warts or which stain on peeling.

Very large domed mushrooms can be stuffed in many delicious ways, smaller mushrooms are best fried gently and briefly with bacon or chopped in omelettes, while tattier leftovers are excellent in soups, stews and make marvellous ketchups. Stalks should not be thrown away but dried with other odds and ends to make mushroom powder, (p.239). If you have picked a mushroom with the complete base throw the stems onto the compost heap but remember that although you may raise a few of your own mushrooms you will deplete the supply in the field.

Do not peel mushrooms unless they are very dirty, just wipe them with a damp cloth and examine them carefully for worm (you should not find any unless the mushroom is too mature or is picked late in the day). Another thing worth remembering is that if you wash mushrooms, particularly the flat ones, they will become flaccid when cooked. Overcooking also causes this to happen.

Commercial button mushrooms do not have anything like the flavour of the wild mushrooms but they pickle well, as do the small closed field mushrooms. I also find that wiped clean and sliced thinly they are marvellous eaten raw in salads. The ketchups and sauces made with mushrooms give a rich, full flavour to sauces, soups and savouries which cannot be bettered by commercial products.

MUSHROOM AND PEPPER CHUTNEY

500g/1lb 2oz small button mushrooms
4 or 5 green peppers
800g/1lb 12oz onions
6 cloves garlic
8 shallots
6 whole cloves

575g/1lb 4oz brown sugar
2 teaspoons ground ginger
3 teaspoons curry powder
1.15 litre/2 pints malt vinegar
½ teaspoon tabasco sauce or pimento
   paste

2 hot, dry, sterile jars with non-metal lids

Clean the mushrooms, de-seed the peppers and cut into thin strips. Peel and chop the onion, garlic and shallots. Bruise the cloves and tie them into a twist of muslin. Put all the ingredients, except the tabasco or pimento, into a stainless steel pan and heat gently, stirring well until the sugar has dissolved. Simmer, still stirring occasionally, for 1 hour and then add the tabasco or pimento. Give another very good stir and leave to cool. Remove muslin bag. Seal when cold.

Leave for at least 2 months before using. Very strong and pungent chutney, and excellent mixed into a cheese dip, particularly a blue cheese.

MUSHROOM KETCHUP

Whereas button mushrooms are the most suitable for making pickles, field mushrooms are without doubt preferable for ketchup as they have a much stronger flavour and also give a dark, rich, brown, juice which is highly satisfying. Any field mushrooms may be used, all the bits and pieces, the stalks and large mushrooms which break easily, but it is important to ensure that they are fresh and dry. If they are damp they will go slimy or mouldy and this will affect the keeping properties of the finished ketchup.

The method for making a ketchup is the important factor, the additions to flavour are added with the vinegar after all the bashing and mashing has been gone through so I will give you the basic method of preparation for the ketchup and follow it with a choice of vinegars.

1kg/2lb 4oz field mushrooms
75g/3oz sea salt

hot, dry, heat-resistant, sterilized bottles and corks

Wipe the mushrooms clean, peel if necessary, remove stalks and examine for worm. Keep all of those that are good and put them with the caps.

Break up by hand and put them in layers with the salt into an earthenware dish. Cover and leave overnight (you can leave them longer but I do not find it necessary). The next day rinse them very briefly, shake in a colander and mash very well. Return them to the clean dish with the prepared vinegar, cover and put into a gentle oven for about 30 minutes – you can turn them into a stainless steel pan and cook them for 30 minutes on top of the oven instead, but I feel that it does not give the same mellow result. When the juice is rich and quite substantial looking, strain it through a fine nylon sieve pressing gently to get a good extraction. You may either bottle it as it is or measure it, and for every 600ml/1 pint take either 300ml/½ pint red wine or port, or 1 tablespoon brandy. Add this to the ketchup and bottle. Although these alcoholic extras are not essential they certainly add strength to the brew. Bottle to within 3cm/1 inch of the top, seal tightly and continue as for sterilized Spiced Apple Ketchup, p.50. If you do not sterilize, you will have a fermentation.

TO MAKE A PUNGENT KETCHUP

1 medium onion	1 teaspoon mixed pickling spice
1 clove garlic	¼ teaspoon grated nutmeg
300ml/½ pint malt vinegar	pinch cayenne pepper (optional)

Peel and chop the onion and garlic before adding to the vinegar.

TO MAKE A MELLOW KETCHUP

600ml/1 pint malt vinegar	small cinnamon stick
2 pieces mace	small piece root ginger
1 teaspoon allspice	1 small onion (optional)
1 teaspoon black peppercorns	½ teaspoon horseradish (optional)
1 teaspoon whole cloves	

Bruise and mix the ingredients together with the vinegar and just bring to the boil, allow to cool before adding to the mushrooms.

PICKLED MUSHROOMS

Pickled mushrooms are very simple to make and are extremely good as *hors d'oeuvre*. Follow this basic method for preparation and ring the changes with the different vinegars. Throw small, hard, clean button mushrooms into salt boiling water (1 litre/1¾ pints water to 50g/2oz salt). Leave for 5 minutes, drain and pack into jars. Then cover with boiling vinegar.

TO MAKE A SAVOURY VINEGAR

600ml/1 pint tarragon vinegar
2 medium-sized onions

1 teaspoon celery seed
fresh tarragon

Peel and finely slice the onion and add it to the vinegar and celery seed. Put into a stainless steel pan and boil until the onion is slightly soft, add a piece of fresh tarragon to each jar of mushrooms.

TO MAKE AN AROMATIC VINEGAR

600ml/1 pint white wine vinegar
2 pieces mace
2 teaspoons mixed peppercorns

1 teaspoon coriander
a few shreds of lemon rind
small bay leaves

Boil all the ingredients together in a stainless steel pan. Strain before using and reserve the bay leaves and lemon shreds, if your preference is such these may be added to the jars when potting.

MUSHROOM POWDER

A very simple powder may be made by drying mushrooms in the oven and grinding them to a powder with the end of a jar but the recipe below gives a stronger substance for flavouring.

1kg/2lb 4oz field mushrooms
2 small onions
$\frac{1}{4}$ teaspoon ground cloves

$\frac{1}{4}$ teaspoon ground mace
$\frac{1}{4}$ teaspoon ground white pepper

small, dry jars

Wipe the mushrooms with a damp cloth, making sure that all pieces, stalks etc., are clean. Peel and chop the onions. Put all the ingredients into a heavy pan and shake continuously over a medium heat. Cook until the mushrooms are quite dry and brittle. Lay out on a baking tray and leave in a slow oven to dry off completely. Either grind to a powder with a blunt instrument or put into a dry liquidizer. Sift through a sieve and pack into jars. Seal tightly.

DRIED MUSHROOMS

Use only the fresh, dry, flat, field mushrooms. Peel them if they are very dirty, otherwise wipe them with a damp cloth after removing the stalks (either dry these separately or use them in soups, stews or for powder). Lay the mushrooms on a flat tray, making sure that they do not touch, and place in a cool oven, 48°C/120°F (gas mark $\frac{1}{4}$) keeping the door ajar, for as long as it takes for them to become crisp and dry. Do not allow the atmosphere to turn steamy or humid. Pack dried mushrooms into airtight containers or into tightly sealed brown paper bags.

Another interesting way to deal with the larger mushrooms is to prepare them as above and to pass a thin cane through the centre of each one until the cane is full up without the caps touching. Rest the ends of the canes on the ledges in the sides of the oven. Although I have not recently seen it practised, my mother used to thread a thin string through the centre of the mushrooms (use a carpet needle) knotting each one as she went to keep them apart. They were then hung in a warm, dry place to become crisp and moisture free. Children will love to go mushrooming and dry the mushrooms by impaling them on a long prickly hawthorn twig. This is then set into a pot of sand and placed near the fire or range where it should be turned once a day to allow all the mushrooms to dry evenly.

To reconstitute the dried mushrooms either steep them in lukewarm water or steam them for a few minutes. They can be added to soups, stews and casseroles just as they are and you will find that they give a good flavour to most dishes making it well worth the effort and saving in both time and money.

Mustard

Mustard powder is the finely ground seeds of *Brassica nigra*, *Brassica juncea* or *Brassica alba*, sometimes mixed and sometimes separate. Although we are all familiar with this pale, golden powder to which we just add water, how many of us are equally familiar with the small seeds? Yet the powder is an annihilator of taste, and the seed a persuasive adjunct to the preserving pan and cold table. A steak spread with crushed mustard seed before cooking is more acceptable than served with a fiery dollop of raw heat.

There are many more imaginative commercial mustards on the market now in the manner of the famous *Moutarde de Meux* which contain the whole mustard seed ground with various emulsive mixtures of herbs and spices, wines, oils or vinegar.

Although I cannot give you specific recipes for making up some original home ground mustards I can give you some good reasonably inexpensive ideas to experiment with.

To start with you will need either black, white or yellow mustard seeds or a mixture of them – some you may even be able to grow yourself. Toast them very lightly in the oven and grind them to a powder in a pestle and mortar. Attempt to sieve or blow away the coarser chaff leaving a fine speckled powder, then put this carefully to one side. Using the same pestle and mortar decide what flavouring you would like – perhaps tarragon, mixed herbs, garlic, black pepper, horseradish or onion – the choice is yours, just use your imagination. Grind this chosen substance to a smooth paste with a little oil – olive, sunflower etc. Add to this paste a little sweetener, brown or white sugar or honey and mix very well. To this mixture add the mustard powder, grinding and pounding for all you are worth and adding a little more oil as you go until the paste is very thick and smooth. For the sharpeners, remember what the original flavouring was and make a choice from wine vinegars, vinegar, wine, dry cider, lemon juice or some of those lovely home-made vinegars like horseradish vinegar whose pungent flavour will not be lost. Add slowly, still beating to ensure a good emulsification, until you have the texture and taste required. I prefer to use very little oil and rather more vinegar but the combinations are endless. Keep in a well sealed jar in the refrigerator and allow to stand at room temperature for a while before using. Black mustard seed is very pungent, the brown mustard less so and the white or yellow mustard seed is relatively mild.

CHOW-CHOW

Chow-chow is a similar pickle in all respects to mustard pickle and piccalilli and these two pickles are known as chow-chow in the USA. However, on the continent, piccalilli is a spicy mixture not a mustardy one, and chow-chow served as a dessert in Chinese restaurants is a different thing altogether.

1kg/2lb 4oz green tomatoes	25g/1oz allspice berries
1kg/2lb 4oz silverskin onions or shallots	25g/1oz coriander seeds
	15g/½oz cardomum
1kg/2lb 4oz small cucumbers	24 whole cloves
1kg/2lb 4oz French beans	2 pieces cinnamon stick
1kg/2lb 4oz cauliflower	12 bay leaves
1kg/2lb 4oz celery	500g/1lb 2oz white sugar
1kg/2lb 4oz hard, white cabbage	175g/6oz mustard powder
sea salt	25g/1oz turmeric powder
3 litres/5 pints white vinegar	100g/4oz plain flour

hot, dry, sterile jars with non-metal lids

Wash all the vegetables. Quarter the tomatoes, peel the onion, leave the cucumbers as they are, string the beans and slice them cross-wise. Divide the cauliflower into florets and cut the celery and cabbage into small pieces. Lay them all on flat dishes and sprinkle fairly liberally with salt. Leave for 24 hours. In the meantime, put the vinegar and spices, with the exception of the turmeric and mustard, into a stainless steel pan and bring to the boil. Put to one side and leave to get cold. Drain the vegetables well, rinse them briefly in cold water and shake dry. Strain the vinegar and put it into a large stainless steel pan, taking a little to add to the sugar, mustard, turmeric and flour. Mix this to a smooth paste. Bring the vinegar to the boil and add the paste stirring continuously to ensure a nice, smooth mixture. Add the vegetables and simmer for 20 minutes. Pot and seal.

Store for at least 2 months before using. The quantities are very large so reduce for preference. All pickles containing mustard powder and flour thicken considerably during cooking and keeping time.

MUSTARD PICKLE AND PICCALILLI

Mustard pickle and piccalilli were the result of a fashionable rise in the popularity of Eastern foods brought about by the British Empire builders. The pickles were extremely ferocious, using quantities of fiery spices which we would now find unacceptable. Paradoxically, the people who may have benefited most from this type of pickling, which both preserved excess vegetables and gave a lift to very plain food, were those who could ill afford the expensive spices required. But despite all drawbacks the liking for these pungent accompaniments persisted and flourished to this day, although the exaggerated seasonings have been adapted to make more palatable and economic pickles.

The common factors in most mustard pickles and piccalillis are mustard powder or seed, and turmeric powder which gives the bright golden appearance. The main differences between the two pickles are that the mustard pickle contains both vegetables and dried or fresh fruit which is left in larger pieces and cooked in the sweetened sauce for some time. Piccalilli has vegetables cut into small dice which are barely cooked at all in a sauce which is rarely sweetened to any degree. As a matter of choice the spices may be left whole in the pickles rather than strained off before adding to the vegetables.

In either of these pickles the basic methods of preparation remain the same, but the differences in the strength or flavour of the sauces give individuality. I have therefore given instructions on preparation followed by suggestions for making several sauces.

apples	peel, core and dice
green beans	string and slice crosswise
carrots	peel and dice
cauliflower	divide into small florets
courgettes	slice crosswise
pickling cucumbers	peel and dice
gherkins	slice crosswise
green tomatoes	quarter and seed
marrows	peel, seed and dice
nasturtium seeds	leave whole
small onions or shallots	peel and slice if large
peppers	seed and small dice
radish pods	leave whole
prunes, sultanas (only for mustard pickle)	chop and add 10 minutes before end of cooking

BASIC METHOD OF PREPARATION FOR PICCALILLI

Prepare the vegetables as above and lay on a large dish or bowl, sprinkle with 100g/4oz sea salt to each 1kg/2lb 4oz of vegetables making sure that the layers get a good helping. Cover and leave overnight. (There are those who prefer to immerse the vegetables overnight in a brine made up with 100g/4oz salt to 1.15 litre/2 pints water but I find that this gives a soft pickle.) The next day put the vegetables into a colander and rinse under cold running water, shake and drain very well. Make up the sauce as shown and mix the vegetables into it while still boiling. For a soft pickle cook the vegetables with the sauce for 5 minutes for a crisper pickle just bring the mixture to the boil and for a very crisp pickle mix the vegetables in off the heat. Pack immediately and seal whilst hot.

An easy way to make Mustard Pickle is to follow the preparation given above but simmer the ingredients gently in the sauce for approximately 1 hour.

TWO GOOD SAUCES

750ml/1¼ pints vinegar	1 tablespoon black peppercorns
1 tablespoon dried red chillies	1 tablespoon cornflour
2 cloves garlic	1 tablespoon turmeric powder
piece root ginger	1 tablespoon mustard powder

Boil together 600ml/1 pint of the vinegar, the spices and bruised garlic. Remove from the heat, cover and allow to become quite cold. Strain and mix to a smooth paste with the cornflour, turmeric and mustard, add the remaining vinegar and continue as in the given method.

2 cloves garlic
25g/1oz fresh horseradish
2 teaspoon black peppercorns
1 teaspoon whole allspice
25g/1oz shallots
2 pieces root ginger

6 whole cloves
750ml/1¼ pints vinegar
1 tablespoon turmeric powder
2 level tablespoons mustard powder
¼ teaspoon cayenne pepper

Bruise the garlic, grate the horseradish and peel and chop the shallots. Lightly bruise the whole spices and ginger. Put these ingredients into a stainless steel pan with 600ml/1 pint of the vinegar and boil for 5 minutes. Mix the remaining ingredients with the rest of the vinegar until it is a smooth paste. Add the strained spiced vinegar and continue as in the given method.

N

Nectarine

The nectarine is a smooth-skinned peach with an apricot to gold-red colour depending on the variety and the flesh is either white or pale gold. To my mind the texture and taste is a cross between a ripe eating plum and an apricot and it is known to be related to the apricot, cherry and plum. Nectarines are often borne on a peach tree, from which they derive, and although I have grown a tree from the stone it has proved to be barren, so it would seem a more sensible idea to buy a small tree from a reputable nursery and take their advice on planting and training. Several varieties grow well in Britain, particularly if you have a south facing wall and, as they are such a delicious fruit, it is worth the time and expense of having a go. Imported nectarines come into the shops during May to September from Britain (usually hothouse), the continent and USA. Larger, luxury varieties come from South Africa during December to March.

Nectarines are really too good to eat in any other way but fresh. However, the recipes given for Apricots and Peaches work very well.

O

Olive

Those grey and ghostly shadows springing from barren rock and fertile plain throughout the Mediterranean regions represent not only a livelihood to those who own them but also symbolize joy, happiness and peace. This most ancient of cultivated trees, squabbled over by the Gods and beloved by the Impressionists brings forth a bitter fruit which, in its varying stages of ripening, green to pale gold, purple pink, red and black, is steeped and treated, cured or brined to give us the olives so necessary to southern European cooking. Some olives are small and green, others black and as large as a walnut, with many degrees of succulence between. Olives also provide us with that most important of oils, from the fruity, rich, green pressings of Greece, Italy and Cyprus to the fine *vierge* oil of Provence.

Traditionally the olives are steeped in a solution of water and wood ash but, more domestically, into a salt and water solution of 100g/4oz salt to 4 litres/7 pints water. They are then left until the colour changes. Removed and drained, each one is then slit carefully several times with a very sharp knife, and submerged in cold water for a further two or three days – the water being gently changed every day. They are then transferred to another, weaker, brine solution and a little olive oil poured on top. Finally, they are sealed and left until they have lost their bitterness. When this has occurred, an amount suitable for immediate use is removed, drained and put into a jar with garlic and vinegar and a little oil is poured on top. They are then left for one week before using. This last is a refinement that purists may not approve of, preferring the olive to be immersed in oil rather than vinegar. Olives are dried in the sun and packed into barrels with salt.

246

Onion

The predominant member of the *Allium* family which includes shallots, leeks, garlic, chives, Welsh onion, rocambole etc. If you have ever been left without onions in the kitchen, you will realize how vital they are to cooking, particularly in the making of pickles and chutneys.
Onions fall into five categories:

The all purpose onion, varies from pale gold to blood red and is the most valuable in cooking and preserving.
The Spanish onion is mild enough to be eaten raw or as a whole braised vegetable. Some pickles specifically require a mild onion.
Button and *pickling onions* are small and fast growing and not to be confused with shallots which are also ideal for pickling, and excellent in preserves and cooking.
Silverskin onions are very small and pure white, and not as popular in Britain as on the continent but ideal for cocktail onions and in mixed pickles.
Spring onions are used principally in salads.
Scallions in southern England are the green top of small onions, in the north of England it is a shallot and in America it is a spring onion.

The first four categories of onion are best grown from sets (tiny onion bulbs prepared from the year before) planted in shallow drills well away from beans and peas with which they are antipathetic. Make sure that they have a good soil, keep well weeded and thinned using the thinnings as you go. Spring onions are grown from seed. In a small garden I find it best to concentrate on growing the small pickling onions particularly silverskins which do not appear so readily on the market. I buy the larger onions from the shops as they are easily obtainable and there is usually a wide choice since Britain is one of the largest importers and growers of onions. Make sure that the onions you buy are dry and firm with no mould, otherwise they are likely to be brown right through.

Although onions are considered to be very good for you they are also repugnant when second hand. Black coffee or fresh parsley will remove any odour from the breath!

247

PICKLED ONIONS

Peel the onions, taking as little from the base and crown as possible as this causes bruising. A very good way of ensuring that the skins come off quickly, and at the same time subduing those dreaded fumes, is to drop the onions into a pan of boiling water, leave for one minute, drain and dip into cold water. Peel under cold water using a stainless steel knife to prevent discolouration. Transfer them to a fresh bowl of cold water as you go. Drain well.

For a crisp pickled onion just lay them in a large dish and sprinkle with 50g/2oz sea salt to each kilogram/2lb 4oz of onions. Cover and leave overnight. The next day, rinse well, drain and dry. I prefer this method as it gives a crisp, well seasoned result.

For a softer pickle, brine the onions by leaving them overnight in a solution of 100g/4oz sea salt to 1 litre/1¾ pints water. Rinse, drain and dry well. An old-fashioned way of preparing the onions instead of using a salt method is to boil them in a mixture of milk and water for 10 minutes in order to soften and reduce the flavour. Very small onions may be peeled and packed without further preparation. This is useful for tiny cocktail onions.

When the onions are prepared, make sure that they are absolutely dry before packing them firmly into dry, sterile jars with non-metal lids. Cover with either hot or cold spiced vinegar of your choice. Once again you will find that a hot vinegar will give a soft pickle whilst the cold vinegar gives a crisp, crunchy pickle. A handy hint if you are using white vinegar is to add a few drops of sweet almond oil to each jar to keep that pristine appearance – the tiny silverskin onions will benefit particularly from this. Silverskin onions should be pickled in a white vinegar and any of the following seasonings may be used: basil, nutmeg, celery seed, chilli, dill, chervil, rosemary. Pickled onions should be left for at least one month before using, to allow the spiced vinegar to penetrate. Try experimenting with your own vinegar, e.g., horseradish, chilli etc.

VINEGARS FOR PICKLING ONIONS

1. 1.15 litre/2 pints brown malt vinegar
    2 tablespoons mustard seed
    2 tablespoons whole cloves
    2 tablespoons black peppercorns
    2 tablespoons whole allspice
    2 tablespoons dried red chillies

2. 1.15 litre/2 pints red wine vinegar
    1 tablespoon dried red chillies
    whole fresh tarragon leaves
    1 teaspoon whole cloves

Boil the vinegar first and leave it to get cold. Pack the chillies, tarragon and cloves into the jars with the onions.

3. 1.15 litre/2 pints white wine vinegar
    a few pieces mace
    1 teaspoon whole cloves
    bay leaves
    sliced pimento

Boil the vinegar, mace and cloves together in a stainless steel pan. Strain before using. Pack the bay leaves and pimento into the jars with the onions.

SWEET PICKLED ONIONS

Add 25g/1oz sugar, white or soft brown, to any of the vinegar variations given previously. Stir it in to the boiling vinegar just before removing from heat but do make sure that it has dissolved properly.

ONION PICKLE

white vinegar   1kg/2lb 4oz medium-sized onions
black peppercorns   100g/4oz sea salt
1 garlic clove

dry, sterile jars with non-metal lids

Boil the vinegar with the peppercorns and thinly sliced garlic and leave to get cold. Peel and slice the onions paper thin and dissolve the salt in the water. Leave the onions to soak in the brine solution for 1 hour. Turn into a colander and run under cold water. Wash and shake well dry. Pack into the jars and cover with the vinegar plus bits and pieces. Seal tightly.

Very good with green salad and not quite so repetitive as pickled onions.

249

HOT ONION SAUCE

1kg/2lb 4oz onions
675g/1lb 8oz red plums
75g/3oz sultanas
4 chillies
piece root ginger
750ml/1¼ pints malt vinegar

1 level tablespoon ground allspice
1½ tablespoons mustard powder
2 teaspoons turmeric powder
2 teaspoons fresh ground nutmeg
175g/6oz brown sugar
3 tablespoons sea salt

hot, dry, sterile bottles with corks

Peel and chop the onions, wash and stone the plums, chop the sultanas, shred the chillies and bruise the ginger. Put all of these together into a stainless steel pan with half the vinegar, bring to the boil and then simmer until very soft. Mix the allspice, mustard, turmeric and nutmeg to a smooth paste with a little of the vinegar. Pass the contents of the pan through a fine sieve and return the purée to the clean pan. Heat gently and add the spiced paste, sugar and salt. Stir in the remaining vinegar and bring to the boil stirring well until the sugar has dissolved. Simmer for approximately 20 minutes. Leave until cold. Bottle and seal.

Better with cold meat than any commercial product and a wonderful fillip to savoury sauces.

MIXED PICKLE

A MILD VINEGAR

1 litre/1¾ pints white or brown malt
  vinegar
50g/2oz shallots

25g/1oz mustard seed
1 tablespoon mixed pickling spice

Peel and chop the shallots and put with the remaining ingredients into a stainless steel pan. Bring to the boil and boil hard for 5 minutes. Remove from heat, cover and leave for 2 hours. Strain before using.

A HOT VINEGAR

1 litre/1¾ pints white vinegar
1 tablespoon mustard powder
2 cloves garlic

2 teaspoon sea salt
a few dried red chillies

Mix the mustard powder with a little of the vinegar. Peel and chop the garlic. Put all the ingredients including the mustard paste into a stainless steel pan and bring to the boil. Boil for 5 minutes. Cover and remove from the heat. Leave for 2 hours and then strain through a double muslin before using. Retrieve the chillies and keep them in reserve to add to each jar of pickle as you cover with vinegar.

Both of these vinegars are fairly pungent but the hot vinegar has the definite edge; on my market stall it is affectionately known as 'The Colonel's Choleric'.

Vegetables to use:

silverskin or shallot onions	peeled
small gherkins	left whole
nasturtium seeds	brine blanched
radish pods	brine blanched
courgettes	unpeeled, thick sliced
small scarlet runner beans	left whole
cauliflower	in florets
carrots	peeled and cut in fine slices
peppers	cut in short thick strips

dry, sterile jars with non-metal lids

Prepare the vegetables and pack them into the jars. Cover with the cold strained vinegar.

VEGETABLE PICKLE FROM FRANCE

FOR THE VINEGAR:

12 silverskin onions	10 black peppercorns
hot red pepper	3 whole cloves garlic
1 litre/1¾ pints white wine vinegar	15g/½oz sea salt
6 branches tarragon	50g/2oz white sugar
8 whole cloves	

Slice the onions, wash and chop the pepper and put all the ingredients into a stainless steel pan. Bring gently to the boil and boil for 5 minutes. Remove from the heat, cover and leave to get cold. Pour into a jar and seal with a non-metal lid. Leave for 15 days to steep.

251

TO MAKE THE PICKLE:

very small gherkins	left whole
cucumber	unpeeled cut into thick slices
cauliflower	cut into florets

large, dry, sterile preserving jars

Boil up 2 litres/3½ pints water with 100g/4oz sea salt. Blanch the prepared vegetables in this boiling brine for 5 minutes. Drain well and pack into jars, cover with the cold strained vinegar. Seal and keep in a very cool place for 1 month before using.

The cucumber goes soft if kept for long but the taste is unimpaired.

BROWN SPICY SAUCE

450g/1lb shallots	1 tablespoon mushroom ketchup
1 clove garlic	1 tablespoon anchovy paste
1 tablespoon black treacle	½ tablespoon whole cloves
1 teaspoon sea salt	600ml/1 pint brown malt vinegar
6 dried red chillies	1 dessertspoon cornflour

2 hot, dry, sterile bottles with corks

Peel and chop the shallots and garlic, and put into a stainless steel pan with all the other ingredients except the vinegar and cornflour. Just cover with water and bring to the boil, then simmer until the shallots are very soft. Press through a sieve and return to the pan. Take 1 tablespoon of the vinegar and mix with the cornflour to a smooth paste. Add the remaining vinegar to the pan and boil for 3 minutes; stir in the cornflour paste and continue to stir until the mixture is smooth and slightly glossy. Bottle and seal. A thinner sauce can be made by omitting the cornflour.

This sauce does not keep for very long unless it is sterilized so if you have made a large quantity it would be best to continue, after bottling, to sterilize as for Spiced Apple Ketchup, page 50.

NUN'S SAUCE

3 cloves garlic
3 shallots
1 tablespoon anchovies
1 rounded tablespoon cayenne pepper

1 tablespoon soft brown sugar
1.15 litre/2 pints vinegar
1 teaspoon whole cloves

dry, sterile stone jar with lid

Peel and chop the garlic and shallots. Pound them to a paste with the anchovies. Mix the cayenne pepper and the sugar to a smooth paste with a little of the vinegar. Crumble the cloves and put everything into the pot. Seal tightly and leave for 1 month, shaking day and night. Strain through a muslin. Bottle and seal with corks.

I cannot believe that the good sisters required such hair raising additions to their diet. Perhaps they saved the sauce for visiting bishops.

STORING ONIONS

If you grow your own onions you will probably need to dry them. Leave the onions in the soil until the leaves turn yellow and drooping, lift them and leave them in the sun to dry. If the weather is not suitable find a warm shelf somewhere. When the leaf has dried right down and the onion skin looks papery, either twist the tops right off and hang the onions in nets or leave the leaf on the onion and plait them one above the other to make a string. Keep stored in a dry, airy atmosphere otherwise they will start to sprout.

DRYING ONION RINGS

Use medium to large onions, peel them and cut them into uniform 5mm/¼ inch slices, making sure that they are all the same otherwise you will have difficulty in preventing scorching. Part the slices into rings and put them into a wire basket, dunk into boiling water for a count of 30 and whip them out again, drain, and plunge them into cold water. Drain well and dry on kitchen towels until all surplus moisture is absorbed. Spread on a sponge rack and leave in a cool oven (65°C/150°F or gas mark ¼) with the door ajar until the rings are just crisp and quite dry. If the temperature is too high or the rings too thin they will burn instantly. Cool and store in an airtight jar.

To reconstitute soak in warm water for 30 minutes. Throw into stews etc. just as they are. A marvellous standby.

Orange

When talking about oranges we generally speak in terms of sweet oranges or those suitable for dessert or culinary uses and bitter oranges, those which are used for making marmalade and with specialized culinary values. Sweet oranges originally came from Asia, but as they gradually evolved a climatic tolerance they became established throughout southern Europe and the Mediterranean. During the seventeenth and eighteenth centuries a considerable vogue arose in Britain among the owners of conservatories for possessing this beautiful tree with shiny leaves and headily perfumed blossom and although the fruit was still a considerable luxury it became popular in the more fashionable areas. Nowadays the demand for oranges and the improvement in transport and storage has ensured a constant supply of reasonably priced fruits throughout the year. The vitamin C content in oranges is enormously high, as is the pectin and acid content. Preserves made from sweet oranges are of the more elegant variety – delicate conserves and jellies, exquisite 'spoon sweets' from Greece, summery curds and light sweet marmalades.

There are three main types of sweet oranges:

navel oranges which have a bumpy little protruberance at one end, hence the name. The rind is usually thick and the flesh of good flavour and nearly always seedless. However they cannot be relied upon to be juicy. Imported from Australia, Brazil, Spain, Morocco and South Africa.

blood oranges as the name implies the flesh has a fiery pigment which becomes more obvious as the fruit ripens. Imported from Malta, Egypt and Spain.

common oranges this description covers a great variety of oranges from different areas. Some of the more familiar are Valencia, Maroc and Jaffa. The thickness of peel, the quantity of juice and degree of sweetness all vary considerably and the colour of the peel unfortunately will give no reliable indication.

Bitter oranges made their appearance originally in southern Europe. They are a much hardier tree and may even be grown against a south-facing wall in frost-free sunny areas of Britain. A neighbour of mine has grown a splendid orange tree which bears a prolific crop. It was grown from a pip and resides on her windowsill. Bitter oranges make the traditional tangy marmalades and are virtually unsuitable for any other preserves, although the peel and juice make exceptional flavourings for savoury dishes. The orange sauce which accompanies duck should properly be made with bitter oranges and it is worth freezing a few for this purpose as the flavour is unique and cannot be copied with sweet oranges. The juice from bitter oranges can be used in the same way as lemons or as an alternative to 'bitters' at the cocktail hour. In France the bitter orange is known as *bigarade*.

Seville oranges   a fruit with a deep orange, pitted skin of sharp and bitter taste. The flesh and juice are sour and inedible when raw. Available from December to February and are imported from Spain.
Bergamot   an orange which is primarily used in the perfume industry for its rind which contains invaluable aromatic oils.

It is always advisable to wash oranges in warm water, even scrubbing them gently with a soft brush as they are frequently sprayed with gas to either improve the colour or for storage. If you are fortunate enough to be picking oranges cut them from the branch, do not break or tear, for once the peel is split it will be useless for storing. The weight of oranges is very difficult to gauge as they vary considerably in size and thickness of pith and this guide is only approximate. Five large, thick-skinned Jaffas will weigh 1 kilogram/2lb 4oz but for a good preserve you will need to use an orange with a thinner rind and less pith. Seven medium, thin-skinned oranges or 8-9 small, thin-skinned oranges should make up to 1 kg/2lb 4oz.
   Orange blossom is used to make orange flower water which is frequently used in more delicate preserves. It is also candied to make the most attractive sweetmeats.

ORANGE JAM USING A PRESSURE COOKER

1kg/2lb 4oz small, thin-skinned	600ml/1 pint water
oranges	1kg/2lb 4oz white sugar
3 lemons	

5 hot, dry, sterile jam jars

Wash the fruit and, working on a large dish, slice the oranges thinly and evenly. Peel the lemon and chop the rind, squeezing out the juice. Remove both orange and lemon pips and tie these into a muslin bag with the lemon rind. Put the orange slices and any excess juice, the muslin bag and the lemon rind into the pressure cooker with the water (remembering to remove the trivet first). Cover and bring to H/15lb pressure for 10 minutes. Reduce at room temperature. Remove the muslin bag and add the warmed sugar, heat gently stirring well until it has dissolved. Bring to the boil and boil hard, uncovered, until a set is obtained. Allow to cool before potting. Seal when cold.

Like many fruits with a thick skin oranges take a long time to soften. A pressure cooker is a quick and economical piece of equipment for this job.

ORANGE JELLY

1kg/2lb 4oz bitter oranges (Sevilles)	7 litres/12 pints water
1kg/2lb 4oz sweet oranges	white sugar
3 lemons	

9 hot, dry, sterile jam jars

Wash the fruit and, working on a large plate, chop it up quite small. Put all this pulp together with any juices that may have been collected into a preserving pan with the water, and cook until the contents are reduced to half their original quantity. This will take quite a while as you should not boil furiously. Turn into a jelly bag and leave to drain overnight into a clean bowl and resist the temptation to prod or poke as this will cause the jelly to become cloudy. The next day measure the juice gained and for each 600ml/1 pint take 450g/1lb warmed sugar. Return the juice to the pan and heat gently, add the sugar stirring well until it has dissolved and bring to the boil. Boil hard until a set is obtained. Pot and seal.

This is a sharp jelly which is as good as a savoury with cold meats as it is excellent for a breakfast jelly.

ORANGE AND BASIL JELLY

500g/1lb 2oz bitter oranges	3 litres/5 pints water
500g/1lb 2oz sweet oranges	a large bunch of fresh basil
2 lemons	white sugar

12 small, hot, dry, sterile jars

Wash the fruit, chop the whole lot – a liquidizer may help the process – and put pulp, peel, juice into a preserving pan with the water. Separate

256

the basil into two halves, wash well and add one half to the pan. Cook until all the fruit is soft and the quantity reduced by half. Turn into a jelly bag and leave to drain overnight into a clean bowl. The next day measure the juice gained and for every 600ml/1 pint take 450g/1lb warmed sugar, return the juice to pan, heat gently and add the sugar stirring well until it has dissolved. Bring to the boil and boil until a set is obtained. In the meantime, make sure that the remaining basil is clean and dry and chop it very finely. Stir it into the finished jelly and allow to cool a little before potting, stir to disperse the bits. Pot. Seal when cold.

This is a lovely jelly with chicken, turkey etc., and, because of the delightful fragrance of basil, it is particularly nice to make. Basil may be added to any of the orange jelly recipes but I prefer this particular one as I feel that the bitter oranges with basil have an aromatic subtlety.

ORANGE AND ROSE GERANIUM JELLY

1kg/2lb 4oz bitter oranges
900ml/1½ pints water

a good handful of scented rose
  geranium leaves
700g/1lb 9oz white sugar

12 small, hot, dry, sterile jars

Wash the oranges, extract the juice and put to one side. Chop up the squeezed orange halves on a chopping board, and put them into a preserving pan with the water. Wash and dry the geranium leaves. Keeping back a few nicely shaped ones, add the rest to the pan, bring to the boil, cover and simmer until peel is very soft. Turn into a jelly bag and leave to drain overnight into a clean bowl. The next day mix the juice gained with the strained orange juice and measure the result – for every 600ml/1 pint gained take 450g/1lb warmed sugar. Return the juice to the pan, heat gently and add the sugar, stirring well until it has dissolved. Bring to the boil and boil hard until a set is obtained. Wash and dry the remaining geranium leaves. Allow the jelly to cool just a little and half-fill the jars. Suspend a leaf in each one and leave to cool just a little more. Fill up with jelly. Seal when cold.

An unusual jelly that is equally good without the geranium leaves.

ORANGE FRUIT CONSERVE

500g/1lb 2oz thin skinned sweet
   oranges
200g/7oz thin skinned lemons
500g/1lb 2oz good raisins (muscatels
   for preference)

200g/7oz walnuts (shelled)
200g/7oz almonds (shelled)
350g/12oz caster sugar
250ml/8fl. oz pineapple juice

4 hot, dry, sterile jars

Wash the oranges and slice very thinly. Squeeze the juice from the lemons. Seed the raisins if necessary. Chop the walnuts and blanch, skin and slice the almonds. Put orange slices, lemon juice, raisins, nuts, sugar and pineapple juice into a preserving pan, bring gently to the boil stirring well and then simmer until thick, cooked and hopefully a set is obtained. Pot and seal.

    As this preserve cannot be recommended for its setting properties it might be better to reduce the quantities by half although it is so good it will disappear like wildfire.

ORANGE AND WATER MELON CONSERVE

1kg/2lb 4oz prepared water melon
1725g/3lb 14oz white sugar
1 lemon

1kg/2lb 4oz prepared, sweet,
   thin-skinned oranges
300ml/½ pint water

8 hot, dry, sterile jam jars

Prepare the melon by removing the rind, seeds, pips and soft flesh. Cut into cubes and weigh. Put into a bowl with 725g/1lb 10oz of the sugar, cover and leave for 3 hours. Chop the lemon and tie it in a muslin bag. Turn the sugary melon into a preserving pan, add the muslin bag and simmer gently for 1 hour, stirring occasionally. To prepare the oranges, work on a large dish and peel, pip and divide them into quarters. Shred the rind of two of the oranges into very fine strips, and weigh to ensure that you do indeed have 1kg/2lb 4oz once they have been robbed of their skins. Boil the remaining 1kg/2lb 4oz sugar with the water in another larger preserving pan. When a thin syrup is formed add the orange segments, juices and shredded peel. Simmer gently for 1 hour until tender and transparent. Turn the water melon into the orange conserve and mix the two jams together and I hope that the bowl is big enough. Simmer gently for 10 minutes when the mixture should be very thick. Remove the muslin bag, giving it a good squeeze. Stir once more. Pot and seal.

A really delicious conserve with a certain touch of class.

ORANGE CURD

Orange curd recipes are simply the same as those recipes given for Lemon Curd, p.200, and although it is perfectly feasible to plug ahead using the same method I would give a word of advice which may be helpful. When taking your 1kg/2lb 4oz bright, juicy, thin-skinned oranges of which there will be approximately 9, use the rinds of all 9 but the juice of only 6. As oranges are usually sweeter and juicier than lemons this will ensure that the mixture is not too soft. Alternatively use the rinds and juice of 7 oranges and the juice of 2 small lemons to sustain a thick mixture which is also sharper.

ORANGE CURD WITH PEEL

1 large, sweet, thin-skinned, juicy
  orange
50g/2oz candied orange peel

100g/4oz caster sugar
100g/4oz unsalted butter
3 large, fresh eggs

4 small, hot, dry, sterile jars

Wash the orange, grate the rind finely and extract the juice. Chop the candied peel very small. Put the orange juice, grated rind, chopped peel, sugar and butter into a double boiler, heat gently and beat well until melted and mixed. Separate the egg yolks from the white and beat them until they are fluffy and golden. Add them to the mixture in the bowl and continue to beat well until the mixture is thick and creamy – take care not to overheat. Pot and seal.

A tasty, surprising curd which is particularly useful as a filling in Victoria sandwich.

ORANGE AND LEMON CURD

Use the Lemon Curd recipe, p.200, but take the rind and juice of 675g/1lb 8oz oranges (approximately 6) and the rind of 350g/12oz lemons (approximately 3).

PICKLED ORANGE RINGS

1kg/2lb 4oz small firm seedless oranges

900ml/1½ pints cider vinegar

900g/2lb white sugar

1 level tablespoon whole cloves

7cm/2¾ inches cinnamon stick

4 hot, dry, sterile jars with wide necks and non-metal lids

Wash the oranges well in warm water, cut them into 5mm/¼ inch slices and place them in a stainless steel pan. Just cover with water and simmer gently for 30 minutes or until the peel begins to soften. Remove with a perforated spoon and leave to drain. Add all the other ingredients to the cooking water and heat gently, stirring well until the sugar has dissolved. Bring to the boil and boil hard for 10 minutes. Remove from heat and return the slices to the syrup and bring back to the boil, trying to ensure that the slices do not disintegrate before your eyes. Immediately remove the slices with the perforated spoon and pack them into the jars. Reboil the syrup until it is very thick and remove the cinnamon stick. Pour the syrup over the fruit to cover well and make sure that there are no air bubbles. A few of the cloves should be allowed to slide into the jars, although they may stain the pickle a little they do add to the flavour. Seal.

This is another very attractive pickle but like most orange pickles etc., it tends to discolour slightly if kept too long. A whole bird glazed and decorated with orange rings makes a very festive centrepiece for a cold buffet.

ORANGE CHUTNEY

1kg/2lb 4oz sweet oranges
500g/1lb 2oz cooking apples
2 large onions
25g/1oz chillies
225g/8oz seedless raisins

225g/8oz preserved ginger
50g/2oz sea salt
1.15 litre/2 pints malt vinegar
450g/1lb soft brown sugar

5 hot, dry, sterile jars with non-metal lids

Wash and peel the oranges, removing all the pith and pips. While the peel is aromatic and bitter the pith can, without the proper processes, be just bitter. Wash, peel and core the apples. Peel the onions and de-seed the chillies. Now, either mince or chop the orange peel and flesh, apples, onions, chillies, raisins and ginger. Put into a stainless steel pan with the salt and half the vinegar. Cook until very soft. Dissolve the sugar in the remaining vinegar and add this to the pan. Simmer until thick and cooked. Pot and seal.

Store for at least 2 months before using. A thick, sweet, fruit chutney.

CUMBERLAND SAUCE FOR KEEPING

2 large sweet oranges
1 lemon
1 shallot
225g/8oz redcurrant jelly

1 teaspoon Dijon mustard (or
  equivalent)
150ml/$\frac{1}{4}$ pint port
2 teaspoons arrowroot

small, hot, dry, sterile jars

Wash the fruit and peel the rind from 1 orange and the lemon, cut into very fine threads and put into a small saucepan. Peel and mince the shallot and add to the saucepan. Just cover with cold water, bring to the boil and cook for 5 minutes. Drain well. Put the jelly into a double boiler or a small china bowl set over a pan of hot water, and heat until the jelly has melted. Pass through a sieve and return to the clean bowl. Continue to cook gently over the pan of hot water and add the mustard, port, the juice from both oranges and the lemon, the cooked rind and shallot. Stir very well and cook for 5 minutes. In the meantime, mix the arrowroot to a smooth paste with a little water. Add it to the mixture in the bowl, stirring well and cook for 3 minutes when it should be blended and look glazed. Pot and seal.

Keep at least 1 week before using and keep in a refrigerator once opened.

PRESERVED ORANGE PEEL

1kg/2lb 4oz oranges
white sugar

earthenware crock or large glass jar

Wash and dry the oranges thoroughly. Remove the peel in neat segments scraping off as much pith as possible. Cut each segment into hair strips and put a 5mm/¼ inch layer into the bottom of the jar, cover with sugar and continue the process until the jar is full. Finish with a layer of sugar. Seal and leave for 1 week, shaking it every time you go by and even standing the jar upside down to obtain a good mixture. Top up with more peel and sugar as it becomes available. Store in a cool dark place.

A wonderful way to use up surplus orange peel. Peel preserved like this makes marvellous flavouring and the longer you keep it the richer it becomes.

PRESERVED ORANGE PEEL IN SALT

sweet or bitter orange peel   a little orange juice
sea salt

wide-necked jar with lid

Cut the well washed and dried peel into small pieces. Put into a jar, sprinkle lightly with salt and enough juice to moisten. Seal tightly and shake well. Every now and again give a good shaking.

Excellent flavouring for soups, stews etc., particularly lamb.

CRYSTALLIZED ORANGE SQUARES

1kg/2lb 4oz sweet firm oranges   4 teaspoons white malt vinegar
575g/1lb 4oz white sugar   300ml/½ pint water

Wash and dry the oranges. Working on a large dish, peel the fruit and discard the peel and pith, pips and skin. A quick way to achieve this is to drop them into boiling water for a few minutes, drain and allow to cool before starting. Cut the fruit into squares (this is rather tricky so do ensure that you have chosen firm oranges) and lay them on a rack to dry for 24 hours. Using a small, deep saucepan make a syrup of the sugar, vinegar and water, and when it is very thick dip each square into the syrup making sure that it is completely covered. Do only one square at a time and use a long skewer to save accidents. Lay the finished squares of orange on a flat tin and place in a cool oven to dry. Store between sheets of greaseproof paper in a wooden box. Keep in a cool dry place.

Although they do not keep long, orange squares make a good addition to the crystallized fruit tray at Christmas.

CANDIED ORANGE PEEL

See Candied Lemon Peel, p.204 or Candied Grapefruit Peel, p.185.

TO DRY ORANGE PEEL

As for Lemon Peel, p.205.

MARMALADE

Prior to the arrival on the preserving scene of a strong-minded and resourceful Scotswoman called Mrs Keiller, marmalade had only a somewhat vague and indeterminate pedigree. Did it really come by its name due to confusion in the minds of Portuguese explorers who called the orange, newly discovered, *marmelo*, the Portuguese for quince? Or was it a corruption of the Greek *meli-*(honey) and *melon* (apple)? Or could it have been the sweet potted oranges which a devoted French chef whipped up for his ailing mistress Mary Queen of Scots – hence *Marie est malade*? By the 1800s marmalade was very firmly established by Mrs Keiller, the wife of a Dundee grocer. Appalled at the apparent mismanagement of her husband who had inadvertantly purchased a large quantity of bitter oranges which would not sell, she set about utilizing them in such a way as to be able to recoup their losses. Enterprising lady that she was, she established a devotion to marmalade that exists to this day and has made Great Britain the leading consumer and exporter of this extraordinary bitter-sweet conserve so dear to our hearts.

A marmalade is made of citrus fruits and sugar using the peel and a percentage of pith to give a tangy result. It can be improved upon and experimented with by the addition of other fruits, spices, alcohol etc., and may be fine and golden, thick, dark and chunky or purely a jelly, but it should always have the same background bitterness that is unique to marmalade. Lime, lemon and grapefruit all make good marmalades but sweet oranges make something more akin to a jam as do other non-citrus fruits.

For ideal results soak the cut fruit overnight in the water that it is to be cooked in, as this gives the best pectin extraction ensuring a good set. Take care when making marmalade not to boil beyond the set – it is easily done and can spoil both flavour and appearance. One of the most common mistakes is leaving the pan still boiling while you are testing for a set, so always remember to remove it, however briefly, from the heat.

SEVILLE ORANGE MARMALADE

1kg/2lb 4oz Seville oranges   2.25 litres/4 pints water
1 lemon   2kg/4lb 8oz white sugar

9 hot, dry, sterile, jam jars

Wash all the fruit and, working on a large dish, either slice thinly, chop coarsely or mince it, collect all the pips and tie them into a muslin bag. Put this with the fruit and water into a deep bowl, cover and leave to stand for 24 hours. Transfer to a preserving pan and simmer gently until the contents are soft and reduced by about half. Add the warmed sugar stirring well until it is dissolved, bring to the boil and boil hard until a set is obtained. Leave to stand for 10 minutes. Pot. Seal when cold.

In my opinion by far the best method.

ORANGE AND TANGERINE MARMALADE

1kg/2lb 4oz Seville oranges   2kg/4lb 8oz white sugar
1 large lemon   4.5 litres/8 pints water
5 tangerines

9 hot, dry, sterile jam jars

Follow the method for Seville Orange Marmalade for a sweeter marmalade with that inimitable taste of tangerine.

OLD-FASHIONED BITTER MARMALADE

1kg/2lb 4oz Seville oranges
1 lemon

2.25 litres/4 pints water
2kg/4lb 8oz brown sugar

7 hot, dry, sterile jam jars

Follow the method for Seville Orange Marmalade. It is worth remembering with any marmalade that if you prefer a very thick and bitter marmalade you should leave all the pith on the peel. Whereas if you prefer a milder flavour carefully remove the pith and put it into a muslin bag with the pips. Great variations on the flavour of marmalade can be obtained by using soft light brown, brown or dark brown Muscovado sugar. Molasses or black treacle used in the proportions of two tablespoons to 1kg/2lb 4oz of oranges also gives a darker result. The browner the sugar the richer and darker the marmalade which is particularly good with alcohol added.

BRANDY, RUM OR WHISKY MARMALADE

Take any of the previous marmalade recipes, particularly those made with brown sugar, and give an extra zing with a little alcohol, which may be added in one of two ways. 150ml/¼ pint of alcohol can be added to the water where the fruit is soaking providing it is to be used in the recipe, or two generous tablespoons of alcohol can be stirred into the marmalade just before taking from the boil. Make sure, however, that it does get a very brief boiling and a good stir before removing from the heat.

MARMALADE USING A PRESSURE COOKER

Any of the previous recipes can be made using a pressure cooker. As the firm peel of all citrus fruit can take a long time to soften by conventional methods this is both economical and time saving. However, in order to extract the maximum amount of pectin from the fruit prior to cooking I would suggest that you choose a recipe in which the fruit is soaked for at least 12 hours before cooking.

Follow the method of preparation suggested by your chosen recipe but because you will require less water reduce the amount given to the proportions of 1.15 litres/2 pints to 1kg/2lb 4oz of fruit. Remember not to overfill the pan (most pressure cookers will not take more than 2kg/4lb). Remove the trivet and place the cut or whole fruit and the water in the pan, cover and bring to M/10lb pressure for 10 minutes. Remove from the heat and allow the pressure to reduce at room temperature. Continue as given in the recipe but do not replace the cover after the sugar has been added. Take care not to overcook the fruit for not only does it become flaccid and uninteresting, losing both colour and flavour, but the valuable pectin content is reduced.

ANGELICA MARMALADE

Chopped, preserved angelica added a few minutes before the end of cooking, adds a sweet and perfumed flavour to any marmalade recipe.

CORIANDER MARMALADE

1 teaspoon to 1 tablespoon of coriander seed crushed and added to the bag of pips gives a delightfully exotic touch to marmalade.

GINGER MARMALADE

Ginger may be added to any of the previous marmalade recipes to give a luxury preserve but there is no magic secret. For every 1kg/2lb 4oz of oranges used add 25g/1oz of root ginger to the pip bag and 225g/8oz preserved or crystallized ginger, well chopped, to the marmalade when the sugar is added. If you feel that preserved ginger is a little expensive, add ground ginger to taste with the sugar instead.

SPICED MARMALADE

Add either 1 teaspoon mixed ground spice or spices of your choice with the sugar. Alternatively add whole spices, e.g., root ginger, mace, cinnamon etc., to the muslin bag with the pips.

FRUIT MARMALADE

2kg/4lb 8oz fruit made up with
grapefruit, sweet oranges, Seville
oranges, lemons and apples

1.15 litres/2 pints water
3.5kg/8lb white sugar

10 hot, dry, sterile jam jars

Wash the citrus fruit, remove peel with a potato peeler and leave to soak overnight in a little of the water. The next day transfer the peel and water to a small saucepan, cover and simmer until soft. Remove without discarding the water and cut into fine shreds. Working on a large dish remove the pith and pips from the citrus fruit and put to one side, chop the flesh and put it with the rind and the water it was cooked in into a preserving pan. Wash, peel, core and chop the apples and add them to the other fruit. Tie the peel and cores into a muslin bag with the pips and pith and add this with the remaining water to the pan. Cover and cook gently until it is all soft and pulpy – about 30 minutes. Remove the muslin bag giving it a good squeeze without burning yourself! Add the warmed sugar stirring well until it has dissolved. Bring to the boil and boil hard until a set is obtained. Allow to stand for 10 minutes. Pot. Seal when cold.

The softness of set will depend upon which fruit you use in the greater proportion. If you are pushed for time mince all the citrus fruit including the peel and go straight into the cooking process, but cook for at least 1 hour to ensure that the peel is soft.

MARMALADE USING A FREEZER

Seville oranges come into the shops for a very limited and rarely opportune period, so rather than losing the opportunity of home-made marmalade throughout the coming year, buy the oranges and freeze them for future use. Wash them with lukewarm water, dry well and pack into heavy polythene bags, extract the air and seal tightly. Unfortunately about 10 per cent of the pectin extract is lost during freezing and to counteract this add 25 per cent more fresh fruit.

Alternatively prepare and cook the fruit to the point at which the sugar should be added. (This can be done speedily using a blender and pressure cooker.) Pack the mixture into rigid polythene containers leaving at least 3cm/1¼ inches headroom. Seal, label freeze. Use as soon as practical.

If using a pressure cooker and a recipe cooking the whole fruit, there is no need to thaw before using.

267

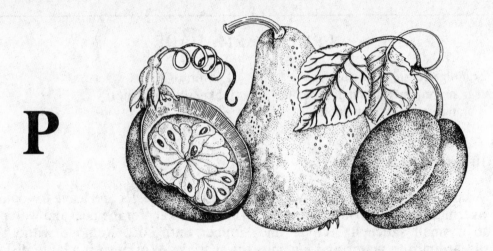

P

Papaw or *Papaya*

The papaw is a strange and irregular, palm-like tree which grows in tropical countries. The fruit is something between a melon and a mango, growing as large as 30cm/1 foot on occasions. Green when unripe and yellow-orange when ripe, the papaw is full of vitamins and has magical and practical properties attributed to it; for instance the milky juice obtained from the leaves, stem or fruit will tenderize meat and alleviate asthma among many other uses. The flesh is usually cut in slices and sprinkled with lemon juice. When unripe it makes excellent chutneys and may be used when ripe in preserves. Experiment by substituting papaw in melon, marrow and peach recipes. I have had success with crystallizing the fruit using the same method as for Candied Marrow, p.220. As imported papaws are expensive, hard, under-ripe peaches may be substituted for the following recipes.

PAPAW CHUTNEY

1kg/2lb 4oz green papaw
500g/1lb 2oz red and green peppers
450g/1lb firm, ripe tomatoes
350g/12oz onions
175g/6oz seedless raisins
6 red chillies
4 cloves garlic

25g/1oz fresh ginger root
½ teaspoon ground allspice
1 tablespoon sea salt
450ml/¾ pint white vinegar
575g/1lb 4oz white or soft light brown
 sugar

6 hot, dry, sterile jars with non-metal lids

Peel the papaw, discard the seeds and very soft flesh and cut the remainder into cubes. Seed and dice the peppers. Peel and chop the tomatoes (drop them into boiling water very briefly – this makes it much easier). Peel and chop the onions, chop the raisins. Peel and finely chop the garlic and finely shred the chilli and ginger. Put all the ingredients except the sugar into a large preserving pan and bring to the boil. Cover and simmer very gently for 30 minutes. Remove the cover and stir in the sugar, continue to simmer, stirring occasionally, until thick and smooth. Pot and seal.

Store for at least 2 months before using. Very hot and fruity chutney that is ideal with barbecued foods.

Parsley

Petroselinum hortense

Parsley is one of those delightful herbs which are an absolute necessity in the garden, and it has a thousand uses from making a pleasant tea to pungent garlic butters. I am sorry to say, however, that it is not the simplest plant to grow, and for some people it just totally refuses – I am one of them. Scurrilous old wives tales reflect upon those who are successful, but I think failure is due to the fact that parsley seed takes so long to germinate – eight weeks – that it is frequently neglected.

To ensure survival, warm the soil with hot water and sow the seed thinly. Cover lightly with soil and mark the spot with fast growing seeds like radishes, keep well watered and protected from strong sunlight. Or grow in deep pots and window-boxes, making sure that there is enough room for the long tap root. Bright, dark-green, curly parsley looks spectacular in hanging baskets. Parsley is best treated as an annual so allow some of the tiny yellow seeds to mature and reseed for the following year. Cover young plants with cloches to protect them from frost. If you grow parsley near spring onions, both will benefit but lettuces will die from contact. There is a choice of parsley for the adventurous – the tightly bunched, dark-green moss-curled parsley which most people seem to prefer for its appearance does make an attractive garnish but it has nowhere near the flavour of the pale, flat-leaved French parsley. This parsley grows much taller than the moss-curled and many endure several winters, being particularly successsful when grown in damp areas.

Another variety of parsley is the Hamburg or turnip rooted parsley and although the leaves may be used as flavouring it is grown mainly for its roots which have a fine flavour. Wild parsley is not to be recommended – not only because it is stringy and indifferently flavoured but also because it too readily resembles fool's parsley and Hemlock which you would not find agreeable.

Parsley is high in vitamin C so use every part of the leaf and stalk, it also has a happy knack of removing odours from the breath, even garlic, and acts as a mild diuretic and blood purifier.

PARSLEY JELLY

2 large handfuls of parsley	white sugar
3 large lemons	green colouring (optional)

2 small hot, dry, sterile jars

Wash the parsley and pick out a few crisp sprigs, put to one side. Wash and peel one of the lemons and put the parsley and lemon peel into a pan with just enough water to cover. Simmer for 1 hour. Strain and measure the liquid, for each 600ml/1 pint take 450g/1lb warmed sugar. Return the liquid and the juice from the lemons to the pan, heat gently and add the sugar, stirring well until dissolved. Bring to the boil and boil hard until a set is obtained. Stir in a few drops of colour if needed. Half-fill the jars and put a sprig of the well dried parsley in each – this is optional but it does look very pretty. Leave to cool a little and fill up the jars. Seal when cold.

TO FREEZE PARSLEY

Wash crisp, firm sprigs of parsley and pack tightly into polythene boxes. Seal, label, freeze and store.

As it is not possible to use frozen parsley as a garnish but only as a flavouring, try grating the frozen block when you need it. The parsley may be blanched before freezing which helps to retain the colour but is not absolutely necessary. Do not chop parsley prior to freezing as it will lose its flavour.

TO DRY PARSLEY

Pick crisp, curly parsley with long stems. Tie into a loose bunch and dip into boiling water for 1 minute. Drain or shake well and lay on a tray in single sprigs. Set the oven at 200°C/400°F or gas mark 6 and put in the parsley, leave for 1 minute only. Turn the oven off immediately and open the door. The parsley is dry when crisp to the touch. Crumble it between finger and thumb (add the stalk although it will not be so fine). Store in small, dark, airtight jars.

TO DRY PARSLEY ROOT

Dry as for Horseradish, p.193. Parsley root, particularly Hamburg parsley, has a good fine flavour slightly akin to parsnip.

Passion fruit or *Granadilla*

The passion flower is a very beautiful climbing plant which originated in South America. It is so called by Spanish missionaries to whom the prominent anthers represented the five wounds Christ received when nailed to the cross: the three styles are the three nails used, the central column represents the pillar of the cross and the filaments surrounding it the crown of thorns. The calyx being seen as the nimbus of light and glory or halo.

During very hot summers the ornamental *passiflora caerula* has fruited in warm areas of the British Isles and many people have wondered to what use the small, yellow egg-shaped fruit may be put. Although not as desirable as the really luscious purple fruit of the *passiflora edulis* and other edible species, it may be experimented with along the lines suggested for the latter and although very pippy it is said to relieve nervous insomnia. The magnificent varieties of passion fruit imported by this country from Kenya and Madeira during January, February and March do make delicious preserves and excellent eating. A properly ripe passion fruit may vary in colour through purple, orange and greeny yellow but at their best they will be wrinkled and rather tatty looking. When fresh passion fruit are not available, tinned fruit make a good substitute.

PASSION FRUIT JAM

1kg/2lb 4oz passion fruit   1kg/2lb 4oz white sugar
2 lemons

3 hot, dry, sterile jam jars

271

Cut the fruit and scoop out the pulp, including the seeds as well, Squeeze the juice from the lemons and put this with the fruit into a preserving pan. Heat gently and add the warmed sugar stirring well until it has dissolved. Bring to the boil and boil until a set is obtained. Pot and seal.

Pippy but fine tasting jam with a good set.

Peach

Another fruit from the ancient garden of civilization, China, the peach still flourishes throughout every temperate zone in the world. In South Africa, Europe, North America and Canada the peach is grown commercially but in areas of the Middle East, Asia and the Mediterranean it can also be found growing wild. The varieties of peach are endless: some are referred to as clingstone or freestone – speaking for itself, this means that the stone either adheres firmly to the fruit or easily comes loose – golden peaches or white, some with a rich full flavour and others with the merest whiff of perfume as delicate as distant wood smoke.

Although peaches are self-pollinating you will get a better result if they are grown in company with a different variety of peach or nectarine. Many people successfully raise peach trees from the stone and common sense would seem to indicate that it is preferable if the original peach was of a known hardy type. One of the worst pests to which peach trees fall victim is peach leaf curl and I have heard that a few cloves of garlic planted beneath the tree will put paid to this. White peaches (Peregrine) are hardier, firmer and have a better flavour than the yellow peach (Hales Early) and these make superb preserves when the character of the fruit is to be recognized, e.g., peach slices in jelly, conserves or brandied peaches. However the rich golden peach (Rochester) is lovely in jams, or spiced and pickled. Although it may seem wicked to do this to a really rather expensive fruit, bear in mind that good fruit properly preserved can be an attractive, satisfying and very appetizing addition to the menu throughout the year.

Holidaymakers travelling back by car from Spain, Italy and the south of France during the summer months will recall the ridiculously cheap trays of peaches for sale in markets and on the roadside, these are really worth buying for although a few may go off on the way home, you can pop them in the refrigerator and organize yourself a few days later to turn out some of the most exciting preserves that are possible to make.

As has been said with apricots, peaches do not set with any great degree of success and nearly all recipes will specify the use of much lemon and little water. Although dried peaches are rarely seen as a separate fruit, usually being in mixed fruit salad, many health food shops will endeavour to obtain them for you and although not economical, make thick and satisfying jams and chutneys – not, I hasten to add, in the same league as an elegantly stoppered jar of golden peaches soaked in brandy or a humble salad of crisp cos lettuce and slices of thin salt beef brightened by a jar of spiced peaches, but nevertheless a preserve which cannot be obtained other than by your own efforts.

PEACH JAMS

Apricots, nectarines and peaches are treated in exactly the same way, therefore simple basic jams can be made for peaches and nectarines following the recipes for apricots. Remember though that both fruits should be skinned before using and the simplest way to do this is to drop into boiling water for 30 seconds, rinse briefly under cold running water and slip the skins off easily. This does not affect the fruit and makes a much less tiresome task of peeling. If you have managed to buy under-ripe fruit at an economical rate it will make very good jam but you must use an additional 150ml/$\frac{1}{4}$ pint water to each 450g/1lb of fresh fruit. Using fresh or dried peaches follow the quantities and methods given for Basic Apricot Jam Using Fresh Fruit, p.57 Basic Apricot Jam Using Dried Fruit and Pressure Cooker, p.57.

However as peaches are such a delicate and exotic fruit I think that it is somewhat cavalier to treat them in this fashion and the following recipes have a more reverent approach.

PEACH JAM USING COMMERCIAL PECTIN

1kg/2lb 4oz ripe peaches
2 large lemons
600ml/1 pint water

1350g/3lb white sugar
$\frac{1}{2}$ bottle commercial pectin

5 hot, dry, sterile, jam jars

Peel the peaches, cut the fruit into slices removing the stone, crack a few of these and extract a few kernels to give that connoisseur touch. Squeeze 3 tablespoons of juice from the lemons and put this with the fruit and water into a large preserving pan. Simmer gently until the peach slices are tender but not soggy. Add the warmed sugar and stir well until it has dissolved.

273

Bring to the boil and boil rapidly. for 2 minutes, add the pectin, stirring well and remove the pan from the heat – you will see why you require a large pan. Add the kernels and skim and stir the jam for 2 minutes. Allow to cool before potting. Seal when cold.

This is an occasion when commercial pectin can have its advantages as the minimum cooking ensures that the fruit keeps its fresh flavour and does not become an unrecognizable mash.

PEACH AND RASPBERRY JAM

1kg/2lb 4oz fresh ripe peaches   150ml/¼ pint water
900g/2lb fresh raspberries   1675g/3lb 12oz white sugar

6 hot, dry, sterile jam jars

Peel and slice the peaches, remove the stones, crack a few and skin the kernels. Pick over the raspberries. Put both fruit into a preserving pan with the water and cook until just tender, watch carefully to prevent burning. Add the warmed sugar and kernels stirring well until the sugar has dissolved. Bring to the boil and boil hard until a set is obtained, continue to stir from time to time to stop it sticking. It should take about 15 minutes to set. Pot and seal.

Spreadable sweet jam. Expensive but delicious.

GEORGIA PEACH CONSERVE

1kg/2lb 4oz peaches   200ml/7fl. oz water
175g/6oz prunes   225g/8oz golden syrup
100g/4oz fat seedless raisins   50g/2oz pecan nuts (hazelnuts or
1 large sweet orange   walnuts)

3 hot, dry, sterile jars

Peel, stone and chop the peaches, stone and chop the prunes and chop the raisins. Grate the rind from the orange and extract the juice. Put all the ingredients except the nuts into a preserving pan and bring to the boil, reduce the heat and cook gently until the fruit is soft and the conserve thick and dark. This will take approximately 1 hour. Skin and chop the nuts, add them to the pan and cook for a further 5 minutes. Pot and seal.

Tinned peaches may be used but drain first and measure the juice using 200ml/7 fl. oz as a substitute for 200ml/7 fl. oz water, also reduce the golden syrup by 50g/2oz. A preserve with a very agreeable taste and texture but unfortunately it does not keep for long.

PERFUMED PEACH CONSERVE

1kg/2lb 4oz fairly hard, ripe peaches
1 lemon
675g/1lb 8oz white sugar

2 teaspoons rosewater
2 teaspoons orange flower water

3 hot, dry, sterile jars with wide necks

Peel and quarter the peaches, remove the stones, use a sharp knife and a clean cloth to hasten a slippery business. Squeeze the juice from the lemon and put this with the peach quarters into a large preserving pan. Cook very gently until the peaches are soft but not broken and take great care not to burn (I find that it is best, right from the beginning of the cooking, to keep giving the pan a shake, which keeps the fruit moving without breaking it). Stir the warmed sugar in very carefully, making sure that it has dissolved, and bring to the boil. Boil hard until a set is obtained, add the rosewater and orange flower water. Boil briefly, but briefly! Pot and seal.

PEACH AND PEAR CONSERVE

4 lemons
2kg/4lb 8oz white sugar
300ml/½ pint water

1kg/2lb 4oz firm peaches
1kg/2lb 4oz firm pears

8 hot, dry, sterile, wide-necked jars

Grate the rind from the lemons and extract the juice, put the rind with the sugar and water into a large preserving pan and boil together to form a thick syrup. Skin, quarter and stone the peaches. Peel, core and cube the pears. Put these into the boiling syrup with the lemon juice and simmer until pears and peaches begin to look transparent. If the fruit is cooked but the syrup gives no indication of setting remove the fruit with a perforated spoon and pack into the jars and reboil the syrup hard until a set is obtained, pour over the fruit to cover. If fruit and syrup reach the same point together pot as usual. In either case leave to get cold before sealing.

PRESERVED PEACHES

1kg/2lb 4oz slightly firm peaches
900g/2lb caster sugar

1 litre/1¾ pints red or white currant juice

4 hot, dry, sterile, wide-necked jars

Peel and cut the peaches into thick even slices. Lay in a large shallow dish one layer at a time. Take half the sugar and dredge each layer with it as you go, finish with a layer of sugar. Leave overnight. The next day put the remaining sugar and the fruit juice into a wide-based preserving pan and bring to the boil to make a thin syrup – do not allow to actually boil. Add the contents of the dish, bring to the boil and reduce the heat. Simmer until the fruit takes on a transparent look. Pot and seal. If you do not have the fruit juice available, take 1 scant litre/1¾ pints of water and the juice of 3 lemons.

PEACHES IN BRANDY AND SYRUP

white sugar
water

firm ripe white or golden peaches
good quality brandy

large, hot, dry, sterile, wide-necked preserving jars

Using a large preserving pan make up a syrup with the sugar and water in the proportions of 1 litre/1¾ pints water to 450g/1lb sugar. In the meantime, prepare the peaches. It is easier to peel the peaches by dipping into boiling water and then holding under cold running water, the skins should then slide off. Cut in half and remove the stone. I have seen very small peaches left whole, in which case wipe them with a damp cloth and, using a silver needle, prick them right through to the stone several times so that they may completely absorb the syrup. When the thin syrup is ready slide the peaches into the pan and bring very slowly to the boil, making sure that you have enough syrup to keep the fruit immersed. Once the boil has been reached remove the peaches with a perforated spoon and pack into the jars. Measure the syrup and for each 600ml/1 pint take 900g/2lb sugar. Return sugar and syrup to the pan and heat gently stirring

276

well until the sugar has dissolved. Bring to the boil and boil hard until it will form a thread when pulled up by the spoon. Measure the syrup and take an equal quantity of brandy. Mix well and pour over the fruit to cover. Paddle the top gently to remove air bubbles. Seal tightly.

Apricots, greengages and cherries may all be brandied in this fashion. Serve with cream or just as they are in their own syrup for dessert.

PEACHES IN WHITE WINE

small firm ripe golden peaches

a bottle of good, sweet, white wine (Sauternes)

a large, wide-necked jar

Wipe the peaches and prick them several times with a silver needle. Pack them loosely into the jar, cover with the wine and seal tightly. Leave for 1 week before yielding to temptation and eat either as a dessert, with the coffee or as your own private little goodies when you need cheering up. This recipe is also particularly good made with fresh apricots.

PEACHES SPICED IN RED WINE

1kg/2lb 4oz golden peaches
whole cloves
150ml/¼ pint red wine
300ml/½ pint water

900g/2lb white sugar
2 cinnamon sticks
150ml/¼ pint white vinegar

hot, dry, sterile, wide-necked jar with non-metal lid

Skin the peaches and stick two cloves into each one. Put the remainder of the ingredients into a large stainless steel pan and bring to the boil. Boil for 20 minutes. Lay the peaches in the syrup, cover and simmer until tender. Transfer the contents of the pan to a large china bowl and leave overnight. The next day pack the peaches into the jars and return the strained syrup to the pan. Bring to the boil and pour over the peaches to cover. Seal.

Lasts remarkably well and is very good with cold rare beef.

FRESH PEACH CHUTNEY

1kg/2lb 4oz peaches
175g/6oz cooking apples
175g/6oz onions
450ml/¾ pint white vinegar
100g/4oz yellow sultanas

275g/10oz white sugar
1 tablespoon sea salt
2 teaspoons ground ginger
2 teaspoons ground cloves
¼ teaspoon cayenne powder

3 hot, dry, sterile jars with non-metal lids

Peel, stone and chop the peaches, crack a few of the kernels and blanch and skin them. Peel, core and chop the apples. Peel and chop the onions. Put the fruit and onions into a stainless steel pan with the vinegar, cover and cook until soft. Wash and chop the sultanas and add them with the sugar, salt, spices and peach kernels to the pan. Stir until the sugar has dissolved and simmer for 30 minutes or until thick. Pot and seal.

Store for at least 2 months before using. A light, mild chutney.

Peanut

As peanuts are only usually roasted or eaten fresh I do not think it is necessary to say very much about them except that they make super butter and this recipe is undoubtedly cheating.

PEANUT BUTTER

salted peanuts
pure oil – sunflower, nut, olive, etc.

small, hot, dry, sterile jars

Using a liquidizer or blender, half fill it with peanuts, add enough oil to give a smooth blend and switch on to high speed for a few seconds. Pot and seal.

Its undoubted advantage over shop-bought butter is your own choice of consistency.

Pear

There are so many varieties of pear both from the British Isles and imported from every temperate area of the world that it would be unnecessarily tedious to list them all with their appropriate culinary uses.

Pyrus communis, however, was the first and original pear which is still to be found growing wild in southern England and Europe. The fruit is green and hard and although low in pectin can be treated in much the same way as crab apples. All cultivated pears are descended from this dark and handsome tree whose rosy wood was frequently used in the making of country furniture and you may still come across its use in northern parts of France. If you decide to grow your own pear trees – a very worthwhile deed – then my advice would be to seek out a good nurseryperson specializing in pears for although they crop well under good conditions, those conditions have to fairly specific for different varieties and many varieties need to be grown in company with another type of pear. Apart from growing freely in orchard conditions they also take well to being espaliered or cordoned and I have seen a long archway to a front door that was a growing mass of white blossoms, an idea that might appeal to those with an eye to the future generations.

Although pears bloom early, the flower frequently appearing before the soft green leaf, the fruit does not mature until well on in the year and are best picked before they are fully ripe. The pear will come easily from the tree when ready but should not be left long as they remain perfect for but a short time and greedy wasps will also appreciate your largesse. When you have picked them – any time from August to October – store them for a while before eating.

In my childhood we had a great and ancient pear tree in our garden, a tree which was goodnatured enough to withstand the onslaught of being Peter Pan's tree house and a Spanish galleon as well as to continue to fruit prolifically. My mother watched this tree with a stern eye on the weather conditions and if the summer was poor the fruit was ruthlessly picked before it reached any state of full maturity and used in chutneys and other well cooked preserves. She rightly maintained that without the sun the fruit would be gritty and, if fully ripened, mealy-centred and sleepy, so it could be used early to advantage rather than wasted at a later date.

A perfect dessert pear – Beurre, Comice, Williams (Barlett) – is as enjoyable as a classic peach and for this reason I would hesitate to use

279

them in cooking although they bottle well and are delicious when preserved in brandy. Catillac (Christmas pear), Conference, Passe Crassane from Italy, Winter Nelis and Black Worcester, now rarely seen, all stew well and will give excellent pickles. Although lacking in pectin these pears will also make delicate, slightly smoky preserves and jams.

The choice of pear is considerable and varies from country to country and county to county, each having its favourite. You may wish to make your choice not only for the type of fruit but also for the foliage, since like the pear itself the leaves can change from the palest silvery green to a deep autumnal russet.

For those ever willing to try a new idea – if you have a good dessert pear tree – do as they do in France. Take a few small clean jars and select several promising looking fruit. By some devious method, and while the pear is still in its early stages, fix the jar over the fruit making sure that it has room for growth. Leave the pear to mature in the jar when it will hopefully have filled it with no room for exit. When it is just mature and ripe enough to leave the tree without force – this will be earlier than usual owing to the hothouse conditions – take both your jar and resident pear off to the kitchen and fill it with the finest brandy or eau de vie. Seal tightly and leave until Christmas, when you can all arm yourselves with spoons and sit silently digging away at this intoxicating lovely. Of course, if you use elegant jars you can serve them up as a very special dessert or gift but I warn you – enough is enough!

BASIC PEAR JAM

Pear jam always has a marvellous mellow flavour but do not make the mistake of believing that apples and pears share the same characteristics. Pears are notoriously low in pectin and for this reason keep water to the minimum and add plenty of lemon. Under-ripe pears make very good jam but they require a long cooking in extra water (at least 150ml/¼ pint per kilogram/2lb 4oz of fruit – maybe a little more). A pressure cooker of course can be used to great advantage for the initial cooking in any of the pear recipes, but make sure that you have at least 150ml/¼ pint water to each 1 kilogram/2lb 4oz pears and cook at M/10lb pressure for 7 minutes before continuing.

1kg/2lb 4oz cooking or hard eating pears	2 large lemons 725g/1lb 10oz white sugar

4 hot, dry, sterile jam jars

Peel, core and chop the pears, do not throw the peelings away. Squeeze the juice from the lemons and tie the pith and pips into a muslin bag with the pear peel and cores. Put the pears, muslin bag and lemon juice into a preserving pan with just enough water to prevent sticking. Bring gently to the boil, stirring and shaking to make sure it does not catch, reduce the heat and simmer until the fruit is soft and has made some juice. Fish out the muslin bag and add the warmed sugar, stirring well until it has dissolved. Bring to the boil and boil hard until a set is obtained. Pot and seal.

PEAR AND ALMOND JAM

Taking the recipe for Basic Pear Jam, add 25g/1oz blanched, skinned and chopped almonds with the warmed sugar. Allow to cool before potting. Seal when cold.

Pear and Hazelnut, Pear and Pecan, and Pear and Walnut Jam (which is particularly super) are all made in the same way.

PEAR AND APRICOT JAM

1kg/2lb 4oz pears
1kg/2lb 4oz fresh apricots
4 lemons

600ml/1 pint water
2kg/4lb 8oz white sugar

8 hot, dry, sterile jam jars

Peel, core and slice the pears. Wash the apricots, cut them in half and remove the stones – if you can crack a few add the skinned kernels to the jam. Squeeze the juice from the lemons, and shred the peel finely, tie this into a muslin bag with the pear peel and cores. Place pears, apricots, lemon juice and muslin bag into a preserving pan with the water and bring to the boil, reduce heat and simmer until the fruit is soft and thick. Remove the muslin bag, giving it a good squeeze and add the warmed sugar, stirring well until it has dissolved. Bring to the boil and boil hard until a set is obtained. Pot and seal.

PEAR AND ORANGE JAM

1kg/2lb 4oz pears
600ml/1 pint water

4 large sweet oranges
1kg/2lb 4oz white sugar

5 hot, dry, sterile jam jars

Peel, core and chop the pears. Tie the cores and peel into a muslin bag. Put fruit and bag into a preserving pan with the water and cook until very soft. Remove the muslin bag and mash the fruit well with a spud masher or pass it through a sieve. Return it to the pan and heat gently. In the meantime, grate the rind from the oranges and extract the juice. Add the warmed sugar to the pear pulp and stir well until it has dissolved, now add the orange rind and juice. Bring to the boil and boil for 10 minutes stirring constantly. When the mixture is thick, pot and seal.

Pleasant mellow, tangy jam which children appreciate at breakfast time.

PEAR, PINEAPPLE AND LEMON JAM

1kg/2lb 4oz pears
small fresh pineapple
5 lemons

1.5kg/3lb 8oz white sugar
small bottle Kirsch

6 hot, dry, sterile, jam jars

Peel, core and slice the pears. Peel and cube the pineapple, grate the rind from the lemons and extract the juice. Place the pears, pineapple, lemon rind and juice in a preserving pan and simmer for approximately 10 minutes. Add the warmed sugar stirring well until it has dissolved and bring to the boil. Boil until setting point is reached and stir in the Kirsch, reheat briefly without boiling. Pot and seal.

Difficult jam to cook without burning but a really super flavour that goes well with vanilla ice cream.

HIGH DUMPSIE DEARIE JAM

1kg/2lb 4oz pears	3 lemons
1kg/2lb 4oz apples	large piece root ginger
1kg/2lb 4oz plums	3kg/6lb 12oz white sugar
water	

14 hot, dry, sterile jam jars

Peel, core and chop the pears and apples, keep them separate and tie the peels and cores in two separate muslin bags. Wash the plums and stone them if you prefer. Put the fruit into three separate pans, the bag of peelings in each appropriate pan. Just add enough water to ensure that the fruit will cook without burning and simmer until tender. Transfer the whole caboodle to a large preserving pan. Grate the rind from the lemons and bruise the ginger which should be tied into a muslin bag. Add lemon rind, ginger and warmed sugar to the pan of fruit and heat gently stirring well until the sugar has dissolved. Bring to the boil and boil hard until a set is obtained, approximately 10 minutes, removing any excess plum stones as they appear. Pot and seal.

Very fruity rich jam with a firm set. There are lots of strange sounding end of season jams which include all those odds and ends of fruit which are going begging – particularly glut fruit. It is wise to remember to treat its making with due reverence, not just throwing the whole lot in and boiling it up for it can deteriorate into a mish-mash of nothingness, particularly if you overboil, and this is a waste of time and money. The fruit can also include damsons, greengages, eating pears and apples but they should always be sound and not squishily over-ripe.

PEAR AND APPLE CONSERVE

1kg/2lb 4oz firm eating pears	50g/2oz mixed glace peel
1kg/2lb 4oz cooking apples	675g/1lb 8oz white sugar
75g/3oz sugar lumps	25g/1oz almonds
2 small lemons	

6 hot, dry, sterile, jam jars

Peel, core, and chop the pears and apples. Rub the sugar lumps over the well washed and dried lemons to remove the zest, extract the juice. Put pears, apples, sugar lumps and lemon juice into a deep bowl. Chop the mixed peel and add this with the warmed sugar to the bowl of fruit. Cover and leave overnight. The next day transfer the contents of the bowl to a preserving pan and heat gently stirring well until the sugar has completely dissolved. Bring to the boil and boil hard until a set is obtained, about 25-30 minutes. Stir in the blanched, skinned and split almonds. Allow to cool a little before potting. Seal when cold.

An alternative way to make this conserve is to cook the fruit first without the granulated sugar for 20 minutes then to transfer it to the bowl. Cover and leave overnight. The next day add the warmed sugar etc., and continue cooking. This is a preferable method when the fruit is very hard.

PEAR AND CIDER MARMALADE

1kg/2lb 4oz eating pears   675g/1lb 8oz white sugar
600ml/1 pint sweet cider

4 hot, dry, sterile jam jars

Boil the cider in a stainless steel pan until it has reduced by half. Peel and core the pears, cut large ones into eighths and small ones into quarters, pop the pieces into the cider as you go. Simmer until the pieces are tender and add the warmed sugar stirring well until it has dissolved. Bring to the boil and boil hard until a set is obtained. Pot and seal.

Another splendid pudding jam. Try spreading it liberally on brown toast, sprinkling finely with brown sugar and sticking it under a hot grill until it bubbles.

PEARS IN SHERRY

675g/1lb 8oz white sugar   1kg/2lb 4oz small pears
600ml/1 pint water   450ml/¾ pint sweet sherry

large, hot, dry, sterile jars with wide necks

Put the sugar and water into a preserving pan and bring to the boil stirring well and continue to boil for 10 minutes. In the meantime, peel the pears and as far as you can, core them without breaking. Pop them into the syrup and simmer for 10 minutes. Remove the fruit with a perforated spoon and pack artistically into the jars. You will probably find that one up, one down, is the easiest way to get them in without taking too much room or squashing. Simmer the syrup for a further 5 minutes and stir in the sherry. Remove from the heat and pour over the fruit to cover. Seal tightly.

Leave for 1 month before using and keep in a fridge once opened. Try other alcoholic additions such as vermouth or martini for a strange effect. Although they may change the colour of the fruit it is a sacrifice well worth enduring.

POTTED PEARS

1kg/2lb 4oz pears
900g/2lb white sugar

3 hot, dry, sterile jars with wide necks

Peel, core and halve the pears but do not discard the peelings and cores. Put the pears in a pan with just enough water to cover and simmer until tender, in other words just poach them. Remove the halves carefully with a perforated spoon and lay on a dish. Turn the pear peel and cores into the water and boil hard until it is reduced by half. Strain and return the liquid to the pan, heat gently and add the warmed sugar stirring well until it has dissolved. Bring to the boil and boil hard until a jelling stage is reached – this will be when the syrup is slow to leave the spoon. Pop the pears back into the pan and bring to the boil. Keep stirring very carefully and cook for 5 minutes, when the pears should be heated through. Too long and you will destroy the set. Pot and seal.

A very good dessert fruit in flans and especially good with meringue and cream. Potted Pears with Ginger is a zingy special treat easily made by adding 50g/2oz diced preserved ginger to the syrup just before you pop the pears back into it.

HOT PEAR CHUTNEY

1kg/2lb 4oz cooking pears	1 small lemon
100g/4oz cooking apples	2 dried red chillies
100g/4oz onions	2 whole cloves
50g/2oz preserved ginger	600ml/1 pint malt vinegar
2 cloves garlic	1 level tablespoon sea salt
175g/6oz seedless raisins	175g/6oz dark brown sugar

3 hot, dry, sterile jars with non-metal lids

Peel, core and cut the pears and apples into respectable chunks. Peel and slice the onions, chop the ginger, finely chop the garlic and chop the washed raisins. Grate the rind from the lemon and extract the juice. Shred the chillies and tie them into a muslin bag with the cloves. Put the vinegar, sugar, salt and muslin bag into a stainless steel pan and bring gently to the boil, boil for 5 minutes. Place all the other prepared ingredients into a large china bowl and cover with the boiling vinegar. Put a plate over the bowl and leave overnight. The next day transfer to a stainless steel pan and cook until thick and smooth, approximately 3 hours, stir from time to time to show you care. Remove the muslin bag. Pot and seal.

Store for at least 2 months before using. Thick traditional chutney that is not overpowering. This recipe is useful for windfall and winter pears.

PEAR KETCHUP

1kg/2lb 4oz cooking pears
225g/8oz white or soft brown sugar
150ml/¼ pint white or brown vinegar
1 teaspoon sea salt

½ teaspoon ground black pepper
½ teaspoon ground cinnamon
½ teaspoon ground cloves

small, hot, dry, sterile jars

Peel, core and chop the pears and put into a stainless steel pan with just enough water to cover, cook until very soft. Mash well and either sieve or liquidize the pears. Return to the pan with all the ingredients and heat gently stirring well until the sugar has dissolved. Simmer until very thick, giving a good stir from time to time. Pot and seal.

Eat in mild cheese or chicken sandwiches. Simply super.

PICKLED AND SPICED PEARS

As far as pears are concerned, pickling or spicing them is one and the same thing, but there are several different ways of preparing the fruit. You may leave the fruit whole and unpeeled, in which case choose small pears, wipe them clean and remove the stalk end. Alternatively peel, core and either halve, quarter or cut into eighths depending on the size of the fruit. As you work, peeled pears should be immediately submerged into a bowl of cold water to which 1 tablespoon of lemon juice has been added, to prevent discolouration. Peeled pears can have a clove inserted into each segment and these should be taken from the original quantity in the recipe.

286

They give a good flavour but cause brown staining on the fruit if the preserve is kept for any length of time. Before you add the pears to the syrup make sure that you pat them dry on a kitchen cloth. Always use hard pears, either Christmas, cooking or Conference.

BASIC METHOD FOR PICKLING OR SPICING PEARS

600ml/1 pint white vinegar
350g/12oz – 900g/2lb white sugar,
  depending on your sweet tooth
12 cloves
large stick cinnamon

the pared rind of 1 lemon
25g/1oz bruised root ginger (optional)
2 teaspoons whole allspice (optional)
1 bay leaf (optional)

Prepare the fruit in one of the methods suggested. Put the vinegar, sugar and spices, tied in a muslin bag, into a stainless steel pan and bring gently to the boil stirring well until the sugar has dissolved. Add the pears and simmer until they begin to look transparent and are just tender enough to be easily pierced with a skewer. Remove the fruit with a perforated spoon and keep warm. Return the pan of syrup to the heat and boil until thick and probably reduced by about half. Remove the spice bag giving it a good squeeze. Cover the pears with the hot syrup, tipping the jars a little to make sure that there are no air bubbles. Add a few fresh spices to the jar if you want a slightly spicier result although they will eventually stain. Top up with more syrup if necessary. Seal immediately.

    Keep at least 1 week before using. Whole unpeeled pears should be kept at least 1 month. Spiced and pickled pears do tend to discolour a little with age but as they become more succulent and spicy this is no great hardship.

GOLDEN PICKLED PEARS

1kg/2lb 4oz small dessert pears
350g/12oz golden syrup
300ml/½ pint white vinegar

piece cinnamon stick
6 cloves
1 lemon

4 dry, sterile jars with wide necks and non-metal lids

Put the syrup, vinegar, spices and a few pieces of the finely pared lemon rind into a stainless steel pan. Bring gently to the boil, stirring well and then leave to cool. Peel the pears, leaving them whole and drop them into a large bowl of cold water and a dash of lemon juice as you work. When you have finished, fish them out of the water, pat them dry and pack into the jars. Cover with the cooled syrup. Seal.

Absolutely delicious way of preserving ripe pears that goes particularly well with cold chicken, turkey and ham.

DRYING PEARS

In Normandy, dry cider and honey is used to make a most unusual concoction for drying pears. Take equal quantities of dry, still cider, water and clear honey and cook the prepared fruit in this until tender. Allow to drain well and then lay on racks in a warm oven until dried out. When resuscitated they have a very pleasant, winey flavour.

Pepper

A native of Central and South America the pepper or capsicum family has established itself well throughout the world. The fruits of this rather shrubby annual are very high in vitamins C and A and provide an important contribution to the diet. The flavour, shape and colour of capsicum has great variation and confusion may arise in the popular names for them in different areas. Some setting out of the regional names and changing appearance may help to avert physical and culinary disaster.

Sweet peppers have a roundly, squared-off shape and vary in size and colour from pale olive green, glossy viridian, yellow, orange, scarlet and crimson. The taste is mild, sweet and very distinctive, in hotter climates becoming more pungent. The flesh varies from firm and thick, to soft and thin walled. The seeds can be very hot and should be removed before cooking. In Great Britain they are known just as sweet pepper or capsicum.

Hot red pepper is another variety of capsicum. It differs from the sweet pepper in its shape which is long and tapering, and although the colour is the same, ranging from green to scarlet, the flavour is much hotter especially when fully ripe. The hot pepper is reputed to be a great internal disinfectant and in some slightly backward countries is used in such a way as to make the imagination boggle. However, there is evidence to suggest that a certain amount of hot red pepper in the diet will control the level of the blood pressure and act as a deterrent against colds and infections.

Fresh hot red peppers are stocked occasionally by specialist shops, but it is more likely that you will find them tinned or bottled, even dried. They are used predominantly as a seasoning and for making hot sauces, vinegars and more exotic dishes perhaps not so suited to western palates. They are colloquially known in parts of Europe as piri-piri, but beware – so is the chilli pepper. This type of capsicum grown in more northern areas is relatively mild but the further south you go so the hotter they become, although never attaining the hair-raising qualities of the chilli pepper.

A good rule to follow with capsicums is that the smaller they are the more virulent they become and this brings me finally to the chilli pepper which is the smallest variety. See Chilli, p.118.

Capsicum are imported into Britain throughout the year but our home grown crops are generally to be found in the greengrocers during the late summer when they should be at their most economical and well worth preserving against the winter when they are astronomically expensive. A rough guide to buying: approximately 4 firm, sweet peppers will weigh 450g/1lb.

RED PEPPER CHUTNEY

1.15 litre/2 pints malt vinegar
25g/1oz pickling spice
1kg/2lb 4oz sweet red peppers
1kg/2lb 4oz aubergines
1kg/2lb 4oz cooking apples
450g/1lb onions
4 large cloves garlic

350g/12oz seedless raisins
15g/½oz root ginger
12 dried red chillies
1½ tablespoons curry powder
2 teaspoons turmeric
2 teaspoons sea salt
100g/4oz soft brown sugar

8 hot, dry, sterile jars with non-metal lids

Boil the vinegar with the pickling spices for 2 minutes. Cover and leave to get cold, strain before using. Wash and dice the peppers, removing seed and white membrane. Wash and chop the aubergines. Peel, core and chop the apples. Peel and chop the onions and garlic. Chop the raisins. Tie the bruised ginger and chillies into a muslin bag and put this into a stainless steel pan with half the vinegar and all the other ingredients except the curry powder, salt and sugar. Bring to the boil, stirring well, cover and simmer until soft. Blend the curry powder, turmeric and salt with the sugar and remaining vinegar, add to the pan and continue to cook uncovered until thick and smooth. Remove the muslin bag, giving it a good squeeze. Pot and seal.

Sweet, hot chutney excellent with cold lamb and chicken or with cold rice salads.

RED PEPPER RELISH

1kg/2lb 4oz red peppers
1kg/2lb 4oz green peppers
675g/1lb 8oz onions
600ml/1 pint malt vinegar

275g/10oz soft brown sugar
1 tablespoon sea salt
1½ tablespoons celery seed

6 hot, dry, sterile jars with non-metal lids

Wash and chop the peppers, removing seeds and membrane. Peel and chop the onions. Put all the ingredients into a stainless steel pan – tie the celery seed in a muslin bag if you prefer – and bring gently to the boil, stirring well until the sugar has dissolved. Simmer until thick and cooked. Pot and seal.

Pineapple

A pineapple, golden, roundly conical fruit surmounted by a tazz of serrated green leaves is not one fruit but made up of many hundreds of small fruit all growing together by some miracle of nature. Indigenous to the tropics, pineapples are also grown under glass by the enthusiastic gardener in more temperate zones and many of us must remember trying to grow pineapples from the green top placed in a saucer of water and living in smelly glory on the windowsill.

In the eighteenth century, pineapples were grown in English conservatories in much the same way as oranges, to provide a delicacy for the rich man's table. However, cultivation on a grand scale (such as in Hawaii) and cheap transportation soon put them within everyone's reach. Although we enjoy them for their sweet, juicy flesh they also have high vitamin A and C content. Fresh pineapples from the Azores, the Africas and West Indies are available in shops throughout the year, but more provincial areas may see them only sporadically. Fresh pineapple make good if somewhat runny preserves and lose much of their sharpness in cooking taking on a mellow flavour and colour. As a large amount of pineapple is bristly skin, leaves and hard core it is impossible to gauge an accurate weight without first preparing it. Never use any part of the fruit which is turning brown for this will cause a fermentation in the finished preserve if kept for any length of time.

As tinned pineapple is more readily obtainable I have included two recipes for its use both delicious and attractive and I might add, reasonably economical.

PINEAPPLE JAM

1kg/2lb 4oz prepared pineapple
2 large lemons

300ml/½ pint water
1kg/2lb 4oz white sugar

4 hot, dry, sterile jam jars

Working on a large dish to catch the juice, peel the pineapple and remove the hard core, dice and weigh the flesh. Put into a preserving pan with the juice. Extract the juice from the lemons and chop the peel, pith and flesh very finely and tie into a muslin bag with the pips. Place this in the pan with 3 tablespoons of the lemon juice and the water. Bring very gently to the boil and then simmer until the pineapple is transparent and tender. Turn into a china bowl and mix well with the sugar, cover and leave for 12 hours (if you leave it in the preserving pan it will take a taint from the metal). The next day remove the muslin bag giving it a good squeeze and transfer the contents of the bowl back to the preserving pan. Heat gently, stirring well until the sugar has dissolved, bring to the boil and boil rapidly until a set is obtained. Allow to cool a little before potting. Seal when cold.

Not a spreadable jam unless you choose to grate the pineapple and if you do, make sure you catch the juices on a plate.

PINEAPPLE AND BLACKBERRY JAM

1kg/2lb 4oz prepared pineapple
500g/1lb 2oz cooking apples
1kg/2lb 4oz blackberries

3 lemons
2kg/4lb 8oz white sugar

9 hot, dry, sterile jam jars

Working on a large dish, peel the pineapple, removing the hard core, weigh and dice the flesh. Peel, core and slice the apples and put pineapple and apples into a preserving pan. Heat very gently until the fruit softens and you have some juices. Simmer for 15 minutes until the pineapple is beginning to soften – add a little water if the operation becomes hazardous. Pick over the blackberries, rinse if necessary and shake dry. Add them to the pan and cook until soft. Extract the juice from the lemons and add it to the pan with the warmed sugar, stir well until the sugar has dissolved. Bring to the boil and boil until a set is obtained. Pot and seal.

Soft jam with a very pleasant flavour.

MINTED PINEAPPLE JAM

1kg/2lb 4oz prepared pineapple
3 lemons
1kg/2lb 4oz white sugar

150ml/$\frac{1}{4}$ pint water
knob unsalted butter
a handful fresh mint

4 hot, dry, sterile jam jars

Peel, core, chop and weigh the pineapple. Wash and chop the lemons removing the pips. Mince the pineapple and lemons, taking care to catch all the juices. Put the minced fruit, any juices, sugar, water and butter into a preserving pan. Wash and dry the mint putting aside a couple of sprigs, tie the remainder together with a piece of fine string and pop it into the pan. Heat gently, stirring well until the sugar has dissolved, add a little warm water if the jam looks like burning and bring to the boil, reduce the heat and simmer very gently until the fruit is soft. Bring to the boil again and boil until set is obtained. Remove the mint leaves, chop the reserved mint and add it to the pan. Leave to cool before potting. Seal when cold.

Fresh, fruity flavour.

PRESERVED PINEAPPLE

1kg/2lb 4oz prepared pineapple
1350g/3lb white sugar

1.15 litre/2 pints water

4 hot, dry, sterile jars

Working on a large dish to catch the juices, peel the pineapple, remove the hard core and cut the weighed flesh into even slices or cubes. Put

292

550g/1lb 4oz of the sugar into a preserving pan with the water, heat gently, stirring well until the sugar has dissolved and boil to a thin syrup. Drop in the pineapple and cook gently until the fruit is just tender – but only just. Have ready a sink of cold water, take the pan from the heat and stand it in the water. Remove, cover and leave for 24 hours. Return to the heat and add another 300g/11oz sugar, bring slowly to the boil stirring with care until the sugar has dissolved. Boil gently for 2 minutes. Remove from the heat, plunge into cold water to cool quickly. Remove, cover and leave for 24 hours. Return to the heat and add the remaining sugar, heat gently stirring with care until the sugar has dissolved, boil gently for 2 minutes and take the pan off the heat and leave it until a skin begins to form. Stir gently several times to disperse the fruit. Pot. Seal when cold.

An arduous task to ensure that the fruit cooks in a thick syrup without breaking up, but worth the effort as you should have lovely, rich, golden jars of sweet fruit. This is a method which can be used very satisfactorily to preserve apricots, strawberries and greengages.

PINEAPPLE MARMALADE

3 large, thick-skinned oranges (Jaffa)
1 lemon
800g/1lb 12oz tin pineapple

600ml/1 pint water
1800g/4lb white sugar

5 hot, dry, sterile jam jars

Wash the oranges and lemon, remove the pips and tie them into a muslin bag; pass the fruit through a mincer. Drain the pineapple reserving the cubes and put the juice with the citrus fruit, muslin bag and water into a china bowl. Cover and leave to stand overnight. The next day transfer the whole caboodle to a preserving pan and add the pineapple cubes, heat gently and add the warmed sugar, stirring well until it has dissolved. Cook until the marmalade is thick and soft – about 45 minutes. Fish out the muslin bag, giving it a good squeeze, and allow the mixture to cool before potting. Seal when cold.

Crushed coriander seeds give an extra splendid touch if added to the muslin bag.

PINEAPPLE CHUTNEY

1kg/2lb 4oz tinned pineapple cubes or
  pieces
500g/1lb 2oz soft brown sugar
900ml/1½ pints wine vinegar
1½ tablespoons mustard seed

1 cinnamon stick
5 whole cloves
1 small teaspoon ground ginger
250g/9oz seedless raisins

4 hot, dry, sterile jars with non-metal lids

Drain the pineapple. Put all the ingredients except the pineapple and raisins into a stainless steel pan and bring gently to the boil, stirring well. Simmer for 15-20 minutes. Strain and return to the pan. Chop the raisins and add them with the pineapple to the vinegar syrup. Cook on a low heat until thick and reduced to a jam-like consistency. Leave to cool before potting. Seal when cold. Store for at least 2 months before use.

CRYSTALLIZED AND CANDIED PINEAPPLE

Peel, core and cube the fresh pineapple. Follow the quantities and method given under Crystallized Apricots, p.64.

Plum

Probably the most versatile fruit tree for a small garden is the plum tree for not only do plums actually prefer garden to orchard conditions but will grow into attractive shapes and take well to being espaliered. This is a great advantage with a tree like the Victoria plum, for though small it may bear a crop heavy enough to break the branches, which must be supported. Generally plum trees are good natured and tolerant although having an aversion to acid soil. As they are one of the first flowering fruits it is wise to plant the tree in a warm spot well protected from late frost. Certain plum trees like the Victoria will not grow too large and it is worth choosing a variety with an eye to the available space.

Although originating in Asia the plum tree has made its mark throughout the western world but those trees which you may find growing wild in

Britain are usually garden escapes or have planted themselves from the discarded stone. The ease with which plum trees grow would seem to explain the great variety available, some of them purely regional, so not only do we have tremendous choice in the shops from our native isles but also many imports such as Gaviota, Santa Rosa and President which will arrive from Italy, Spain, South Africa and the USA etc., when our own plums are out of season.

Plums reach glut proportions and are used mostly for jam making and bottling, however a word of warning: unless over-ripe or very ripe fruit is specifically called for, you will find that a sharper, thicker jam with a good set is obtained if under-ripe or just ripe fruit is used. The sharp, dark, cooking plums and the Quetsche-type plums make excellent sweet-sour pickles with a darkly mysterious appearance and of course give some of the best fruits preserved in alcohol particularly traditional in France. Another plum more likely to be found in France is the tiny, scented, golden Mirabelle which makes delicate apricoty conserves. There are also specific varieties of purple plums for drying to prunes. Over-ripe fruit can be used to make superb plum sauces, ketchups and purées while a mixed bag of cooking plums will ensure a supply of rich fruity chutneys for the winter. Although dessert plums, particularly the Victoria, are frequently cooked and used in preserves it is only common sense to keep them for very special recipes.

Many English recipes still refer to raisins as plums particularly if they are traditional and the French for plum is confusingly prune so – think twice!

The list of plums given below, mainly from the British Isles may help with instant identification and suggest their prime uses.

Victoria	Golden red	dessert, special culinary and preserves
Marjorie	blue black	dessert
Coe's golden drop	golden orange	dessert
Kirkes Blue	blue black	dessert
Laxtons Delicious	crimson	dessert
Jefferson	green gold	dessert
Monarch	purple red	culinary, preserving
Czar	dull red	culinary, preserving
Early Rivers	dark crimson	culinary, preserving, bottling
Pershore Egg	yellow green	culinary, preserving, bottling

Warwickshire Drooper	yellow gold	culinary, preserving, bottling
Belle de Louvain	purple red	culinary, preserving, bottling

Quetsche-type plums:

'Zwetchen, Switchen, Switzen' and Mussell Plum	purple black	culinary, pickling, spicing, in alcohol

Prune Plums:

Prune D'Agen, Prince Engelbert Fellenberg	purple black	steeping in alcohol, drying

---

PLUM JAMS

Several small items of interest to store away: plums are not miracle setters, they require little water and constant watching. Very ripe, over-ripe or bruised fruit just will not do unless the recipe specifies otherwise. Over-ripe fruit lacks pectin and the quantity of sugar will have to be reduced – 900g/2lb sugar to 1kg/2lb 4oz plums. Bruised fruit will cause the jam to ferment on keeping. Should you prefer to cook the plums without first stoning them, you will find that it gives a better flavour and set although causing inconvenience at the tea table, that is why stones should be tied into a muslin bag. If you leave the fruit whole, either slit it or prick several times with a needle and try to remove stones as they rise to the surface. The kernels added to the jam will give a slight almondy taste which will put the jam above the mundane.

1kg/2lb 4oz under-ripe plums
900g/2lb white sugar

3 hot, dry, sterile jam jars

Wash the plums, cut them in half and remove the stones. Tie half the stones in a muslin bag and crack the other half and winkle out the kernels – the best way to do this is to wrap them in a heavy cloth or thick polythene bag and bash them with a hammer or similar object; try not to be too abusive for you will crush them completely. Put the plums and kernels into a deep bowl and layer with the sugar, cover and leave overnight. The next day turn into a preserving pan, add the muslin bag and heat gently stirring well until all the sugar has dissolved. Bring slowly to the boil. Boil hard until a set is obtained. Remove the bag. Pot and seal.

This is one of the best ways to make plum jam, nearly always giving perfect results and I would particularly recommend using Victoria plums.

PLUM JAM USING COMMERCIAL PECTIN

1kg/2lb 4oz ripe plums
1 lemon
150ml/¼ pint water

1400g/3lb 2oz white sugar
¼ bottle commercial pectin

5 hot, dry, sterile jam jars

Wash the plums and remove as many of the stones as you can. Squeeze the juice from the lemon and put the fruit, water and lemon juice into a large preserving pan. Bring to the boil. Cover and cook until the plums are soft. Add the warmed sugar stirring well until it has dissolved. Bring to a full rolling boil for 3 minutes, stirring occasionally without being burnt by erupting jam. Remove from the heat and stir in the pectin. Skim and stir for 2 minutes. Allow to cool before potting. Seal when cold.

Before everyone shrieks that plums do not need the encouragement of commercial pectin I would say in defence that I do not find plums to be the super setters that they are cracked up to be. In fact I think that they can be downright temperamental and I believe that this is caused by several factors. A wet, sunless summer will cause the fruit to become plump and succulent with little sweetness or pectin build up – very deceptive. Or during a hot summer the fruit ripens very rapidly and has practically fallen from the tree before picking commences and over-ripe fruit does not give a satisfactory set.

PLUM AND ELDERBERRY JAM

850g/1lb 14oz elderberries
300ml/½ pint water (scant measure)

1kg/2lb 4oz plums
1700g/3lb 12oz white sugar

6 hot, dry, sterile jam jars

Rinse and remove the elderberries from their stalks. Put into a preserving pan with 150ml/¼ pint of the water. Bring to the boil and simmer until soft – no longer than 5 minutes. Turn into a jelly bag and leave to drain overnight into a clean bowl. The next day wash and stone the plums, crack a few stones and remove the kernels. Put the plums into the remaining 150ml/¼ pint of water. Simmer until just soft and add the elderberry juice. Bring to the boil stirring well and add the warmed sugar, continue to stir until it has dissolved and then bring to the boil again. Boil rapidly until a set is obtained. Stir in the kernels. Pot and seal.

If you use black or blue plums you will have a jam that is dark purple and deliciously autumnal.

PLUM JELLY

1kg/2lb 4oz ripe plums   lemons
water   white sugar

6 medium size, hot, dry, sterile jars

Wash the plums and put them in a casserole with enough water to half cover the fruit. Cover and cook in a moderate oven until the plums are collapsed, soft and juicy. Turn into a jelly bag and leave to drain overnight into a clean bowl. The next day measure the juice gained and for each 600ml/1 pint take 450g/1lb warmed sugar and the juice of 1 lemon. Return the juice to the pan with the lemon juice and heat gently, add the sugar stirring well until it has dissolved. Bring to the boil and boil hard until a set is obtained, approximately 30 minutes. Pot and seal.

If it is impractical to use the oven, cook in a covered pan on the top of the cooker.

VICTORIA PLUM CONSERVE

1kg/2lb 4oz Victoria plums   150ml/¼ pint water
1kg/2lb 4oz white sugar

4 hot, dry, sterile jam jars

Wash, halve and stone the plums, crack as many of the stones as possible and blanch and skin the kernels. Put the sugar and water into a preserving pan and bring to the boil, stirring well until the sugar has dissolved. When this is the consistency of a thin syrup add the plums. Boil gently until the conserve has set (this will not be a jammy set). Stir in the kernels. Leave for 5 minutes before potting. Seal when cold.

This is also an excellent method to use for preserving those delightful, tiny, golden plums which in France are called mirabelles but these should be left whole. Almost too good to eat as a bread and butter conserve, pour a little on to home-made ice cream or in tiny tartlets.

PLUM WALNUT CONSERVE

1kg/2lb 4oz red or gold plums
2 large sweet oranges
1 small lemon
25g/1oz seedless raisins

25g/1oz currants
675g/1lb 8oz white sugar
25g/1oz unsalted butter
100g/4oz walnuts

6 hot, dry, sterile jam jars

Wash, halve and stone the plums. Wash the oranges and lemon, chop up discarding the pips and put the flesh, peel, pith through a coarse mincer with the raisins and currants. Put all the ingredients except the nuts into a preserving pan and bring gently to the boil stirring well until the sugar has dissolved. Reduce the heat and simmer until the jam is thick and a set is obtained. Stir in the nuts. Leave to cool before potting. Seal when cold.

Two tablespoons of brandy or sherry stirred in with the nuts will give an extra richness.

CHINESE MARMALADE

1kg/2lb 4oz golden plums
1 small sweet orange
1 small lemon
150ml/¼ pint water

1350g/3lb seedless raisins
1350g/3lb demerara sugar
75g/3oz preserved ginger
1 tablespoon brandy

8 hot, dry, sterile jars

Wash and stone the plums. Grate the rind from the orange and lemon and extract the juice. Put plums, rinds and juice into a preserving pan with the water and simmer gently until soft, taking care that the fruit does not stick. Pass through a fine sieve, return the pulp to the pan and heat gently. Chop the raisins and add them to the pan with the warmed sugar, bring slowly to the boil, stirring continuously until the sugar has dissolved and simmer gently for 30 minutes. Chop the ginger and stir it into the thick, brown marmalade. Boil rapidly for 5 minutes and then leave to cool. Stir in the brandy. Pot. Seal when cold.

Treacly, rich, gooey preserve that has strong overtones of Christmas pudding. Tinned plums may be used instead of fresh. Drain them well and substitute some of the syrup for the water.

THE EVERLASTING RUM POT

mixed fruit   granulated sugar
1 bottle or so of light or dark rum

large stone crock or jar

Take a selection of plums, greengages, apricots, raspberries, cherries strawberries, redcurrants, peaches, grapes, using only the very best fruit. Wipe the fruit and weigh it. Do not peel or remove the stones. Take an equal quantity of sugar and as you place the fruit in the jar sprinkle it with sugar. Just cover with the rum. Seal tightly with waxed paper and a cork or wooden lid and as you find more fruit to add to the collection just take off the lid and repeat the process until the pot is full but not crammed. Always replace the lid tightly and keep in a cool place. Allow at least 3 months before using, so I suggest that making it remains a dark secret until then!

Expensive but so simple. One of the great pleasures of making this delightful concoction is either buying a few of the best and expensive fruits as they come into season or picking a selection from your own garden – it gives a great feeling of luxury. Melon may also be used peeled, seeded and cut into chunks but I find that it can go slimy. Never use apples, pears, bananas or citrus fruit. Although there are many ways of using this extraordinary potent mixture I find that just two or three fruits with a little of the syrup and a spot of fresh cream is enough to knock the coolest customer sideways. Any syrup that you may have left over is a tremendous booster to fresh or frozen fruit salads. Decant the fruit into small decorative pots to give as presents. They will be much appreciated!

SPICED PLUMS

1kg/2lb 4oz purple or dark red plums
cinnamon stick
whole cloves
450ml/¾ pint red wine vinegar

150ml/¼ pint water
350g/12oz soft, light brown sugar
2 teaspoons sea salt
a few blackcurrant or raspberry leaves

3 hot, dry, sterile, preserving jars with wide necks and non-metal lids

Wipe the plums and prick them with a needle several times. Pack the plums, standing upright, into the jars. At the bottom of the jar put a layer of leaves and between each layer of plums put a few of the spices and another leaf or two. Finish off with a leaf. Put the vinegar, water, sugar and salt into a stainless steel pan and bring gently to the boil. Boil for 5 minutes and pour it hot over the plums to cover well. Seal tightly.

Leave for 8 weeks before using. Delicious with any cold meats particularly meat loaf, roll, pie or with sausage meats. Should you wonder about the 'leaves', not only do they add an aromatic touch, they also act as firming agents in much the same way as oak or vine leaves do.

SPICED VICTORIA PLUMS

750ml/1¼ pints white wine vinegar
1100g/2lb 8oz white sugar
large piece cinnamon
25g/1oz allspice berries

1 teaspoon whole cloves
several blades mace
1kg/2lb 4oz Victoria plums

4 dry, sterile jars with wide neck and non-metal lid

Put the vinegar, sugar and spices into a stainless steel pan and boil together until syrupy and thick, leave to cool. Wipe the plums and prick through with a needle several times. Place them in the jars, keeping them upright. Pour the cool syrup over the plums, cover with a cloth and leave overnight. The next day drain off the syrup and return it to the pan. Bring to the boil for 2 minutes and leave to cool. Pour over the plums to seal completely. Seal when quite cold. Store in a cool dark place.

Leave for 3 months before using. It is a wise woman who does not throw away the surplus syrup – bottle it and keep it to top up with. These are the most attractive and succulent plums imaginable but they must not be allowed to dry out.

PLUM AND GINGER CHUTNEY

1kg/2lb 4oz plums
1kg/2lb 4oz soft brown sugar
900ml/1½ pints vinegar
450g/1lb sultanas
225g/8oz shallots
2 cloves garlic

50g/2oz sea salt
1 tablespoon ground allspice
25g/1oz ground ginger
1 tablespoon whole mustard seed
50g/2oz preserved ginger

5 hot, dry, sterile jars with non-metal lids

Wash and stone the plums and put them into a pan with the sugar and vinegar. Bring gently to the boil, stirring well until the sugar has dissolved. Continue to simmer until the fruit is soft and mushy. Chop the sultanas, peel and finely chop the shallots and garlic. Mix the ground spices to a paste with a little of the hot liquid and add all of these to the pan with the mustard seed. Stir well and bring to the boil. Boil for 30 minutes, stirring frequently. Chop the preserved ginger very fine and add it to the pan. Cook for a further 15 minutes. Pot and seal. Store for at least 2 months before use. For a basic chutney omit the preserved ginger.

COUNTRY GARDEN CHUTNEY

1kg/2lb 4oz plums
1kg/2lb 4oz cooking apples
675g/1lb 8oz red tomatoes
350g/12oz onions
2 ridge cucumbers
2.25 litres/4 pints malt vinegar
350g/12oz brown sugar
75g/3oz sea salt

1 dessertspoon fresh ground nutmeg
1 teaspoon ground cinnamon
1 tablespoon mustard seed
2 small pieces root ginger
1 tablespoon black peppercorns
2 teaspoons whole cloves
4 dried chillies

6 hot, dry, sterile jam jars with non-metal lids

Wash, stone and chop the plums. Peel, core and chop the apples and skin the tomatoes (drop into boiling water, then cold water, to help this process). Peel and chop the onions and wash and chop the cucumbers. Put the vinegar into a stainless steel pan with the sugar, salt, nutmeg, cinnamon and mustard seed. Bruise the remaining spices and tie them into a muslin bag. Add this to the pan and bring the syrupy solution to the boil, stirring well. Add the prepared fruit and vegetables to the pan and heat gently until boiling.

Reduce the heat and simmer until thick and smooth, stirring occasionally, which will take approximately 2 hours. Pot and seal.

SWEET AND SOUR PLUMS FROM FRANCE

1kg/2lb 4oz blue plums
2 sprigs tarragon
12 whole green peppercorns
4 whole cloves

1 piece cinnamon
900ml/1½ pints white wine vinegar
1 teaspoon sea salt
100g/4oz white sugar

3 dry, sterile, preserving jars with non-metal lids

Wash and dry the plums, cut them in half and remove the stones. Arrange them in the jars with the tarragon and spices nicely dispersed amongst them. Put the vinegar, salt and sugar into a stainless steel pan and boil together for 10 minutes. Leave to cool uncovered, then pour over the fruit to cover completely with no air bubbles. Seal hermetically (this means using a clip top or equivalent which will completely exclude air). Leave to macerate for 1 month.

Excellent with cold meats, chicken etc. Tarragon is a very useful herb to add to pickled fruit of all kinds. This recipe may also be made with greengages or small green plums. A mixture of green and purple would look extremely attractive.

CANDIED PLUMS

1kg/2lb 4oz just ripe dessert plums
1kg/2lb 4oz white sugar

1.15 litre/2 pints water

a non-porous stone or earthenware jar or crock

Wipe the plums and prick them through several times with a silver needle. Pack into the jar. Dissolve half the sugar in half the water and bring gently to the boil. Pour this syrup over the plums, cover and put into a cool oven, 115°C/240°F or gas mark ½. Leave overnight. The next day drain the syrup from the plums and pour into a pan, bring to the boil and once again pour over the plums. Cover and leave in a cool oven 110°C/225°F or gas mark ½ overnight. Repeat this process twice more, making four times in all. The final day drain the plums once more, although this syrup is not used again I am sure that you can find a good use for it. Take the remaining 0.5kg/1lb

2oz sugar and 600ml/1 pint water, using a preserving pan, make a new syrup. Transfer the plums to the boiling syrup and immediately remove from the heat. Do not cover (unless with a fine muslin) and leave to get cold. Remove the plums one by one and lay them on a wire mesh to dry, leave in a warm place where the air circulates freely and is nice and dry. They will be ready when they are firm to the touch and are not tacky. Store between layers of waxed paper in a box or tin (preferably not airtight).

Greengages may be candied by this excellent method which keeps the fruit juicy and soft.

Pomegranate

The pomegranate, which resembles an orange with a calyx, has a tough golden skin which encases a large amount of pink-fleshed seeds embedded in acidulous pith. The flesh surrounding the seeds is juicy and delicious but, while children thoroughly enjoy the messy hassle of extracting the maximum amount of refreshment from these, adults find it rather tedious. However the seeds encased in flesh have an attractive crystalline appearance and are often served sprinkled with rose water as a dessert in Middle Eastern countries. The history of the tree is ancient, originating in Persia and, although it grows well in warm areas of Britain, bearing remarkably beautiful blossoms, it will not fruit. Pomegranate seeds have been used for centuries in English cooking particularly as decoration and for making wines and syrups. Although the seeds do become more soft and edible as the fruit ripens the pomegranate is really only suitable for making a jelly. Most pomegranates are imported from Cyprus during October-November.

POMEGRANATE JELLY

1kg/2lb 4oz very ripe pomegranates	water
2 large sweet oranges	white sugar
2 large thin-skinned lemons	rose water (optional)

3 small, hot, dry, sterile jars

Working on a large dish to catch the juice, halve the fruit and scoop the seeds into a sieve, stand it on the dish and, using a wooden spoon squeeze and prize the juicy flesh from the seeds. When you have collected all the flesh and juice pass it through the sieve again and put into a bowl. Extract the juice from both oranges, grate the rind from 1 lemon and extract the juice from the 2 lemons. Strain and add to the pomegranate juice, measure and for each 600ml/1 pint take 450g/1lb warmed sugar and 600ml/1 pint water. Return the juice and water to a preserving pan, simmer for 15 minutes and add the sugar, stirring well until it has dissolved. Bring to the boil and boil until a set is obtained. For a perfumed jelly add 2 small teaspoons of rose water and bring briefly to the boil. Pot and seal.

A beautiful, golden-red jelly.

Primrose

Primula vulgaris

Pale-golden primroses peeping from beneath banks of green are the most heartlifting flowers for this is when we feel that spring is really with us and we can look forward to warmer days of sunshine and showers. There are few recipes for using primroses because the primrose has not the heady perfume of cowslips, violets or roses which can be used to flavour vinegars and syrups, and those that do exist are very ancient and impractical. However, they do make the most enchanting decorations for cakes and I would suggest that to avail yourself of an abundant supply without robbing the countryside of its fast decreasing flowers you plant a few seeds in a partially shaded part of the garden or rockery.

CRYSTALLIZED PRIMROSES

fresh primrose heads   caster sugar
egg

Make sure that your flower heads are clean and dry and have a small piece of stalk to hang on to. Separate the egg white from the yolk and whisk it until it is fluffy but not crisp. Using a soft paintbrush 'paint' each primrose thoroughly with the egg white and dip it gently and carefully into the sugar, twizzle it between finger and thumb to remove excess sugar and lay it on a sponge rack covered with greaseproof paper. Put to dry in an airing cupboard or very cool oven with the door ajar. Leave until completely dry and crisp to the touch. Store between layers of waxed paper in airtight tins.

Primrose heads 'painted' with a mixture of gum arabic and rose water last longer but I prefer to use egg white.

Prune

Although we know what the prune is – the dried plum – to any reader who as a child has been institutionalized in hospital or boarding school etc., the name may well send a shudder down the spine. Well meaning adults, insisting that 'it will do you good' have ruined the reputation of prunes, spinach, liver and milk puddings. Yet properly cooked and lovingly cared for, these so-called nursery foods should attain culinary heights. Prunes to my mind are not the most suitable fruit for small palates for they have a rich, strong, sophisticated taste which should be acquired rather than thrust upon one. Prunes stuffed, prunes as stuffing, prunes on horseback, devilled, concocted and soaked in alcohol, prunes with game, fish, pork and eel, lit or soused, all make splendid dishes. Nowhere though do they display their virtues better than when preserved in various soothing syrups for feast days or made into rich chutneys and thick dark jams.

Although prunes come from various corners of the world either loose or in packets, in need of soaking or not, expensive or cheap, the majority are imported from the USA and Australia. Several very special kinds of prune come to us from Europe but these are more in the manner of a sweetmeat and not only a very expensive luxury but too delicious to recommend experimenting with except, perhaps, to soak them in the best brandy.

To rescuscitate prunes soak them in cold water, tea or brandy depending on taste, temperance and how flush you may be.

PRUNE JAM

1kg/2lb 4oz prunes	white sugar
1.15 litre/2 pints water	lemons

3 hot, dry, sterile jam jars

306

Soak the prunes in the water overnight. The next day transfer the prunes and water to a preserving pan and cook gently until very soft. Pass through a fine sieve and measure the purée, for each 600ml/1 pint take 450g/1lb warmed sugar and the juice of 1 lemon. Return the purée to the pan, heat gently and add the sugar and lemon juice, stirring well until dissolved. Bring to the boil and boil hard until a set is obtained. Pot and seal.

A very good sandwich and biscuit jam.

PRUNE AND NUT CHUTNEY

1kg/2lb 4oz prunes
900g/2lb cooking apples
600ml/1 pint wine vinegar
2 teaspoons curry powder
2 teaspoons ground cinnamon

2 teaspoons ground allspice
¼ teaspoon cayenne powder
575g/1lb 4oz dark brown sugar
225g/8oz hazelnuts

5 hot, dry, sterile jars with non-metal lids

Put the prunes into a deep bowl with cold water to cover and leave overnight. The next day peel, core and chop the apples and put them in a stainless steel pan with just enough water to prevent sticking. Cook until soft. Drain the prunes, discard the stones, chop the flesh and put it into the pan with the apple, add the spices and half the vinegar. Simmer until very soft, approximately 30 minutes. Dissolve the sugar in the remaining vinegar and stir it into the mixture, bring to the boil and then simmer for 10 minutes. Chop the hazelnuts and add them to the chutney, continue cooking until thick and smooth. Pot and seal.

Keep at least 2 weeks before eating. Hot, spicy, crunchy chutney which accompanies cold lamb very well.

PICKLED PRUNES

1kg/2lb 4oz fat, good quality prunes
225g/8oz white or soft brown sugar
¼ teaspoon fresh grated nutmeg
1 blade mace

1 teaspoon ground black pepper
600ml/1 pint malt vinegar
brandy (optional)

3 hot, dry, sterile jars with non-metal lids

Put the prunes into a deep bowl and cover completely with cold water.

Leave for at least 12 hours. They must be properly plumped out before using. Drain them well and pack into the jars. Put the remaining ingredients except the brandy into a stainless steel pan and bring to the boil, simmer for at least 10 minutes and pour while very hot over the prunes to cover completely. Add 1 tablespoon of brandy if used to each jar. Seal when cold.

Leave at least 2 months before using.

DRIED FRUIT PICKLE

1kg/2lb 4oz dried prunes, apricots,
   apples, figs, dates
25g/1oz pickling spice

1.15 litre/2 pints malt vinegar
225g/8oz white sugar

6 hot, dry, sterile jars with non-metal lids

Put all the fruits except the dates into a deep bowl and cover with a lot of water, make sure that you have room for expansion. Leave overnight. Put the spices and vinegar into a stainless steel pan and bring to the boil. Simmer for 5 minutes. Remove from the heat, cover and allow to get quite cold. Strain before using. The next day drain the fruit and reserve a small amount of water to cook them in. If the dates are in a block, chop them first, otherwise just add them to the pan with the other fruit and the water, simmer until tender. Drain well. Put the spiced vinegar and sugar into a stainless steel pan and bring to the boil, stirring well until the sugar has dissolved. Simmer until syrupy and add to the fruits. Remove immediately from the heat and stir well. Pot and seal.

Store for at least 2 months before use. For a hotter pickle add 1 dried chilli to each jar. Keep for at least 2 months before using. Very delicious with cold meats, a cross between chutney and pickle.

SHERRIED PRUNES

1kg/2lb 4oz good quality prunes
1 lemon
1kg/2lb 4oz white sugar
1.15 litre/2 pints water

1 teaspoon vanilla essence
2 whole cloves
1 bottle sherry

dry, sterile jars with wide necks

Put the prunes into a deep bowl and cover with cold water. Leave overnight. The next day drain well. Take 4 slices from the lemon and put this into a preserving pan with the sugar, water, vanilla essence and cloves, stirring well bring to the boil and then simmer for 15 minutes. Add the prunes and continue to simmer for a further 30 minutes or until they are just tender – you may need to add a little more warm water. Remove the prunes with a perforated spoon and pack into the jars leaving enough room for the sherry and syrup. Half-fill each jar with sherry and then add the strained syrup to cover completely. Seal.

Prunes and sherry combine remarkably well to make a rich and pleasant dessert fruit.

PRUNES IN PORT

fat luxury prunes   cheap port
lump sugar

sterile, dry, wide necked, preserving jar

Pop the prunes into the jar, leaving plenty of room for expansion. Add 3 lumps of sugar, 1 at the bottom, 1 in the middle and 1 at the top. Cover with port and seal tightly. Top up with more port as it is absorbed during the macerating period.

Leave for 3 months and eat as a dessert but not advisable for children. Do not waste the liquor, it is superb.

Pumpkin

In recent years there has been a tremendous resurgence in the popularity of this traditional fruit. In America the pumpkin, along with the other squashes, has always been made much of, in fact there are markets, fairs and festivals given over to just the pumpkin, splendid creations of gargantuan size. They are transformed into pies, puddings, ice cream, jams and preserves. But in Great Britain we have been more conservative and only use pumpkins for Halloween masks when the flesh is gouged out and a face cut into the peel, a nightlight placed in the middle gives the desired flickering effect. Do not waste the firm flesh; after all that hard work you can use it for any of the recipes below.

Pumpkin is also sold by the piece in many greengrocers. They are totally recognizable being large, roundly squat with a lumpy bumpy skin of soft orange. The flesh when it is fully ripe is a deep golden orange, with something of the taste between marrow and a cantaloupe melon. Related to marrows and squashes, pumpkin should be planted and grown in much the same way but they usually mature in the autumn.

Pumpkins in preserving have no appreciable setting qualities so their chief virtue is that they are pleasantly mildly flavoured and provide plenty of bulk for other fruit. Although I have given specific recipes, the marrow and melon recipes work equally well with pumpkins.

PUMPKIN AND CRANBERRY JAM

1kg/2lb 4oz prepared pumpkin
225g/8oz cranberries
1 lemon

300ml/½ pint water
1225g/2lb 12oz white sugar

5 hot, dry, sterile jam jars

Peel the pumpkin, remove the soft flesh and seed. Dice and weigh the firm flesh. Wash the cranberries and put them into a preserving pan with the pumpkin, the juice from the lemon and the water. Bring to the boil, cover and simmer until soft. Add the sugar, stirring well until it has dissolved. Bring to the boil and boil hard until it is very thick. Do not overboil. Pot and seal.

PUMPKIN AND QUINCE JAM

1kg/2lb 4oz prepared pumpkin
500g/1lb 2oz quinces
1 lemon

450ml/¾ pint water
1450g/3lb 4oz white sugar

7 hot, dry, sterile jam jars

Peel the pumpkin, discard the soft flesh and seeds. Dice and weigh the firm flesh. Peel, core and chop the quince and tie the peelings and cores into a large muslin bag. Squeeze the juice from the lemon and put this with both fruits and the muslin bag into a preserving pan, add the water and bring to the boil. Cover and simmer until soft – quince take absolutely ages and absorb loads of water so do not be alarmed if you have to add a drop more warm water, but do not overdo it. Remove the muslin bag giving it a good squeeze and add the warmed sugar, stirring well until it has dissolved. Bring to the boil and boil gently until a set is obtained. Pot and seal.

A very good tasty recipe. One cookery book, published during the last war, recommends that for economy's sake you mince the quince to cut down on cooking time. A pressure cooker is not much help as it causes the pumpkin to disintegrate and both fruits should be cooked together for a good result.

PUMPKIN MARMALADE

1kg/2lb 4oz prepared pumpkin
2 Seville oranges

300ml/½ pint water
1kg/2lb 4oz white sugar

5 hot, dry, sterile jam jars

Peel the pumpkin and discard the soft flesh and seeds. Dice and weigh the firm flesh. Wash and finely slice the oranges. Put the oranges in one bowl with the water and the pumpkin in another bowl with the sugar. Cover both and leave for 24 hours. Place the oranges and water in a preserving pan and bring to the boil, add the pumpkin and sugar, stirring well until the sugar has dissolved. Bring to the boil and boil gently until the pumpkin is transparent and tender. Pot and seal.

A very good syrupy breakfast preserve. For a thicker marmalade you can try mincing the oranges but do not forget to remove the pips.

PUMPKIN PICKLE

1kg/2lb 4oz prepared pumpkin
750ml/1¼ pints white vinegar
750g/1lb 10oz white sugar
3 teaspoons celery salt

1 piece root ginger
1 stick cinnamon
3 teaspoons white mustard seed
6 whole cloves

3 hot, dry, sterile jars with non-metal lids

Peel the pumpkin and discard the soft flesh and seeds. Cut the firm flesh into dice and weigh. Put the sugar and vinegar into a stainless steel pan and boil until it becomes a thin syrup. Place the pieces of pumpkin in a large china bowl and cover with the boiling liquid. Leave for 24 hours. The next day drain off the syrup and pour it into a stainless steel pan with all the spices. Bring to the boil and throw in the pumpkin. Simmer for 3 hours. Pot and seal.

This is a very good sweet pickle with cold ham, tongue and spiced beef. For a dark pickle use brown sugar and vinegar.

PUMPKIN CHUTNEY

1kg/2lb 4oz prepared pumpkin
450g/1lb ripe tomatoes
225g/8oz onions
50g/2oz sultanas
350g/12oz white sugar
350g/12oz soft, dark brown sugar
2 tablespoons sea salt
1 rounded teaspoon ground ginger

1 rounded teaspoon fresh ground
   black peppercorns
1 rounded teaspoon fresh ground
   allspice berries
2 cloves garlic
600ml/1 pint tarragon, cider or wine
   vinegar

5 hot, dry, sterile jars with non-metal lids

Peel the pumpkin, remove the soft flesh and seeds. Dice and weigh the firm flesh. Prick the tomatoes with a needle and dunk quickly into boiling water and then into cold water (this will help you to whip the skins off easily without undue nerve snapping), cut them into wedges. Peel and chop the onions and garlic. Put all the ingredients into a stainless steel pan and bring gently to the boil, stirring well. Reduce the heat and simmer until the mixture is thick, smooth and cooked, stir frequently to prevent sticking. Pot and seal.

A very pleasant, mild chutney.

Quince

One of my warmest childhood memories is that of the spicy, sweet, sharp smell of ripening quinces on the kitchen dresser mingling with wood smoke and baking cakes, the last of the summer sun and the promise of good things to come. It therefore came as no surprise to learn that this most ancient fruit was considered an emblem of love and happiness by the Gods. The perfume is all pervading and if you like it, it has a supremely tranquillising effect. The fruit, something of a cross between apple and pear, deep gold and rather irregularly shaped, has an odd and unmistakable flavour which goes well with apples and pears (add a few to a golden apple pie) and gives a unique touch to savoury dishes particularly pork. If you have one of the strange gnarled and knotted trees in your garden then you will have discovered the value of quince in the kitchen for not only are they excellent in cooking but make superior preserves traditional in both Britain and Europe ranging from the membrillo and cotignac paste of Spain and France to the old-fashioned preserves of Great Britain, deep amber or glowing cornelian in colour, which give as much pleasure to the eye as to the palate.

Quinces have several drawbacks. They should be picked when just ripening and be allowed to mature indoors for if they ripen on the tree the granular cores become hard and woody. If however they become too soft they are difficult to use in preserves for the centre takes on a fibrous quality which does not improve on keeping. To balance the odds in their favour though, quinces are very high in pectin and make a trouble-free set but as the peels and cores take up a substantial part of the fruit – approximately 50g/2oz to each 450g/1lb – they are usually made use of in the making of the preserve both for the extract and to add the colour. The best basic proportions for quince preserves are 0.5 litre water, 1.25kg/2½lb sugar and the juice of 1 lemon to each 1kg/2lb 4oz fruit. If the fruit is hard you will find that it will absorb a deal of water, this being so, more warm water may be added with discretion.

Quince is not a fruit to be eaten raw nor should it be stored in close proximity to other foods for, as I have said, the scent is all pervading and powerful.

QUINCE JAM

1kg/2lb 4oz quinces
1 lemon

water
1225g/2lb 12oz white sugar

6 hot, dry, sterile jam jars

Wash, peel, core and chop the quinces into small pieces. Extract the juice from the lemon, gather up the pips and tie them into a muslin bag with the cores and peelings from the quinces. Put the fruit and the muslin bag into a preserving pan and just cover with water. Bring to the boil and simmer until very soft. This takes quite a long time and it will hasten the process if you cover the pan, but do not let it boil dry while you are not watching. Also – quince seems to absorb water with alarming rapidity – if you feel that it is absolutely necessary then add a little more warm water but use your discretion. When the fruit is very soft remove the muslin bag giving it a good squeeze. Add the warmed sugar and lemon juice, heat gently stirring well until it has dissolved and bring to the boil. Boil hard until a set is obtained. Pot and seal.

For economy's sake you may wish to use a pressure cooker. Take the same quantity of fruit prepared in the same way and just, but only just, cover with water. Cook at M/10 1lb pressure for 8 minutes. If you do not have a pressure cooker try grating the quince, particularly if they are firm. Quince jam has a unique and delicious taste which children will say tickles the nose. It also sets well and is a great family favourite.

SPICED QUINCE JAM

Following the ingredients and method given for Quince Jam but use 625g/1lb 6oz white sugar, 625g/1lb 6oz soft brown sugar and add 1 rounded teaspoon of ground mixed spice.

QUINCE AND CRANBERRY JAM

1kg/2lb 4oz quinces
500g/1lb 2oz cranberries

750ml/1¼ pints water
1675g/3lb 12oz white sugar

7 hot, dry, sterile jam jars

Wash and roughly chop the quince and put into a preserving pan with the water. Bring to the boil and then simmer until very soft. Pass through a sieve and return the purée to the pan. Wash the cranberries and add them to the quince purée, simmer for 20 minutes by which time the skin on the cranberries should be tender. Add the warmed sugar and heat gently stirring well until it has dissolved. Bring to the boil and reduce the heat immediately, continue at a gentle boil until a set is obtained. Pot and seal.

Fabulous colour for a jam that is equally good eaten as sweet or savoury.

QUINCE JELLY

1kg/2lb 4oz quinces
1 litre/1¾ pints water

1 large lemon
white sugar

3 hot, dry, sterile jam jars

Wash and cut up the quinces quite small. Put into a preserving pan with the water and cook until very soft. As with all quince recipes, especially if the fruit is hard, it may be necessary to add more warm water during cooking but do not overdo it. Turn the cooked fruit into a clean muslin bag and leave to drain overnight into a china bowl. The next day measure the juice gained and for each 600ml/1 pint take 450g/1lb warmed sugar. Pare the rind from half the lemon and tie it into a muslin bag, take a few fine shreds from the remaining peel and put them to one side. Squeeze out the lemon juice and put this into a preserving pan with the quince juice and muslin bag, heat gently and add the sugar stirring well until it has dissolved. Bring to the boil and boil rapidly until a set is obtained, remove muslin bag and leave the jelly to cool a little. Skim and half-fill the jars, add a piece of the reserved lemon peel to each jar and fill up. Seal when cold. Quince jelly frequently looks cloudy during the straining process, it will clear once the sugar is added unless, of course, you have been prodding it! A scented geranuim leaf may be added to the jars instead of the lemon, either way it gives an added distinction which is not essential but very nice.

This fiery gold jelly has a mouth watering flavour which goes superbly well with game and cold meats as well as being smashing on hot brown toast. Use sieved pulp to make quince cheese or if you would prefer to be economical and do not mind a softer jelly, then reboil the pulp with half the original quantity of water, allow the pulp to drain overnight in a jelly bag and add it to the first collection of juice, measure and continue as above.

JOANNA'S QUINCE PRESERVE

1kg/2lb 4oz quinces   1 large lemon
1kg/2lb 4oz parsnips   1 litre/1¾ pints water
1 large orange   1kg/2lb 4oz white sugar

5 hot, dry, sterile jars

Peel, core and slice the quinces, drop them into a bowl of cold water to which a dash of lemon juice has been added to prevent discolouration. Wash and chop the parsnips. Slice the oranges and lemons finely and put them into a preserving pan with the parsnips and water. Cover and simmer until very soft and limp looking. Turn into a fine sieve and press gently to extract the maximum amount of juice but no pulp. Collect the juice and return it to the clean pan with the well drained quinces and the sugar. Heat gently, stirring well until the sugar has dissolved, bring to the boil and then reduce the heat to simmer gently until the fruit is quite soft. Remove the quince slices with a perforated spoon and pack into the jars. Reboil the syrup until it is thick and pour it over the fruit to cover. Seal when cold.

I first bought a jar of this preserve about a year ago at a country fair and I could not believe my eyes – parsnip in a fruit preserve – but after I had wangled the recipe out of the cook I realized that the partnership of the rich sweetness of parsnip and the citrus elements complement the offbeat flavour of quince very well to give a delicious preserve.

QUINCE MARMALADE

1kg/2lb 4oz quinces
1kg/2lb 4oz white sugar
250ml/8fl. oz water

1 small lemon
vanilla essence (optional)

4 hot, dry, sterile jam jars

Peel the quinces and grate coarsely. Put into a pan with the water and cook until soft. Add the warmed sugar, stirring well until it has dissolved and bring to the boil. Squeeze the juice from the lemon, add it to the quince and continue to simmer until the marmalade is thick, syrupy and a jellified sort of set is obtained. Stir in the vanilla. Allow to cool before potting. Seal when cold.

A very beautiful cornelian preserve which spreads well and is very good on brown toast. Simple, almost foolproof, and I can thoroughly recommend it.

SPICED QUINCE

1kg/2lb 4oz large, ripe quinces
50g/2oz sea salt
white sugar

wine vinegar
coriander seeds

3 hot, dry, sterile jars

Wash, then peel, core and cut the quinces into eighths, do not discard the peels and cores. Put the fruit into a saucepan and cover with cold water, add the salt and boil hard for 10 minutes. Drain well. Put the peels and cores into another pan and cover with cold water, boil until very soft. Strain and measure the juice – for each 600ml/1 pint take 450g/1lb sugar, 150ml/¼ pint vinegar and 1 good teaspoon of coriander. Return these ingredients to a stainless steel pan with the juice and bring gently to the boil, add the quinces and simmer until tender but do not allow the fruit to break up in any way. Pour fruit, juice etc., into a china bowl, cover and leave to stand overnight. The next day drain off the syrup, return it to the pan and bring to the boil. Pour over the fruit, cover and leave overnight. The next day drain of the syrup and return it to the pan, bring to the boil and boil hard until reduced and thick. Pack the fruit into the jars and cover with the hot syrup. Seal.

One of the very best pickles with cold white meats and excellent for cutting the richness of lamb or mutton.

R

Radish

The familiar red or red and white radish are those most frequently grown in Britain and may be either round or long depending on variety, however there are also some variation of pure white radish that are equally good. As most radishes, particularly the elongated kind, become woody, hot and hollow if kept too long in the ground or stored in any way, it is wise to look for some of the newer varieties which can be left in. Otherwise, plant your radish seeds at intervals to prevent them all maturing in one fell swoop. Leave some radishes to go to seed and pickle the pods. In fact there is a variety of radish – Munchen Bier – that has been cultivated specifically to produce edible pods which can be eaten as a green vegetable. Winter radish – Spanish Black and China Rose – take longer to grow and may be lifted and stored in the winter as you would any root vegetable and with no adverse effects. These exotic ladies are crisp, large and mildly hot. Grated into winter salads they are a tremendous boon. The familiar salad radish is really quite versatile and if you do have an unfortunate glut remember that not only can the fresh young leaves be cooked as you would spinach but the root itself can be blanched, braised or put into stews and sauces (there is a particularly good one using chopped egg and asparagus with radish). A handy tip – when you cut a radish decoratively for a salad, drop it into a bowl of iced water where it will open out into an attractive shape.

Do not grow brassicas on ground that radish has occupied. In order to subdue the little monsters that chew their way through each root of radish, grow a few cress between the rows, this will distract the pest long enough for the radishes to mature unscathed.

STORE WINTER RADISH

As for Jerusalem Artichokes, p.68.

PICKLED RADISH PODS

radish pods
100g/4oz sea salt
1 litre/1¾ pints water

dried red chilli peppers
white vinegar

small, dry, sterile jars with non-metal lids

Pick tender radish pods and make sure that they have no greenfly on them. Use them immediately. Boil up the water and salt and drop the pods into this. Leave until cold when miraculously they should turn bright green; if they do not – then just reboil the brine and drop the pods in again until cold. In the meantime, boil up the vinegar in a stainless steel pan and leave that to get quite cold. Wash the brine from the radish pods, drain well and pack them into the jars with the chillies. Cover with the cold vinegar. Seal.

Add to hors d'oeuvres, salads or use in mixed pickles at a later date.

Raspberry

The raspberry – closely related to the blackberry – is another fruit which although well known to gardeners grows very frequently in the wild. The fruit, made up of soft one seeded drupelets, is carried on canes and is usually red, although there are other varieties such as the golden raspberry, black raspberry or thimleberry, more familiar in the USA, and the purple or red-black raspberry. Two other related species are the Golden Mayberry and the Japanese Wineberry – the latter grown mainly for decoration. Raspberries are without doubt the most rewarding fruit to grow in any garden and I find that if you look after them they are very little trouble. Most modern raspberries come from Malling stock but two names worth remembering, particularly with an eye to preserving are Norfolk Giant and Zeva. The red-black raspberries are also to be recommended for their small seeds.

The soft, sweet-acid berries come to fruition in mid-summer and although they make excellent preserves with an adequate amount of pectin they are at their very best eaten fresh. When picking raspberries leave the hull and stalk on the stem – in this way you can be sure that they are ripe for if they are not they will not slip easily from the cane. If you fear the presence of wriggly things inside do not be tempted to soak them out, just lay the raspberries out flat on a dish and leave it in a cool place when hopefully the tiny maggots will leave home. Raspberries of course make the most delicious puddings – raspberry cream, ice cream, summer pudding, fool, bavarois, in kissel, in beautiful decorative flans and many other mouthwatering goodies.

Raspberry tea made with the leaves and berries also makes a very ancient brew – as small scruffy children we were held spellbound by an equally nasty little girl who regaled us chapter and verse with the maternity benefits of the raspberry as used by her infinitely witch-like grandmother. Awestruck, we never for a moment doubted that were another raspberry to pass our lips, so we would be smitten down by instant pregnancy! The berries of the raspberry contain a fair amount of iron, potassium and vitamins A and C. Raspberry leaves are both tranquillizing and effective in treating skin rashes.

Raspberries in the shops early in the season are usually from France, later in the year they are home-produced.

RASPBERRY JAMS

In the following recipes the ingredients are basic but the methods are varied and much depends on personal preference and the quality of the fruit used. Squishily over-ripe fruit should not be used for jam making as it can cause mould. Even if you have used perfect fruit you may find a mould forming on top – this can be caused by a wet summer which causes raspberries to retain a great deal of water. It is not dangerous but should be removed immediately before it goes too far, to prevent the flavour spoiling. I have been told that the mould, removed in one piece, may be laid upon wounds to heal them.

BASIC INGREDIENTS

1kg/2lb 4oz raspberries
1kg/2lb 4oz white sugar

3-4 hot, dry, sterile jam jars

GENERAL PREPARATION

Do not wash the fruit but pick it over well and make sure soft centres and stalk pieces are removed. To remove suspected maggots place the fruit in a very cold place for several hours (not the deep freeze).

METHOD 1 (FOR VERY SOFT FRUIT)

Place the prepared raspberries in a china bowl in layers with the sugar. Cover and leave in a cool place (not the refrigerator) for 24 hours. By this time there should be quite a lot of juice. Turn the contents of the bowl into a preserving pan and bring gently to the boil, stirring well. Boil for 3 minutes only and remove instantly from the heat, making sure that you give it a good stir. Leave to cool. Pot. Seal when cold.

The best flavour.

METHOD 2

Place the prepared raspberries in a preserving pan and heat gently until some of the juices are beginning to run. Simmer until the fruit is soft and then pass through a fine sieve. Return the pureé and juices to the clean pan and heat gently, add the warmed sugar, stirring well until it has dissolved. Bring to the boil and boil hard until a set is obtained. Pot and seal.

Seedless jam that is a necessity if you have small children, stomach ailments or dentures.

RASPBERRY JAM USING COMMERCIAL PECTIN

1kg/2lb 4oz ripe raspberries
1400g/3lb 2oz white sugar

150ml/¼ pint commercial liquid pectin

5 hot, dry, sterile jam jars

Pick over the raspberries removing hulls, stalks etc., if necessary. Put them into a large preserving pan and mash down well with a wooden spoon or spud basher, add the sugar and heat slowly stirring continously until it has dissolved. Bring quickly to a full boil and boil for 2 minutes, still stirring. Remove from the heat and add the pectin. Skim and stir for 2 minutes. Allow to cool a little before potting. Seal when cold.

If the raspberries are very ripe and soft you will find that it is necessary to use pectin in order to obtain a set without waste. For a different flavour add 2 small teaspoons of orange essence to the jam when the pectin is stirred in.

RASPBERRY AND REDCURRANT JAM

1kg/2lb 4oz raspberries   150ml/¼ pint water
1kg/2lb 4oz redcurrants   2kg/4lb 8oz white sugar

8 hot, dry, sterile jam jars

Pick over the raspberries. Wash the redcurrants and remove the stalks, put them into a preserving pan with the water and cook for approximately 5 minutes. Add the raspberries and bring quickly to the boil, stir in the warmed sugar and continue stirring until it has dissolved. Bring to the boil and boil hard until a set is obtained. Pot and seal.

Finest, freshest flavour of all but take care not to overcook at any stage of the proceedings. Marvellous on summer flans, in sweet souffles or for topping cheesecake.

RASPBERRY AND RHUBARB JAM

1kg/2lb 4oz raspberries   450ml/¾ pint water
1kg/2lb 4oz rhubarb   2kg/4lb 8oz white sugar

8 hot, dry, sterile jam jars

Pick over the raspberries, wash and strip the fibrous skin from the outside of the rhubarb, taking off the leaf and the bulbous end of the stalk. Cut the sticks into pieces and put into a stainless steel pan with the water, simmer until soft. Add the raspberries and cook until they are just soft. Stir in the warmed sugar and continue to stir until it has dissolved then bring to the boil and boil hard until a set is obtained. Pot. Seal when cold.

Rhubarb has a fine sharp flavour that goes well with raspberries and if you grow rhubarb yourself this is a very economical jam indeed.

HIGH SUMMER JAM

500g/1lb 2oz raspberries
500g/1lb 2oz strawberries
500g/1lb 2oz blackcurrants

500g/1lb 2oz redcurrants
2kg/4lb 8oz white sugar

6 hot, dry, sterile jam jars

Hull and pick over the raspberries and strawberries, do not wash although you may need to wipe the strawberries. Wash the blackcurrants and redcurrants and remove them from the stalks using the prongs of a fork. Put the blackcurrants into a preserving pan with just enough water to prevent sticking and simmer until just soft. Add the other fruit and cook until they are tender. Stir in the warmed sugar and continue stirring until it has dissolved. Bring to the boil and boil hard until a set is obtained. Pot and seal.

This same method may be applied to any soft fruit, e.g., loganberries, white currants, raspberries, cherries, strawberries, gooseberries, black-currants (these last two should be cooked before the others – see above) and in any quantity but if you do not use any high pectin fruit then add the juice of 1 lemon to each 450g/1lb fruit. This is a jolly good way of using up fruit that is not at its best for the table.

OLD FASHIONED RASPBERRY JELLY

1kg/2lb 4oz raspberries
white sugar

4 small, hot, dry, sterile jars

Put the clean raspberries into a covered dish and leave in a warm oven until the juices begin to flow. Turn into a thick muslin bag and leave to drain until the surplus juice has run out. Now wring the bag – absolutely forbidden in other circumstances – until all the juice is extracted, which has the same effect as putting the fruit into a press. Measure the liquid gained and for each 600ml/1 pint take 575g/1¼lb very warm sugar. Return the juice to the pan and heat gently, add the sugar, stirring well until it has dissolved. Bring to the boil and boil hard for 5 minutes. Pot and seal.

If you use small moulds instead of jars this jelly should be firm enough to turn out and use as decoration or eaten with cream cheese and sugar – a truly Victorian country recipe.

RASPBERRY AND APPLE JELLY

1kg/2lb 4oz raspberries
500g/1lb 2oz cooking apples

450ml/¾ pint water
white sugar

4 hot, dry, sterile jam jars

Pick over the raspberries. Wash and chop the apples and place both fruit into a preserving pan with the water. Cook until very soft and turn into a jelly bag, leave to drain overnight into a bowl. The next day measure the juice gained and for each 600ml/1 pint take 450g/1lb warmed sugar. Return the juice to the pan and heat gently, add the sugar, stirring well until it has dissolved. Bring to the boil and boil hard until a set is obtained – approximately 10 minutes. Pot and seal.

A good easy way to use up small or very soft raspberries and windfall or under-ripe apples. Gooseberries may be substituted for the apples.

RASPBERRY PRESERVE

1kg/2lb 4oz raspberries
1kg/2lb 4oz white sugar

4 tablespoons water
¼ teaspoon vanilla essence

4 hot, dry, sterile jars

Pick over the fruit and put it into a china bowl with the sugar. Cover and leave for at least 12 hours. The next day turn the contents of the bowl into a preserving pan and add the water, bring to the boil stirring gently and then boil for 7 minutes. Remove the fruit with a perforated spoon and lay on a sieve, transferring any juices that drip through to the pan. Continue to boil the syrup until it is very thick. Add the raspberries and a few drops of vanilla essence. Remove from heat and allow to cool before potting. Seal when cold.

BOTTLED SUMMER FRUIT SALAD
USING PRESSURE COOKER

675g/1lb 8oz raspberries   450g/1lb redcurrants
675g/1lb 8oz strawberries   450g/1lb blackcurrants
450g/1lb black cherries   caster sugar
450g/1lb loganberries   water

8 450g/1lb-size sterilized preserving jars and lids

Although this recipe sounds complicated it is very easy indeed and it is by far and away the best method of bottling soft fruit like raspberries and strawberries. For each jar you will need approximately 1 litre/1¾ pints boiled water. That means it must have boiled once and should be very hot but not boiling when you use it. Prepare the fruit by wiping or washing, removing stalks, hulls and stones where necessary, taking care not to lose any of the juices.

Start off with a layer of halved cherries adding a few kernels if liked. Sprinkle with 2 heaped teaspoons of sugar, follow with loganberries, then blackcurrants, next redcurrants and make sure that each layer of fruit has its quota of sugar. Finish up with the strawberries and lastly raspberries – neither of these two need sugar. As you work, tap and shake the fruit to encourage it to settle down. Fill the jars with the very hot water giving ample time for it to work right through and ousting any air bubbles. Seal with clip or screw tops which should be given a half twist back to allow for expansion.

Take a pressure cooker and reverse the trivet rim side up within the pan. Fill with 900ml/1½ pints boiling water, adding a dash of lemon juice or vinegar to prevent discolouration. Take the hot jars straight to the cooker, making sure that they do not touch, a twist of newspaper around each will act as a buffer. If you are fiddling about a lot and the jars show signs of cooling before you can get them into the pan then pop them into a bowl of very hot or simmering water as you fill each one, they can then be transferred, boiling hot, to the pressure cooker but do take care not to burn yourself. Cover and bring to 5lb/L pressure for 1 minute only. Allow the pressure to reduce at room temperature. When you move the cooker take care that the jars do not crash about. Lift the jars out onto a wooden board or several layers of cloth. If you transfer boiling jars to a cold surface you may either lose the bottom of the jar or cause an uneven cooling of the fruit. Tighten screw bands and repeat again later. The next day test the jars for a correct seal by removing bands or clips and lifting jars by the glass lid. If the top comes off, use straight away. If not then replace screw bands and clips and store. N.B. The jars are sealed during processing.

Served chilled in their own syrup, a very agreeable surprise in the heart of winter, and served with a crème brûlée, a sophisticated supper sweet.

I have given large quantities here but it is worth reducing the amounts to take advantage of a few punnets bought in season.

Rhubarb

As I cannot pretend to be a fiercely dedicated gardener, I have not done unto my rhubarb all those things like feeding it well and forcing it early in the year, but it has stood like Goliath on the remmants of an old compost heap in full sunshine at the bottom of my garden for ages. The only protection it has been offered has unwittingly been provided by the annual fall of bay leaves under which it becomes snugly buried. The gargantuan green leaves are a decorative composition of their own and the long, thick, red, juicy stems without fibre or toughness are picked by the kilo week after week. I know that the plants are supposed to be divided after five years and that they must be buried into well manured soil, that flower stems should be removed and that black boxes, tubs or pots covered with manure should encourage an early growth, which is said to be sweeter and more tender. However, I have done none of these things and, having had my one rhubarb crown (bought originally in a penny store) for years without hassle, I do not now wish to tempt providence by over-indulging it.

Things which everyone should know about rhubarb: the leaves are deadly poisonous, so do not eat them yourself or give them to the rabbit; the bulbous bright base of the stem must also always be removed; rhubarb has a high oxalic acid content as does spinach and sorrel – this is why it sets the teeth on edge.

Rhubarb makes the most delicious puddings ranging from the humble pie to the elegant sorbet. Stewed rhubarb in pies, fools and crumbles can be given a sweet life by the addition of angelica or ginger and a stick of rhubarb stirred through a pan of gooseberry jam, or a few pieces added to stewed gooseberries will impart a glorious glowing pink to the fruit. The tart yet sweet flavour of rhubarb is very refreshing, particularly as a cold drink and as the basis of fruit punch.

Rhubarb in preserve making is economical but not always very accommodating, for the pectin content is fairly low and consequently it should be cooked without water to achieve a set. Early rhubarb will need a little water to soften it and will set better, but late rhubarb will need no water and requires the addition of lemon to bring about a set. Nevertheless, it is one of those fruit – like plums – which cannot be one hundred per cent guaranteed to co-operate, unless used in conjunction with apple, blackcurrant or lemon.

326

It stands to reason that if rhubarb leaves affect us adversely, they might do the same with garden nasties. Aphis and sucking pests come particularly to mind. Make up this thoroughly lethal concoction to spray on roses etc. If, however, you also spray on fruit, vegetables and herbs for the table, they must be left at least two weeks before being eaten. Cut up 1kg/2lb 4oz rhubarb leaves and boil in 2 litres/4 pints water for 30 minutes. Strain and add 125g/5oz soft laundry soap, dissolve it well and leave to cool. Safer on the whole than chemical sprays.

Here is a very handy hint which may well cause roars of rage amongst the purists, but is an economical godsend for rhubarb jam that refuses to set. Add it to chutney – particularly apple or marrow – in this way: for each 1kg/2lb 4oz main fruit used in the chutney recipe, take 675g/1½lb jam, reduce the amount of sugar by at least half according to taste, and add the jam when the sugar is added, stir well to ensure that it is completely mixed. The same method can be applied to plum jam which also gives problems. Most chutneys are much improved by this deception.

RHUBARB JAMS

When using rhubarb in jam making, try to wait until the second crop which has a better flavour. Ripe fruit requires the addition of lemon juice (4 tablespoons to each kg/2lb 4oz fruit) but no water. Unripe fruit requires water (2 tablespoons) but no lemon. Early spring rhubarb requires both. Make sure that you remove every scrap of leaf which is very poisonous – in one part of the UK a whole battalion of enemy soldiers were once removed wholesale by the serving of rhubarb leaves as a green vegetable. Also remove the bulbous pink base. If the sticks of rhubarb are large and ripe it will probably be necessary to strip off a percentage of the skin – rather like stringing beans. The setting properties of rhubarb are not great but the flavour is fine and blends admirably with other fruit. Weigh the sticks after the leaf and base have been removed. Do not cook in aluminium.

RHUBARB JAM USING COMMERCIAL PECTIN

1kg/2lb 4oz rhubarb	50g/2oz crystallized ginger
200ml/7fl. oz water	1500g/3lb 6oz white sugar
2 lemons	150ml/¼ pint commercial pectin
piece root ginger	

7 hot, dry, sterile jam jars

Wash and chop the rhubarb and put it into a large preserving pan, stainless steel or enamel, with the water. Extract 3 good tablespoons of juice from the lemons, bruise the root ginger and tie it into a muslin bag. Add the lemon juice and muslin bag to the pan and bring to the boil. Simmer gently until the rhubarb is tender. Chop the crystallized ginger and add it to the pan with the warmed sugar, stirring well until the sugar has dissolved. Bring to the boil and boil quickly for 3 minutes. Remove the pan from the heat and retrieve the muslin bag. Add the pectin and stir well with a long handled spoon to avoid its effervescent qualities. Continue to stir and skim for 1 minute and leave to cool a little. Stir well and pot. Seal when cold.

An economical jam.

RHUBARB AND ANGELICA JAM

1kg/2lb 4oz rhubarb
2 large lemons

1kg/2lb 4oz white sugar
50g/2oz preserved angelica

5 hot, dry, sterile jam jars

Wash, trim and cut the rhubarb into pieces, put in layers with the sugar into a china bowl. Leave overnight. Squeeze the juice from the lemons and add this to the fruit, stir well, transfer to a preserving pan and bring to the boil. Boil rapidly until a set is obtained. Remove from the heat, chop the angelica and add it to the jam. Allow to cool a little. Stir well. Pot. Seal when cold.

Fresh young angelica can be used instead of preserved angelica. Just chop it finely and add it to the pan when the cooking commences. This is a good basic recipe. Chopped almonds can be substituted for the angelica.

RHUBARB AND ELDERFLOWER JAM

1kg/2lb 4oz ripe rhubarb
1 large handful elderflowers

1 large lemon
1kg/2lb 4oz white sugar

5 hot, dry, sterile jam jars

Wash and cut the rhubarb into small pieces, put into a large china bowl. Tie the well inspected, shaken and clean flowers into a muslin bag, allowing just a few to escape as they look so attractive, but do not leave any thick stalk. Bury the bag in amongst the rhubarb and pop the sugar on the top, turn over gently with a wooden spoon, cover and leave for 24 hours. Every 6 hours or so give a good stir. Turn the contents of the bowl into a stainless steel pan. Heat gently to the boiling point, stirring occasionally and then remove immediately from the heat. Return to the bowl, cover and leave for a further 24 hours. Grate the rind from the lemon, retrieve the muslin bag giving it a good squeeze and once again turn the contents of the bowl into the pan. Add the lemon rind, bring to the boil, stirring occasionally and boil hard until a set is obtained. Pot and seal.

All this to-ing and fro-ing does ensure a good set and that delicious elderflower fragrance.

RHUBARB AND GRAPEFRUIT JAM

1kg/2lb 4oz rhubarb   1kg/2lb 4oz white sugar
1 large grapefruit

5 hot, dry, sterile jam jars

Wash the rhubarb and cut into small chunks. Wash the grapefruit and, working on a dish to catch the juices, grate the rind, remove the pith and pips and press the flesh through a coarse sieve. Put the rhubarb, grapefruit peel and juice into a china bowl with the sugar, mix well and cover. Leave to stand overnight. The next day turn the contents of the bowl into a stainless steel pan and bring to the boil, stirring well until the last little bit of sugar has dissolved. Boil hard until a set is obtained. Pot and seal.

A strong sharp jam, very acceptable for breakfast after an over-indulgent evening.

RHUBARB AND RAISIN JAM

1kg/2lb 4oz rhubarb   225g/8oz fat seedless raisins
1 large lemon   1kg/2lb 4oz white sugar

5 hot, dry, sterile jam jars

Wash, trim and cut the rhubarb into pieces. Squeeze the juice from the lemon and mix it together with the rhubarb and remaining ingredients in a china bowl. Cover and leave for 24 hours. Turn the contents into a stainless steel pan and bring to the boil, stirring continuously. Boil until a set is obtained. Leave to cool before potting. Seal when cold.

GLENCAR JAM

1kg/2lb 4oz rhubarb
225g/8oz dried block figs
100g/4oz candied lemon peel

1 small lemon
1kg/2lb 4oz white sugar

6 hot, dry, sterile jam jars

Wash, trim and cut the rhubarb into pieces. Chop the figs very small and shred the candied lemon peel. Squeeze the juice from the lemon and put all the ingredients into a china bowl. Cover and leave to stand for 24 hours. Transfer to a stainless steel pan and heat gently, stirring well, until all the sugar has dissolved. Bring to the boil and boil hard until a set is obtained. Pot and seal.

A very tasty, bright clear jam which improves on keeping. If you keep all those squeezed lemons and candy the peel you will be able to make an inexpensive jam.

RHUBARB JELLY

1kg/2lb 4oz red autumn rhubarb
1 large lemon

white sugar

6 medium size, hot, dry, sterile jars

Wash, trim and cut the rhubarb into pieces. Pare the rind from the lemon and put the rhubarb and lemon peel into a casserole or covered heatproof jar. Leave to stand in a low oven until the juices are flowing and the fruit is very soft. Turn into a muslin bag and leave to drain overnight into a china bowl. The next day measure the juice gained and for each 600ml/1 pint take 675g/1½lb warmed sugar. Return the rhubarb juice to a stainless steel pan with the juice from the lemon, heat gently and add the sugar, stirring continuously until it has dissolved. Bring to the boil and boil hard until a set is obtained. Pot and seal.

A very good, old fashioned recipe. You will need much more than 1kg/2lb 4oz rhubarb to catch an appreciable amount of juice and the set will be very soft.

MRS MERRYWEATHER'S RHUBARB PRESERVE

1kg/2lb 4oz ripe red rhubarb   1kg/2lb 4oz white sugar
110g/4oz good quality mixed peel

5 hot, dry, sterile jam jars

Wash, trim and cut the rhubarb into pieces. Chop the mixed peel finely – please do not use the flaccid ready cut peel in plastic pots unless you absolutely have to, as it just does not impart the same subtle flavours. Put the rhubarb, sugar and peel into a china bowl, neatly layered, cover and leave overnight. The next day strain off the syrupy juice and put it into a stainless steel pan, boil until it is thick – about 10 minutes. Pour it over the bowl of fruit, cover and leave for 24 hours. The mixture should now be thick and soft. Turn it into a stainless steel pan and heat gently, stirring occasionally, taking great care not to burn. Cook in this fashion until a set is obtained. Pot and seal.

A really delicious preserve, almost oriental in taste.

SPICED RHUBARB

1kg/2lb 4oz rhubarb   1 teaspoon whole cloves
150ml/¼ pint water   1 teaspoon whole allspice
150ml/¼ pint malt vinegar   675g/1lb 8oz white sugar
¼ teaspoon ground nutmeg   350g/12oz fat seedless raisins
1 piece cinnamon

4 hot, dry, sterile jars with non-metal lids

Put the vinegar and water into a large stainless steel pan, tie the spices into a muslin bag and add to the pan with the sugar. Bring to the boil and simmer for 20 minutes. In the meantime, wash, trim and cut the rhubarb into 4cm/1½ inch pieces. Remove the muslin bag from the pan and add the rhubarb and raisins. Simmer until thick and delicious. Pot. Seal when cold.

Store for at least 2 months before use. Most unusual pickle that complements roast lamb.

FRUITY RHUBARB CHUTNEY

1kg/2lb 4oz rhubarb	25g/1oz mustard seed
100g/4oz seedless raisins	1 large piece root ginger
100g/4oz currants	15g/½oz sea salt
25g/1oz candied citron or lemon peel	600ml/1 pint vinegar
225g/8oz onions	225g/8oz soft brown sugar

4 hot, dry, sterile jars with non-metal lids

Wash, trim and cut the rhubarb into pieces. Chop the currants, raisins and peel. Peel and finely chop the onions. Bruise the mustard seed and ginger and tie them into a muslin bag. Put all the ingredients into a stainless steel pan and heat gently, stirring well. Bring slowly to the boil and then simmer, stirring regularly, for approximately 45 minutes or until the chutney is soft and thick. Remove the muslin bag. Pot and seal.

Store for at least 2 months before use. The peel and juice of 1 small lemon may be substituted for the candied peel, but do remember to tie the peel into the bag with the spices. This chutney thickens on keeping.

Rose

The Englishman has an affinity with the rose – that most British of flowers – and they have a well deserved place in our affections for their colour, shape and delicious perfume. Daily the list of roses grows longer as bright new stars are added to it but I must admit to a passion for the old fashioned roses: the cabbage, the damask, moss rose and Rugosa, to say nothing of the pale dog rose and wild sweet briar. These are the roses with their full, fair petals, soft and wrinkled or flat and gleaming in the wild which lend their breath of fragrance to the kitchen. Generally speaking they are also the gardener's friend for plants such as parsley, garlic, lavender, lupins, mignonette, onion and many others will grow happily in proximity with roses each benefiting each other considerably in some unique way, improving the soil conditions and repelling insects.

Every native born Briton will recognize rosehip syrup, the staple source of vitamin C for bonny babies, obtained from the wild rosehip, crammed with health-giving vitamins. A tea made from the hip has wonderful diuretic properties and rosehips, particularly in the northern counties, have long had a traditional use in tarts and pastries. However, great care must be taken in preparing rosehips for they have, gathered around the seeds inside, a multitude of minute bristly hairs. These are a disastrous irritant – remember old fashioned itching powder? – which is not only unpleasant if ingested but could be positively damaging to babies and small children. Split the hip open and remove every scrap of the inner seeds leaving only the flesh and skin. Wash them time and time again. If you are making syrup and jelly this is not necessary but the juice must then be strained in a many layered muslin or flannel bag to ensure that no hair wriggles through. Rosehips should be left until just after the first frost before picking when they are then bright orange, perfect and nearly impossible to find as the birds have had them all!

An incredible list of delicacies are made from the petals of the soft, fat, highly perfumed roses, ranging from brandy or liqueur to sweets and preserves, many from the Middle East, so be prepared for them to be rather sticky. Rose petals must be picked before the full sun is upon them, they should be full but not waning, dry and cleaned of insects (if you grow sage under your rose bushes you will not suffer this problem). Pull the petals from the rose and cut off the white base which is bitter if added to the preserve. Apart from the recipes included below there are some very ancient methods which are fascinating but totally impractical so I have stuck to those that are reasonably easy. Deep red, highly scented rose petals are the best to use, but the pink and whites will do equally well although not giving the glorious ruby colour. Some damask rose petals are tough but you will find that the petals of eglantine or wild rose dissolve without trouble. It is also considered that rose petal conserve made with white roses is more laxative than that made with red.

The loveliest thing of all to remember about roses is that from them, it is believed, are descended all the fruits of the earth.

ROSE PETAL JAM

100g/4oz rose petals
1 lemon
675g/1lb 8oz white sugar

150ml/¼ pint rose or orange flower
water
150ml/¼ pint water

8 small, hot, dry, attractive, sterile jars

Make sure that you use unmarked rose petals and wash and dry them only if necessary. Remove the white base ends from all of them. Extract 1 good tablespoon of juice from the lemon and put this with the sugar, rose water and water into a medium sized, heavy based pan – do not use aluminium. Stir well and leave until the sugar has dissolved of its own accord and without heat. Add the rose petals and cook over the lowest possible heat, stirring continuously until the petals are transparent. Allow to cool a little before potting.

Sweet and perfumed.

WILD ROSE JELLY

100g/4oz wild rose (eglantine) petals
450g/1lb white sugar
150ml/$\frac{1}{4}$ pint water

2 tablespoons clear honey
1 lemon
1 tablespoon orange flower water

6 small, hot, dry, sterile jars

Cut any hard base pieces from the petals (very slight with wild roses). Place the sugar, water, honey, 1 tablespoon of juice from the lemon and the orange flower water into a stainless steel pan with a heavy base. Leave to stand without heat until the sugar has dissolved. Add the rose petals and heat very, very gently, using an asbestos mat if necessary. Continue to cook in this gentle fashion stirring continuously until the rose petals melt. Allow to cool a little before potting. Seal when cold.

Damask rose petals will not dissolve. 50g/2oz of extra sugar may be substituted for the honey but the flavour will suffer. Fresh juice squeezed from the orange may be substituted for orange flower water in this recipe. An absolutely fabulous jelly, pot it up in small jars and cover with pink and white caps for exclusive gifts.

ROSE HONEY

100g/4oz rose petals
450ml/$\frac{3}{4}$ pint water
500g/1lb 2oz clear honey

1 lemon
150ml/$\frac{1}{4}$ pint commercial pectin

4 medium size, hot, dry, sterile jars

Boil the water. Cut the white pieces from the clean and insect-free petals. Put them into a colander, rinse quickly and put into a china bowl. Pour the boiling water over them, cover tightly and leave for at least 6 hours. Strain the juice from the petals, pressing well to extract every last drop. Pour the honey into a large stainless steel pan and add 1 tablespoon of juice from the lemon and the rose juice. Heat gently stirring well for 30 minutes. Bring to the boil and stir in the pectin. Boil for 3 minutes.

Remove from heat and skim and stir for a second or two. Allow to cool a little, stir once more and pot. Seal when cold.

Marvellous for sore throats and tonsilly children.

Rosemary

Rosemarinus officinalis

The shrubby evergreen rosemary is one of the most ancient of cottage garden herbs. From formal knot gardens to rambling beds of lily and lupin, this pretty bush with its dark green, silver-backed, spiky leaves and blue-lipped flowers has perfumed the air of England on many hot summer days with the pungent aromatic scent. The bush, if allowed to, will grow to 7 feet but it can also be trained to live happily in a pot. Seen from a distance behind other plants, it shimmers in a blue green haze. In Elizabethan days rosemary was burnt in rooms to purify and sweeten the air. The oil from rosemary is used in cosmetics and medicines, rub rosemary oil on the temples to alleviate headaches and smooth out those poor tired wrinkles, drink rosemary tea on those grotty days to restore your equilibrium.

I know that rosemary has a reputation for being unreliable but I find that on the warm south coast it will grow freely in the garden without trouble. If you live in colder areas then grow your plant in a pot and bring it in during the winter where it will provide you with fresh rosemary spikes. Like many herbs from the Mediterranean, rosemary prefers to grow in a loose, gravelly well drained soil in a nice hot spot. Keep it well watered and clip it well back – you can dry the clippings for later use or give them to those who do not have a ready source throughout the year.

Woody herbs like rosemary dry very well if tied into a bunch and hung upside down in a dry airy room but as the plant is evergreen this is not really necessary, better to use fresh. Fresh or dried, rosemary is very strong in taste and smell; a little is enough. It is excellent when laid on charcoal under grilling meat or oily fish and a few tiny spikes added to roasting pork, lamb, chicken, veal or bunny will give a moderate lift. To my mind though, the very best way of using rosemary is to dip a branch of it in oil to baste with, or alternatively, baste with rosemary oil. This not only gives a subtle result but also reduces the danger of swallowing spiky pieces of leaf. When used in stock it should be tied into a muslin bag unless you do as I do and grind the dried leaves to a fine powder when a mere *soupçon* can be added to sauces etc., biscuits or bread. Pack fresh branches of rosemary in among stored linen and clothes, not only does it smell good but it will give every moth for miles a fit of the shudders.

Rosemary is for remembrance and the most discreet and useful way of remembering is to make delightful sugars, vinegars and oils with it. Make Rosemary Flower Vinegar as for Lavender Flower Vinegar, p.196 and Rosemary Oil as for Marjoram Oil, p.214.

Dry Rosemary as for Sage, p.338. See also Herb Jellies, p.51.

ROSEMARY SUGAR

rosemary sprigs
caster sugar

dry, sterile, screw-topped jar

Clean and dry the rosemary, it is especially nice if you have pieces of flower left on. Place them in the jar and cover with sugar. Shake well and leave for 24 hours. Shake again and leave for 1 week.

Super in milk puddings or sprinkled on cakes.

S

Sage

Salvia officinalis

There are over five hundred species of sage, most of which have their uses in the kitchen or cure cupboard. Sage is a familiar and well loved herb from the grey-green, leafed variety with the startling blue and purple flowers to the variegated leafed, scarlet, mauve, pink, silver, red, single, bush and shrub varieties. Every garden should have at least one of the sages for not only are they useful but the bees will make whoopee amongst them. They also make extremely attractive, shrubby shapes as a background to the flowerbeds, growing most accomodatingly in the grottiest soil but appreciating full sunshine which few other plants will. Leave a few flowers to scatter their seeds and you will have enough small plants the following year to stock up the neighbourhood. Your friends will love you if you tell them that these plants, once established, will discourage slugs and aphid.

The medicinal properties of this Mediterranean herb are far-reaching, the name alone – salvia – means to heal, so not only is it considered a great antiseptic, a ward against colds, senility, failing memory, failing strength, but it counteracts shock and stress, prevents the hair and teeth from falling out, and so on and so forth. French cooks make a heartwarming soup from sage to alleviate the cold, and beauticians use sage for many purposes of vanity.

Although I love the smell of blue sage and find the pungency of red sage quite remarkable, I am not overfond of it in cooking particularly if it is used to excess. If great care is not used, delicate meat or fish dishes may be

337

overwhelmed, so I find that the sage jellies given below are a very satisfactory accompaniment to roast meats etc., and I save my sage for other fancies.

SAGE AND CIDER JELLY

50g/2oz dried sage
150ml/¼ pint water
450ml/¾ pint sweet cider
900g/2lb white sugar

yellow colouring (optional)
150ml/¼ pint liquid pectin
a few pieces fresh sage

8 small, hot, dry, sterile jars

Crumble the dried sage (do not use powdered sage) and put it into a china bowl. Boil the water and pour it over the sage. Cover and leave for 15 minutes. Strain through a muslin cloth. If necessary, add enough water to make up to 150ml/¼ pint liquid. Put into a large saucepan and add the cider and sugar. Heat gently to boiling point, stirring well until the sugar has dissolved and add enough colouring to satisfy your artistic taste. Pour in the pectin stirring constantly and take care that the whole lot does not boil over. Boil hard for 1 minute. Skim and leave to stand for a minute or two. Half-fill the jars with the cooling liquid. Make sure that the pieces of fresh sage are prettily shaped, clean and dry, place one in each jar and then fill up with the jelly. Seal when cold.

    Absolutely delicious and unique flavour – superb with cold pork.

SAGE VINEGAR

As for Tarragon Vinegar, p.353.

TO DRY SAGE

Pick the herb on a fine warm day before the sun is high – with certain herbs such as sage or rosemary it does not matter if you pick them with their flowers on, especially if they are to be dried in a bunch. Take care to remove all wildlife and try not to wash the leaves unless absolutely necessary. Tie into a bunch, not too tightly (the air must be able to circulate easily), and hang upside down in a dry airy room well away from steam or grease. Sage may be dried in sunlight but make sure that it is not too scorching for this will destroy the precious oils. If the atmosphere proves dusty tie the bunch into a large bag with holes pierced in it. Drying herbs in this manner takes about 1 week. If you prefer to dry them on a frame then strip the leaves from the stalk and leave the drying frame in a dry, airy room, stir and turn them for 4 or 5 days by which time they are ready for storing in dark airtight containers.

Satsuma

Another of the mandarin species of citrus fruit, small, segmented, sweet, lacking in pith and pips and with a loose soft skin. If satsumas are kept long they become dry and disappointing. Not such a good flavour as mandarin or tangerine. Satsumas come to Britain from Spain during October-December.

Follow recipes given for Clementines or Tangerines.

Sloe

Blackthorn (*Prunus spinosa*) is the true wild plum of Europe. Small, dense, spiny and dark, the flowers, which appear before the leaves, are small and white turning to purple-black plum-like fruit with a frosty white bloom. The acid flesh is green and if bitten into will cause teeth, tongue and tonsils to shrivel with shock. However unpalatable the fruit may be, it makes very good gin and several astringent preserves. Many years ago the fruit was roasted and eaten as it was – tough times!

It is best to pick sloes after the first frost when they are soft and juicy, if you pick them before that they should be pricked with a needle to allow the juice to escape. Arm yourself with gloves and stick when gathering sloes and be beady-eyed for not only is the sloe bush well protected by sharp thorns but the single fruit lurk underneath the leaves and are frequently missed by all but the birds who have usually stripped the bush by the time you come along.

The blackthorn blossom is said to presage the return of winter after a false spring and therefore has a black reputation in the world of folklore.

SLOE AND APPLE JELLY

1kg/2lb 4oz sloes
350g/12oz cooking apples

water
white sugar

5 medium size, hot, dry, sterile jars

Wash and prick the sloes unless they have been picked after the first frost.
Wash and chop the apples and put both fruit into a preserving pan with
just enough water to cover. Simmer until very soft, turn into a jelly bag
and leave to drain overnight into a bowl. The next day measure the juice
gained and for each 600ml/1 pint take 675g/1lb 8oz warmed sugar. Return
the juice to the pan, heat gently, add the sugar, stirring well until it has
dissolved. Bring to the boil and boil hard until a set is obtained. Pot and
seal.
  Delicious with mutton, hare and rabbit.

SLOE CHUTNEY

1kg/2lb 4oz sloes
1 stick cinnamon
1 teaspoon whole cloves

450g/1lb brown sugar
225g/8oz seedless raisins
300ml/$\frac{1}{2}$ pint malt vinegar

3 hot, dry, sterile jars with non-metal lids

Wash the sloes and put them into a casserole, cover tightly and cook in a
slow oven until they are very soft. Pass through a sieve. Tie the spices in a
muslin bag and put this with the puréed sloes and the remaining ingredients
into a stainless steel pan. Bring to the boil, stirring well until the sugar has
dissolved. Simmer gently for 30 minutes. Remove the muslin bag from the
pan. Pot and seal.
  Store for at least 2 months before use. A very pleasant, mild chutney.

SLOE GIN

a quantity fat, black sloes
1 bottle gin

white sugar

Wash the sloes thoroughly and prick them through with a needle to release the juice. Drink one third of the gin and, if you are now in any fit state, continue thus. Put enough sloes in the bottle to reach one third of the way up. If you have a sweet tooth add 4 tablespoons of sugar, if you are a more aesthetic drinker 2 tablespoons will do. Seal tightly and shake every day until Christmas. If you collect your sloes in October this will do very well for the macerating period must not be less than 3 months.

Damson Gin or Mulberry Gin which is absolutely gorgeous may be made in the same way but there is no need to prick the latter. Sloes and damsons may also be transformed in the same way with a bottle of vodka. These alcoholic potions get better the longer you keep them but chance, as they say, would be a fine thing.

Strawberry

Strawberries, when they are cultivated lovingly and domestically, are the most delicious sweetly acid and tasty fruit imaginable; when they are grown in warm and sunny fields for local consumption on a small scale they are equally good and a bonus for jam makers for you can usually pick your own at a reduced cost. However, grown for the polythene-packed, vast, commercial market, bombarded with science, frozen and forced, they are too often tasteless, scarlet shells of awe-inspiring glossiness and uniform size filled with watery pap.

Grow your own strawberries: grow Cambridge Vigour, Sans Rival and Gento for heavy crops of well flavoured fruits suitable for all purposes; Royal Sovereign and Grandee, for large, well shaped dessert fruit; Little Scarlet for the firm, sweet fruit which are particularly good in jam making, and plant the glorious wild, wood or Alpine strawberries for their unusual varying flavours and colour and the unique richly flavoured sweetness which is quite unlike the cultivated strawberry. Well recommended varieties are Baron Solemacher for its very heavy crops, Hauteboy which is a rare wild fruit, Alpine Yellow for producing a golden yellow fruit or Alexandria because the strawberries are bigger.

Apart from some difficult diseases strawberries are remarkably easy to grow, some varieties like Sans Rival and Gento are called remontants and flower and fruit throughout the whole summer. Other varieties such as Royal Sovereign or the Climbing Strawberry throw runners from which new plants can be taken – the best way is to train these runners into pots filled with a light soil and allow them to become firmly established before detaching from the parent plant. Strawberries will thrive in a warm open well drained soil that has been carefully prepared with a good manure or compost. In summer they should be mulched with grass cuttings and in winter surrounded with an amount of manure. During the growing time they should be kept moist but bedded down with a good layer of straw under the fruiting plant to protect it from muddy conditions. Plants which continue fruiting into late autumn can be covered with cloches and this will give you fruit until November. Pots and tubs are admirable containers for strawberries particularly Alpines and climbers, which will thrive under these conditions as they afford extra protection against birds and insects – strangely enough Alpine strawberries are not plagued with the havoc wreaked by birds that so affects the ordinary strawberry. One way of overcoming this is to cover with nets or make a big, fluffy cat with terry towelling and sit it amongst the strawberries. It does not fool them for long but just enough. I have grown a mass of Baron Solemacher in a multi-storey container, especially designed for the purpose, on a windowsill – the crop was enormous and everlasting. I have also used a large hanging basket to grow a mixture of red, white and yellow wood strawberries which did very well indeed but must be fed and watered properly. If you have a very small garden bear in mind that strawberries will thrive in the light shade provided by runner beans and spinach and will grow happily in company with lettuce but abhor cabbage and gladioli.

Cultivated strawberries, make delicious preserves and jams from the simple to the highly complex. Despite all the recipes and ideas put forward to obtain a good set, strawberries are so low in pectin that this is virtually impossible – even with the aid of lemon juice. The most that one can hope for is a gorgeous goo which will spread well and taste authentic. Strawberries need no water for cooking unless specifically stated and will reduce considerably during cooking giving an uneconomical result but preferable I feel to the bright, super sweet, commercial product. I could write a separate book on all the imaginative and entertaining recipes for sweets and desserts made with both the fresh strawberries and the jam, from crêpes to gateaux, ice cream, chantilly, mousse, jam rissoles, poached in wine or frozen in cream. To say nothing of all the ingenious purposes that the herbalists have discovered from soothing teas to calming face packs.

British cloche and hothouse strawberries are in the shops from January to June. Outdoor strawberries from Britain are available from May to October whilst strawberries from practically every country in Europe and from the USA, New Zealand and Kenya run throughout the year but because they do not travel or keep well and the spoilage is great, these latter fruit are usually expensive.

WHOLE STRAWBERRY JAM FROM FRANCE

1kg/2lb 4oz small sharp strawberries   2 tablespoons water
1kg/2lb 4oz white sugar   a few drops of vanilla essence

3-4 hot, dry, sterile jam jars

Clean and hull the strawberries and put them into a china bowl with the sugar. Cover and leave for 12 hours. The next day transfer the fruit and sugar to a preserving pan, add the water and heat gently, shaking and stirring with a wooden spoon but not breaking the strawberries. As soon as the fruit sinks to the bottom of the pan (this means it is soft, and takes approximately 10-15 minutes) lift them out with a perforated spoon and pack into the jars. Add the vanilla to the syrup and simmer until it is thick enough to coat the back of a spoon. Stir well and pour over the fruit to cover. Seal when cold.

A very good recipe especially for the smaller strawberries. Wild strawberries are particularly good when preserved in this fashion but omit the water and vanilla and substitute the juice of 1 lemon instead. Wild strawberries will take only 5 minutes, if that, to become soft and to be removed to the pots.

STRAWBERRY JAM

1kg/2lb 4oz strawberries   675g/1½lb white sugar
1 large lemon

3 hot, dry, sterile jam jars

Clean the strawberries by removing hulls and rinsing briefly. Squeeze the juice from the lemon and put it into a preserving pan with the sugar. Boil gently stirring well until a thick syrup is formed. Add the strawberries and boil gently stirring carefully until the syrup begins to jell. Take care not to squash the fruit. Allow to cool. Stir well. Pot. Seal when cold.

Sweet and syrupy with whole fruit.

STRAWBERRY JAM WITH COMMERCIAL PECTIN

1kg/2lb 4oz small strawberries
2 lemons
1350g/3lb white sugar

small knob unsalted butter
½ bottle liquid commercial pectin

5-6 hot, dry, sterile jam jars

Clean and hull the strawberries. Squeeze 3 tablespoons of juice from the lemons and put the strawberries, lemon juice and sugar into a large preserving pan. Leave for 1 hour stirring occasionally. Heat gently, stirring well but carefully until the sugar has dissolved. Add the butter and bring to a full rolling boil for 4 minutes stirring a little to prevent sticking. Remove from the heat and stir in the pectin. Skim and stir for 2 minutes. Leave to cool for 15 minutes and stir well before potting. Seal when cold.

Sometimes there is no other way to ensure an economical and firm set with strawberries, particularly if they are sweet and ripe, than by using commercial pectin. The strawberries should stay whole which looks good especially if you are making jam for sale or show.

HONEYED STRAWBERRY JAM

1kg/2lb 4oz strawberries
750g/1lb 10oz white sugar

100g/4oz clear honey
200ml/7fl oz redcurrant juice

3 hot, dry, sterile jam jars

Clean and hull the strawberries and put them into a preserving pan with the sugar. Heat gently, shaking and stirring carefully until the sugar has dissolved. Add the honey, mixing well and then the warmed redcurrant juice. Bring to the boil and boil rapidly until a set is obtained. Allow to cool a little. Stir well before potting. Seal when cold.

Not a very firm set but the honey gives the jam a super 'wild' taste.

ROUMANIAN STRAWBERRY JAM

1kg/2lb 4oz ripe firm strawberries
850g/1lb 14oz white sugar

150ml/¼ pint redcurrant juice
small knob unsalted butter

3 hot, dry, sterile jam jars

Clean and hull the strawberries and put them into a bowl with the sugar. Stir gently, cover and leave overnight. The next day transfer the contents of the bowl to a preserving pan, heat slowly stirring with care until the sugar is well dissolved. Boil hard for 5 minutes, being sure not to burn. Add the warmed redcurrant juice and boil for a further 2 minutes. Remove from the heat, stir in the butter and continue to stir for 5 minutes. Skim. Pot and seal.

  The same quantity of gooseberry, apple or 2 tablespoons pure lemon juice can be substituted for the redcurrant juice.

STRAWBERRY AND APPLE JAM

1kg/2lb 4oz strawberries
1kg/2lb 4oz cooking apples
2 lemons

450ml/¾ pint water
2kg/4lb 8oz white sugar

8 hot, dry, sterile jam jars

Clean and hull the strawberries. Wash, peel, core and chop the apples. Squeeze the juice from the lemons. Put the strawberries in one pan and the apples, lemon juice and water into another. Heat the strawberries very gently until the juices begin to flow, allow them to become just tender then remove from heat. Bring the apples to the boil and simmer until very soft. Turn the strawberries into the pan of apple, add the warmed sugar, stirring well until it has dissolved and bring to the boil. Boil hard until a set is obtained. Pot and seal.

  Very economical and spreadable jam – excellent on hot steamed puddings, in jam roly poly, pancakes and tarts. Gooseberries may be substituted for the apples in which case omit the lemons.

STRAWBERRY AND REDCURRANT JELLY

1kg/2lb 4oz strawberries
500g/1lb 2oz redcurrants

200ml/7fl. oz water
white sugar

6 medium size, hot, dry, sterile jars

Clean and hull the strawberries. Wash and drain the redcurrants and put both fruit into a preserving pan with the water. Simmer until very soft and then turn into a clean jelly bag. Leave overnight to drain into a china bowl. The next day measure the liquid gained and for each 600ml/1 pint take 450g/1lb warmed sugar. Return the juice to the pan, heat gently and add the sugar stirring well until it has dissolved. Bring to the boil and boil hard until a set is obtained. Pot and seal.
   Very fine colour, flavour and set.

SPECIAL STRAWBERRY JELLY

1kg/2lb 4oz small firm ripe
   strawberries

caster sugar

4 medium size, hot, dry, sterile jars

Clean and hull the strawberries, put them into a heatproof jar or crock, cover and stand in a pan of boiling water. Bring to the boil and then simmer until the strawberries are very soft and there is plenty of juice (this is a preferable way to cook the fruit for all strawberry jellies). Lay a muslin cloth over a colander and turn the fruit into this, extract the juice quickly, measure and for each 600ml/1 pint take 450g/1lb warmed sugar. Return the juice to the pan, heat gently and add the sugar, stirring well until it has dissolved. Bring to the boil and boil hard until a set is obtained, this should not take longer than 30 minutes. Pot and seal.
   A good recipe for those small sharp strawberries. It is sometimes thought that strawberry jelly will not set if the juice is allowed to cool before the sugar has been added, hence the admonishment to extract the juice quickly, although this does not mean you may squeeze it.

PRESERVED STRAWBERRIES

1kg/2lb 4oz strawberries
1kg/2lb 4oz white sugar

450ml/¾ pint water – generous measure
a few whole cloves (optional)

4 hot, dry, sterile jam jars

Clean and hull the strawberries. Put the sugar and water into a preserving pan and tie the cloves into a muslin bag if used (personally I find the flavour unwelcome). Add them to the pan, heat gently stirring well until the sugar has dissolved and then boil hard until a little dropped into cold water will form a soft ball. Add the fruit, stir well and cover the pan. Remove from the heat and allow the strawberries to soak up the syrup for 15 minutes. Return the pan to the heat, remove the cover and boil quickly until the foaming syrup covers the fruit, take the pan away from the heat and let the syrup become clear and skim. Repeat this last process of bubbling and skimming twice more. Have ready a large, dry, nylon sieve laid over a bowl. Remove the strawberries with a perforated spoon and lay them on the sieve. Catch the drained syrup and return it to the pan. Bring to the boil and boil hard until you judge it to be at setting point. Return the strawberries to the syrup and boil for 5 minutes. Remove the muslin bag if used. Pot and seal.

A really delicious preserve to use as a topping for exotic desserts or in flans and gateaux.

STRAWBERRIES IN MADEIRA

1kg/2lb 4oz fresh ripe strawberries
225g/8oz caster sugar

madeira or sherry

dry, sterile, wide-necked preserving jar

Clean and hull the strawberries discarding any that are bruised or over-ripe. Pack into the jars in layers with the sugar, filling up to the top. Pour in the liquor until the fruit is covered, do this slowly to ensure that there are no air bubbles. Seal tightly and store in a cool dry place.

Quite delicious and silly-making strawberries.

Swede

Swede is an abbreviation of Swedish turnip, and is also known as Russian turnip, turnip rooted cabbage and rutabagas, depending on where you live. A hefty root vegetable of deep orange colour and sweet mild flavour which comes into the same category as parsnip and turnip – useful and flavoursome in casseroles and stews and a handy standby on its own mashed or creamed. Not a delicate little creation for growing amongst the flowerbeds but usually inexpensive to buy and available throughout autumn, winter and early spring. Store as for Jerusalem Artichokes, p.68.

SWEDE CHUTNEY

1kg/2lb 4oz swedes
225g/8oz shallots
1 tablespoon sea salt
1.75 litres/3 pints malt vinegar – white
 or brown

25g/1oz pickling spice
175g/6oz white sugar
2 teaspoons turmeric

6 hot, dry, sterile jars with non-metal lids

Wash and peel the swede and cut into cubes. Peel and chop the shallots and put both of these into a bowl, sprinkle with the salt and allow to stand overnight. Boil the vinegar with the spices in a stainless steel pan, cover and leave to get cold. The next day drain the swedes and shallots well and put them into a stainless steel pan with the strained vinegar and the sugar. Heat gently, stirring well until the sugar has dissolved. Bring to the boil and then simmer gently for 1 hour. Mix the turmeric to a smooth paste with a little water and add it to the pan. Boil for 5 minutes. Pot and seal.

T

Tangerine

A very interesting confusion arises over the tangerine. Botanically it is classed as a mandarin (*Citrus Reticulata*) as apparently are clementines and satsumas. It is also hybridized extensively with other citrus fruits to provide some quite extraordinary offspring. However I feel that the flavour of this loose-skinned citrus fruit is very distinctive, the colour is a deeper, more fiery orange than the other varieties but undoubtedly mandarins are one and the same fruit or as close to make little difference. The finer points do not worry me unduly for I am only concerned that I can buy nice juicy, fine-tasting fruit for the Christmas table and to pop in the toe of the children's stockings.

Originating in China, these fruits and related varieties are now commercially produced in southern Europe and the United States, making their appearance in Britain during the winter months. When buying tangerines take care to examine the fruit before choosing, if they have been allowed to mature incorrectly, poorly stored or kept too long they will either be sadly dry or will go mouldy very rapidly.

Tangerines make delicious preserves, particularly when crystallized. Although low in pectin they also make, with the help of an additional setting agent, light and refreshing marmalades and jams.

Calamondine, another variety of tangerine, can be used to make a good marmalade – follow the recipe for Tangerine Marmalade.

Tangers should you come across these varieties of fruit which are a cross between a sweet orange and a tangerine you can make them into preserves following the recipes for sweet oranges.

349

Tangelos   varieties are a cross between tangerine and grapefruit and can be preserved as for sweet oranges.

Naaerje   South African for tangerine.

TANGERINE JAM

1kg/2lb 4oz tangerines   300ml/½ pint water
1kg/2lb 4oz white sugar

4 hot, dry, sterile jam jars

Wash the fruit. Remove the peel and put it into a bowl of boiling water for 5 minutes. Drain and mince. Divide the tangerines into sections and remove tissues, pith and pips, tying the pips into a muslin bag. Put the sugar and water into a preserving pan and heat gently stirring well until it has dissolved. Bring to the boil and add the tangerine rind, segments and the muslin bag. Stir well and boil gently for approximately 45 minutes. Pot and seal.

   A light and refreshing jam with a distinctive flavour. Not only a good breakfast preserve especially at Christmas but an excellent filling for shortcrust tarts.

TANGERINE JELLY

1kg/2lb 4oz tangerines   2.5 litres/4¼ pints water
2 large lemons   white sugar
1 thin skinned grapefruit

8 medium size, hot, dry, sterile jars

Wash all the fruit and either chop the peel and pulp very finely or put it through a coarse mincer. Take care not to lose the juices. Place in a preserving pan with the water and cook gently until the peel is soft – obviously the smaller the pieces the shorter the time. Turn into a jelly bag and leave overnight to drain into a clean bowl. The next day measure the liquid gained and for each 600ml/1 pint take 450g/1lb warmed sugar. Return the juice to the pan and heat gently, add the sugar stirring well until it has dissolved. Bring quickly to the boil and boil rapidly until a set is obtained. Pot and seal.

   A pleasant, light breakfast jelly.

TANGERINE CURD

10 tangerines
2 lemons
450g/1lb caster sugar

100g/4oz unsalted butter
5 fresh eggs

6 medium size, hot, dry, sterile jars

Wash the fruit very well and grate the rind from the tangerines using the fine side of the grater. Extract all the juice and strain. Squeeze the juice from the lemons and strain. Put the tangerine rind and juice, the lemon juice, sugar and butter into a bowl. Beat the eggs and strain them – this keeps out those funny little stringy bits – and add to the bowl of ingredients. Put the bowl over a saucepan of boiling water but do not let it actually touch, or use a double boiler for preference. Cook over a low heat, beating and stirring with a wooden spoon all the time until the mixture is thick and smooth. Remember that at no time must the mixture become too hot for it will curdle and that will be the end of that. Pot and seal.

Tangerine has a unique taste which makes a very good curd – one which children particularly like.

TANGERINE AND LIME MARMALADE

1kg/2lb 4oz tangerines
4 limes

1.75 litres/3 pints water
900g/2lb white sugar

6 hot, dry, sterile jam jars

Wash the fruit, squeeze out all the juice, remove the pips and tie them into a muslin bag. Either shred the rinds and remaining pulp very finely or put through a mincer. Put the rind, fruit, muslin bag and the juice into a preserving pan with the water and bring to the boil. Simmer until the peel is soft, anything between 1-1½ hours. Add the warmed sugar, stirring well until it has dissolved. Bring to the boil and boil hard until a set is obtained, approximately 5 minutes. Leave to cool before potting. Stir well. Seal when cold.

One of the most delicious marmalades with a sharp, fruity, fragrant taste.

Tarragon

Tarragon is not as widely grown as it deserves to be, in fact I have frequently heard it referred to as the snob herb and I suspect that this is sour grapes, for French Tarragon (*Artemisia dracunculus*) is not the easiest plant in the world to grow and because it rarely sets seeds it has to be obtained by cuttings or root divisions. Despite other advice I have found that tarragon will only grow well in rich, well drained, sunny soil and it must be kept moist – a large container or tub will suit it well. The bush can become quite sturdy – and although the tight, little, white flowers never amount to much the smooth, dark grey, lanceolate leaves are an attractive asset in the garden. It has a reputation for keeping the digestion and blood pure and although I have never put it to the test it is also said to cure scorpion stings and snake bites! I find that its greatest advantage is in the kitchen where the distinctive taste, similiar to aniseed, lends enchantment to chicken, eggs and creamy sauces. It also adds to the most supreme of *fine herbes* – a mixture of chervil, chives, tarragon and parsley (purists omit the parsley) – which can be added to butters, sauces, omelettes, stuffing and marinades. Tarragon also combines well with garlic, tomatoes and pot vegetables. However it is wise to remember that if left too long cooking in a dish it will become bitter. The French use tarragon extensively in pickles, a habit which is worth copying. For example, one extraordinary idea that I have seen is a small sprig added to a jar of pickled plums.

Never be waylaid into growing or buying Russian tarragon, it has none of the attributes of the French tarragon and it is a waste of time.

TARRAGON JELLY

2 good sprigs fresh tarragon
600ml/1 pint apple juice made from
   cooking or crab apples

2 tablespoons red wine vinegar
350g/12oz white sugar

4 small, hot, dry, sterile jars with non-metal lids

Wash and dry the tarragon and put it into a stainless steel pan with the apple juice and vinegar. Bring to the boil and boil gently for 10 minutes. Add the warmed sugar, stirring well until it has dissolved, bring to the boil and boil hard until a set is obtained. Pour straight through a nylon sieve. Pot and seal.

Some variations on this very mild jelly: a small sprig of clean, dry fresh tarragon added to the half-set jelly; chop some fresh tarragon and add it to the jelly before potting; 4 teaspoons of dried tarragon instead of fresh may be left in the jelly or sieved. These jellies are delicious with cold chicken, fish etc.

TARRAGON VINEGAR

50g/2oz fresh tarragon

600ml/1 pint white wine or cider vinegar

dry, sterile, glass jar with non-metal lid

Pick the tarragon before it blooms and before the full sun has had time to draw out the aromatic oils. Wash, dry and strip the leaves from the stalk, pack into the jar and cover with the vinegar. Seal tightly and leave to infuse for at least one month shaking it occasionally. Strain into a clear bottle and add a fresh branch of tarragon. Seal with a cork.

Hopefully it will look like those elegant and mysterious bottles in good delicatessens. Tarragon vinegar is essential in sauces such as tartare and béarnaise. It also makes an excellent dressing for tomatoes, fish and chicken salads. If there is no fresh tarragon available then 1 heaped tablespoon of dried tarragon may be used instead. Tarragon vinegar can be given a more pungent flavour by the addition of 1 sliced clove of garlic and 2 whole cloves to the prepared vinegar, which are then left for 24 hours before being removed and the vinegar left to steep in the usual fashion. Many very delicious vinegars are made in the same way.

Thyme
Thymus vulgaris

When writers speak of a warm breeze scented with wild herbs it is ten to one that they are referring to more southern shores than those of Britain.

The wild thyme of those hot hillsides has a pungent, fierce scent which is not reproduced in the wild thyme of mossy British banks. Although our native thyme is delightful and far more subtle, the stronger thyme, frequently grown in gardens, is much more similar to the continental variety. Thyme has been cultivated for centuries for its rich oils which have great antiseptic properties – a sprig was always placed in the posy carried by the Monarch on Maundy Thursday to give some protection from infection – and thyme has been used as a remedy for practically everything from indigestion to whooping cough. Used in the kitchen, it is one of those herbs which, if not taken with discretion, can overwhelm the pot and once again I would say use only a sparing sprig or make it into jellies and oils where its aroma can be further spread. Lemon thyme is far more delicate and can be used with less caution.

For my money, thyme brings its greatest reward when several varieties are planted in a sunny rockery position. The shrubby, grey shape and tiny leaves disport themselves well and are a splendid foil for small bright plants whilst the pink thyme blossom will attract many bees and the sun will bring out the heady fragrant oils to perfume your garden whether it be a Versailles or pocket handkerchief. Thyme can be grown quite well from seed but is better taken in cuttings. Either way, plant where you wish the thyme to grow and make sure that you have chosen a sunny well drained position, water well until either the seedlings appear or the cutting has set. I also cover my thyme over with leaves in the winter, particularly the lemon thyme, wild thyme and other less hardy varieties.

THYME JELLY

3 tablespoons fresh thyme   ½ bottle commercial pectin
300ml/½ pint water   675g/1½lb white sugar
6 tablespoons vinegar

6 small, hot, dry sterile jars with non-metal lids

Put the thyme into a bowl and cover with the boiling water. Put a plate over the top and leave to infuse for 15 minutes. Strain, add the vinegar and measure, add enough extra water to ensure that you have 300ml/½ pint in all. Pour into a large pan and heat gently, add the sugar and stirring well until it has dissolved. Bring to the boil for 1 minute and stir in the pectin. Boil for a further 2 minutes, stirring and skimming constantly. Allow to cool before potting. Seal when cold.

A small sprig of thyme may be added to the half set jelly for decoration. Infuse with more thyme if you prefer a stronger taste. Serve with chicken.

To make Thyme Oil follow the method for Marjoram Oil, p.214.

To make Thyme Vinegar follow the method for Tarragon Vinegar, p.353 – especially recommended using Lemon Thyme.

To make Lemon Thyme Sugar follow the method for Rosemary Sugar, p.336.

To Dry Thyme follow the method for Drying Sage, p.338.

Tomato

The tomato has had a chequered start in life. Thought to have originated in Peru where the Indians called it the tomatl, it then blazed its trail of glory from Southern and Central America to Europe where the Italians, with typical exuberance, christened this fiery fruit *pomo d'oro* or golden apple but in Spain it gained another name – *pome di mori* or Moors' apple. There on to France where the French either misunderstood or just considered the tomato to be another heaven-sent aphrodisiac and named it *pomme d'amour* or love apple! By the late nineteenth century however the name had reverted back to the original tomato, which makes it easier for everybody.

While in southern Europe the tomato thrived and became an important part of the diet, in the northern countries it did not gain in massive popularity until this last century. The tomato should have a ripe, thick, juicy flesh of good flavour, which sadly does not always occur. Depending on the variety, tomatoes have a high vitamin 'C' content and this also affects the sweetness. There is such a wonderful selection of tomatoes available and so many marvellous ways of using them that every household should grow at least two plants, if only in a pot on the windowsill: large, fat tomatoes for stuffing and baking; smooth, round, garden-grown, scarlet or gold for salads; juicy plum tomatoes for casseroles, stews, ratatouille, sauces, ketchups and preserves; cherry, currant and olivette tomatoes for pickling, or crystallizing; tiny, baby tomatoes for little mouths, fat firm tomatoes for man-sized sandwiches; special varieties for bottling and freezing, compact hybrid varieties for pickles and chutneys – the list is endless. Even the unripe fruit, green and hard, is not wasted and makes a myriad of imaginative preserves.

My great-grandfather believed that the fruit of tomatoes was poisonous because the plant was of the nightshade family. However he did grow them for their appearance and one of the most attractive sights that I have ever seen was a hanging basket overflowing with tiny scarlet tomatoes. They were placed against a white wall and in the partial shade thrown by a climbing rose – an extravagant and mouthwatering sight.

A few guidelines to reliable or original buys:

Outdoor girl	outdoor recommended
Ailsa Craig and Big Boy	greenhouse only, but reliable and prolific
Arctic	excellent outdoors in northern counties
Small Fry and Tiny Tim	recommended for window boxes
Pixie	bush variety prolific and compact for pot growing, frost resistant
Super Roma	heavy cropper, very thick and juicy, plum shaped
Mamande	outdoor variety, very fruity rich continental flavour
Gardeners' delight	superb flavour, good for deep freezing as it will freeze whole
Golden sunrise	bright golden colour
Sub-Arctic Cherry	bush variety – a good cropper and a superb choice for hanging baskets, window boxes, tubs etc.
Currant tomatoes	really tiny and decorative
Tiger Tim	really tiny and decorative
Sugar Plum	small and sweet, suitable for baskets and pots
Pear tomato	golden pear-shaped fruit
Tree tomato	golden-red to purple pear-shaped fruit

There are of course hundreds of other very reliable varieties to choose from and seed catalogues these days are mouth-watering publications.

Tinned tomatoes can be used as a good substitute for fresh tomatoes in cooked dishes. Plum tomatoes have a better flavour when cooked than the traditional English tomatoes, and also go much further particularly when making a fresh tomato sauce. Remember, should you be ambitious enough to make your own tomato paste as they do in Italy and Greece you must use plum tomatoes or a variety such as Mamande. The quantity of paste that you eventually reap after all that bubbling and boiling will be approximately one seventh of the quantity of fruit you started with, so bear that in mind! A handy hint – green tomatoes ripen quicker in the dark, particularly in a brown paper bag.

Although the prices of tomatoes vary considerably they are always available throughout the year coming mainly from the Canaries or Channel Islands. In the summer they are home produced and at other times they may also come from Europe, Israel and Malta.

You will, of course, find that everyone's tomatoes ripen at the same time and you have a glut situation. Should that occur then I hope that you will find this section useful for there are a thousand imaginative ways of putting the excess to good use. Many of the best are those used by our great-grandmothers before the invention of deep freezers and, as I do not think that tomatoes either bottle or freeze particularly well, I find the old fashioned methods still excel.

RED TOMATO JAM

1kg/2lb 4oz red ripe tomatoes   2 large lemons
1kg/2lb 4oz white sugar

5 hot, dry, sterile jam jars

Scald, peel and chop the tomatoes into quarters. Lay them in a bowl with the sugar, cover and leave overnight. The next day transfer to a stainless steel pan and heat gently, stirring well until the sugar has dissolved. Simmer until the tomatoes are soft. Extract the juice from the lemons and add it to the pan. Bring to the boil and boil rapidly until a set is obtained – rather soft and sticky. Pot and seal.

A blood curdling colour that would interest Count Dracula but a pleasant preserve for all that. Ring the changes with ground ginger or cinnamon, the grated rind from the lemon, cinnamon stick with a few drops of vanilla essence or several grams of crystallized ginger. All of these additions flavour in a different and delicious way. I do not consider this preserve as a jammy jam but more to be used in sandwiches with other fillings such as cream cheese – my American friends eat it with peanut butter – or as a flan filling with other fruit. If any of your family suffer from tummy trouble it might be a good idea to squeeze the pips out of the tomatoes as you peel them but do not waste the flesh or juice.

TOMATO JELLY WITH HERBS

600ml/1 pint pure tomato juice   1 tablespoon celery seed
50g/2oz fresh basil   1350g/3lb white sugar
50g/2oz fresh tarragon   1 bottle commercial liquid pectin
600ml/1 pint water   1 extra handful fresh herbs
2 lemons

10 small, hot, dry, sterile jars

357

Make sure that the basil and tarragon are clean and put them into a pan with the water, bring to the boil and continue to boil gently until the liquid is reduced by half. Cover and leave to stand for 1 hour. Strain through a muslin cloth. Squeeze the juice from the lemons and tie the celery seed into a muslin bag. Combine all the ingredients except the pectin and the extra herbs, in a large pan and heat gently, stirring continuously until the sugar has dissolved. Bring to the boil and add the liquid pectin. Boil for a further 5 minutes and then remove from the heat. Discard the muslin bag. Skim the top of the pan well and leave to cool for 5 minutes. Add the clean, fresh herbs either chopped and stirred in before potting or one or two tiny sprigs in each jar. Seal when cold.

A very pretty preserve which makes a lovely present particularly at Christmas time. Marjoram or oregano also make a very pleasant tomato and herb jelly.

SPICED TOMATO JELLY

1kg/2lb 4oz ripe, red tomatoes	600ml/1 pint water
2 whole cloves	4 tablespoon white malt vinegar
1 small piece cinnamon stick	1kg/2lb 4oz white sugar

12 small, hot, dry, sterile jars with non-metal lids

Wash the tomatoes and put them into a stainless steel pan with the spices and water. Cook gently until very soft. Discard the spices and pass the tomatoes through a fine sieve, return the purée to the clean pan with the vinegar and heat gently, add the warmed sugar, stirring well until it has dissolved. Bring to the boil and boil hard until a set is obtained. Pot and seal.

A superb savoury jelly with cold meat although it is a little on the soft side. You can make it with drained tinned tomatoes using the measured juice instead of water although this gives a sweeter, softer jelly.

RED TOMATO AND APPLE CONSERVE

1kg/2lb 4oz ripe red tomatoes	225g/8oz mixed candied peel
1kg/2lb 4oz apples	225g/8oz preserved or crystallized
2 large lemons	ginger
1500g/3lb 6oz white sugar	

10 hot, dry, sterile jam jars

Scald, peel and slice the tomatoes. Peel, core and chop the apples. Wash the lemons and put them through a mincer, discarding the pips but catching the juice. Put tomatoes, apples and lemon mince into a stainless steel pan and cook gently until soft – approximately 15 minutes. Add the warmed sugar, stirring constantly until it has dissolved and continue to cook gently until the mixture is thick. Chop the peel and ginger and add it to the pan, cook very slowly – use an asbestos mat if need be – for 10 minutes. Pot and seal.

Delicious filling for pies, particularly at Christmas, this conserve also has a very attractive appearance.

TANGY TOMATO MARMALADE

1kg/2lb 4oz red tomatoes
6 sweet oranges

3 lemons
white sugar

8 hot, dry, sterile jam jars

Scald and peel the tomatoes. Wash and peel the oranges and lemons, scrape away some of the pith and cut the rind into hair strips. Put the rind into a small pan with a little water, bring to the boil and then simmer for 15 minutes. Drain well. Put the tomatoes through a coarse mincer with the orange and lemon flesh making sure that you catch the juice and discard the pips. Place this terrible squashy mixture into a stainless steel pan with the softened rind and bring to the boil. Cover and simmer for approximately 20 minutes then uncover and boil rapidly for 10 minutes. This should cause a reduction in quantity so measure the pulp with a measuring jug and for each 600ml/1 pint take 450g/1lb warmed sugar. Return the purée to the pan, heat gently and add the sugar, stirring continuously. Bring to the boil and boil hard until a set is obtained. Pot and seal.

CURRIED RED TOMATO CHUTNEY

1kg/2lb 4oz red tomatoes
1kg/2lb 4oz cooking apples
400g/14oz onions
1 clove garlic
275g/10oz seedless raisins
15g/½oz mustard seed

15g/½oz curry powder
1 level teaspoon cayenne pepper
1 teaspoon sea salt
400g/14oz sugar
900ml/1½ pints malt vinegar

6 hot, dry, sterile jars with non-metal lids

Scald, peel and chop the tomatoes. Peel, core and chop the apples and cook them in a covered pan with very little water until they are tender. Peel and chop the onions and garlic. Wash the rasins. Tie the mustard seed into a muslin bag. Put all the ingredients into a stainless steel pan and bring gently to the boil, stirring well. Continue to cook slowly for approximately 2 hours, stirring occasionally to prevent burning, until the chutney is thick and smooth. Pot and seal.

Store for at least 2 months before use. Curry powder may be omitted and you will still have a very pleasant mild chutney.

SWEET TOMATO AND CELERY CHUTNEY

1kg/2lb 4oz ripe, red tomatoes
1 large head celery
450g/1lb onions
1 tablespoon sea salt
225g/8oz soft brown sugar

¼ teaspoon ground allspice
¼ teaspoon ground nutmeg
¼ teaspoon dry mustard
900ml/1½ pints brown malt vinegar

4 hot, dry, sterile jars with non-metal lids

Scald, peel and slice the tomatoes finely. Scrub the celery and cut into very small pieces (discard the leaves and use them in a stock). Peel and finely chop the onions. Put all the ingredients into a stainless steel pan and bring to the boil, stirring well. Continue to simmer for 1½ to 2 hours and still stir occasionally to prevent burning. The chutney should be thick and smooth. Pot. Seal when cold.

Store for at least 2 months before use. Remember that red tomato chutneys tend to thicken considerably on keeping, so make sure that the chutney is reasonably moist before potting.

RED TOMATO, APPLE AND RAISIN CHUTNEY

1kg/2lb 4oz red tomatoes
275g/10oz cooking apples
100g/4oz onions
300ml/½ pint white malt vinegar
100g/4oz seedless raisins
2 teaspoons sea salt

½ teaspoon ground allspice
½ teaspoon cayenne pepper
½ teaspoon ground cinnamon
½ teaspoon ground ginger
½ teaspoon paprika
225g/8oz white sugar

3 hot, dry, sterile jars with non-metal lids

Scald, peel and chop the tomatoes. Peel, core and chop the apples. Peel and chop the onions. Put all the ingredients except the sugar into a stainless steel pan with half the vinegar and bring very gently to the boil. Cook slowly for approximately 1-1½ hours. Add the sugar and remaining vinegar and once again bring to the boil, stirring constantly. Simmer until thick and smooth. Pot and seal. Store for at least 2 months before use.

RATATOUILLE NICK'S GREAT MIXTURE

1kg/2lb 4oz red tomatoes
675g/1lb 8oz green and red peppers
450g/1lb aubergines
100g/4oz fresh green and red chillies
450g/1lb onions
3 large cloves garlic

2 rounded teaspoons mustard seed
2 teaspoons sea salt
2 teaspoons paprika
1 rounded teaspoon cayenne
225g/8oz white sugar
600ml/1 pint white malt vinegar

5 hot, dry, sterile jars with non-metal lids

Scald, peel and chop the tomatoes. Remove seed and pith from the peppers and chop the flesh. Wash the aubergines and cut into small pieces, sprinkle with 1 teaspoon of the salt and lay them in a colander with a plate on the top whilst you get on with the rest. Shred the chillies taking care not to get the burning oil on the sensitive areas of the face. Peel and chop the onions. Peel the garlic and put it into a pestle and mortar with the mustard seed and remaining salt, grind away merrily until fairly well crushed. Put the tomatoes into a large stainless steel pan with the onions and the garlic/mustard seed mixture, add half the vinegar and just simmer gently until the onions become soft. Shake the aubergines free of salt and put them with the other ingredients into the pan of tomatoes, bring gently to the boil, stirring constantly and then simmer approximately 2 hours or until soft, thick and pungent. Pot and seal.

Keep for 3 months before using. White sugar and white vinegar will give a clear, bright and colourful effect. Ratatouille Nick was one of the world's worst overbuyers which gave rise to the fact that he was also one of the greatest innovators. This hot tasty and cheerful chutney goes well with practically everything but is particularly good with crusty bread, firm cheese and red wine.

TOMATO AND HORSERADISH RELISH

300ml/½ pint vinegar
1 dessertspoon mixed pickling spice
1kg/2lb 4oz firm red tomatoes
1 large cooking apple
1 medium onion

2 teaspoons sea salt
½ teaspoon cayenne pepper
3 tablespoons fresh horseradish
225g/8oz sugar

3 hot, dry, sterile jars with non-metal lids

Before you start, put the vinegar and pickling spice to boil in a covered pan. Scald, peel and chop the tomatoes. Peel, core and chop the apples. Peel and chop the onion. Put all of these ingredients together in a large stainless steel pan and cook very gently without burning and until thick and pulpy – it will help to stir constantly with a wooden spoon. Strain the hot vinegar and add it to the pan with the salt and cayenne pepper. Cook until thick and soft – approximately 40 minutes. Make sure that your horseradish is clean and then grate it, bear in mind that the quantity you use is a matter of taste but have at least 3 tablespoons ready and then you can stir and taste as you go. Add the horseradish and sugar to the pan and bring to the boil, stirring constantly. Boil for 15 minutes. Pot and seal.

Very hot, very tasty and super in cold meat sandwiches or with sausage meats.

TOMATO SAUCES AND KETCHUPS

There are many recipes for tomato sauces and ketchups and in all of them either the ingredients or the method vary in some way. To do separate justice to the finer points of each would require a complete volume on the subject, therefore I have taken all of them and tried to find a basic method which will give the best results. I have not tampered with the ingredients for half the joy of preserving is in experimenting with new flavours.

Tomato sauce recipes fall into three stages and to start with you will require heat resistant, wide-necked bottles with corks. Make sure that both are dry and clean – the corks must be new. Put the bottles into a cool oven and bring the temperature up to 115°C/240°F or gas mark 1. Other essentials are a clean plastic funnel to fit the neck of the bottle, a large nylon sieve and two wooden spoons – one wide and flat for sieving and one with a long handle for stirring the thick eruptive mixture (if you do not have this then you should use an oven glove to protect your hand). Use a heavy wide based pan – not copper – and an asbestos mat to help control the very low heat required and to prevent burning.

Prepare your vegetable and/or fruit. Tomatoes and apples do not need to be peeled or cored. Put these ingredients with any whole spices and herbs into the pan and cook gently without added liquid, unless stated, until they have reached a point of total dissolution. You will have to watch carefully and stir a lot to stop the mixture sticking to the bottom. Soft, ripe tomatoes without added vegetables or Italian and plum tomatoes will probably take only an hour to cook but do not be surprised if some ingredients take three hours or so. This cooking can also be done in a covered casserole left in a very slow oven, this reduces the chances of burning but is only economical if you have a fire oven in use for it can take a whole day or more.

When the mixture is very soft either sieve, or liquidize and then sieve. Clean the pan thoroughly and return the purée to it. You now add the remaining ingredients as they may be; for example, sugar, salt, vinegar, spices and herbs, dry and liquid seasonings and flavourings. Bring gently to the boil, stirring constantly and continue to boil gently until the mixture is the correct consistency, thick yet still runny enough to pour – you will know how you like it but remember that tomato sauce thickens on cooling and also on keeping.

Bottle the hot sauce using the funnel and leaving a good space at the top. Pop in the cork but do not push right down. Put a wire rack or a false bottom in a sterilizer or a metal pail. Place the bottles on this, well supported by twists of newspaper or skirts of heavy card to prevent them knocking together. Fill the pan with hot water to just above the level of the sauce in bottles. Bring to the boil and hold at simmering for 30 minutes.

Remove the bottles from the pan and stand them on wooden boards or thick cloths – if you plonk the hot bottle on to a cold surface it will disintegrate leaving your floor looking like a battlefield. It will also ensure an even overall reduction in temperature.

Push the corks down tightly and leave to get cold. Prepare melted candle or paraffin wax and when the bottles are quite cold make sure that the corks are absolutely tight then cut them down to the level of the top of the bottle. Brush over thickly with the melted wax to at least 1cm/½ inch down the neck. Repeat this waxing process once again to give a complete seal right over the cork and neck edge.

If you sterilize the sauce you can be completely sure that it will last for ages. However, if you are making small quantities which are going to be rapidly consumed the easy way is to transfer the cooked purée to a china bowl and leave it to get quite cold. Then bottle and cork. Seal with wax as above but this is by no means foolproof and can cause disappointment and be a waste of time and money.

If all this sounds time consuming and expensive on fuel remember that home-made tomato sauce is an absolute joy. This is the sweet sticky sauce which children like and not to be confused with the fresh tomato sauce made for pasta etc. I say this because tomatoes lose much of their fresh flavour when cooked for a long time and become a different creation altogether, suitable to adorn everything from fish and chips, bread and butter, meat pies, cold buffets, breakfasts, picnic parties and excellent as barbecue sauces and dips, or as relishes for grills and seasoning for meats.

TOMATO SAUCE

cook together:

1kg/2lb 4oz ripe red tomatoes	200g/7oz onions
1 sharp cooking apple	

add after sieving:

1 tablespoon sea salt	½ teaspoon ground mace
2 teaspoon ground black pepper	50g/2oz sugar
½ teaspoon ground cloves	200ml/7fl. oz vinegar

TOMATO KETCHUP

cook together:

1kg/2lb 4oz ripe red tomatoes	1 clove garlic
1 small onion	

add after sieving:

½ teaspoon paprika powder	75g/3oz white sugar
½ teaspoon cayenne pepper	1 tablespoon fresh orange juice
½ teaspoon sea salt	150ml/¼ pint white malt vinegar

SPICED TOMATO RELISH

1kg/2lb 4oz red tomatoes
1kg/2lb 4oz onions
6 cloves garlic
1kg/2lb 4oz cooking apples
2 large green peppers
600ml/1 pint white malt vinegar
450g/1lb white sugar

1 rounded tablespoon sea salt
2 teaspoons cayenne pepper
2 level tablespoons paprika powder
2 level tablespoons mustard powder
1 teaspoon mixed ground spice
350g/12oz tomato purée (thick)

8 hot, dry, sterile jars with non-metal lids

Scald, peel and chop the tomatoes. Peel and finely chop the onion and garlic. Peel, core and chop the apples. Remove the pith and seed from the peppers and cut the flesh into dice. Put all these ingredients into a stainless steel pan and add the vinegar except 2 tablespoons. Simmer gently until thick and soft. Mix the remaining ingredients together with the vinegar until it is a smooth paste and add it to the pan. Bring to the boil, stirring constantly and boil for 3 minutes. Pot and seal.

A fruity, tomato relish that children will like. Reduce the quantities if necessary.

RIPE TOMATO PICKLE

1kg/2lb 4oz firm, ripe tomatoes
2 tablespoons sea salt
1 clove garlic
350g/12oz soft brown sugar

400ml/14fl. oz vinegar
1 blade mace
1 small piece cinnamon
3 teaspoons whole allspice

3 hot, dry, sterile jars with wide necks and non-metal lids

Wipe the tomatoes and cut them into thick slices, put into a bowl and layer with the salt. Cover and leave for 24 hours. Drain very well – shaking gently in a colander is the best way. Peel and chop the garlic. Put the garlic, sugar and vinegar together in a stainless steel pan and bring gently to the boil. Tie the spices into a muslin bag and add this to the pan. Now slide the tomatoes gently into this vinegar syrup without breaking them. Return gently to the boil and simmer for a brief 2 minutes. Using a perforated spoon or a slice transfer the tomatoes carefully to the jars, packing them into neat layers. Boil the syrup and spices rapidly until thick enough to almost jell. Pour over the fruit to cover. Seal.

Delicious way of using tomatoes – better even than chutney.

GREEN TOMATO AND LIME JAM

1kg/2lb 4oz small green tomatoes   1 fresh lime
725g/1lb 12oz white sugar   vanilla pod

4 hot, dry, sterile jam jars

Wash, wipe and slice the tomatoes thinly (Italian olivette if possible). Place in a bowl in layers with the sugar and leave for 24 hours. Wipe the lime and slice it thinly removing pips. Place all the ingredients in a stainless steel pan and bring to the boil. Skim and continue to simmer very gently, stirring occasionally until the jam is golden, cooked and a set is obtained, this will take approximately 2 hours. Remove the vanilla pod and allow the jam to cool before potting. Seal when cold.

    Glorious colour, all greeny-gold and glowing. A delicious, tangy taste worth making for presents.

GREEN TOMATO JELLY

1kg/2lb 4oz green tomatoes   2 lemons
600ml/1 pint water   white sugar

8 small, hot, dry, sterile jars

Wash and roughly chop the tomatoes, put them into a stainless steel pan – in case you wonder why stainless steel, tomato reacts against copper and will not make a set, which is a pity because it keeps the green colour well. Add the water and simmer gently until the tomato is quite soft, turn into a jelly bag and leave to drain into a china bowl overnight. The next day squeeze the juice from the lemons and add it to the tomato juice. Measure the liquid gained and for each 600ml/1 pint take 450g/1lb warmed sugar. Return the juice to the pan, heat gently and add the sugar, stirring well until it has dissolved. Bring to the boil and boil hard until a set is obtained. Pot and seal.

    If like me you are extremely fond of herb jellies then read about Crab Apple and Herb jellies p.51. You will find that they work equally well with tomatoes although giving a softer set. The result is sharp and light which carries the flavour of the more delicate herbs very well. Basil, tarragon, apple mint, marjoram are a few excellent examples. Red tomato jelly can also be made in the same way with a sweeter result so try adding spices instead – ginger, cinnamon, coriander, allspice.

GREEN TOMATO AND ORANGE MARMALADE

1kg/2lb 4oz green tomatoes   1.25kg/2lb 12oz white sugar
3 sweet oranges

5 hot, dry, sterile jam jars

Wash the tomatoes and oranges and pass them both through a coarse mincer, catching the juice and removing orange pips as you go. Put the minced fruit into a stainless steel pan and add the sugar, heat gently stirring well until the sugar has dissolved. Bring to the boil and boil rapidly until the conserve looks clear and thick. Pot. Seal when cold.

BASIC GREEN TOMATO CHUTNEY
USING A PRESSURE COOKER

1kg/2lb 4oz green tomatoes   1 level teaspoon sea salt
350g/12oz cooking apples   small piece root ginger
50g/2oz onions   450ml/$\frac{3}{4}$ pint vinegar
225g/8oz block dates   50g/2oz sugar

3 hot, dry, sterile jars with non-metal lids

Scald, peel and chop the tomatoes. Peel, core and chop the apples. Peel and chop the onions. Chop the dates and tie the bruised ginger into a muslin bag. Remove the trivet from the pan and pop in all the ingredients except the sugar and using only half the vinegar. Cover and cook for 10 minutes at 15lb/H pressure. Reduce pressure immediately in cold water. Remove the muslin bag and add the remainder of the vinegar and the sugar. Bring to the boil, stirring well and simmer in the open pan remembering to give an occasional stir until the chutney is thick and smooth. Pot and seal.

This basic method can be followed for most of the chutney recipes. Make sure that you use only half of the vinegar to cook the fruit and vegetables under pressure and add the remainder with the sugar after this stage. Once the sugar has been added the pan must not be covered.

GREEN TOMATO AND APPLE CHUTNEY

1kg/2lb 4oz green tomatoes
1kg/2lb 4oz cooking apples
350g/12oz onions
1 large green pepper
175g/6oz sultanas
1 dessertspoon sea salt

1 small piece root ginger
12 dried red chillies
25g/1oz mixed pickling spice
1 litre/1¾ pints malt vinegar
175g/6oz soft brown sugar

5 hot, dry, sterile jars with non-metal lids

Scald and peel the tomatoes. Peel and core the apples, peel the onions. Wash the peppers and remove the pith and seeds. Wash the sultanas. Put all of these through a coarse mincer. Bruise the spices and tie them into a muslin bag. Place all the ingredients in a stainless steel pan and bring gently to the boil. Continue to simmer, stirring from time to time until the mixture is thick and soft. Fish out the muslin bag. Pot and seal.

Makes up equally well with red tomatoes. 25g/1oz mustard seed can be substituted for the pickling spice. 1 teaspoon cayenne powder can be used instead of the chillies. A gloriously easy recipe that is an excellent standby and a great family favourite even though it is a bit hot!

GREEN TOMATO AND BANANA CHUTNEY

1kg/2lb 4oz green tomatoes
1kg/2lb 4oz windfall apples
1kg/2lb 4oz onions
1kg/2lb 4oz sultanas
3 litres/5 pints malt vinegar

1kg/2lb 4oz bananas
500g/1lb 2oz crystallized ginger
1350g/3lb soft brown sugar
4 tablespoons sea salt

hot, dry, sterile jars with non-metal lids

Scald, peel and chop the tomatoes. Peel, core and chop the apples, peel and chop the onions. Chop the sultanas. Put all of these into a stainless steel pan with half of the vinegar and cook until just soft. Peel and chop the bananas and chop the ginger, add them to the pan with the rest of the vinegar and the remaining ingredients. Bring to the boil, stirring continuously. Reduce the heat and simmer, stirring frequently until the chutney is smooth and thick. Pot. Seal when cold.

Delicious sweet chutney. Reduce the quantities for manageable amounts but I find it worth making in large quantities even if it is rather expensive because it keeps well becoming thick and syrupy. Children love it and it is very good with curries.

GREEN TOMATO CHUTNEY WITH LEMON

1kg/2lb 4oz green tomatoes
225g/8oz sultanas
100g/4oz onions
1 large lemon
1 teaspoon mustard seed

1 teaspoon ground ginger
1 teaspoon fresh grated horseradish
   (optional)
500g/1lb 2oz soft brown sugar
450ml/¾ pint malt vinegar

4 hot, dry, sterile jars with non-metal lids

Scald, peel and chop the tomatoes. Wash and chop the sultanas. Peel and chop the onions. Grate the rind from the lemon and extract the juice. Put all the ingredients into a stainless steel pan and bring gently to the boil stir constantly until the sugar has dissolved. Simmer until the chutney is thick and soft – you will have to judge to a nicety the height of the flame or use an asbestos mat otherwise you are going to have to crouch hotly over the pan for the next hour, for this chutney dries out quickly and sticks like fury. Add more warm vinegar if necessary. Pot. Seal when cold.

A super flavour and particularly good if kept for some time. If you do intend to keep the chutney for longer then put extra vinegar in during the cooking for you will find that it does thicken during storing.

HOT INDIAN CHUTNEY

1kg/2lb 4oz green tomatoes
725g/1lb 10oz prepared marrow
500g/1lb 2oz onions
100g/4oz shallots
1 large clove garlic
25g/1oz sea salt
500g/1lb 2oz sugar

725g/1lb 10oz cooking apples
25g/1oz root ginger
4 teaspoons dried red chillies
4 teaspoons whole cloves
4 teaspoons black peppercorns
2 tablespoons mustard seed
900ml/1½ pints malt vinegar

6 hot, dry, sterile jars with non-metal lids

Scald, peel and chop the tomatoes. Dice the peeled and seeded marrow. Peel and chop the onions, shallots and garlic. Lay them all on a plate and sprinkle with the salt and sugar. Leave overnight. The next day peel, core and chop the apples and put them into a large stainless steel pan with the prepared vegetables and fruit, Bruise the spices and tie them into a muslin bag, add this to the pan with the vinegar and bring gently to the boil, stirring well and then simmer until thick and soft – approximately 2½ hours. Retrieve the muslin bag. Pot and seal.

A hot traditional chutney.

GREEN TOMATOES FOR THE FREEZER
AND HOW TO USE IN A BASIC CHUTNEY

If you can persuade your greengrocer to supply you with green tomatoes at a reduced rate he will probably obtain them by the box. As you may not wish to start in on 14kg/32lb tomatoes in one go I suggest you freeze them by this method and put them away for future use. Remove the stalk ends and wash and dry the tomatoes, plunge them into boiling water for 2 minutes and slip off the skins. Chop them roughly and pack them into polythene bags – pack them in manageable quantities of approximately 1kg/2lb 4oz per bag which will save a lot of bother later on. Do not keep longer than 3 months.

To make the chutney follow any suitable recipe given but put the tomatoes into a large stainless steel pan and thaw out gently over a low heat before adding the rest of the ingredients.

GREEN TOMATO PICKLE

1kg/2lb 4oz medium size green
  tomatoes
2 large Spanish onions
50g/2oz sea salt
1 small lemon
1 firm sweet red pepper
1 teaspoon celery seed

1 teaspoon whole allspice
1 teaspoon mustard seed
1 teaspoon whole cloves
1 teaspoon black peppercorns
100g/4oz brown sugar
300ml/½ pint malt vinegar

3 hot, dry, sterile jars with non-metal lids

Wash the tomatoes and slice thinly crossways. Peel and slice the onions in thin rings. Lay tomatoes and onions in alternate layers on a flat dish, sprinkling each layer with the salt. Leave to stand overnight in a cool place. The next day drain the dish of vegetables, rinse them well in cold water and drain again. Using only a quarter of the lemon, slice it very finely and discard the pips. Wash the pepper and slice thinly removing the seeds and pith as you work and try and make sure that you keep it in nice rings. Bruise the spices and tie them into a muslin bag, put this into a stainless steel pan with the sugar and vinegar and bring to the boil, stirring well to dissolve the sugar. Add the vegetables and lemon and return to the boil, stirring gently to prevent it from catching the bottom of the pan. Cook slowly for 30 minutes still stirring from time to time. Remove the spice bag giving it a good squeeze. Pack the pickle into the jars. Cover with hot excess liquid if any – if you do not have enough make up another

370

solution using vinegar and sugar in the proportions above and the old spice bag. It is important to make sure that the pickle is covered as it absorbs the liquid during storage. Seal.

This is a very pleasant pickle, crunchy and sweet. If you prefer a clear effect use white vinegar and white sugar.

HOT TOMATO PICKLE

1kg/2lb 4oz green tomatoes
500g/1lb 2oz sour cooking apples
2 large onions
2 teaspoons sea salt
100g/4oz seedless raisins

1.15 litre/2 pints vinegar
225g/8oz soft brown sugar
25g/1oz mustard seed
1 teaspoon ground ginger
¼ teaspoon cayenne pepper

3 hot, dry, sterile jars with non metal lids

Wash and thinly slice the tomatoes. Peel core and slice the apples, peel and slice the onions into rings. Lay all these on a shallow dish and sprinkle with the salt. Cover and leave overnight. The next day drain off the salty liquid, rinse and drain the fruit and onions well. Chop the raisins and put them with all the ingredients into a stainless steel pan. Bring slowly to the boil stirring well and then simmer very gently until soft. Pot and seal.

Hot and fruity pickle. Excellent with cheese.

Turnip

A root vegetable, white in colour, round and slightly squat with green tops also used as spring greens. The flavour is quite strong and the turnip is used primarily in stews. A spring stew made with lamb, barley, onions, baby carrots, first peas and tiny turnips is one of the highlights of everyday cooking. Although large turnips are easily obtainable throughout the winter and are very useful as either a separate vegetable or incorporated in other dishes or maybe even stuffed and baked, it is the young small turnips which are in a class of their own – delicious served as they are, hot with butter, pepper and a dash of nutmeg or cold in a salad or hors d'ouevres tray. One variety, Tokyo Cross, is ready for sowing from February to October and will produce small turnips within one

371

month and an added advantage is that they will not become wormy in that short time. As turnips are reasonably cheap to buy and are available throughout the year from British growers or from France it does not seem worthwhile, unless you have a lot of space, to let them grow larger, just keep planting seeds in rote for a never ending supply of tiddlers.

White Rutabaga is the American term for turnips.

TURNIP CHUTNEY

1kg/2lb 4oz turnips
1 tablespoon turmeric powder
1 teaspoon mustard powder
¼ teaspoon ground pepper
50g/2oz sea salt
500g/1lb 2oz onions

500g/1lb 2oz cooking apples
1.15 litre/2 pints vinegar
225g/8oz sultanas
100g/4oz seedless raisins
225g/8oz soft brown sugar

8 hot, dry, sterile jars with non-metal lids
Peel the turnips, chop roughly and cook in a little salted water until soft. Drain and then beat well with a wooden spoon until a soft pulp. Peel the onions, peel and core the apples and pass both through a mincer. Mix the spices and seasonings to a smooth paste with a little of the vinegar. Put all the ingredients into a stainless steel pan and bring gently to the boil, stirring well. Boil slowly for 1 hour stirring occasionally. Pot and seal.

The turnip gives a slightly hot flavour to this mild sweet chutney.

PICKLED TURNIP

600ml/1 pint white or white wine
  vinegar

pickling spice
2 round turnips

small, hot, dry. sterile jars with non-metal lids

Boil the vinegar and pickling spice together for 5 minutes. Remove from heat allow to get quite cool and strain before using. Peel and grate the turnip coarsely and pack it into the jars. Cover with the strained vinegar. Seal.

Keeps well and makes a hot and tasty addition to white cabbage salad.

Violet

Viola odorate

'Where oxlips and the nodding violet grows'
'When daisies pied and violets blue'

Just two quotations out of many from Shakespeare's works but similar references have been made throughout history by poets, authors, nature lovers and gardeners on that most delightful of flowers – the violet. There is something about the sweet shyness of the violet which brings out the eloquence in all of us. Whether it is the heart-shaped leaves or the velvety little face lifted to welcome the spring, the grassy banks that it thrives on or the heady perfume, I really could not say, but to the house-wife of Elizabethan days it was also looked upon with pleasure as a herb and a delicacy to be cossetted for the kitchen. The violet has many medicinal properties, both the leaves and the flowers can be used to help remedy kidney problems, sleeplessness, ailments of the throat, mouth and chest and as a laxative, while in the kitchen the list is extensive. For example, violets have been used to make wine, liqueur, vinegar, tea, honey, creamed milk puddings, ice cream, delicate cakes and sweet confections, pastilles, fritters, potages, added to meat dishes, salmagundy or more latterly salads, and the leaf added to marmalade, honey, syrup, oil, conserve, and of course the most attractive of all decorations – crystallized violets.

A last word on violets – grow a delightful bank in your garden where you can choose your varieties from the deep purple to palest pink and

373

white and where you may pick as many as you can steel yourself to. Please do not pick quantities for preserving from the wild.

VIOLET MARMALADE

225g/8oz perfumed violet flowers   500g/1lb 2oz white sugar
600g/1lb 6oz cooking apples

5 medium size, hot, dry, sterile jam jars

Wash and chop the apples finely, put them into a pan with just enough water to prevent sticking, cover and cook until very soft. Pass through a sieve. Nip the bitter base from the violets and put the flowers into a pestle and mortar, pound to a smooth and perfumed paste. Place the sugar in a preserving pan with 4 tablespoons of water and heat gently until it has dissolved and slightly thick but do not allow to colour or become cracked. Add the violet paste and mix well, now stir in the apple purée and bring gently to the boil, stirring continuously. Boil gently until a set of sorts is obtained, it should be very thick. Pot and seal.
    Reputed to once have been a favourite with Queen Victoria.

VIOLET TEA

Pour 300ml/½ pint boiling water onto 1 teaspoon of dried violets. Cover and leave to infuse for 5 minutes. Strain and add honey to taste. I do not know how good violet tea is for you but a little bit of pampering is very soothing for the soul.

TO CRYSTALLIZE VIOLETS

Follow the method given for Candied Borage Flowers, p.93, and Crystallized Primroses, p.305.

W

Walnut

The walnut tree is not indigenous to the British Isles for it came originally from Asia, yet it has established itself well enough in the last remnants of country estates and large gardens to be looked upon as one of our native treasures. The walnut is a beautiful tree with an attractive leafy spread and fine wood which, to its own detriment, makes most superior furniture, having a lovely colour and grain. Sadly, because of its value as timber, most walnut trees in Britain have now been cut down, however in France the farmers give them a value above pearls for the walnut fruit when ripe is an extremely valuable and nutritious nut., having a high calorific yield and a fine oil which has many uses. As walnuts rarely ripen satisfactorily in Britain most of our Christmas and winter supplies come from France although other countries do produce export crops. The best way of using the green or unripe walnut – which is the most that one can expect in Britain – is to pick them before the end of July whilst they are still soft and wet, with outer skin, soft shell and kernel and to use them in pickle, ketchup or liqueur. A word of warning about walnuts – the shell, kernel, juice and anything they are used in, stain abominably on fingers and fabric, so take care – marvellous way of impersonating Eastern gentlemen! The leaves of the walnut tree are said to make a pleasant tea.

GREEN WALNUT PRESERVE

1kg/2lb 4oz fresh green walnuts   1 large lemon
1kg/2lb 4oz white sugar   4 cloves
900ml/1½ pints water

4 hot, dry, sterile jars with non-metal lids

Pick the walnuts before July. Peel away the soft green skin or shell and prick the fruit delicately several times with a needle. Leave to soak in a bowl of cold water for 6 days, changing the water twice a day. Put the sugar and water into a stainless steel pan with the juice from the lemon and boil until thick and really syrupy. Remove from the heat and allow to cool. Drain the walnuts very well and add them to the syrup. Return to the heat and bring gently to the boil. Simmer for half an hour, transfer to a bowl and leave overnight – if the walnuts show a tendency to bounce up, slip a plate on to them to hold them beneath the syrup. The next day return the nuts and syrup to the pan and bring gently to the boil, simmer for half an hour. Add the cloves, stir well and pot. Seal when cold.

CRYSTALLIZED WALNUTS

1kg/2lb 4oz green walnuts   300ml/½ pint water
1kg/2lb 4oz white sugar

Make sure that the walnuts are small and tender. Pierce with a needle several times and put into a bowl of water to which a dash of vinegar has been added. Leave to soak for 10 days changing the water twice daily. Drain well. Have a pan of boiling water ready and dip the walnuts into this, drain well once again. Put the sugar and water into a pan and boil until it is a very thick syrup. Add the walnuts and boil for 10 minutes. Remove from the heat and transfer to a basin. Leave to stand overnight. The next day return the contents of the bowl to the pan and boil for 10 minutes. Transfer to the basin and leave overnight. Repeat this process once more or until the walnuts have completely absorbed all the sugar and no syrup remains. Lay on drying screen or racks and leave in a cool oven for several days to dry out. Turn twice a day. Store in tins.

Index

Index